Greetings From ST. LOUIS

Mary L. Martin
Dinah Roseberry
Kim Hufford

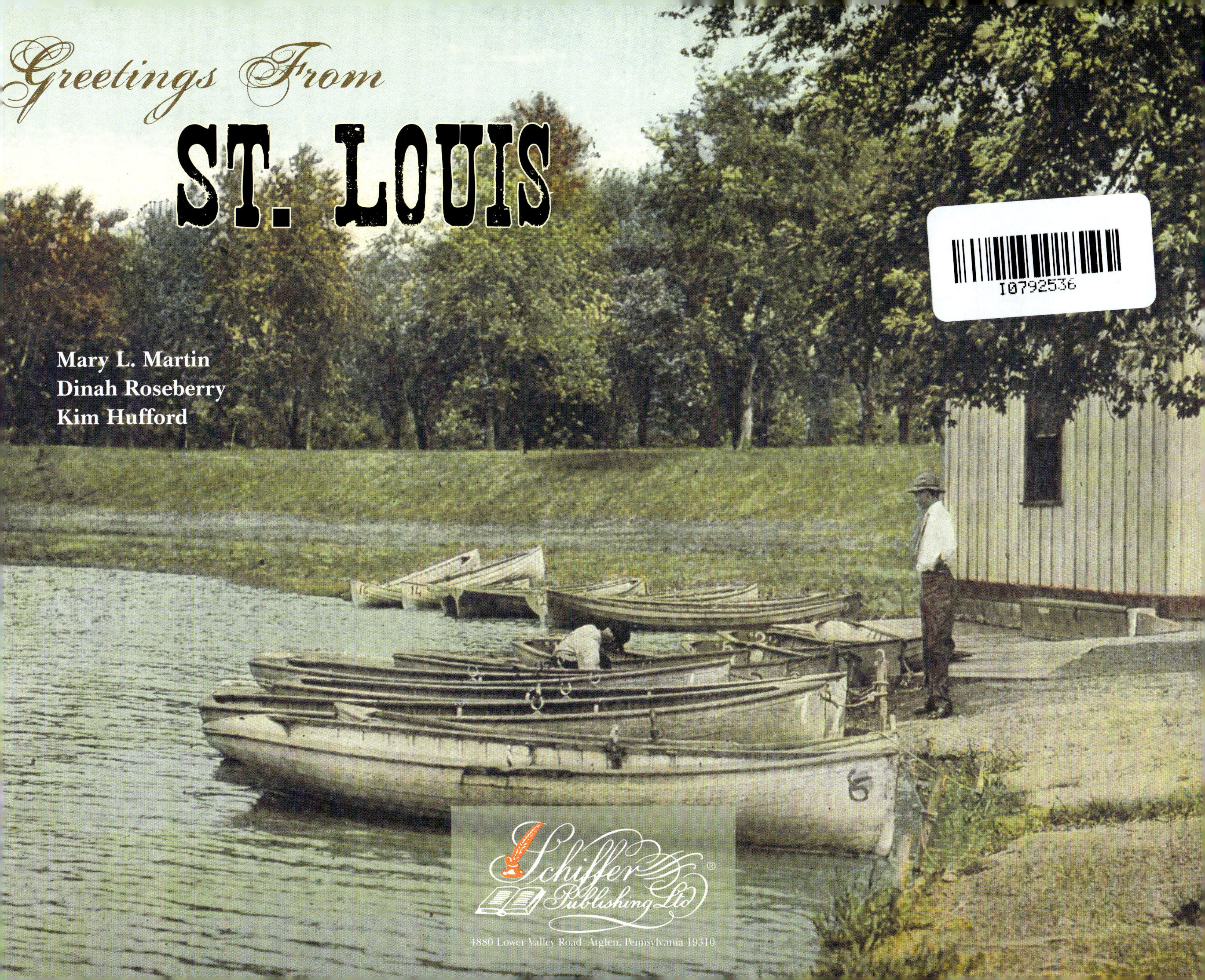

Schiffer Publishing Ltd ®
4880 Lower Valley Road Atglen, Pennsylvania 19310

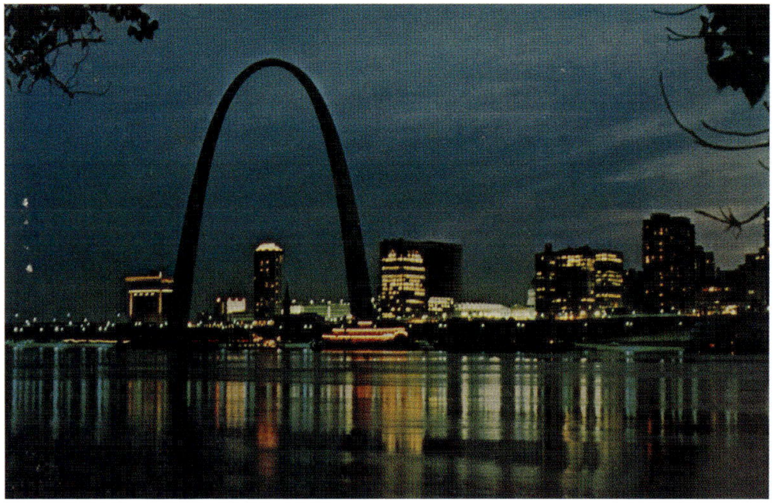

Library of Congress Control Number: 2007934672

Designed by John P. Cheek
Cover design by Bruce Waters

Type set in NewBskvll BT

ISBN: 978-0-7643-2824-4

Printed in China

Published by Schiffer Publishing Ltd.
4880 Lower Valley Road
Atglen, PA 19310
Phone: (610) 593-1777; Fax: (610) 593-2002
E-mail: Info@schifferbooks.com

In Europe, Schiffer books are distributed by
Bushwood Books
6 Marksbury Ave.
Kew Gardens
Surrey TW9 4JF England
Phone: 44 (0) 20 8392-8585; Fax: 44 (0) 20 8392-9876
E-mail: info@bushwoodbooks.co.uk
Website: www.bushwoodbooks.co.uk
Free postage in the U.K., Europe; air mail at cost.

Contents

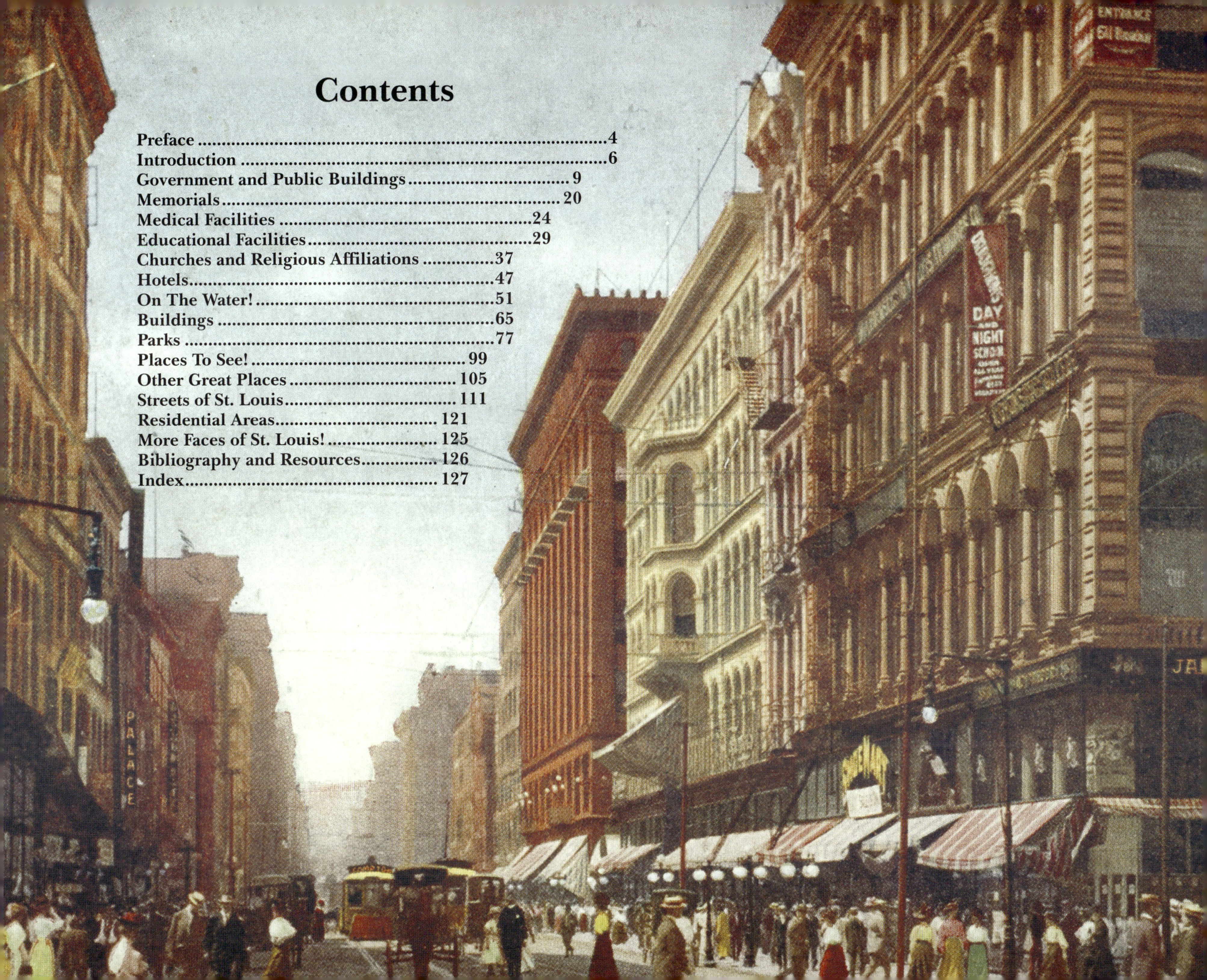

Preface

Historic Images Through Postcards

Postcards are said to be the most popular collectible history has ever known. The urge to horde them sprang up with the birth of this means of communication at the turn of the twentieth century, and has endured great changes in the printing industry. Today, postcard shows take place every weekend somewhere in the country, or the world, and millions of pieces of ephemera lie in wait for those who collect obscure topics or town views.

Postcards once served as the email of their day. They were the fastest, most popular means of communication beginning in the 1890s in the United States. These timely cards provided a way to send visual scenes through the mail along with brief messages—a way to enchant friends and family with the places travelers visited, to send local scenes, or to share favorite topics of imagery. They even provided the latest breaking news, as images of fires, floods, shipwrecks, and festivals were often available in postcard form within hours of an event. Moreover, mail was delivered to most urban homes in the United States at least twice a day. So someone might send a morning postcard inviting a friend to dinner that evening, and receive an RSVP in time to shop for food.

The messages shared and the beautiful scenes combined to create the timeless appeal of postcards as a collectible. Most importantly, history is recorded by the pictures of the times, moments in time reflecting an alluring past.

Dating Postcards

Pioneer Era (1893-1898): Most pioneer cards in today's collections begin with cards placed on sale at the Columbian Exposition in Chicago on May 1, 1893. These were illustrations on government-printed postal cards and privately-printed souvenir cards. The government cards had the printed one-cent stamp, while souvenir cards re-

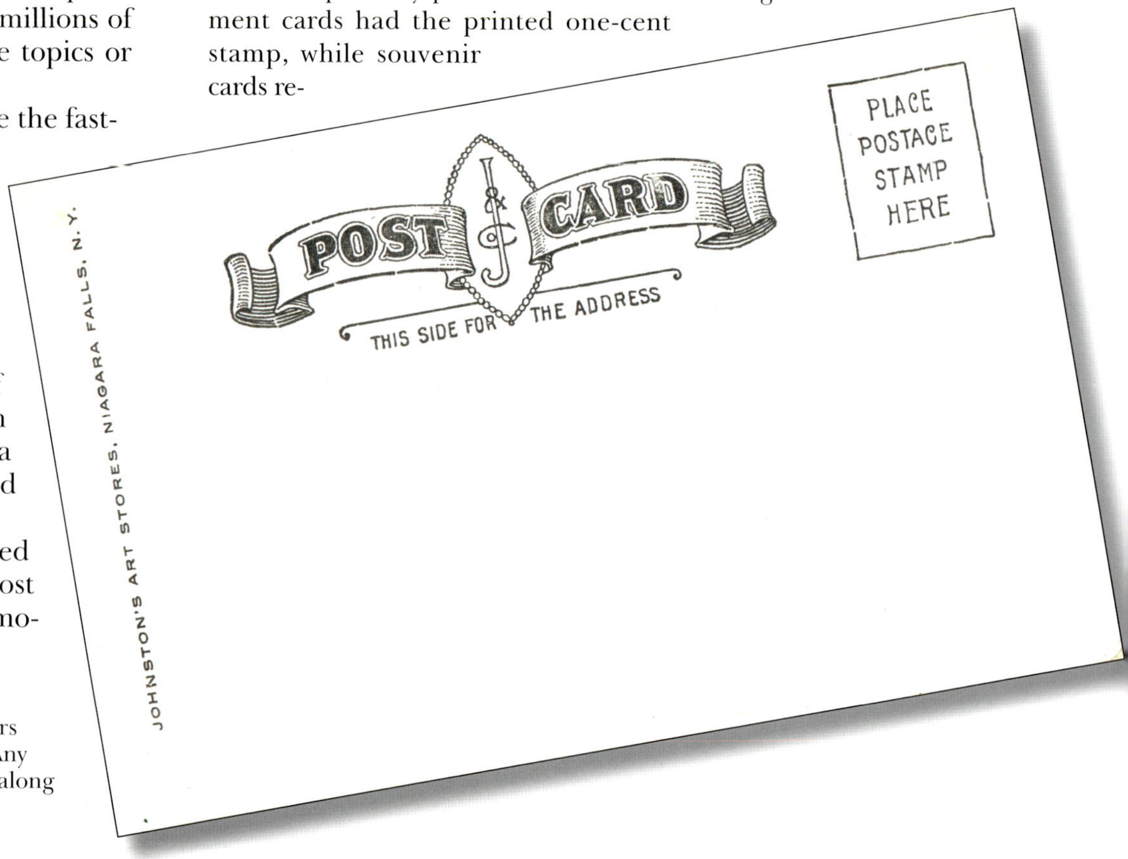

Example of a postcard with an undivided back. Senders could only write the address on this side of the card. Any message needed to be written on the front of the card along with the picture.

quired a two-cent adhesive postage stamp to be applied. Writing was not permitted on the address side of the card.

Private Mailing Card Era (1898-1901): On May 19, 1898, private printers were granted permission, by an act of Congress, to print and sell cards that bore the inscription, "Private Mailing Card." A one-cent adhesive stamp was required. A dozen or more American printers began to take postcards seriously. Writing was still not permitted on the back.

Post Card Era—Undivided Back (1901-1907): New U. S. postal regulations on December 24, 1901 stipulated that the words "Post Card" should be printed at the top of the address side of privately printed cards. Government-issued cards were to be designated as "Postal Cards." Writing was still not permitted on the address side. In this era, private citizens began to take black and white photographs and have them printed on paper with postcard backs.

Early Divided Back Era (1907-1914): Postcards with a divided back were permitted in Britain in 1902, but not in the United States until March 1, 1907. The address was to be written on the right side; the left side was for writing messages. Many millions of cards were published in this era. Up to this point, most postcards were printed in Germany, which was far ahead of the United States in the use of lithographic processes. With the advent of World War I, the supply of postcards for American consumption switched from Germany to England and the United States.

White Border Era (1915-1930): Most U. S. postcards were printed during this period. To save ink, publishers left a clear border around the view, thus these postcards are referred to as "White Border" cards. The relatively high cost of labor, along with inexperience and changes in public taste, resulted in the production of poor quality cards during this period. Furthermore, strong competition in a narrowing market caused many publishers to go out of business.

Linen Era (1930-1944): New printing processes allowed printing on postcards with high rag content that created a textured finish. These cheap cards allowed the use of gaudy dyes for coloring.

Photochrome Era (1945 to date): "Chrome" postcards began to dominate the scene soon after the Union Oil Company placed them in its western service stations in 1939. Mike Roberts pioneered with his "WESCO" cards soon after World War II. Three-dimensional postcards also appeared in this era.

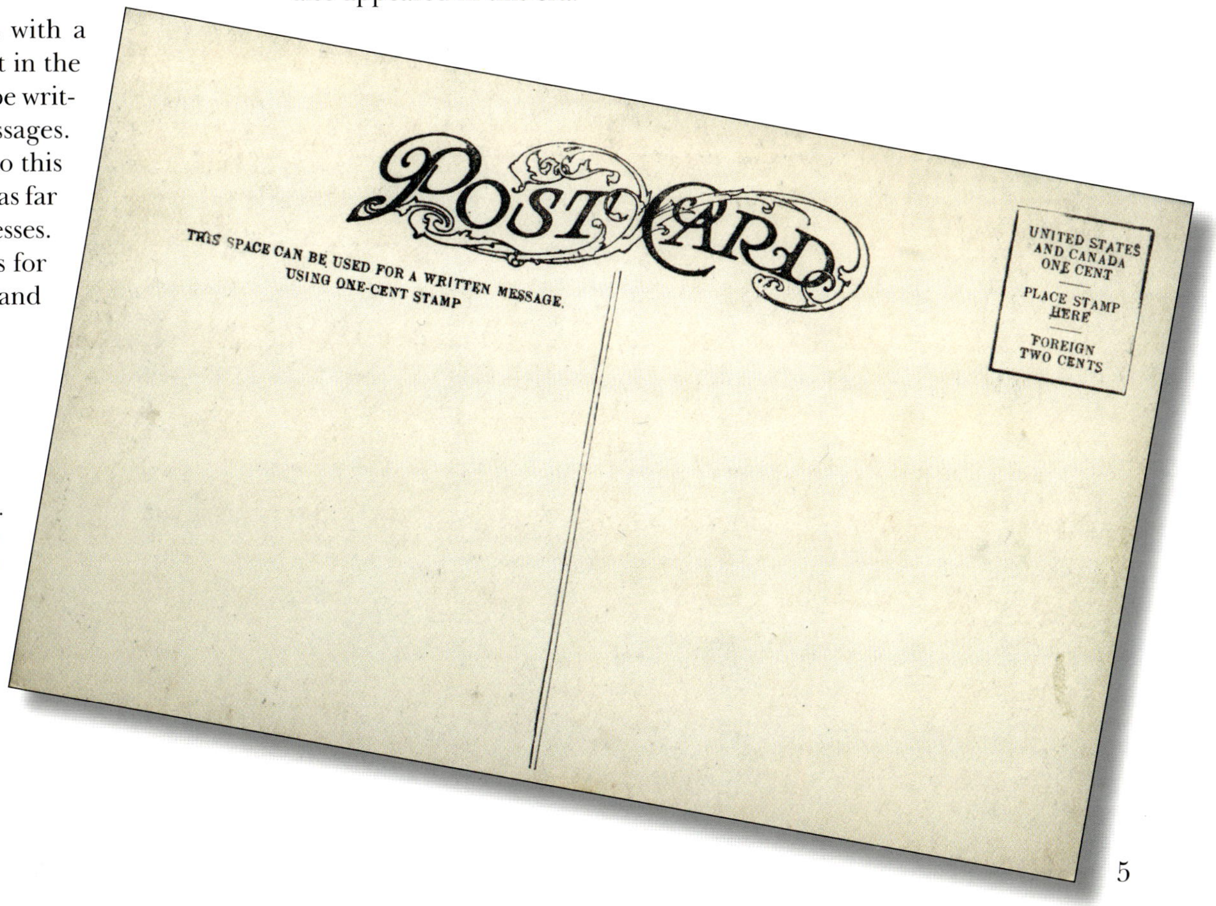

Sample of a postcard with a divided back. Senders were allowed to put an address on the right hand side of the postcard and a message on the left side.

Introduction

St. Louis, a majestic Midwestern center of industry and trade, is located right on the mighty Mississippi River. Situated on the Mississippi, but just below the mouth of the Missouri River, it holds the center of the city nearly eighteen miles downstream from the meeting point of these two great bodies of water. It has been called the "Gateway City," and "Gateway to the West," because it is a most important stopover for travelers going westward. It is also often called "Mound City" because of the Native American burial mounds that were once ordinary sights, though mostly destroyed as the city grew.

The French fur trader, Pierre Laclede Ligueste, established his post in St. Louis in 1764. This was a handy place to reach the water—a significant part of transportation at the time. And later, the location of the city became even more key, as it became a prominent port for shipping via paddle-wheeled steamboats along the Mississippi to outbound and inbound locations—both for fur and other supplies.

St. Louis became an important center for exploration of the Northwest and the ever-vital fur trade during the first ten years of becoming a city. Not only did Lewis and Clark start their expeditions here, but The American Fur Company of St. Louis sent out traders (and trappers) into the great Rocky Mountain country. In 1849, when the Gold Rush was bringing excitement to the eyes of those hoping to get rich quick, many found their way to St. Louis to buy supplies and mining materials. This was the case for those seeking overland routes to the Oregon Trail, as well. These things provided steady growth for the city—growth that you will see through this collection of beautiful historic images.

But whether it's the draw of the gateway Arch (completed in 1965) or the historic World's Fair that has you turning the following pages, St. Louis will captivate you with its growth and the wondrous hearts of its citizens!

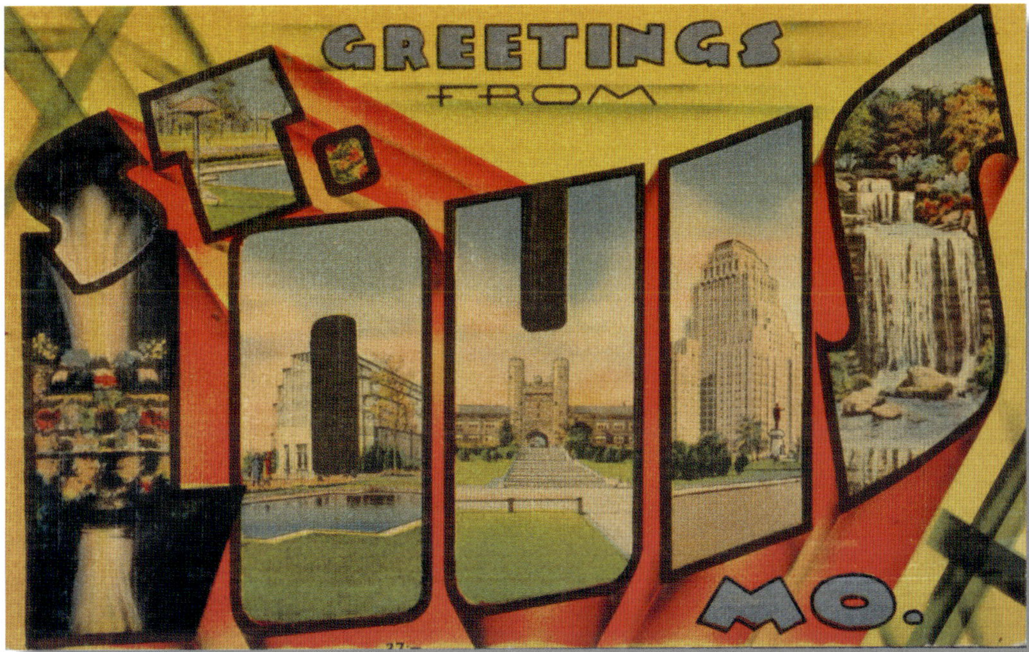

One of the letter postcards showing the best that St. Louis has to offer. At the turn of the century, postcards and other greetings often displayed images that spelled out varied words and names. Cities, towns, and states followed suit as people found the idea an engaging way to announce where they were visiting to the "folks back home." Most of these cards had the words "Greetings From" preceding the lettered card as this one.

circa 1930s, $2-4

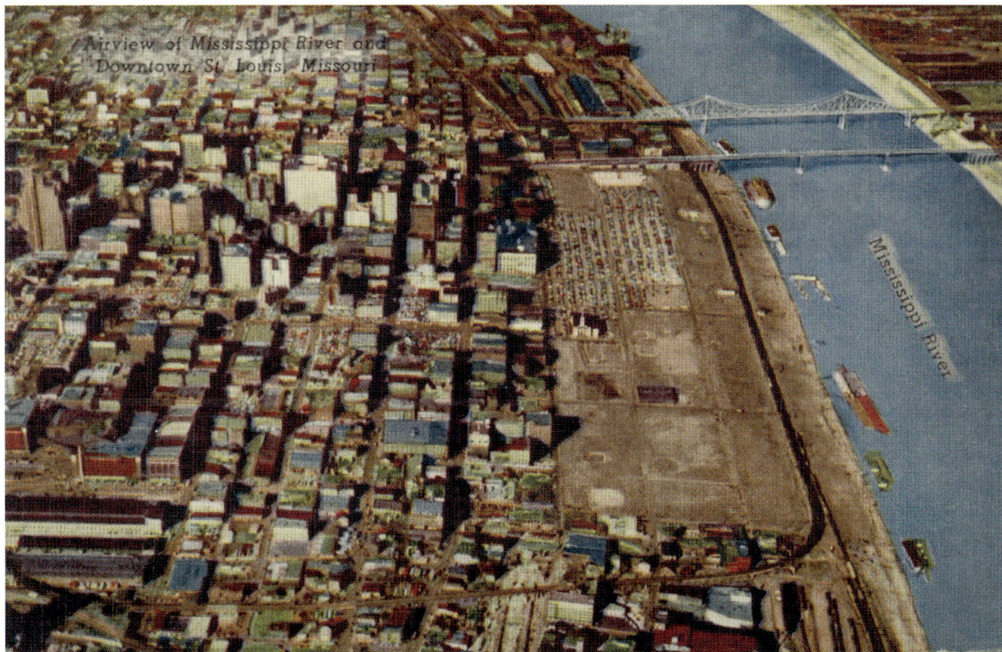

Founded in 1764, this view of St. Louis shows the Mississippi River waterfront with Eads Bridge in the background.

Cancelled 1957, $2-4

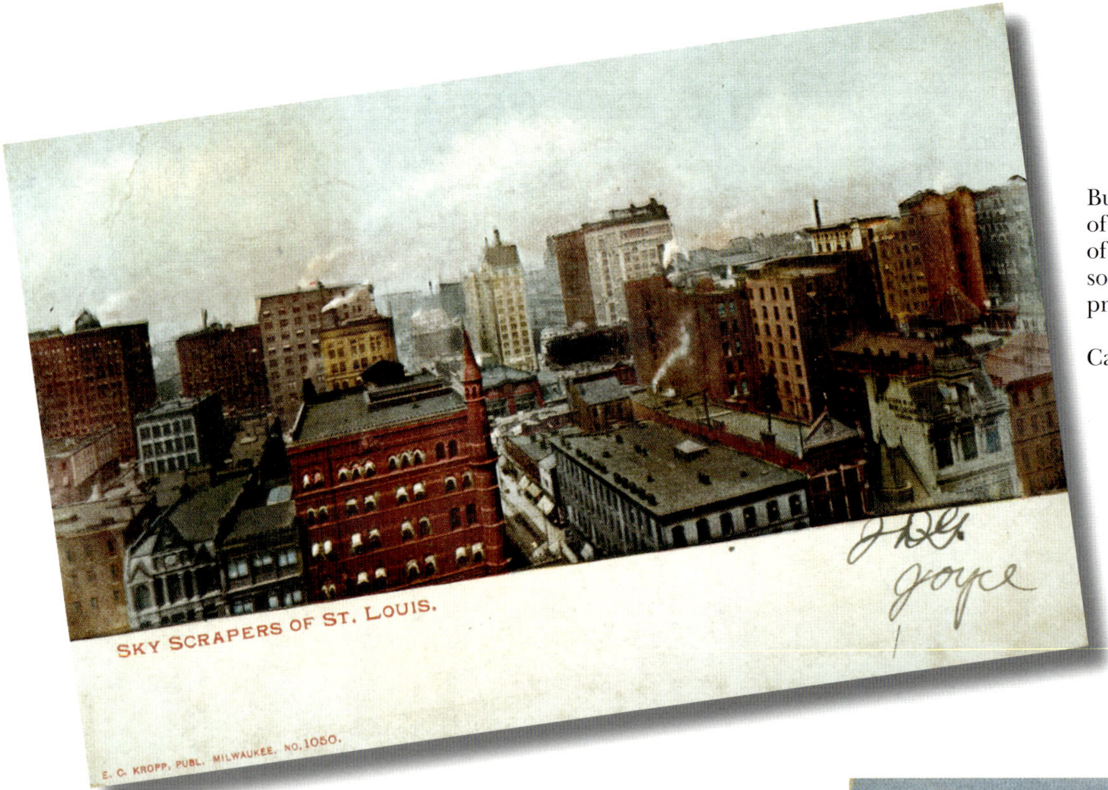

Buildings seem to reach for the sky in this view of skyscraper buildings of St. Louis. On the rear of this card, there is only space for an address, so any personal message had to be written in the provided white space on the front.

Cancelled 1908, $2-4

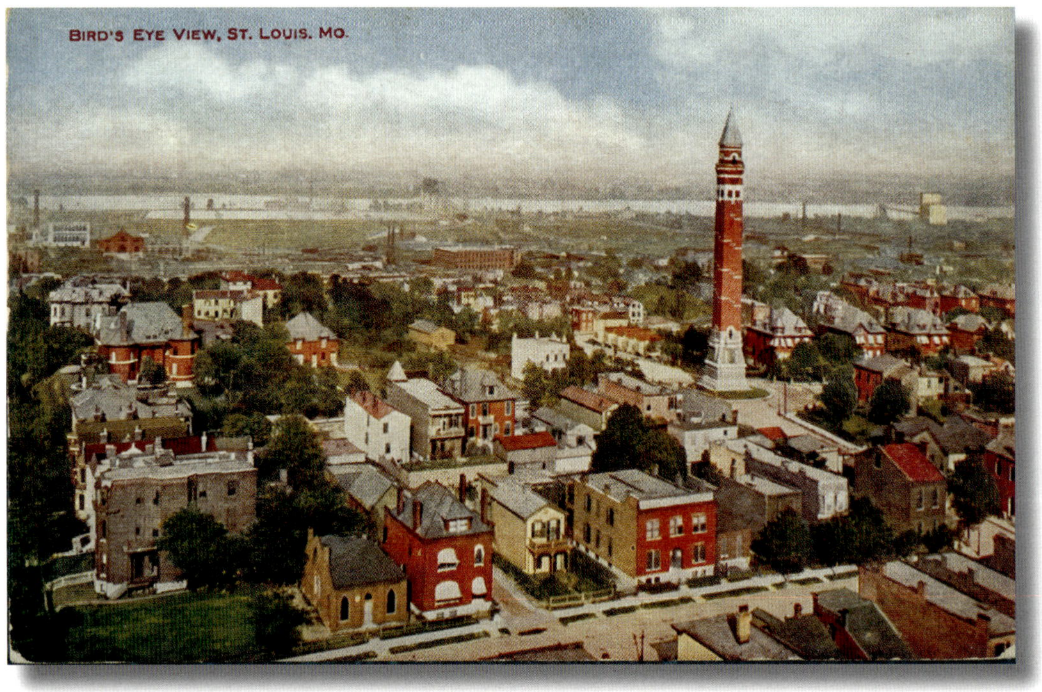

This bird's eye view shows a residential area, with the water tower being the most prominent structure in the scene and the Mississippi River in the far distance.

Circa 1910, $2-4

Government and Public Buildings

From the beautiful Memorial Plaza to the expansive Union Station, the government and public buildings of St. Louis have aroused patriotism, practicality, and general interest through the years.

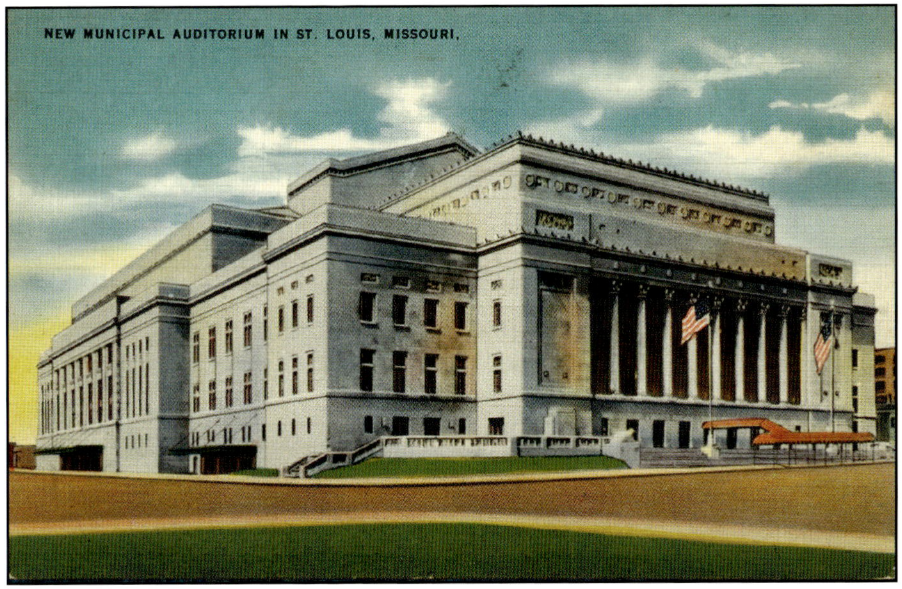

Labeled as the New Municipal Auditorium, this building was erected at a cost of about $7,000,000. Large conventions, meetings, and entertainment events found this facility to be an important venue for the needs of the city.

Circa 1930s, $2-4

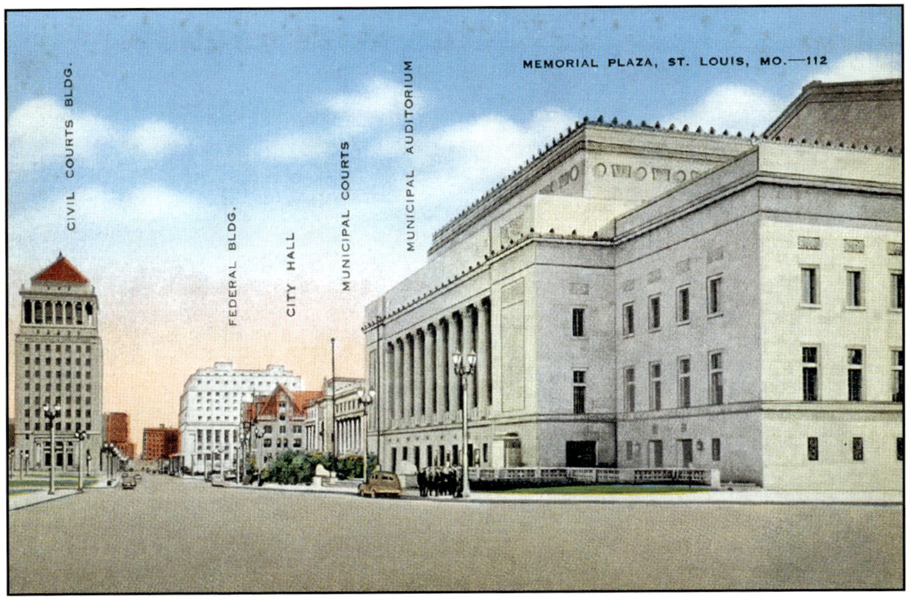

This view of Memorial Plaza, comprised of over seven and a half blocks in the heart of the city, labels the varied government buildings: Civil Courts Building, Federal Building, City Hall, Municipal Courts, and the Municipal Auditorium.

Circa 1930s, $2-4

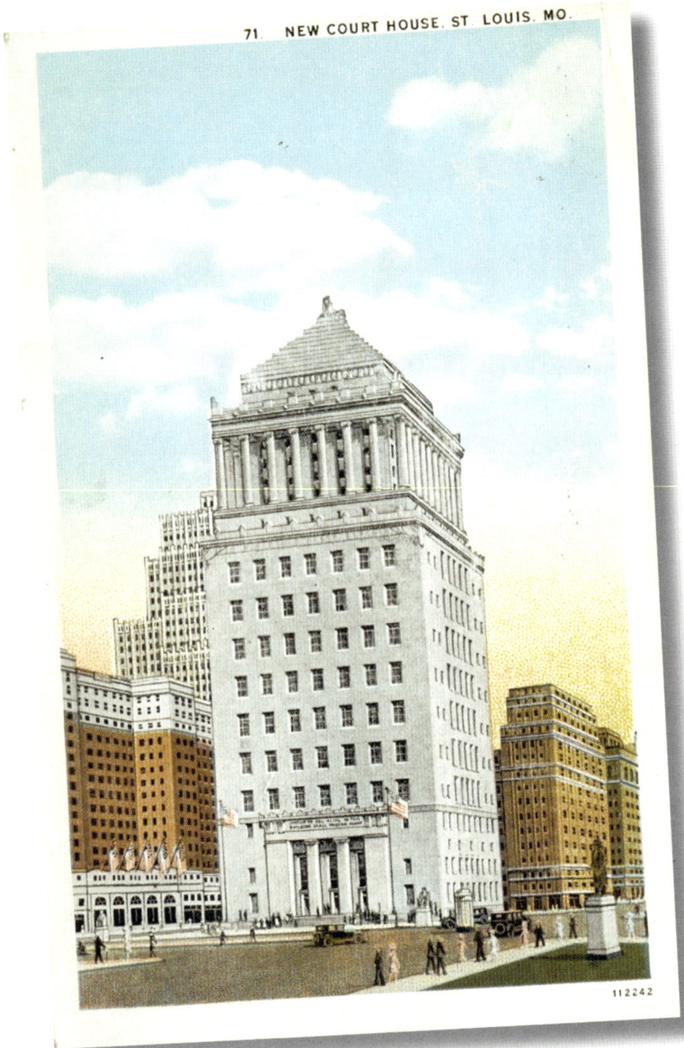

The Old Court House in St. Louis is prominently known for controversial involvement with the Underground Railroad. Prior to the Civil War, slaves were sold at auction from the front steps. A famous trial in this vein includes that of Dred Scott and his wife, Harriet, who were granted their freedom in 1847 at this Court House.

Cancelled 1912, $2-4

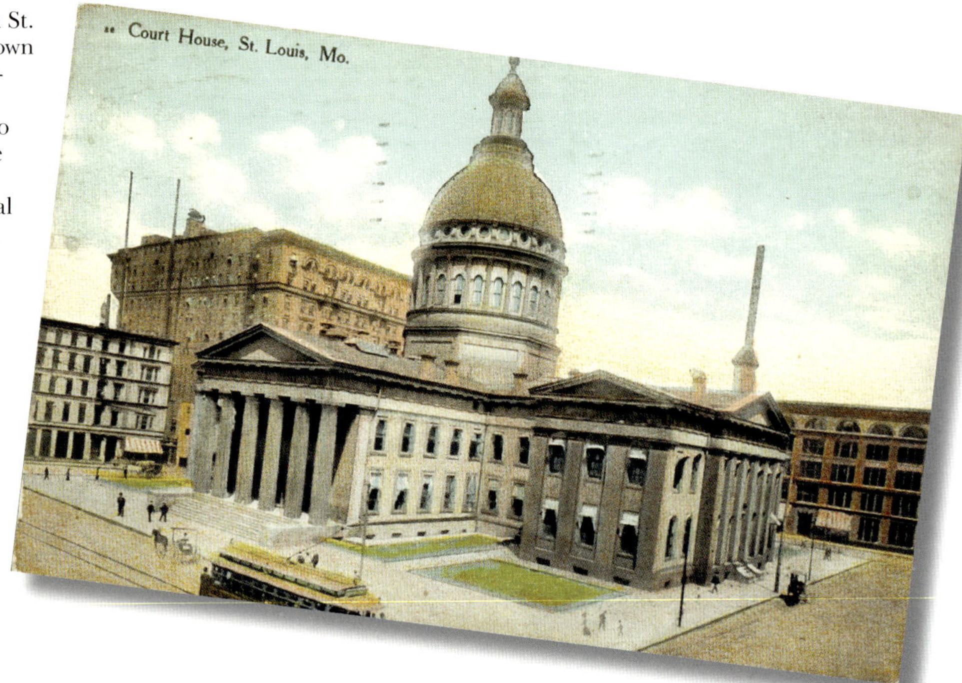

The Civil Courthouse, shown here, now uses the latest equipment in courtroom technology and is noted as a prime example of leading edge, twenty-first century accomplishment.

Cancelled 1930, $2-4

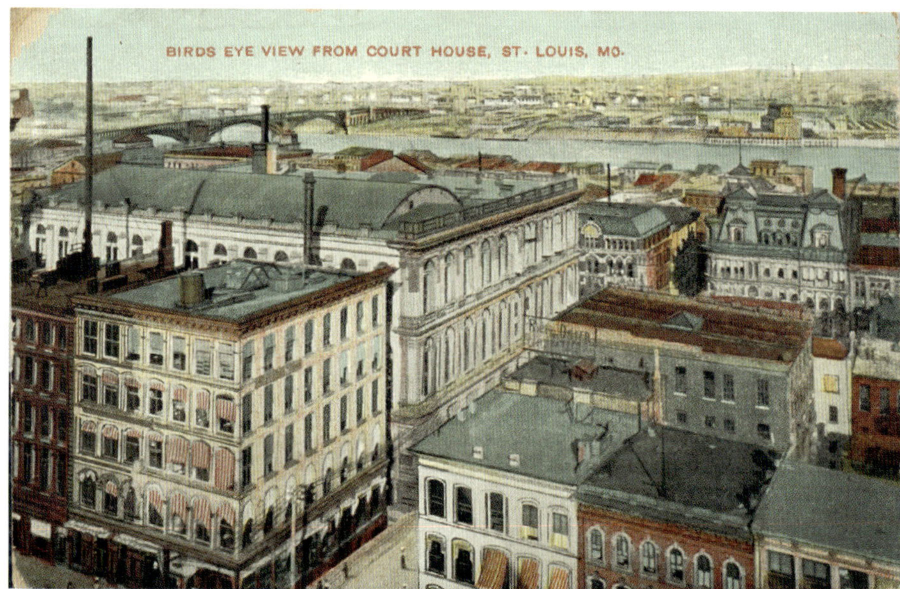

This bird's eye view looking toward the Mississippi River was taken from atop the Court House.

Circa 1910, $2-4

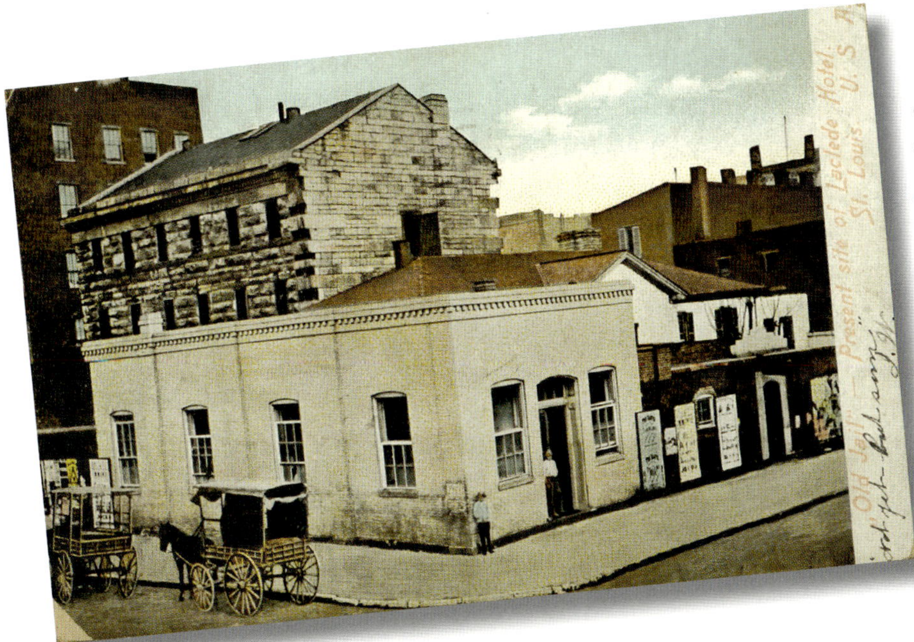

The old stone jail of St. Louis. Later, this structure was replaced by the Laclede Hotel.

Cancelled 1908, $2-4

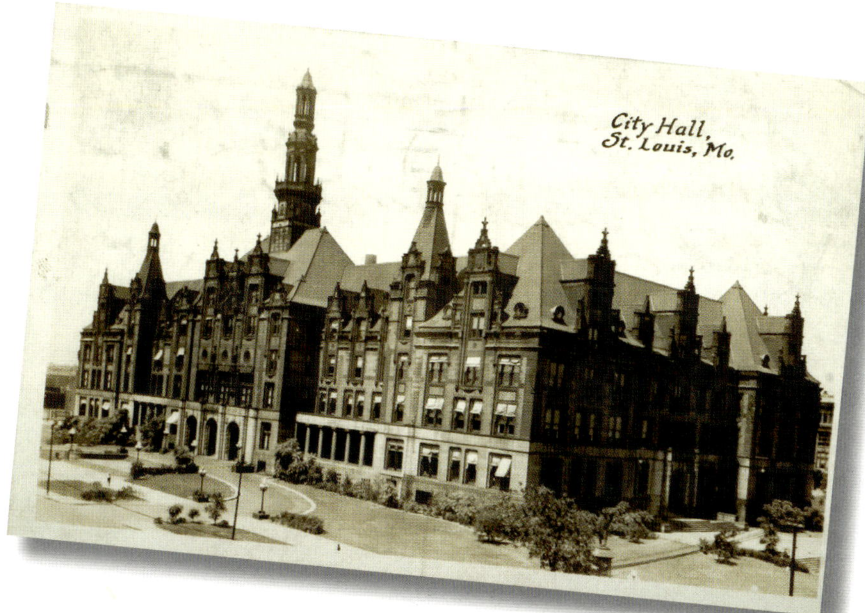

The City Hall was built in 1898, after the original City Hall was destroyed by a cyclone storm in 1896.

Cancelled 1924, $10-12

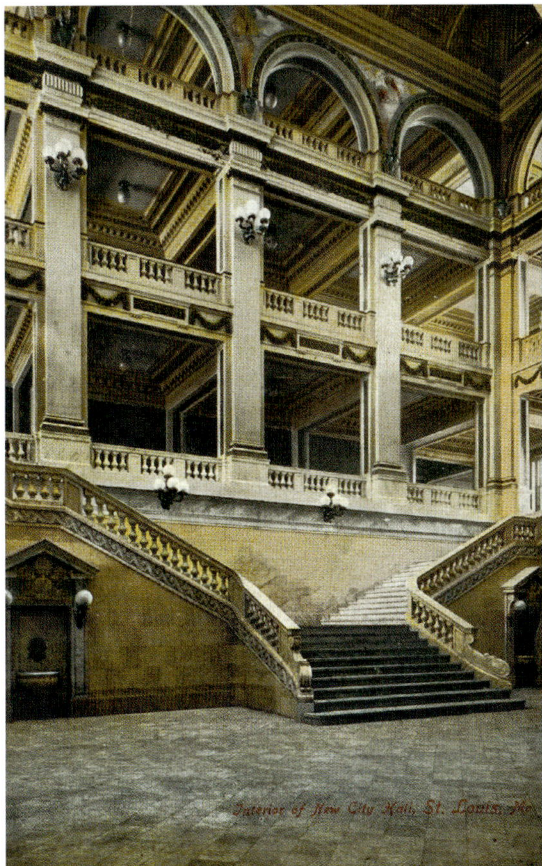

The interior of City Hall was quite majestic, showing elegant design.

Circa Early 1900s, $2-4

The Public Library in St. Louis, like many libraries around the country, began as a subscription service and was established in 1865. The general public, in 1874, was able to take advantage of reading and research materials, but could only use them onsite. In 1893, the administration of the library went from the board of education to an independent library board. At that time, the library became a free service, open to all residents of St. Louis.

Cancelled 1914, $2-4

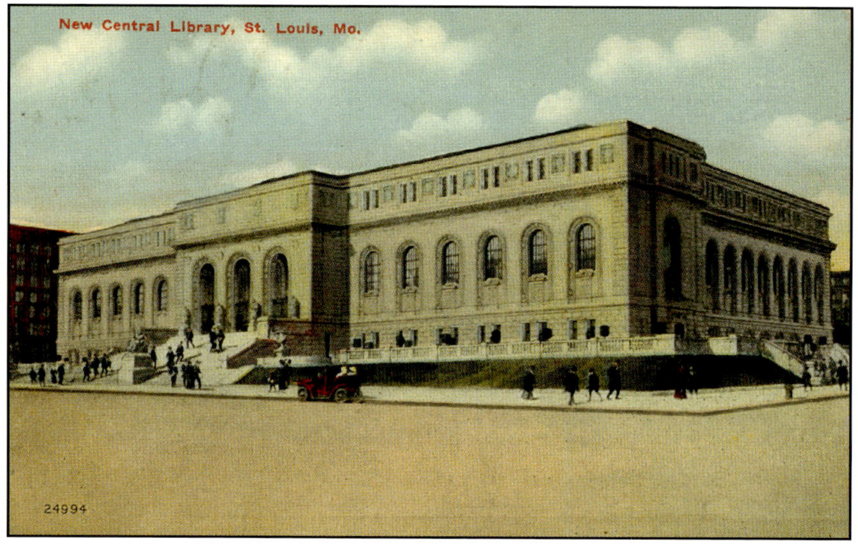

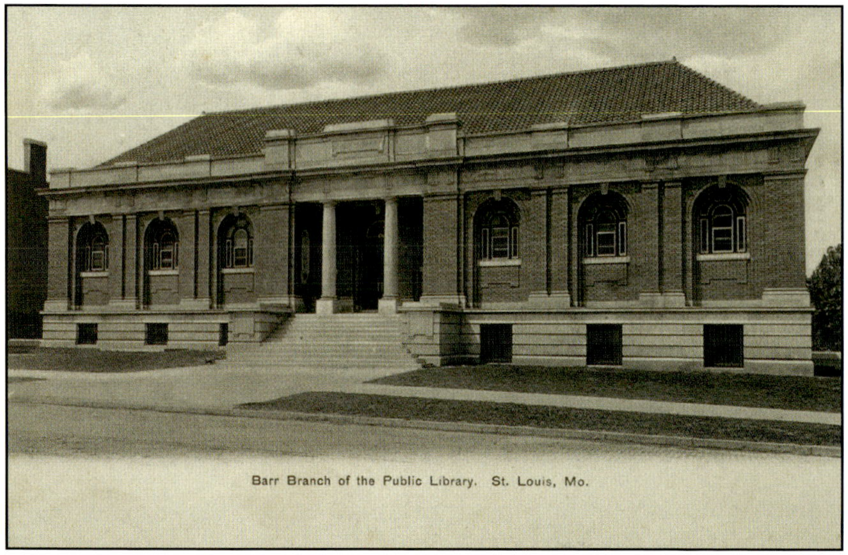

The Barr Branch of the Public Library system was opened in 1906, with the help of grant funding from the famous philanthropist, Andrew Carnegie. Carnegie was known to fund library development across the country.

Circa Early 1900s, $2-4

Known as the Old Post Office, the U. S. Custom House and Post Office was open to the public in 1884, after many years of construction beginning in 1873, with an expenditure of about six million dollars. Originally, the intent was for this building to house varied Federal offices as well as other important entities.

Circa Early 1900s, $2-4

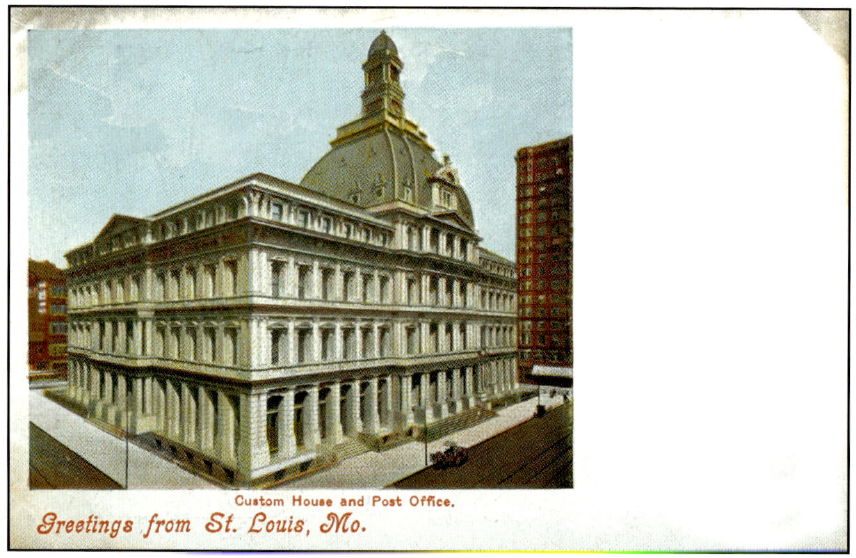

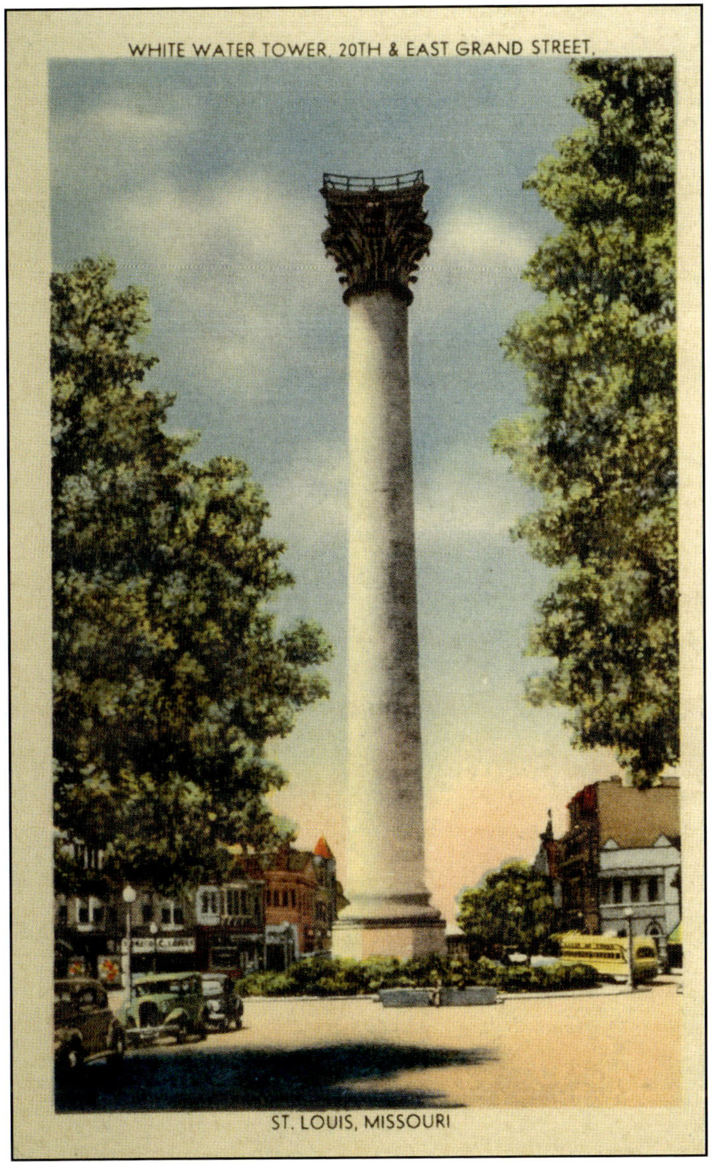

The old white water tower was built in 1871, and is one of the few Victorian-era water towers that still stand today in the U. S. Built to a height of 154 feet, the rear of the card notes it to be the largest Corinthian column in the world.

Circa 1914, $2-4

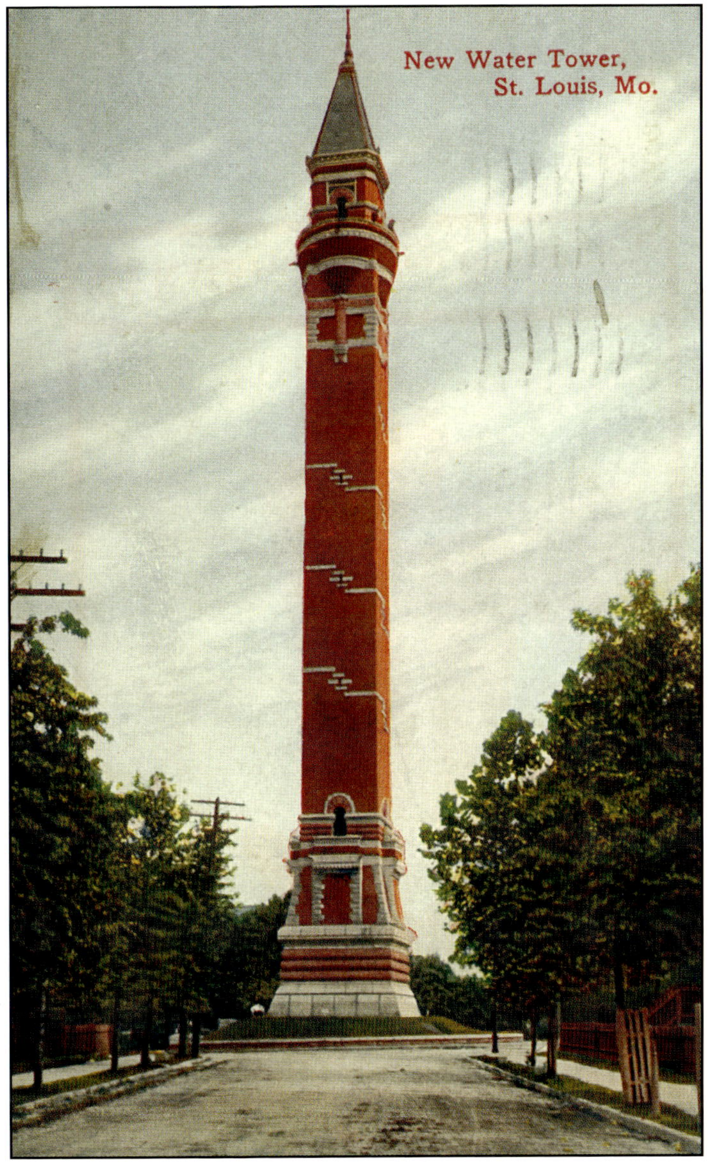

Located at Bissell and Blair Avenues, the New Water Tower—often called the Red Water Tower because it is made of brick—was built 1885-1886.

Cancelled 1909, $2-4

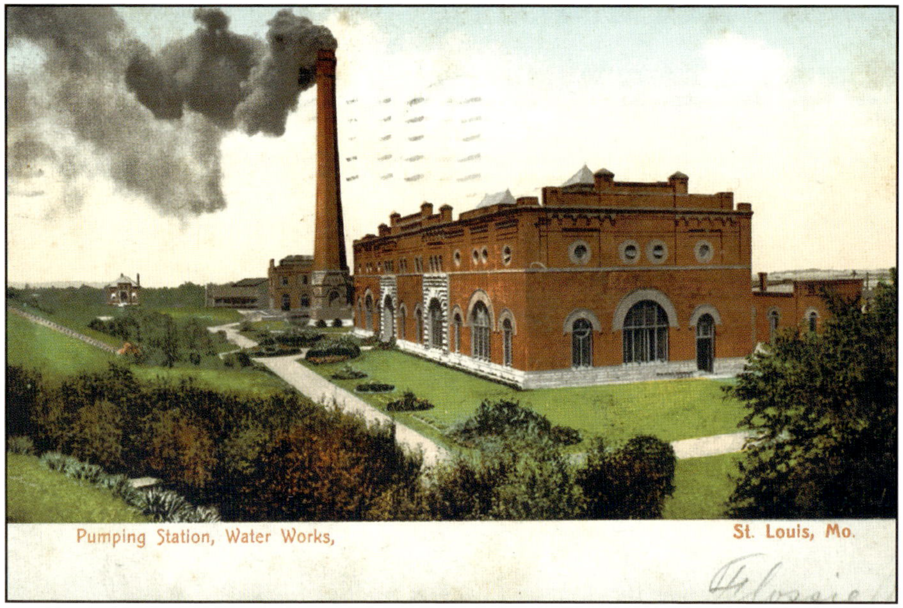

The Chain of Rocks Water Works was noted as a great and powerful facility kept in constant operation, pumping millions of gallons of water through the mains of the city.

Cancelled 1908, $2-4

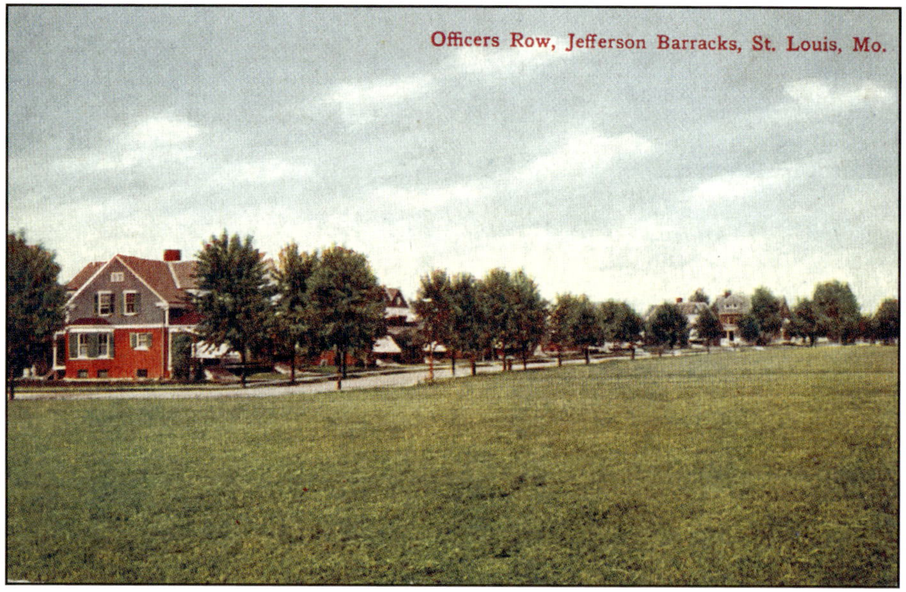

The Jefferson Barracks, named for Thomas Jefferson, was established in 1826. Noted as the first U. S. "Infantry School of Practice," it continued as a key military installation until 1946. Originally, the post was built to replace Fort Bellefontaine.

Circa 1914, $2-4

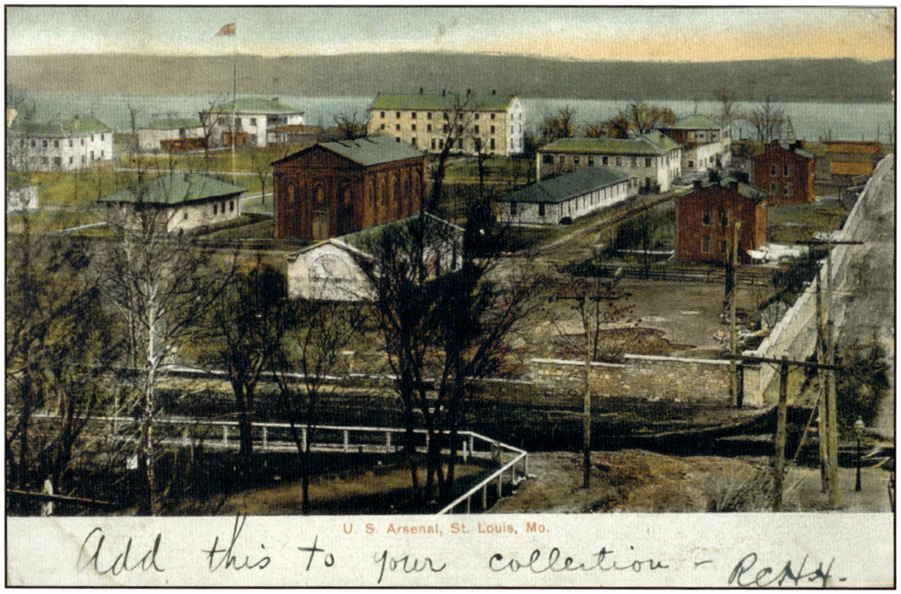

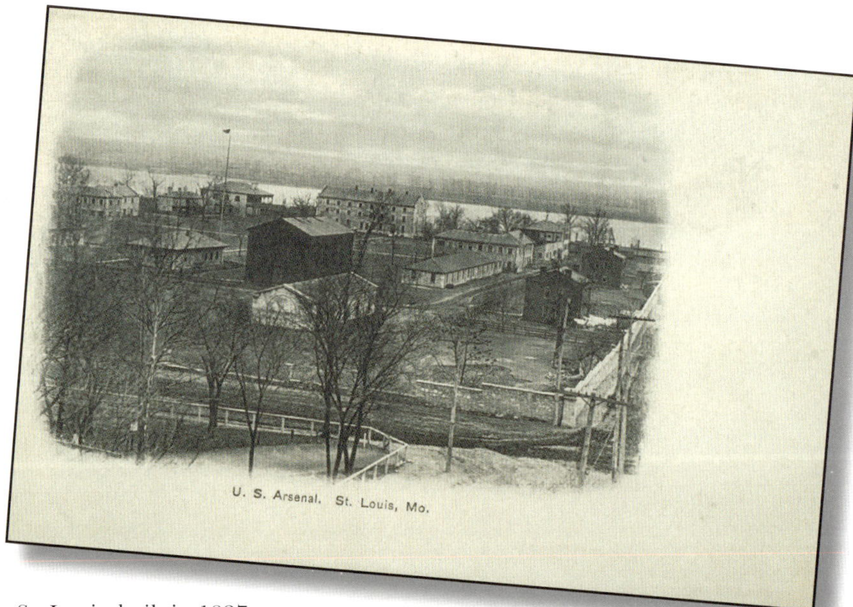

Two views of the U. S. Arsenal in St. Louis, built in 1827.

Cancelled 1907, $2-4 (left)
Circa Early 1900s, $3-5 (right)

Union Station

Union Station, one of St. Louis's most popular tourist attractions, was once the largest and busiest passenger rail terminal in the world. It was first opened in 1894, but by 1978, it ceased operation as an active train terminal. Since being re-opened in 1985, it has become the largest adaptive re-use project in the United States, featuring such things as a 539-room Hyatt Regency Hotel, luxury offices, a ten-screen movie theater, and a lake.

At the turn of the twentieth century, Fred Harvey opened the Fred Harvey Restaurant in, what was then, the Terminal Hotel. The travelers' food orders were taken by the brakeman while they were still onboard the train. By being wired to the restaurant manager, it made it possible for travelers to enjoy a nice meal with plenty of time to catch their next train. Appealing even more so to the public were the "Harvey Girl" waitresses, Fred Harvey's most popular "attraction." Although a delightful feature of the restaurant, the Harvey Girls had strict guidelines to follow once employed. They had to be of high moral character and between eighteen and twenty years old. Although they needed to be attractive and intelligent, they also had to take a vow not to marry for a year after they were employed. A housemother chaperoned the girls to be sure they stuck to their ten pm curfew.

Fred Harvey Restaurant is now the Station Grille, the highly-acclaimed restaurant located in the Hyatt Regency Hotel in Union Station. This 130-seat restaurant, which has been restored to its original grandeur, serves some of the finest cuisines in the city.

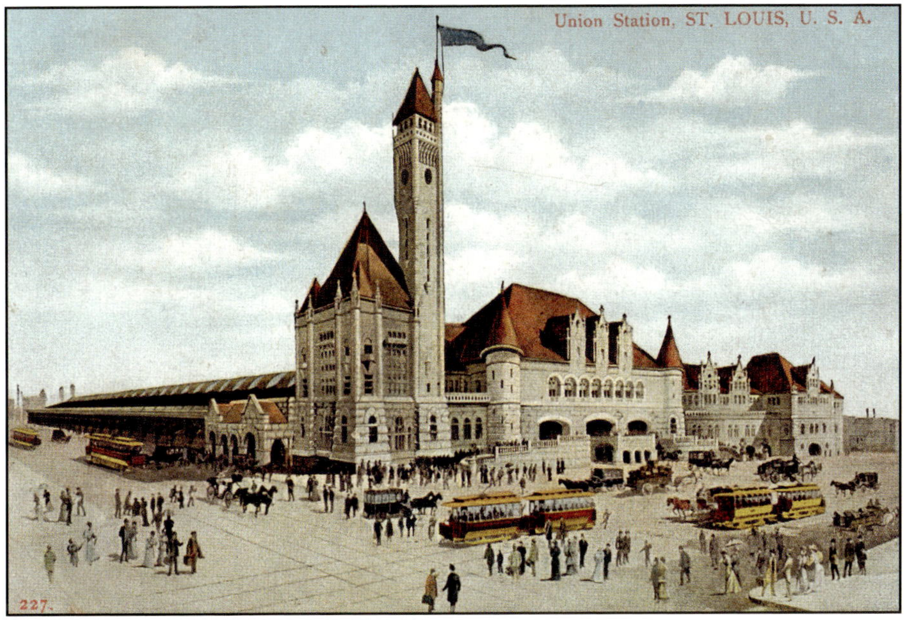

Union Station, stretching over eleven and one half acres, was once the largest and busiest railroad terminal in the world. After a major reconstruction, in was reopened in 1985, with a hotel and marketplace providing shops, restaurants, and cafes. Live entertainment and a lake with boats are also must-see features at the new Union Station.

Circa 1907, $2-4 (above)
Circa 1930s, $3-5 (right top)
Circa 1914, $2-4 (right bottom)

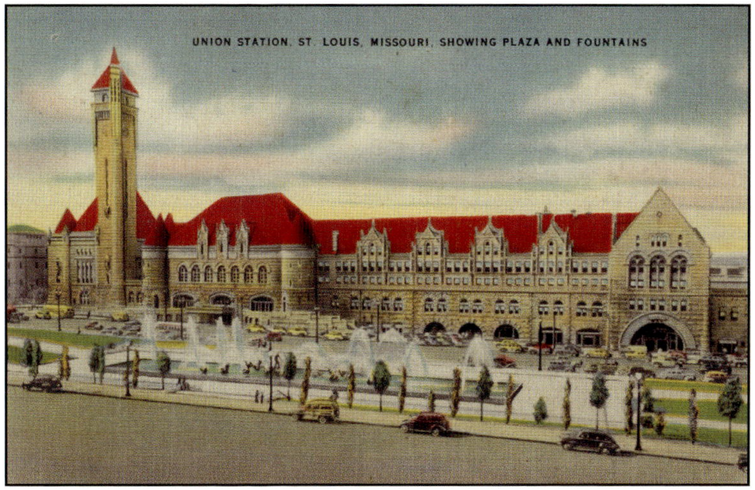

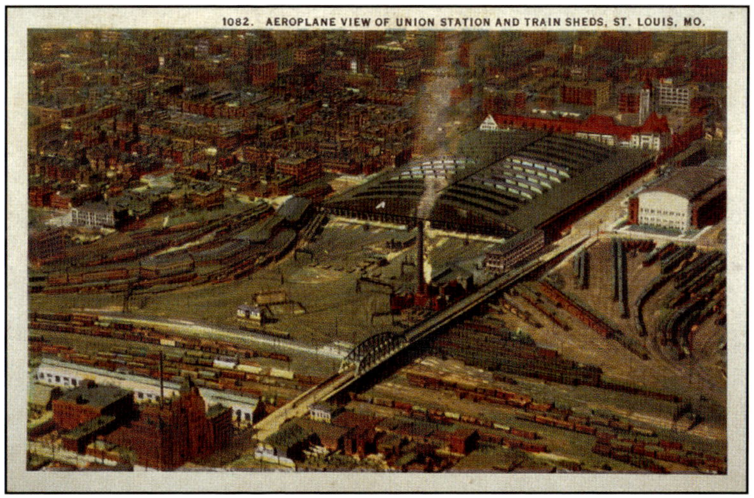

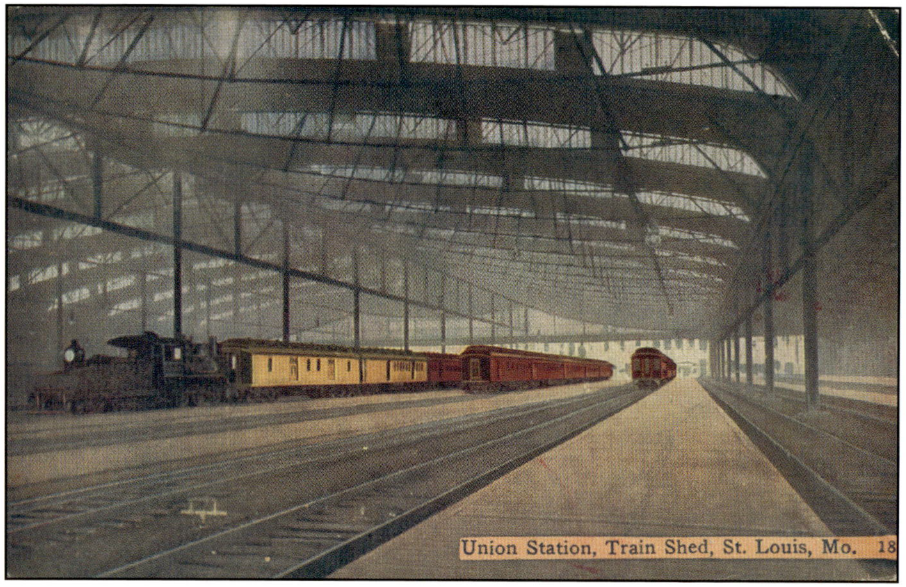

Cancelled 1924, $2-4

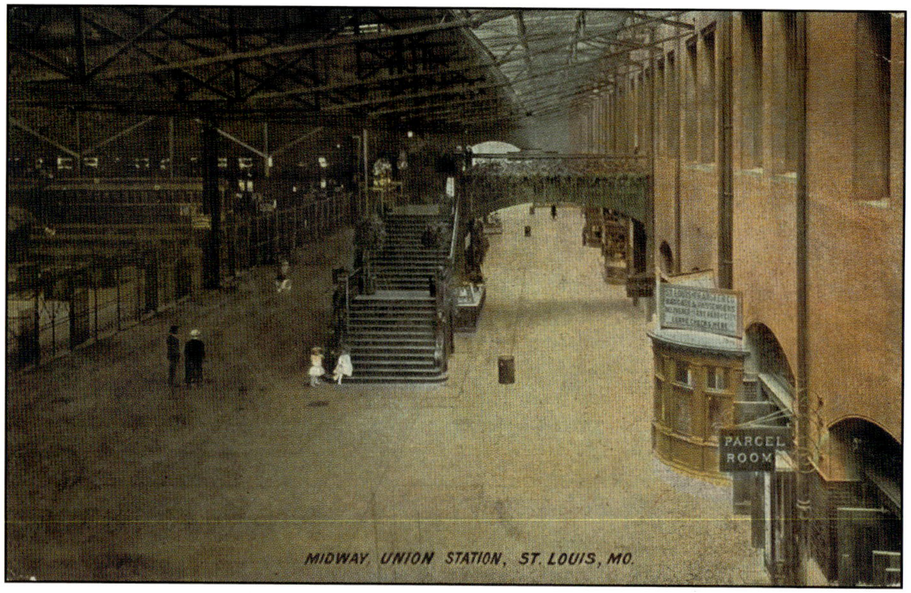

Cancelled 1912, $2-4

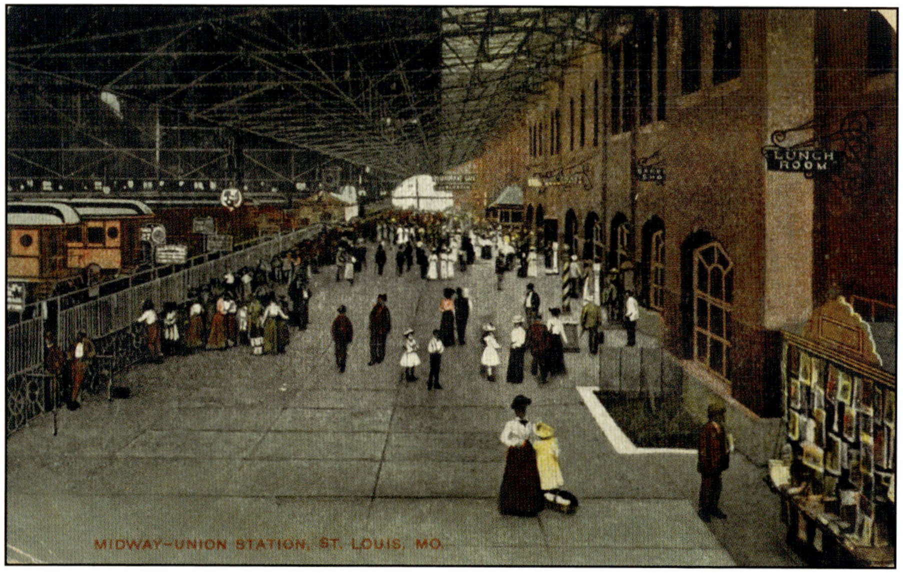

Cancelled 1912, $2-4

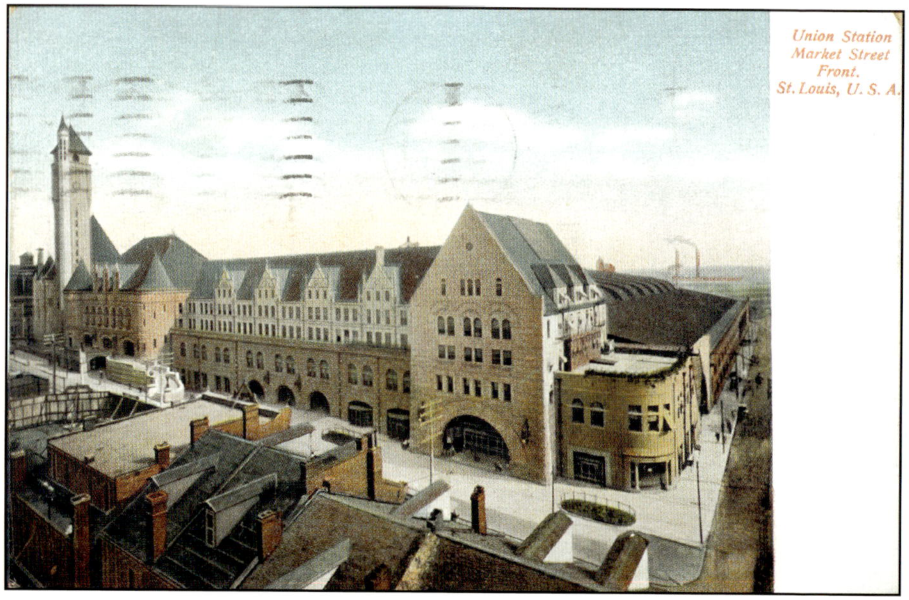

Cancelled 1906, $3-5

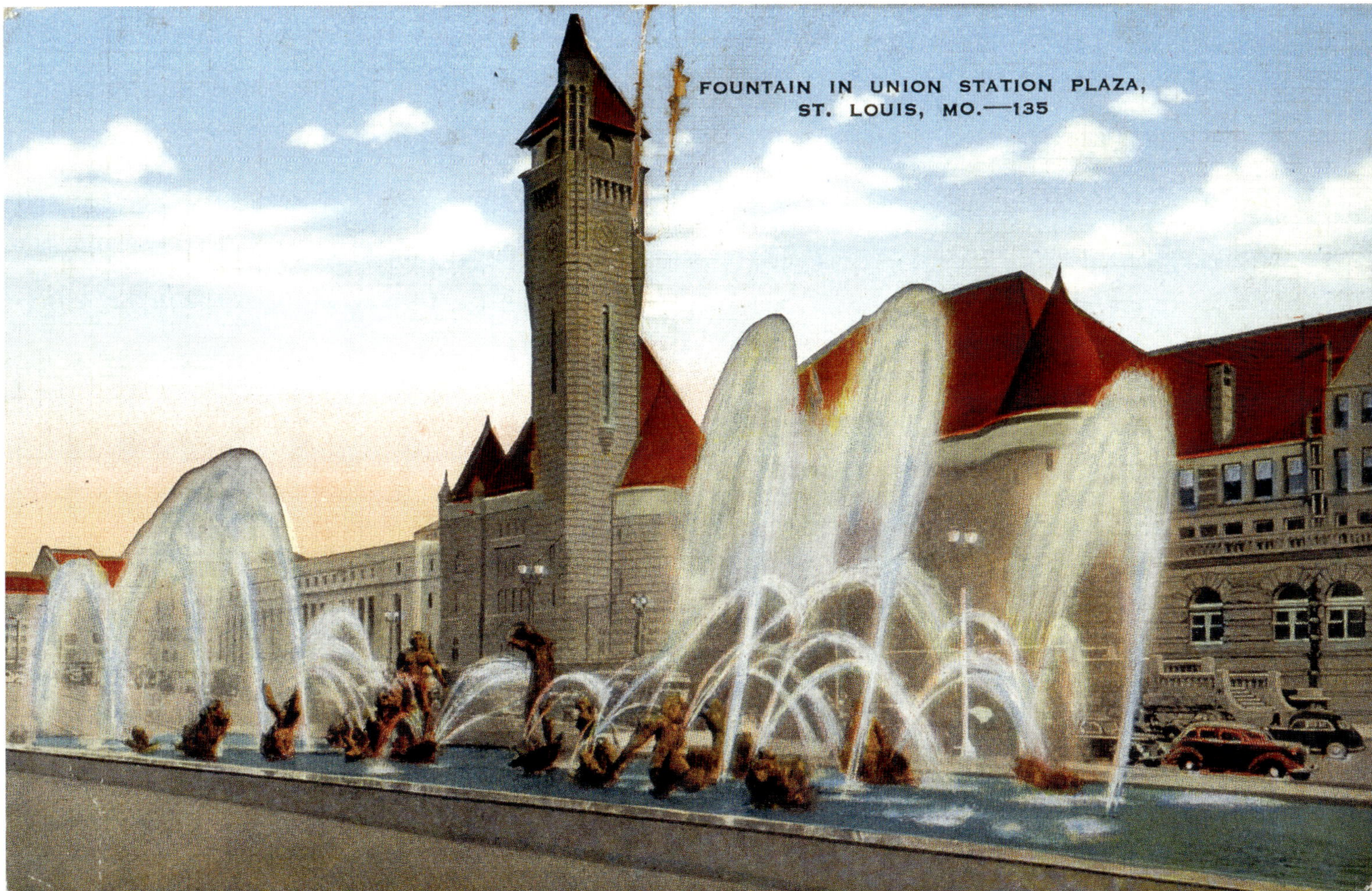

This view of the fountain at Aloe Plaza shows the entrance to Union Station. The fountain features nineteen bronze figurines that were designed by Carl Milles. The sculptures are used to depict the meeting of the waters, the Missouri, and the Mississippi. The name *Aloe* comes from the husband of Mrs. Louis P. Aloe, who set the plans in motion for the fountain and made a large contribution toward it.

Circa 1940, $3-5

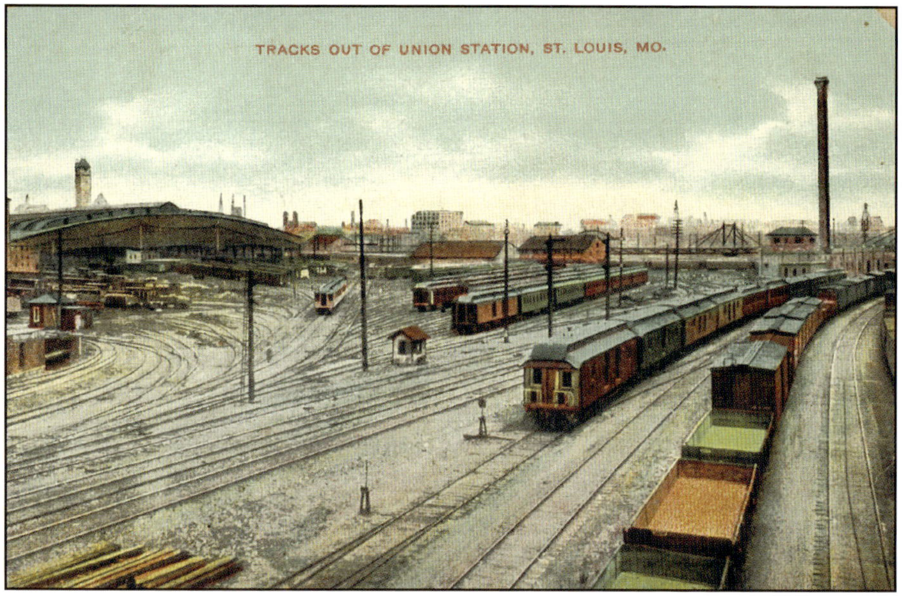

Circa 1910, $2-4

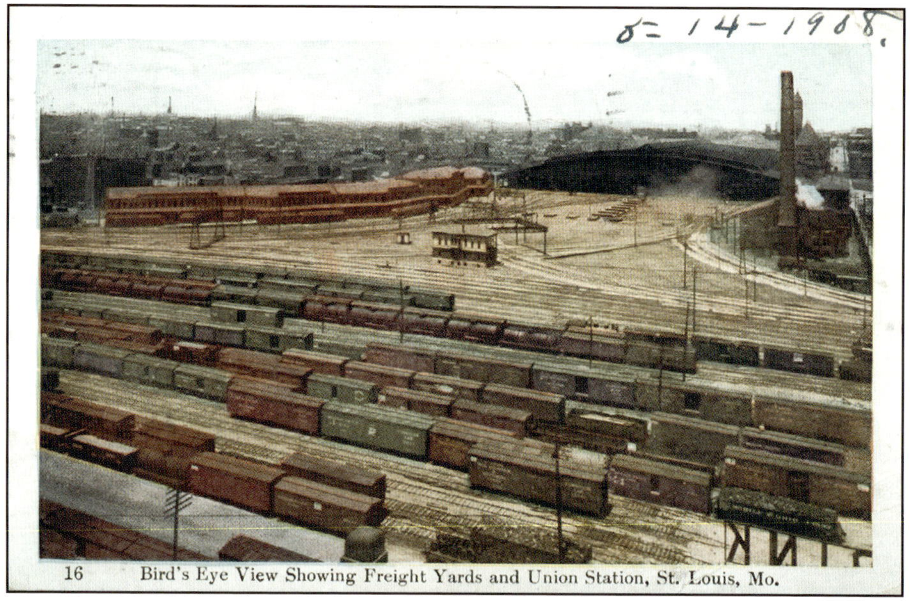

Cancelled 1910 (twice), $2-4

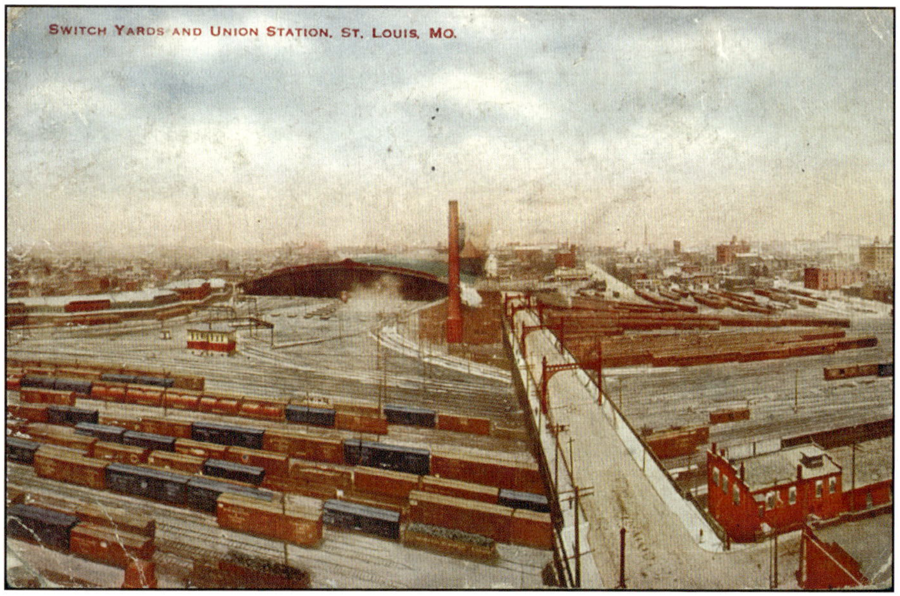

Cancelled 1911, $2-4

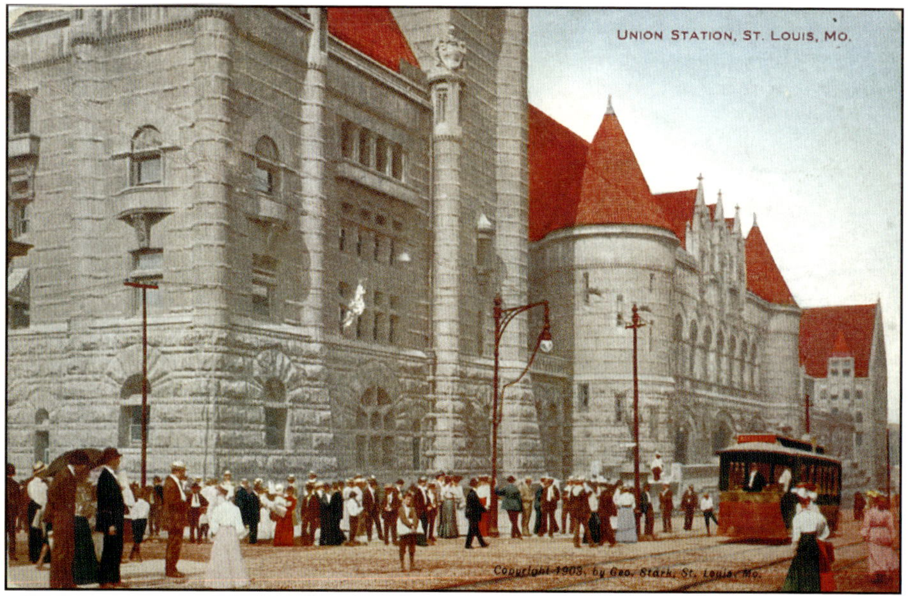

Cancelled 1907, $2-4

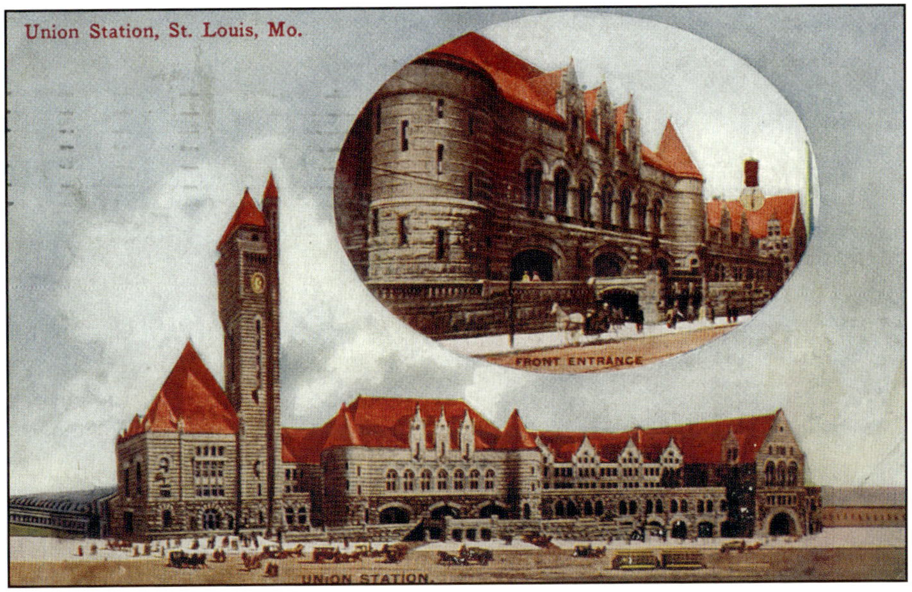

Cancelled 1910, $2-4

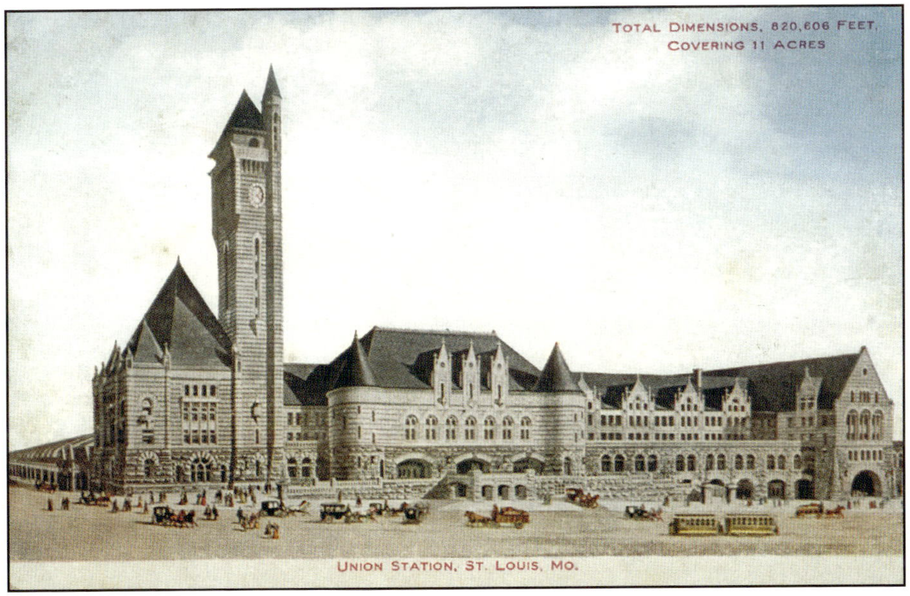

Cancelled 1908, $2-4

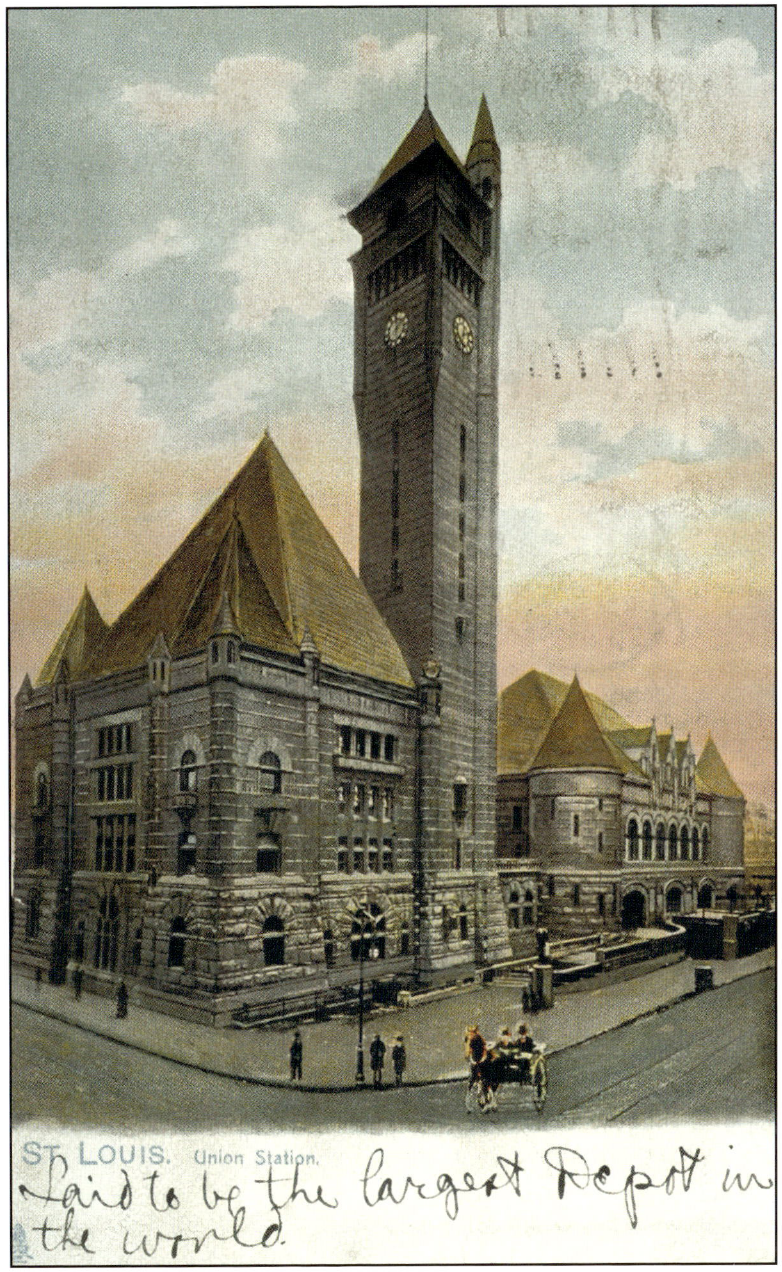

Cancelled 1908, $3-5

Memorials

St. Louis found it important to memorialize the many people who helped her reach her current thriving status of today. See here, The Soldiers Memorial, cemeteries, and statues that continue to describe the depth of heart in St. Louis.

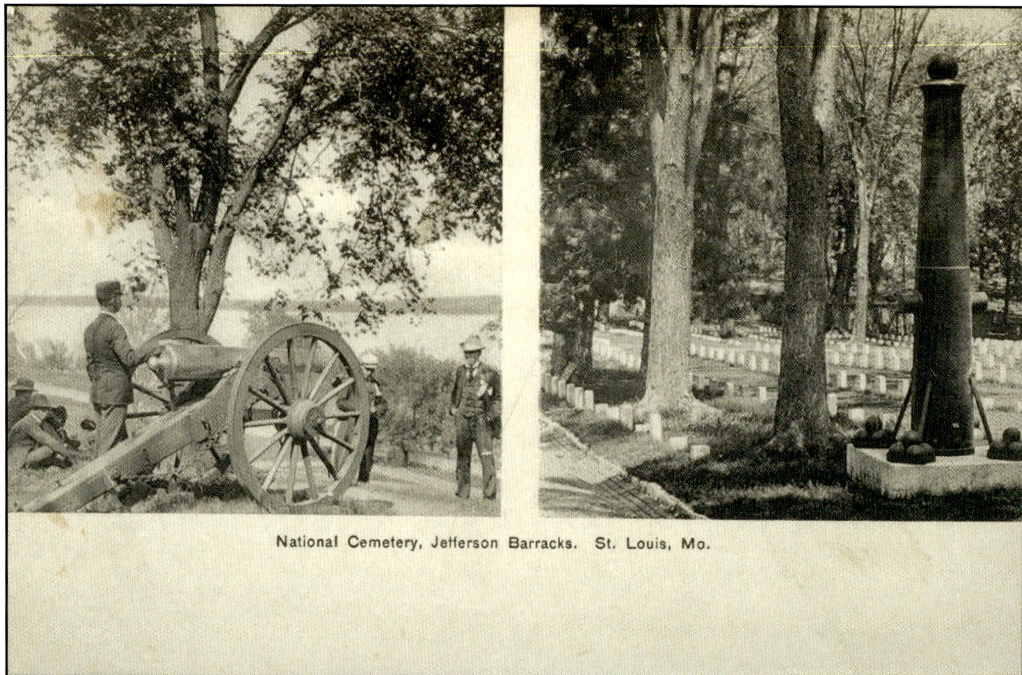

One of the oldest grave sites of the National Cemetery Administration, soldiers from all wars have been memorialized at the Jefferson Barracks Cemetery.

Cancelled 1906, $3-5

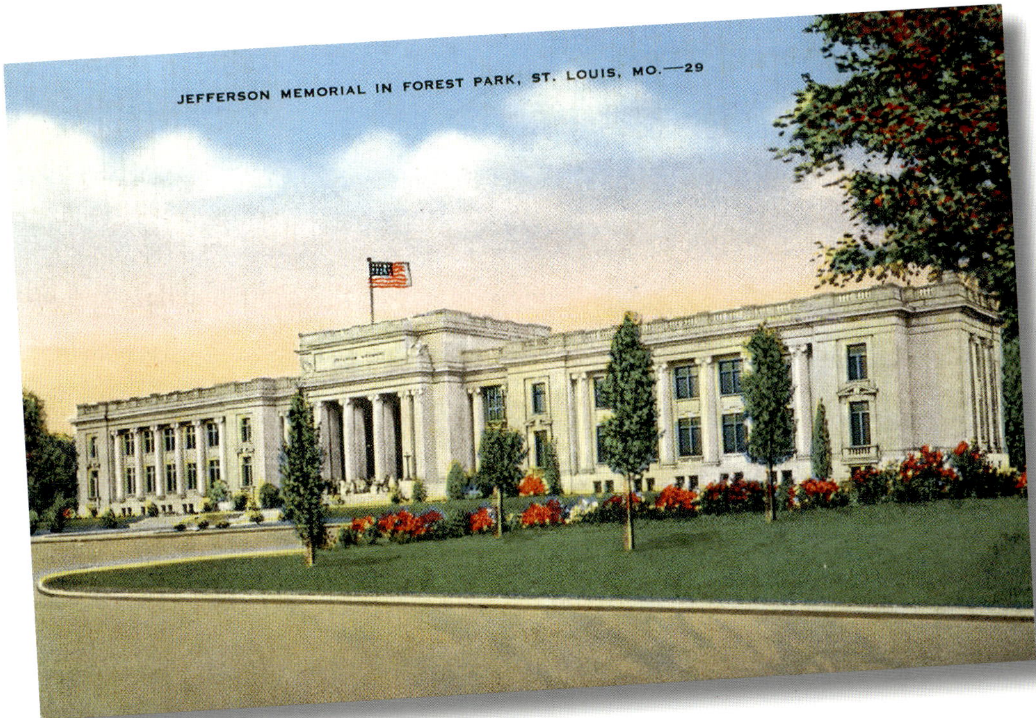

The Jefferson Memorial, located in Forest Park, is home to the Missouri Historical Society, which has been active since 1866.

Circa 1907, $2-4

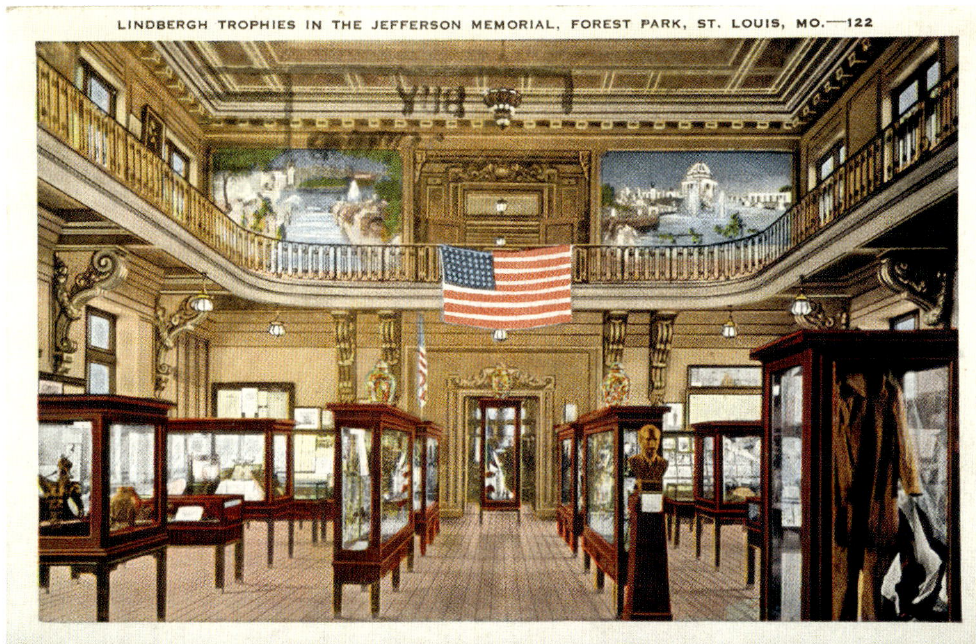

One of the famous exhibitions found at the Jefferson Memorial is the historic presentation of Charles A. Lindberg and his solo transatlantic flight in the Spirit of St. Louis from New York to Paris. Lindberg's original book manuscript, *We*, is also among the treasures to be found there.

Cancelled 1943, $2-4

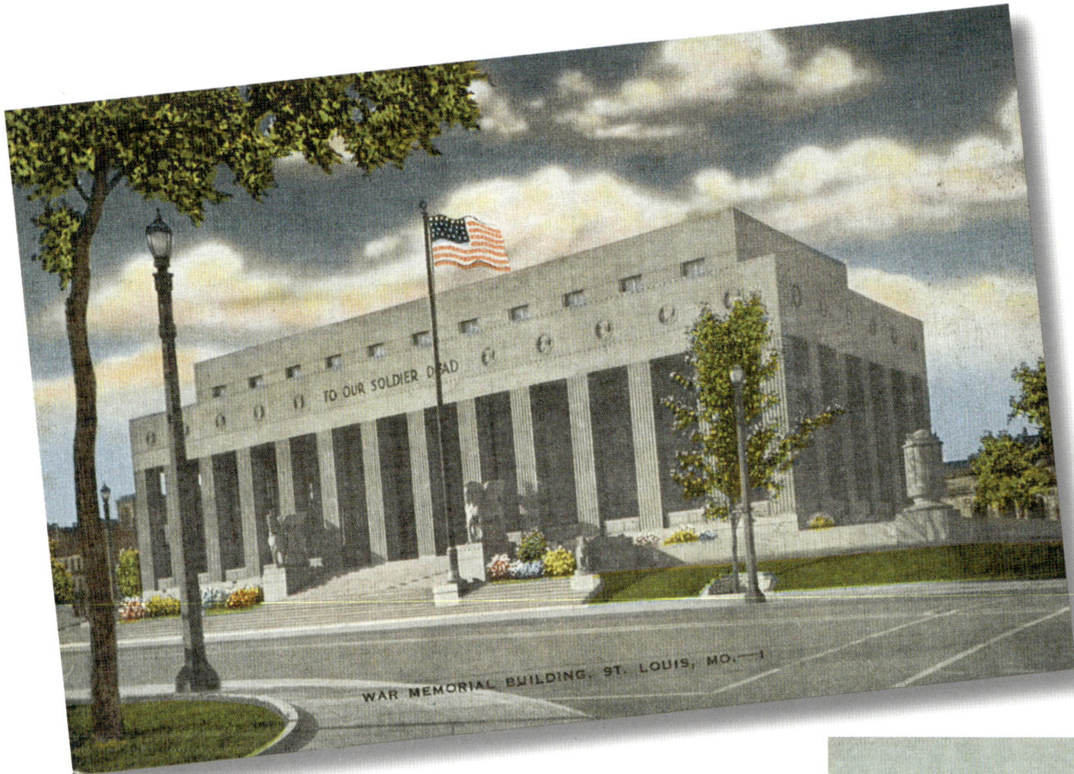

The Soldiers Memorial, erected in 1936, was the first of two war memorials completed to pay tribute to World War I veterans. There are two halls to house museum-type memorabilia and an assembly room in the building.

Circa 1930s, $2-4

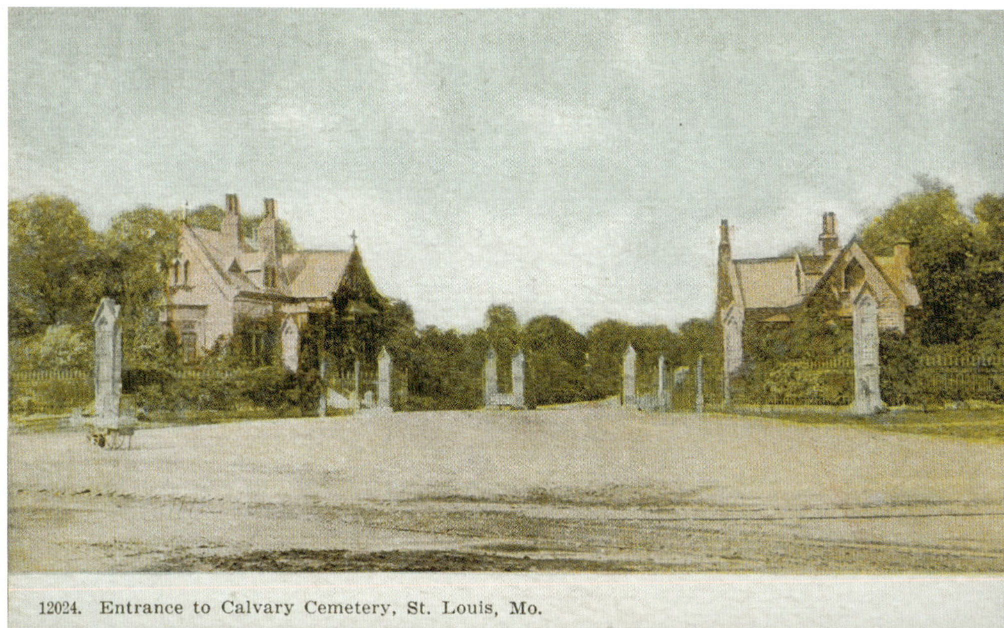

The Calvary Cemetery was established in 1857. Noted as a Catholic cemetery containing graves of important people in St. Louis history, there were also old burials and tombstones relocated from downtown locations to this cemetery.

Circa 1907, $2-4

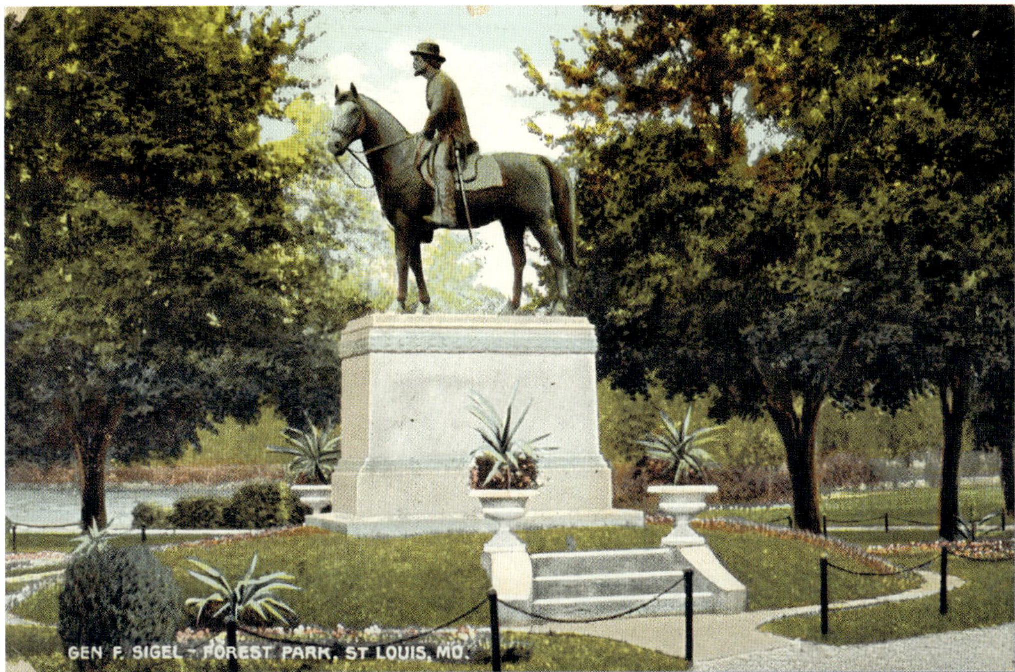

General F. Siegel lead an impressive battle display at the Battle of Carthage during the beginning of the Civil War. He had his men form a line of battle and then moved within 800 yards of State Guard Troops. Though this particular conflict had little meaning, pro Southern factions in Missouri were anxious for any good news—and found this particular win a victory to celebrate.

Circa 1907, $2-4

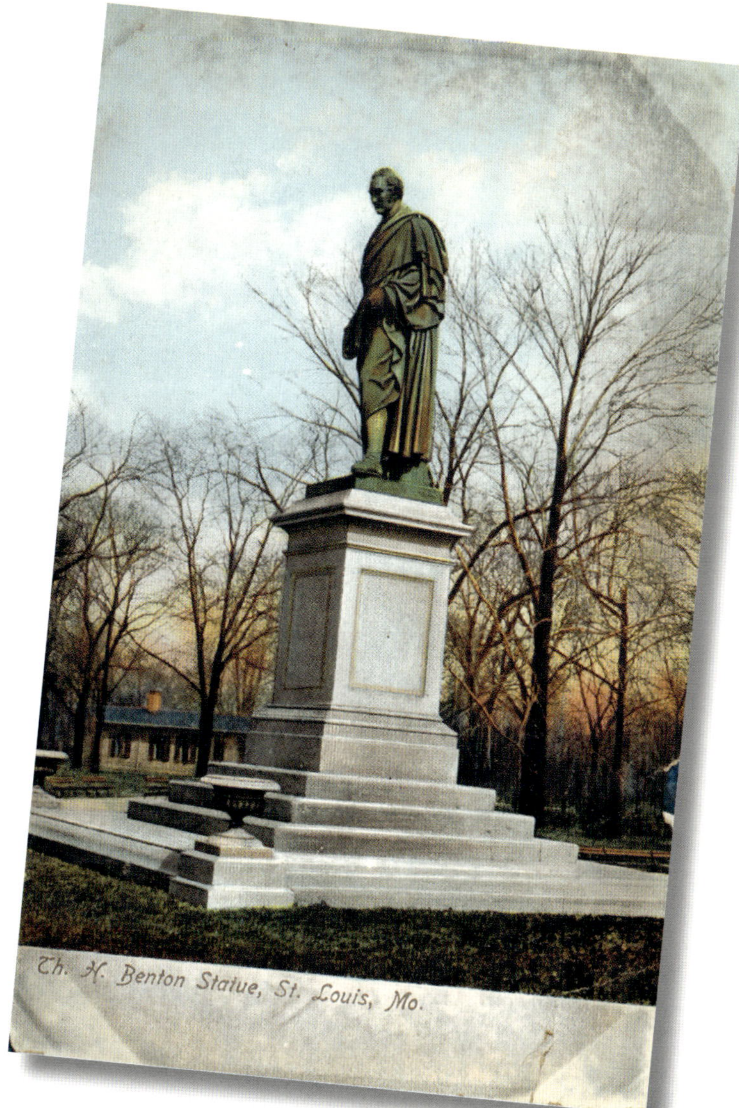

The Thomas Hart Benton Statue located in Lafayette Park. Benton, nicknamed "Old Bullion," was an advocate of westward expansion as well as a senator. Another statue honoring him is one of two for Missourians at the U. S. Capital building in Washington, D.C.

Circa Early 1900s, $2-4

Medical Facilities

Some of the most prestigious medical facilities in the world are located in St. Louis. Whether helping the sick poor, the children, or the general public, this city has been ahead in medical practices from the very beginning. Among those pictured here are: The St. Alexius Hospital, Shriners Hospital, The Barnes Hospital, City Hospital, DePaul Hospital, and others spanning from the late 1800s to the 1900s.

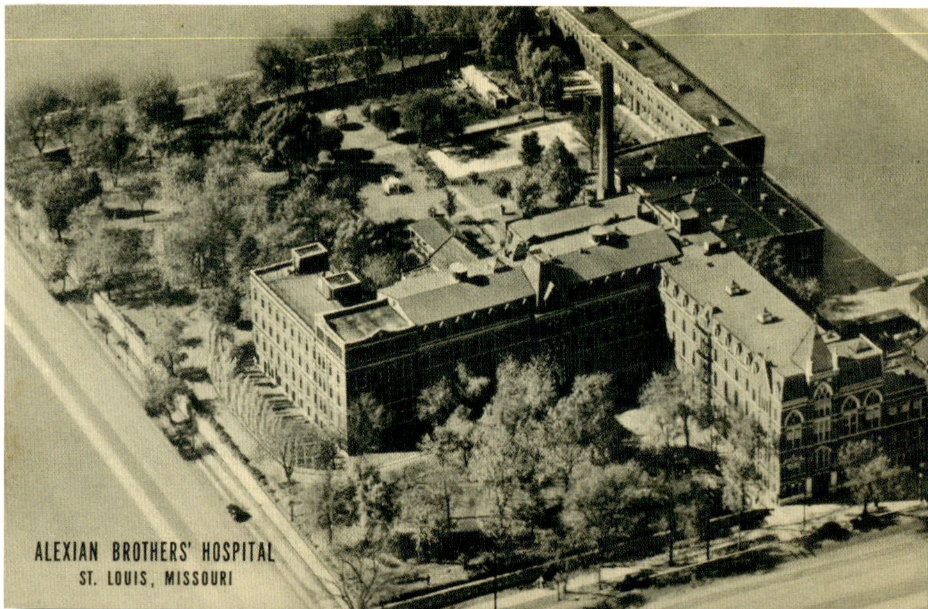

The St. Alexius Hospital, Broadway Campus, was formerly The Alexian Brothers' Hospital displayed here. The mission is rooted in Christianity and is shown by the compassion and respect those working there give to the medical treatment provided for residents in St. Louis.

Circa 1907, $3-5

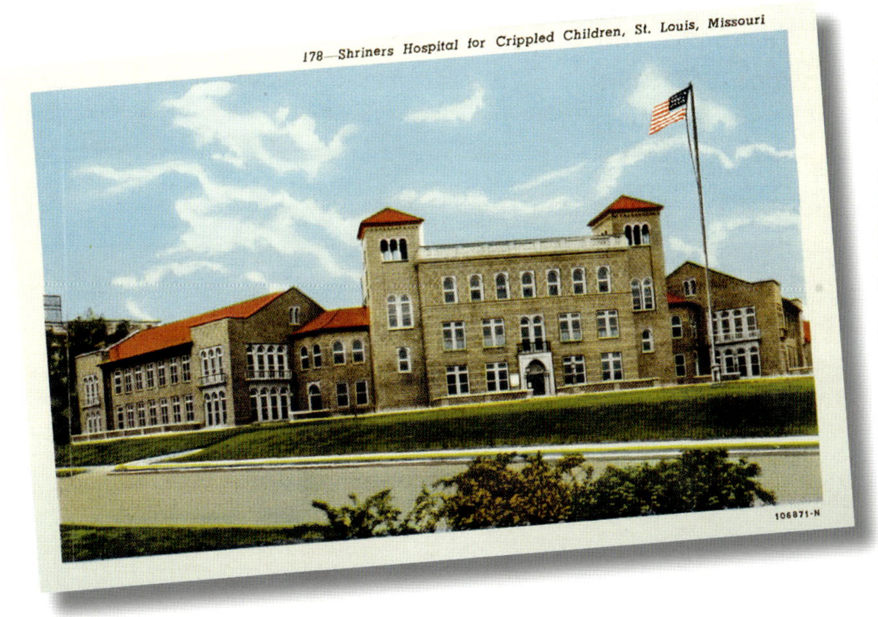

Shriners Hospitals total twenty-two in an international hospital system that specializes in the expert healthcare of children under eighteen years of age. At their 1919 Imperial Council Session, it was voted that not *one* hospital should be developed, but *many* throughout the world. In 1921, the proposal passed. The first hospital was located in Shreveport, LA in 1922, but within ten years, thirteen more would be in operation—pictured here is the St. Louis hospital.

Circa 1914, $2-4

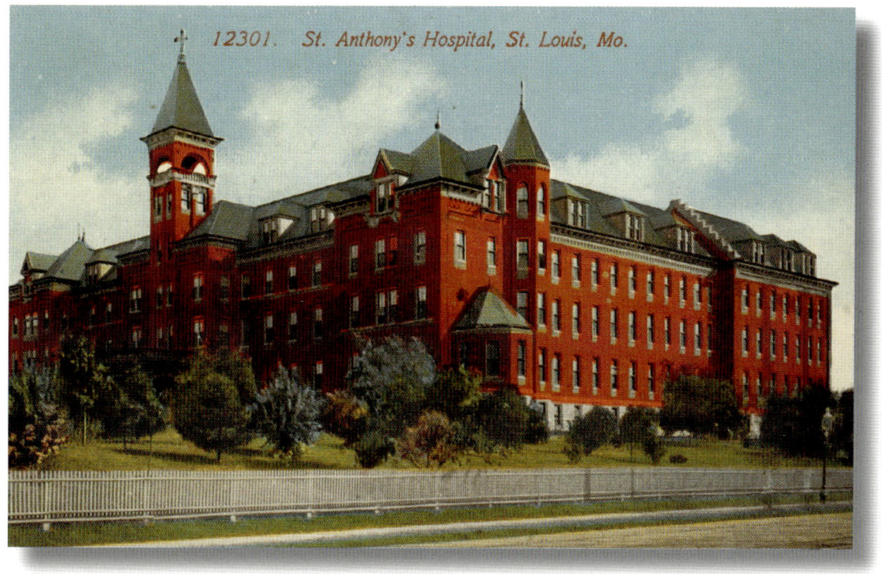

In 1900, the Franciscan Sisters of Germany opened this Catholic faith-based medical facility, named after St. Anthony of Padua. The hospital was expanded in 1904 and 1905, as the community surrounding it grew. In the 1940s and 1950s, it became well known for treating polio patients.

Circa 1907, $2-4

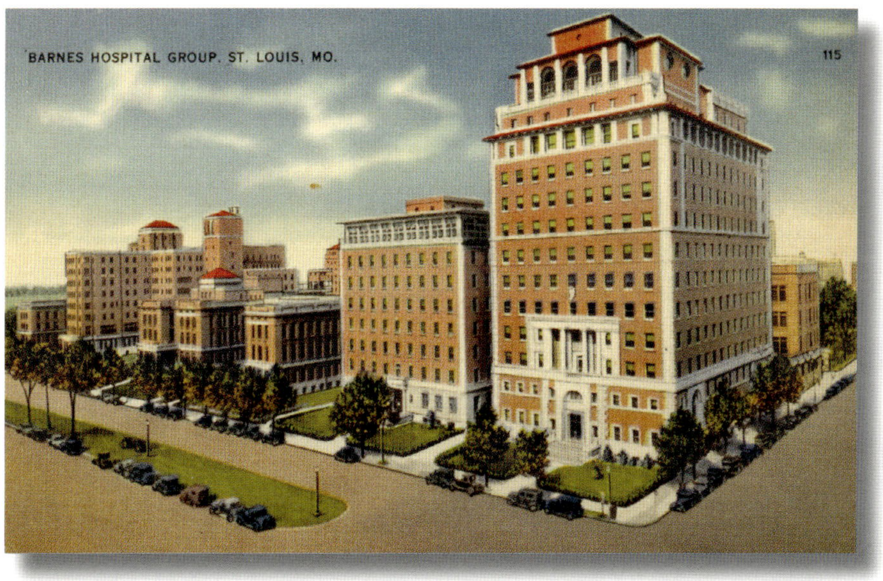

The Barnes Hospital group was named after Robert Barnes, who moved from Washington, D. C. to St. Louis in his youth. Working himself up from the grocery wholesaling and banking businesses, he amassed his fortune. At his death, he bequeathed $850,000 for the construction of a "modern, general hospital for sick and injured persons, without distinction of creed." The Barnes Hospital was dedicated in 1912.

Circa 1930s, $2-4

City Hospital, built in 1846 in the city, cared for the poor sick and emergency cases of all kinds.

Cancelled 1913, $2-4

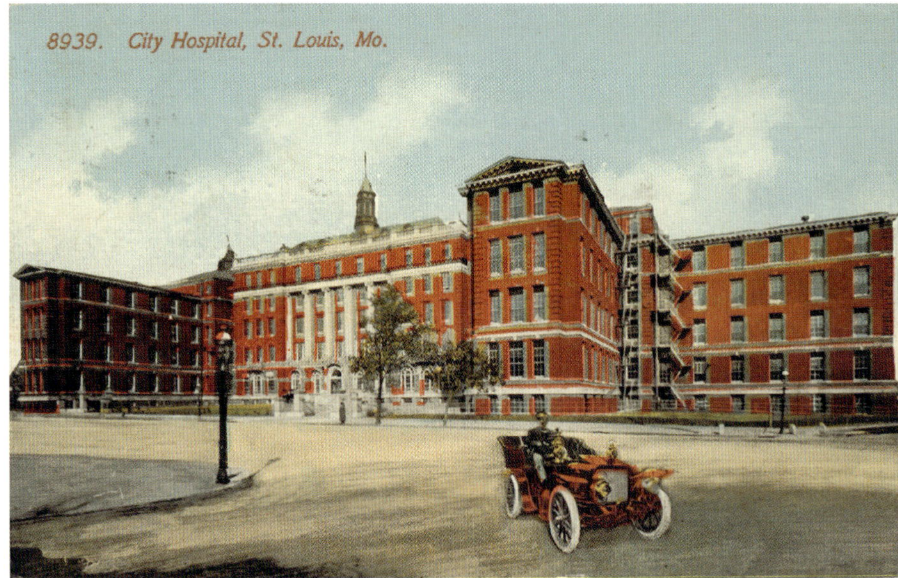

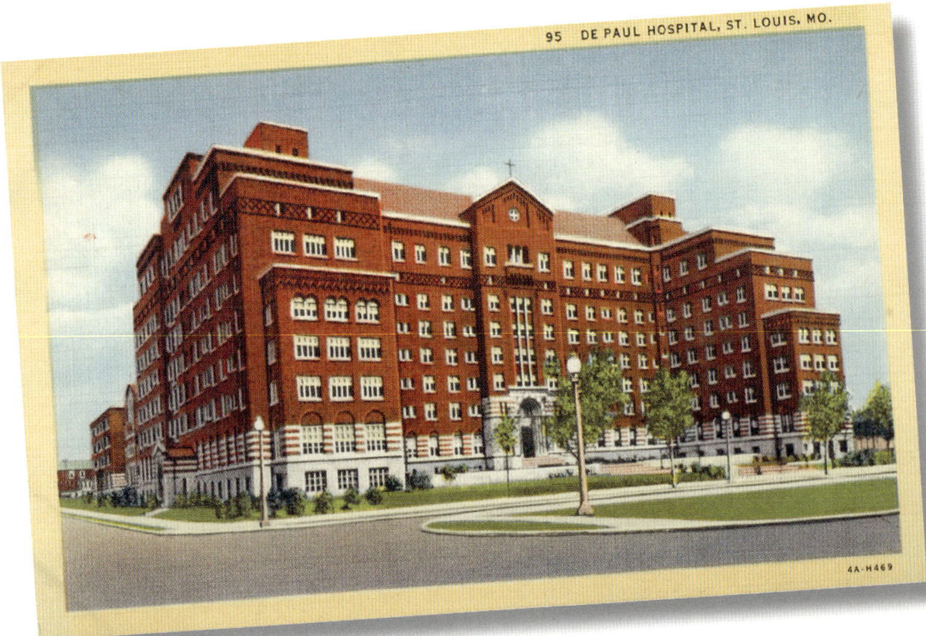

The De Paul Hospital, opened in 1828, was the oldest Catholic hospital in the country. Owned by the Daughters of St. Vincent de Paul, it was originally known as the Sisters' Hospital.

Circa 1914, $2-4

The Frisco Hospital was a large and modern facility built to serve the railroad employees of the Frisco Lines.

Cancelled 1916, $2-4

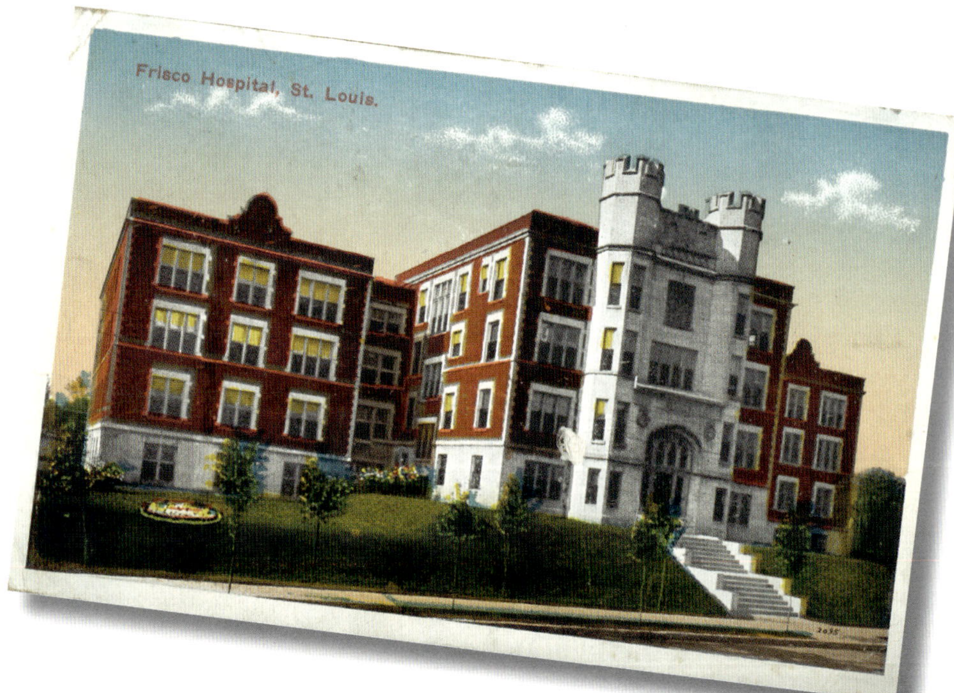

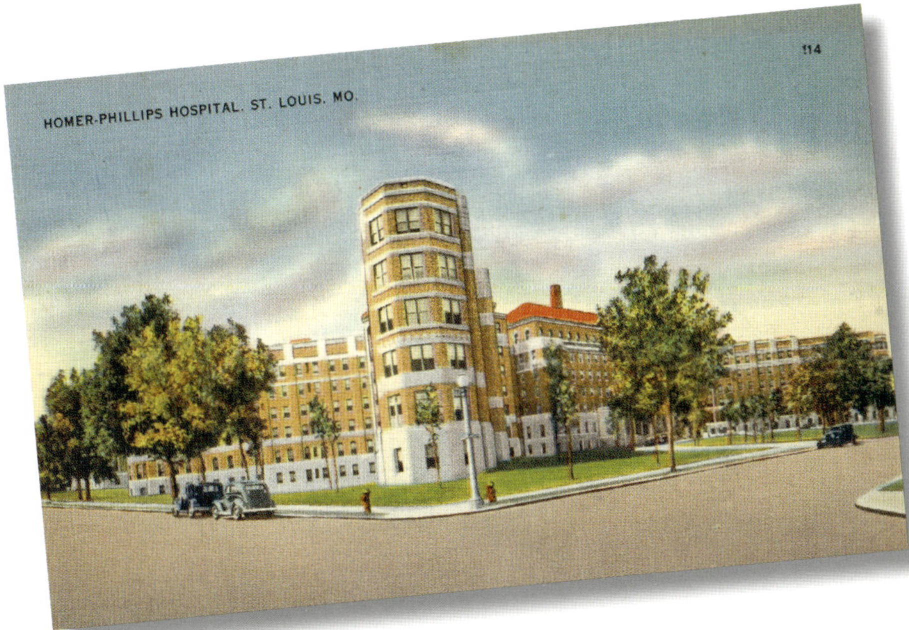

Built in 1932, the Homer G. Phillips Hospital served the poor black population in the city. Situated on over four acres, the hospital had a bed capacity of 685.

Circa 1930s, $2-4

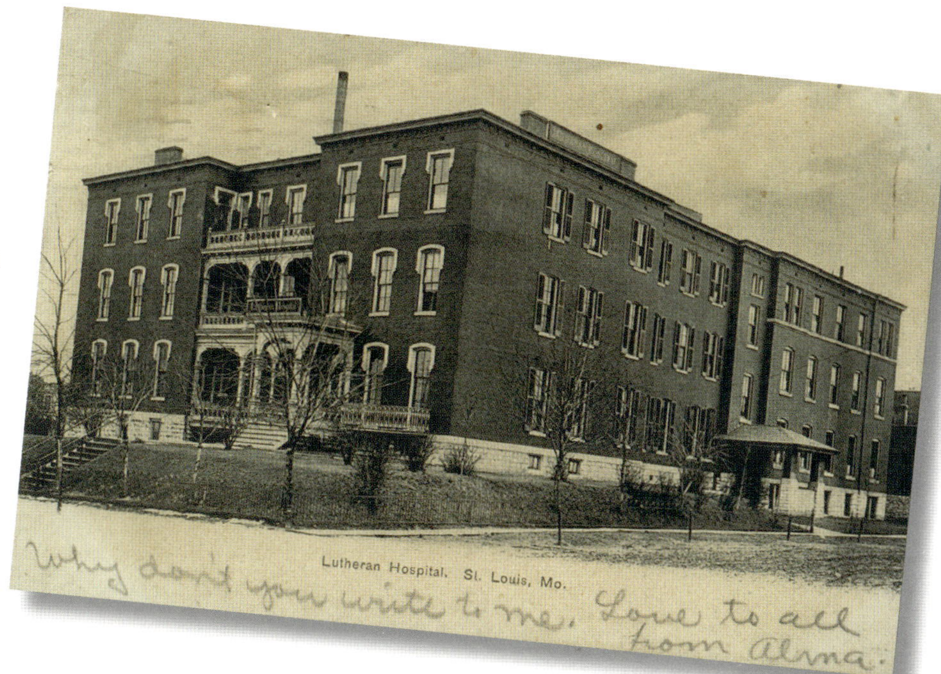

The Lutheran Hospital was opened in 1858.

Cancelled 1908, $3-5

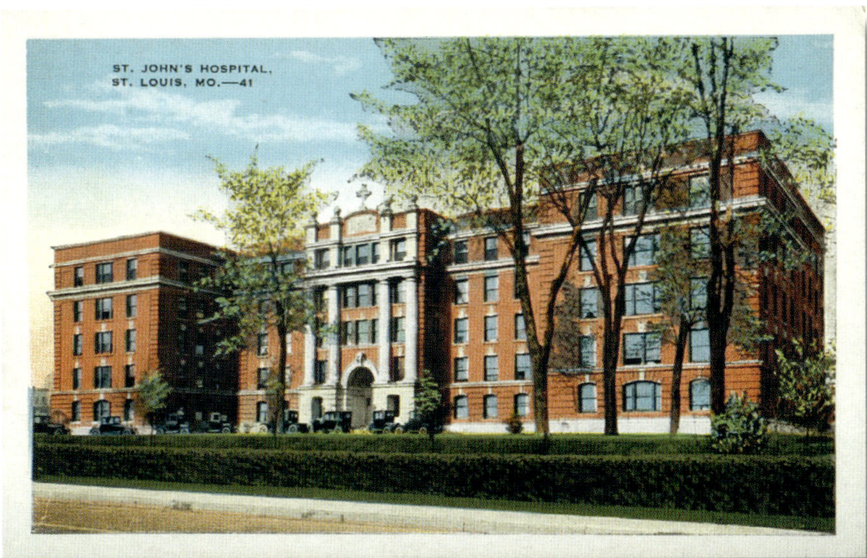

Opened in 1871, St. John's Hospital was a private medical facility and free clinic run by the Sisters of Mercy.

Circa 1914, $2-4

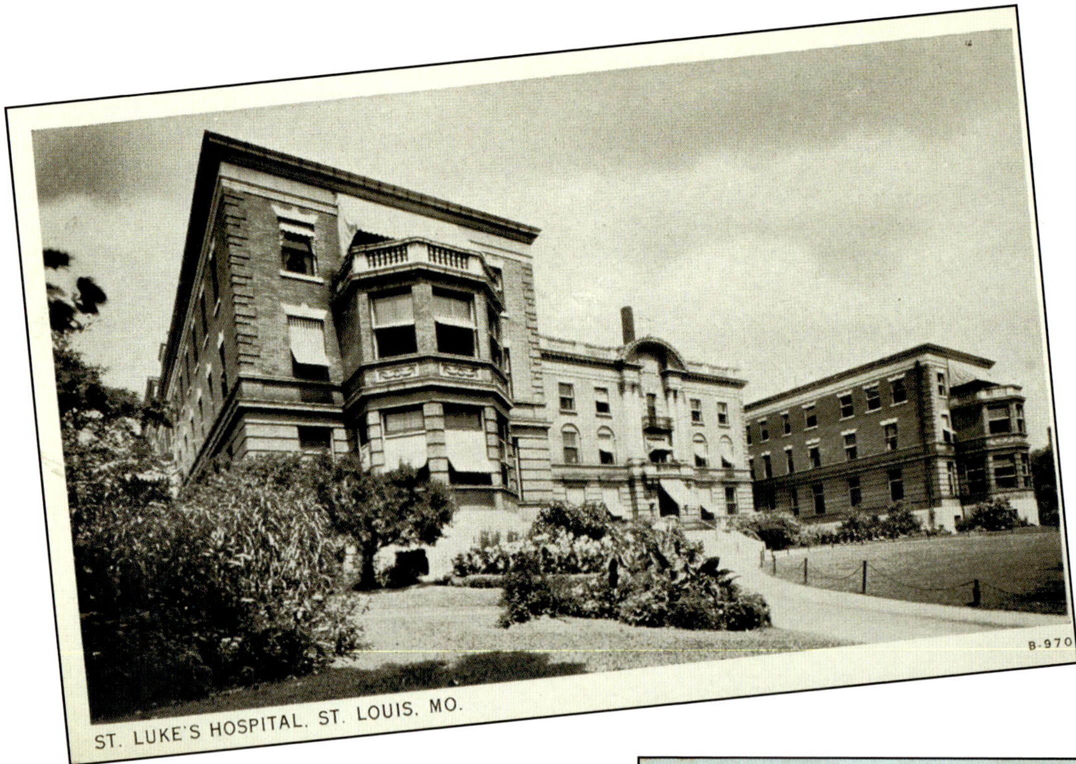

St. Luke's Hospital opened in 1866 as a privately-run medical institution of the Episcopal Church. It was known for accepting charity cases and its fine nursing school.

Circa 1907, $2-4

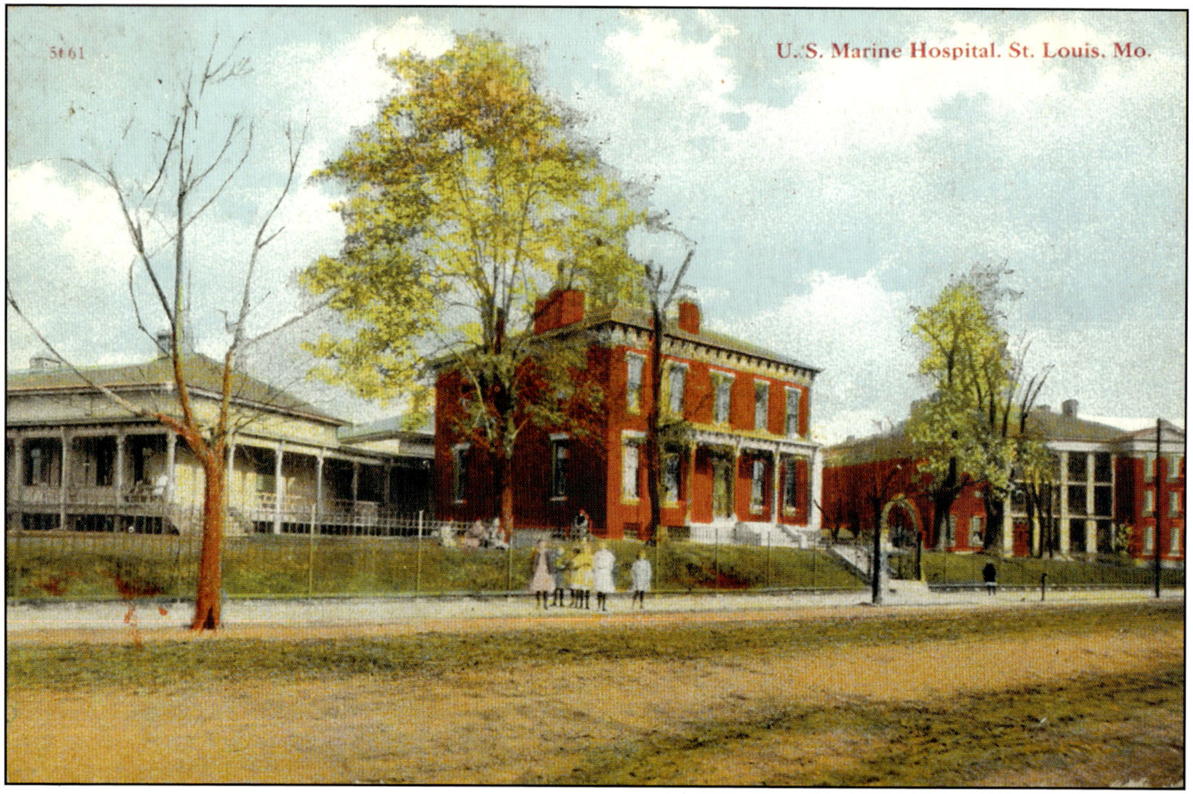

The U. S. Marine Hospital, erected in 1846, was a hospital for sick and disabled seamen. A free government facility, the seamen had to meet specific eligibility requirements to be treated—sixty days of service on a registered vessel. The hospital was, in 1953, taken over by the Sisters of St. Joseph of Carondelet, and its name was changed to St. Joseph's Hospital.

Cancelled in 1912, $2-4

Educational Facilities

In 1838, the first public schools were opened in St. Louis, and by the 1850s, the number of students had quadrupled. By 1900, the population in St. Louis was 575,238 and the need for both public and private education became clear. Shown here are not only some of the primary schools, but the colleges that have provided consistent high educational standards to flourish in St. Louis over the years.

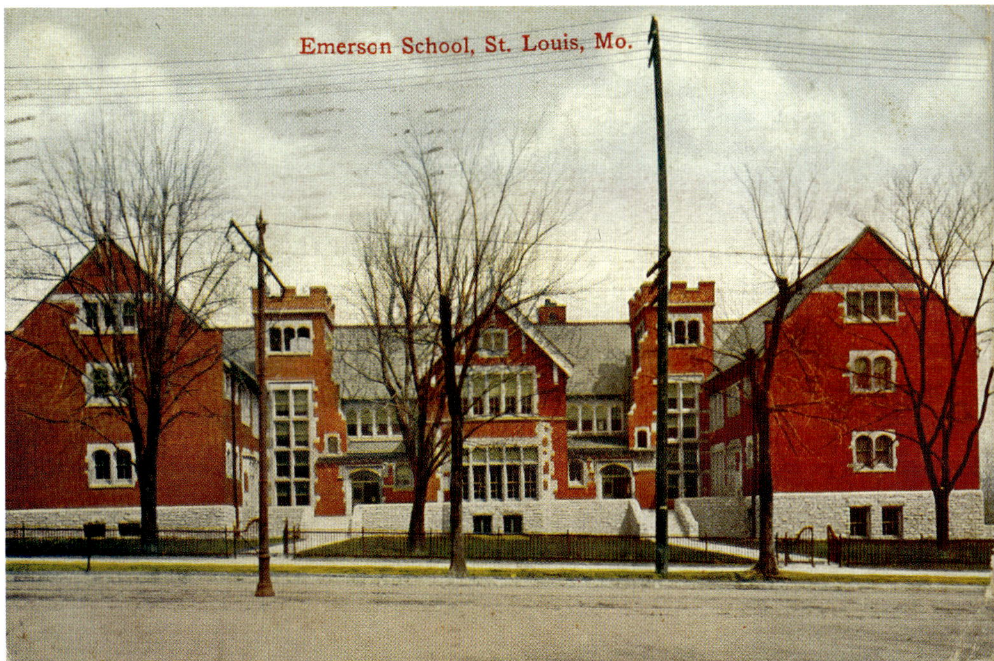

Emerson School.

Cancelled 1913, $2-4

Garfield (Public) School.

Circa Early 1900s, $6-8

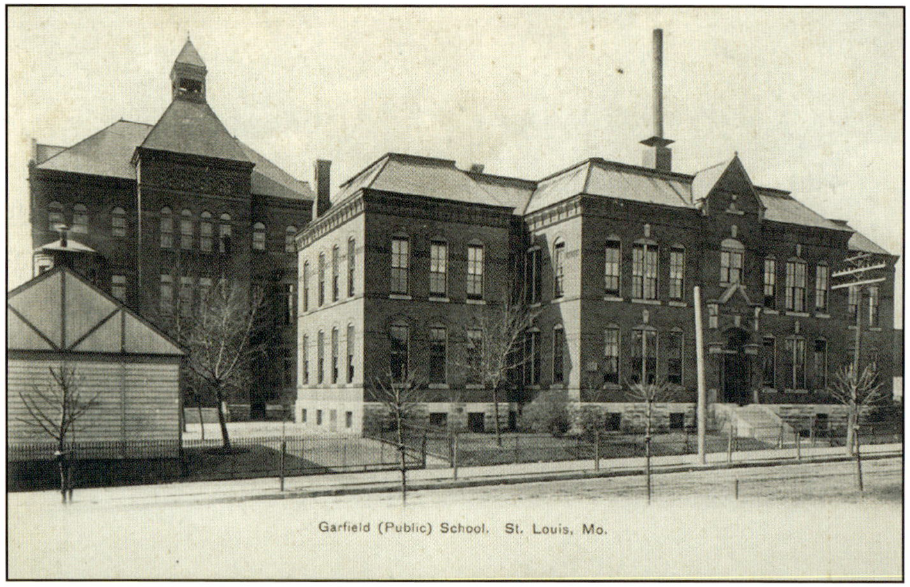

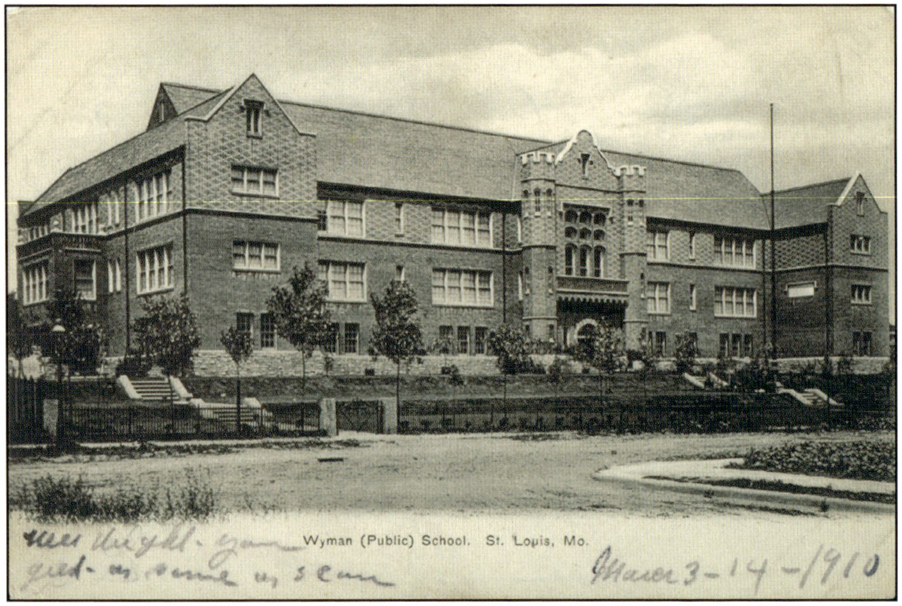

Wyman (Public) School.

Cancelled 1910, $3-5

Central High School.

Circa 1907, $2-4

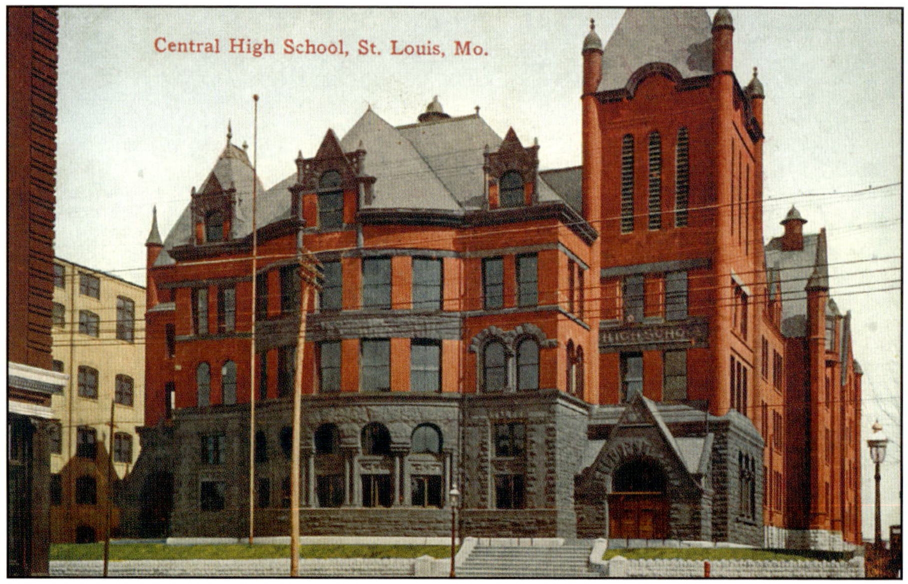

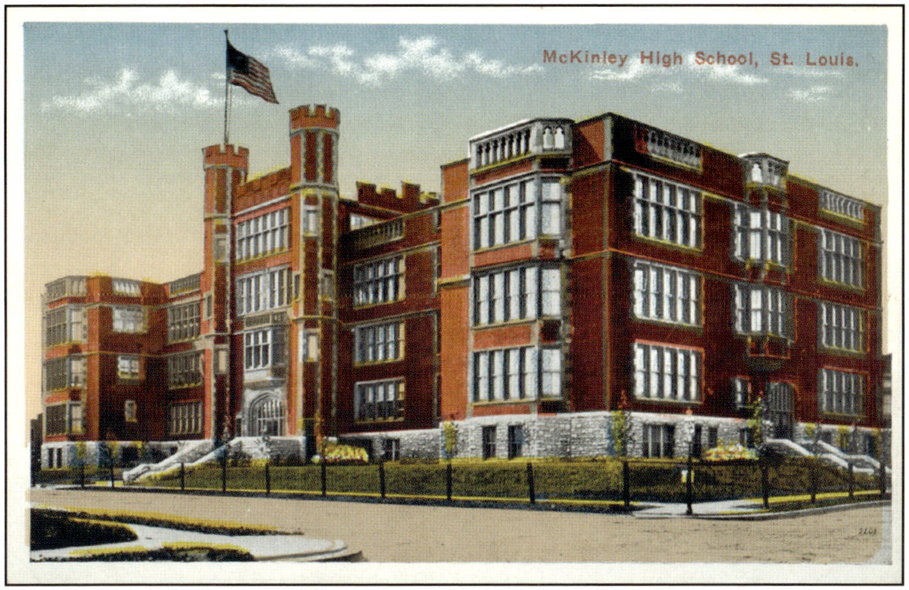

McKinley High School.

Circa 1907, $2-4

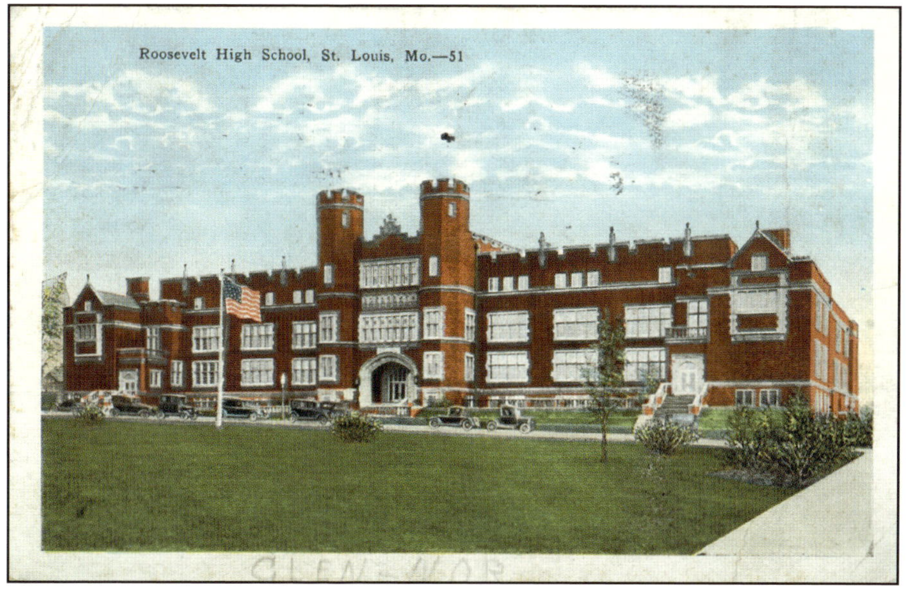

Roosevelt High School.

Cancelled 1928, $2-4

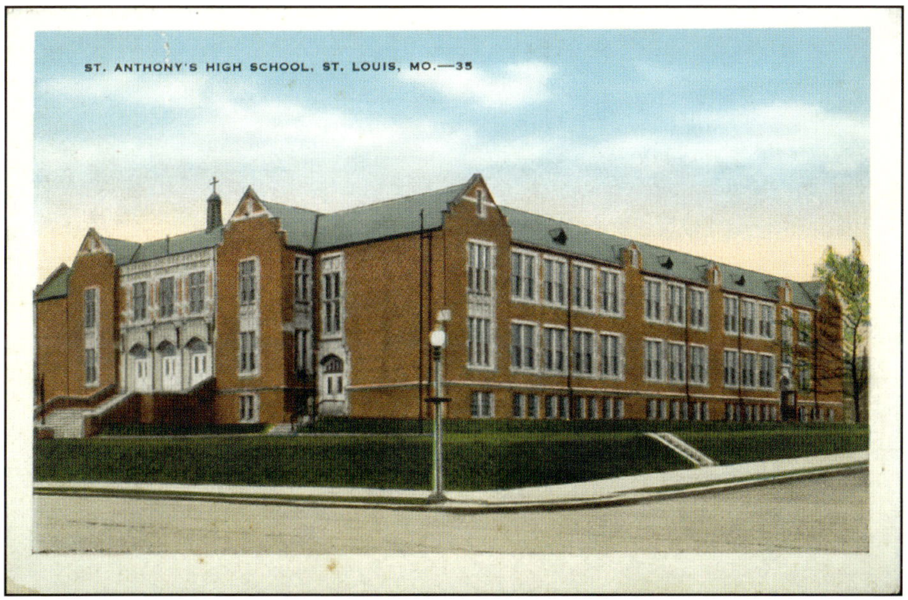

St. Anthony's High School.

Circa 1907, $2-4

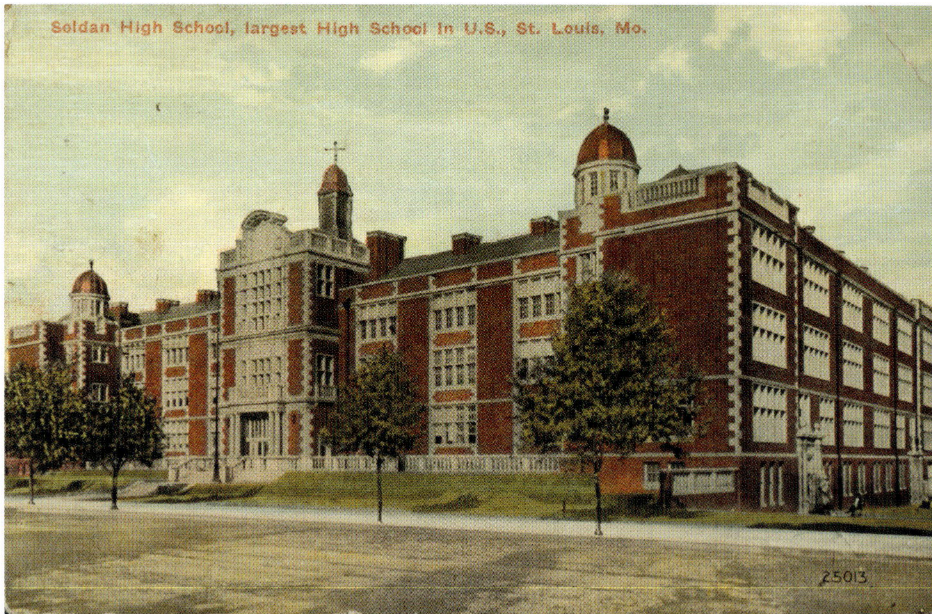

Soldan High School.

Cancelled 1912, $2-4

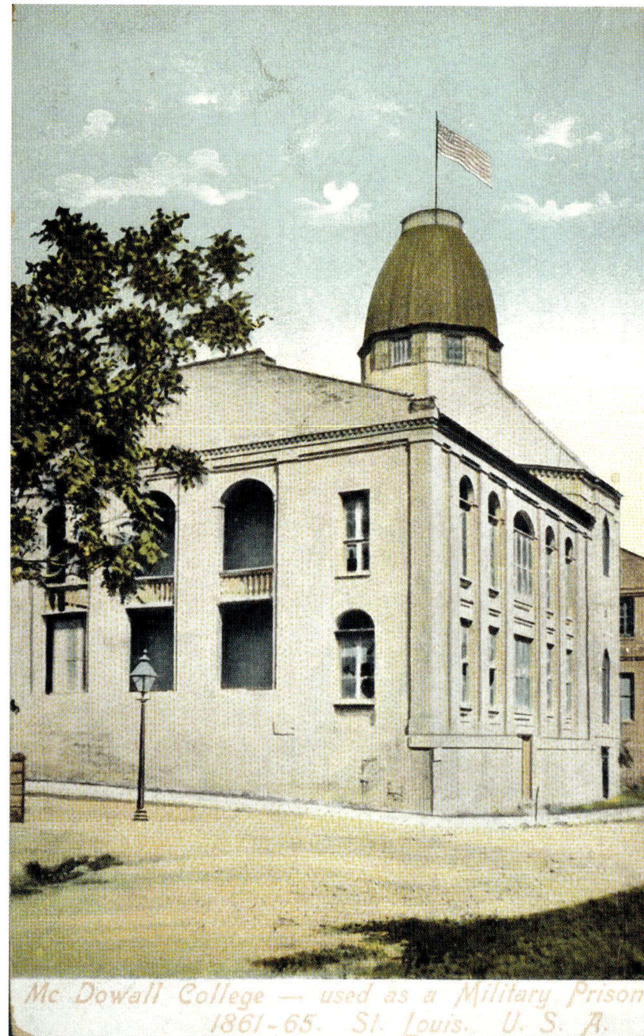

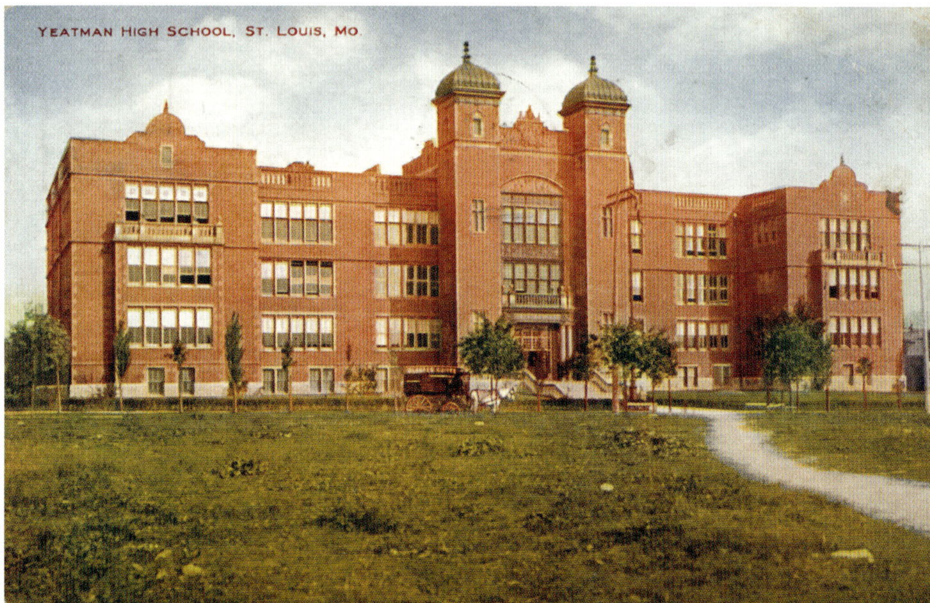

Yeatman High School.

Cancelled 1910, $2-4

The McDowell Medical College housed the school in the north wing of the facility and the McDowell family home in the south wing. Then, in 1861, it became the Gratiot Street Prison. The prison building was demolished in 1878.

Circa 1907, $2-4

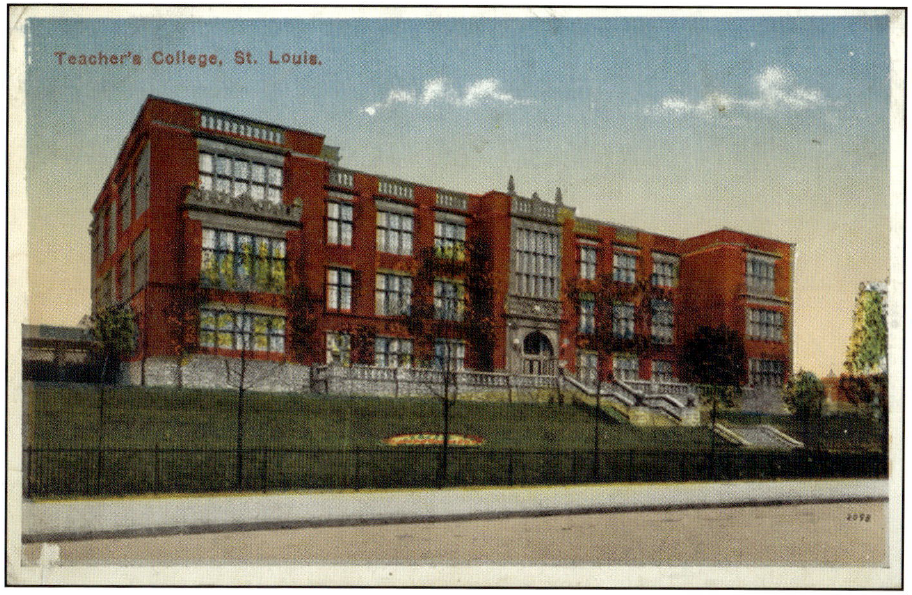

The Harris Teacher's College was established by the St. Louis Public School System in 1857, and was slated for the education of white teachers only. Later, in 1890, the school system established an extension of Sumner High School (called Sumner Normal School) that was specifically designed for the education of black elementary school teachers. In 1924, Sumner became a four-year college with a change in name five years after that to Stowe Teacher's College (honoring abolitionist Harriet Beecher Stowe). Currently, the school is named Harris-Stowe State College after a merger between Harris Teacher's College and Stowe Teacher's College (1954).

Cancelled 1914, $2-4

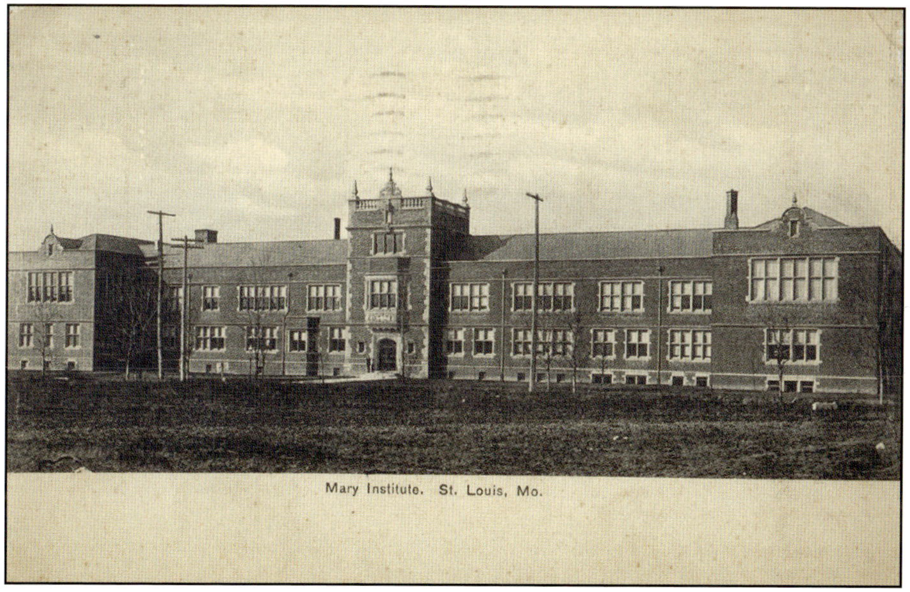

Mary Institute, established by William Greenleaf Eliot (founder, in 1853, of Washington University), in 1859, was the first girls' school west of the Appalachians. Named for his daughter, Mary, he inserted his philosophy that the same education slated for males of the time, should also serve the female population. It was a strange notion in this era, but the school still prospered.

Cancelled 1912, $3-5

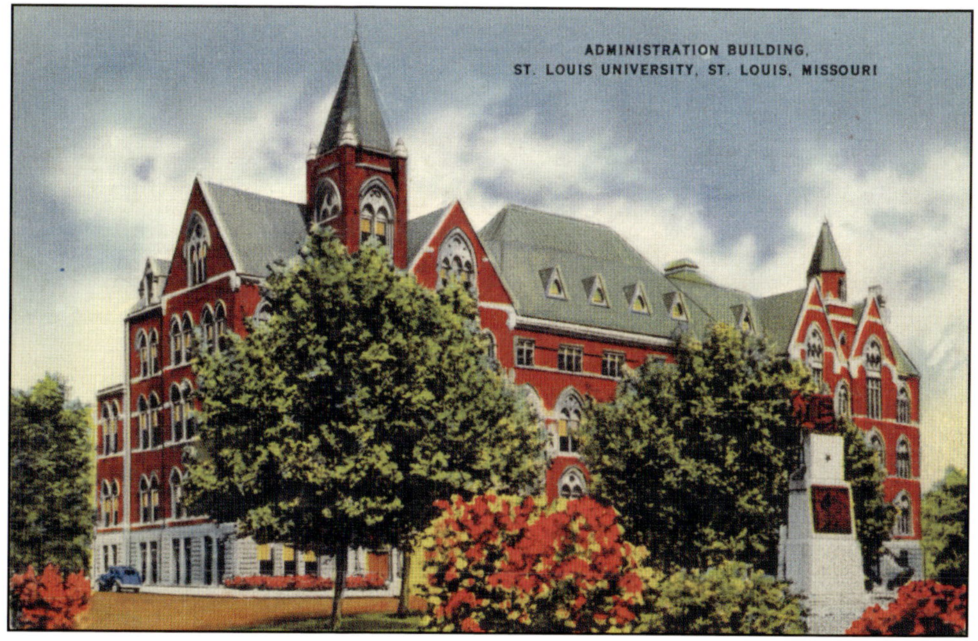

St. Louis University opened its doors in 1818 within a private residence. From 1826, the college held a purpose to offer a Jesuit education, teaching students "how to become practical, socially responsible, humanistic and spiritual human beings." This approach to education has been carried forth into the new century.

Circa 1907, $2-4

The Washington University, located in the western part of the city near Forest Park, is particularly known for its excellent medical school. The administration, hearing the national cry for the improvement of education for doctors, established a medical department in 1891. In 1909, the medical department turned into a modern medical school. These postcard views are of the administration building of the university, constructed in Gothic architecture.

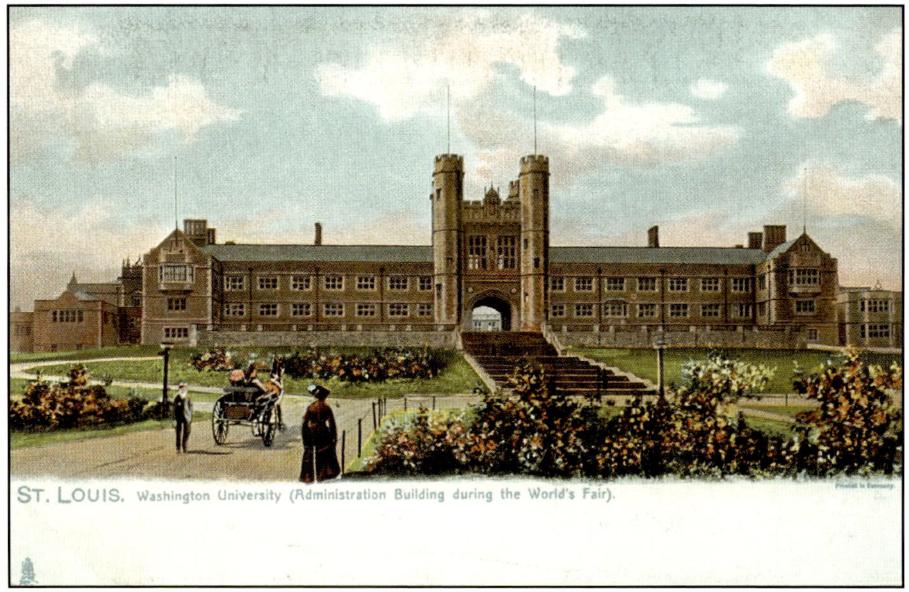

Circa Early 1900s, $3-5

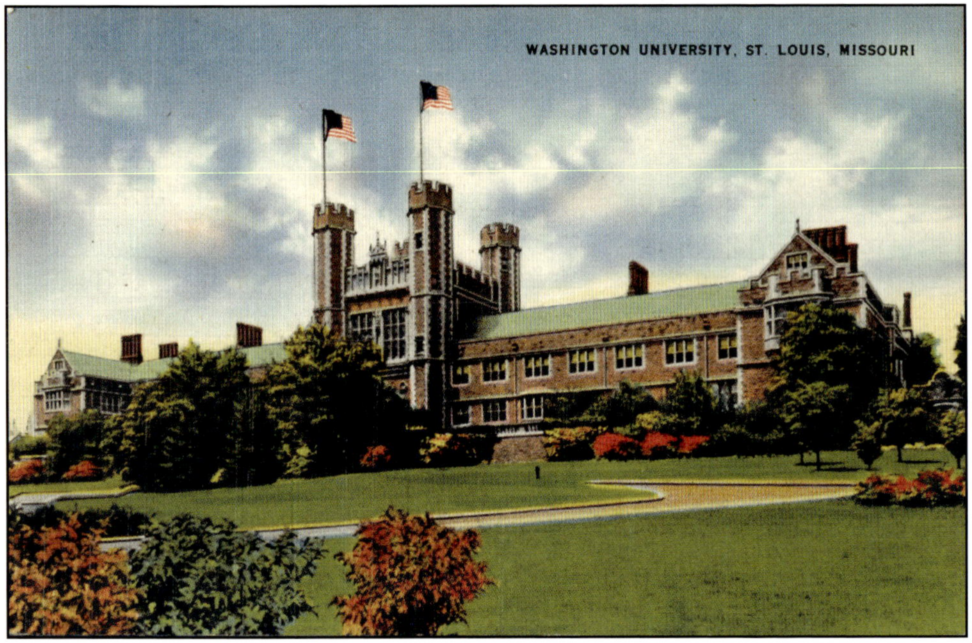

Cancelled 1944, $2-4

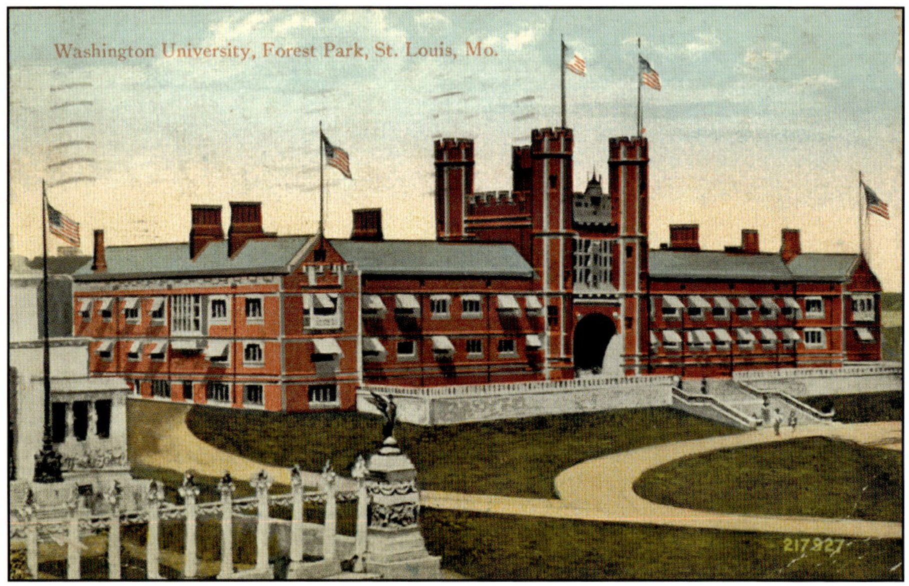

Cancelled 1914, $2-4

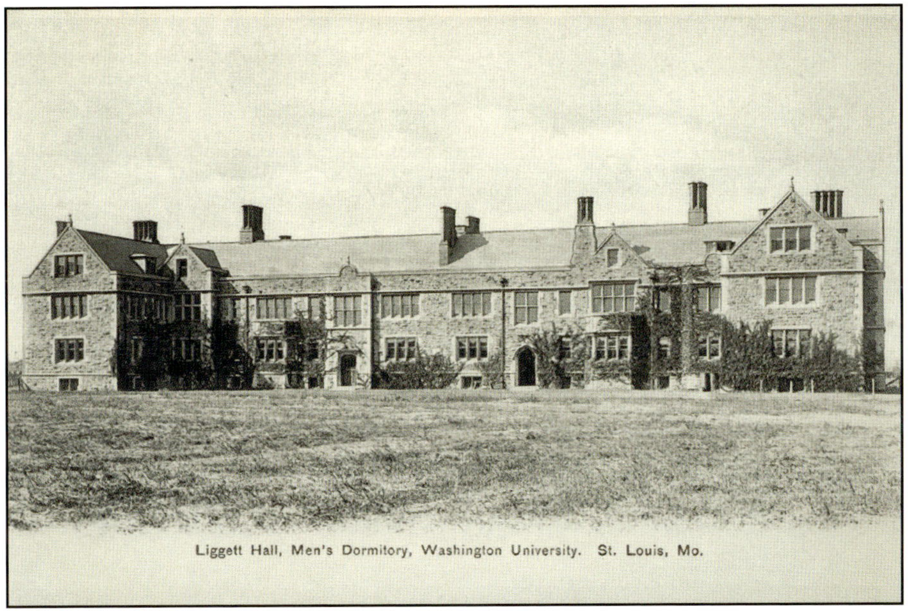

Liggett Hall, Men's Dormitory, Washington University. St. Louis, Mo.

Liggett Hall, a men's dormitory of the Washington University, was built in 1901 with funding from Eliza Liggett, in memory of her husband. It was renamed in 1960, and the original name was given to a multi-story residence hall.

Circa Early 1900s, $3-5

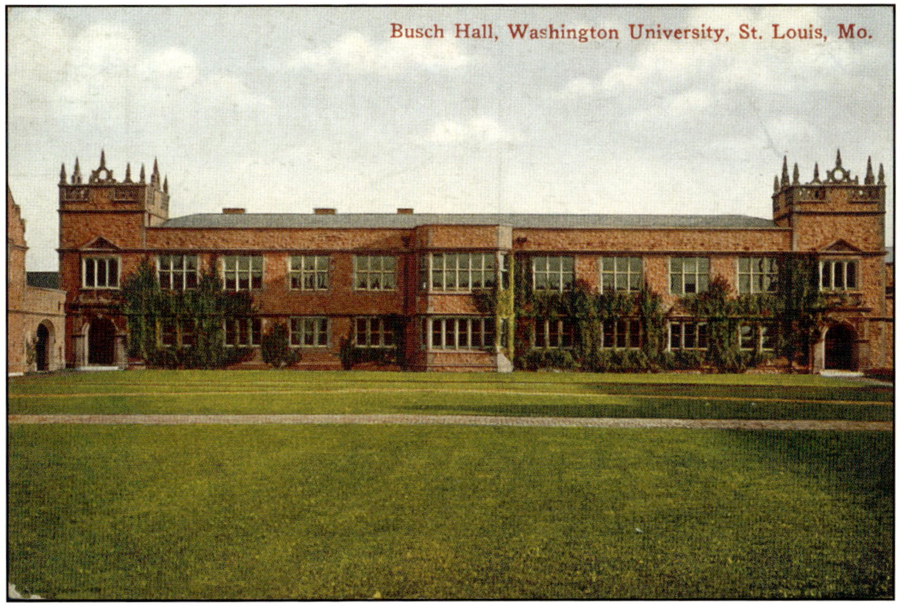

Busch Hall, Washington University, St. Louis, Mo.

Busch Hall, named for Adolphus Busch, was erected in 1900, and served as the Chemistry Building for the university from 1902 until the 1950s.

Circa 1907, $2-4

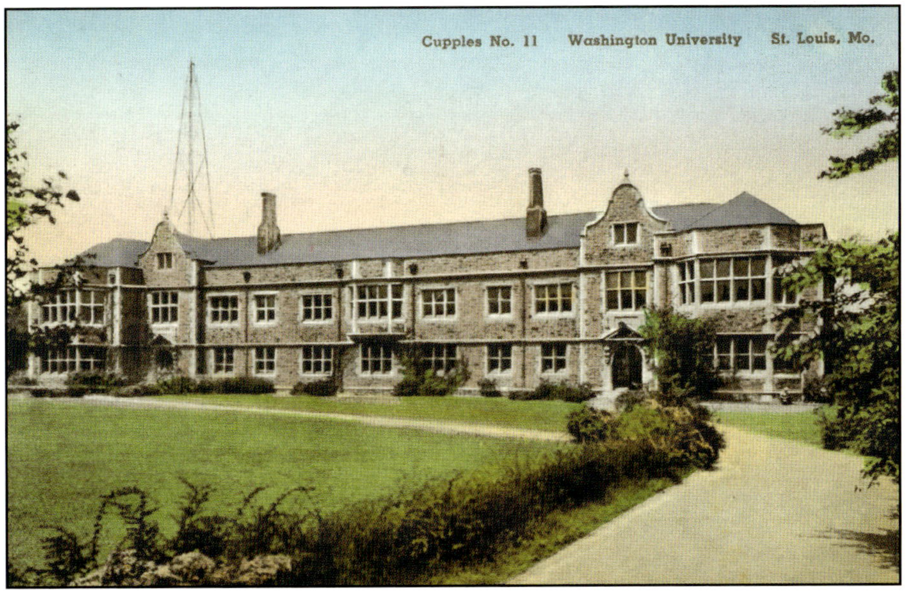

Cupples No. 11 Washington University St. Louis, Mo.

The Cupples II Building (given to the school by Samuel Cupples) is the oldest of the engineering buildings at Washington University, built in 1901. During the 1904 World's Fair, the building was used as the Jefferson Guard Building.

Circa 1907, $2-4

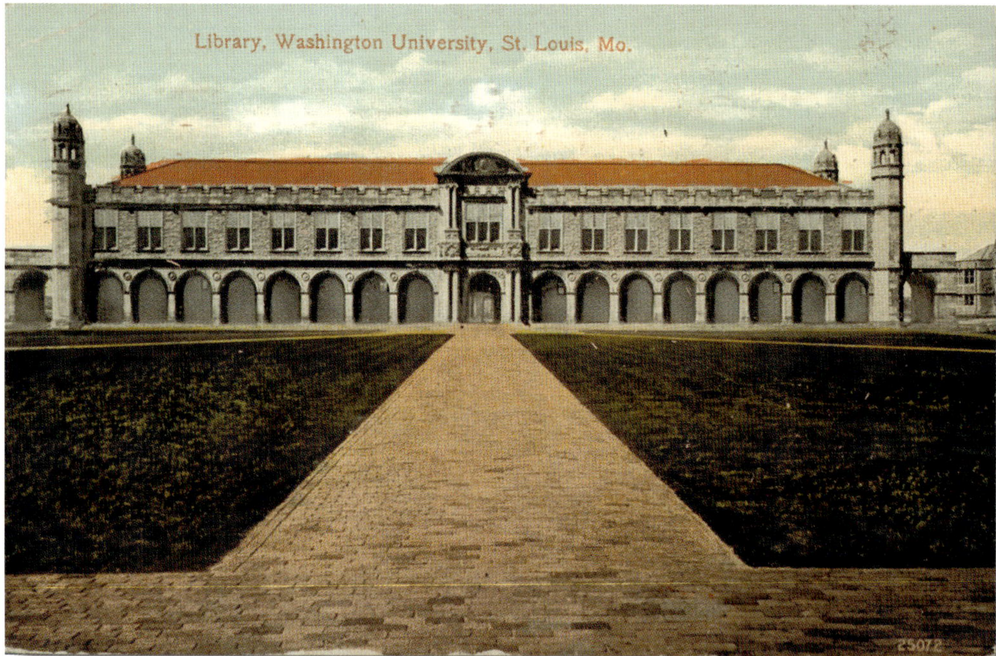

Cancelled 1913, $2-4

Shown here, two views of Ridgley Hall, which was the University's first library building. In the early 1960s, the reading room of Ridgley was turned into lounge space when the Olin Library was completed. Its name now is Holmes Lounge.

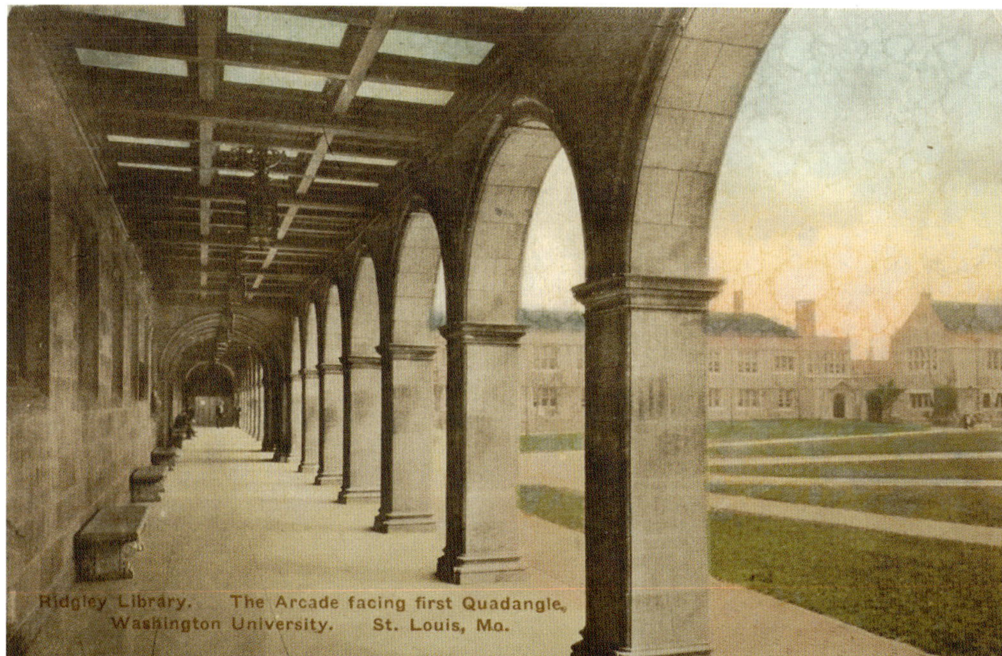

Cancelled 1925, $2-4

Churches and Religious Affiliations

There have always been strong religious affiliations in the St. Louis area including Catholic, Jewish, Episcopalian, Methodist, Lutheran, Presbyterian, and others. Many times, buildings would need to be moved to accommodate larger congregations or a fall of bad luck due to weather or fire, and this would necessitate the redevelopment of a church. Regardless, St. Louis has continued to meet the needs of the population through the years.

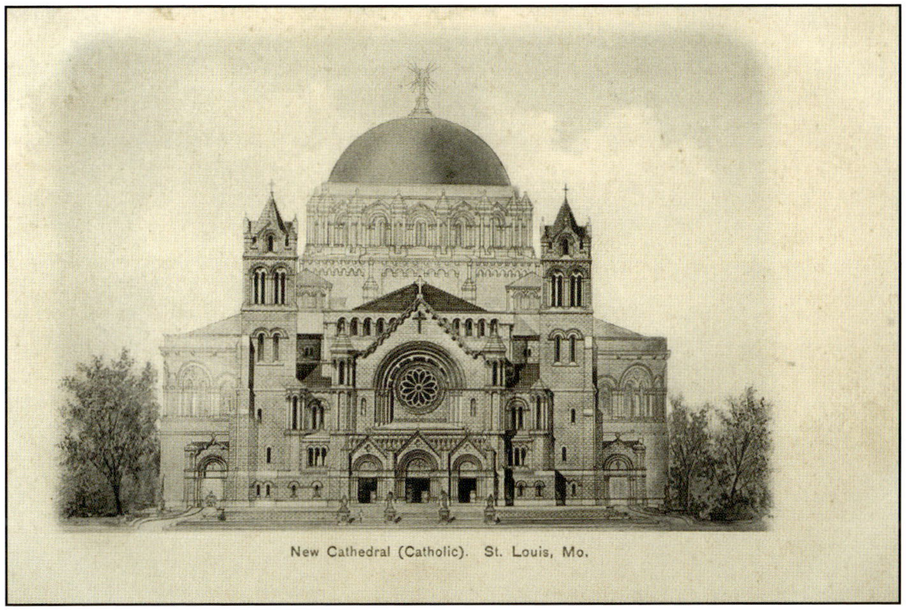

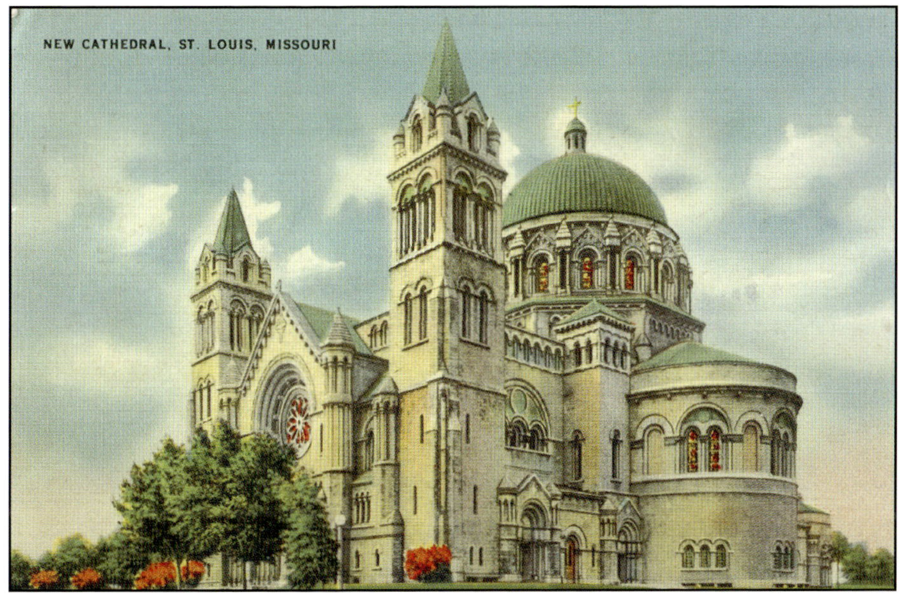

Though the cathedral was proposed in 1896, the church would not see its superstructure (nor its first mass) completed until 1914. The building is noted as being 365 feet long and 212 feet wide, costing $3,250,000 to build, with the mosaic work alone costing $2,000,000. Today, the cathedral contains the largest mosaic collection in the world, created by twenty different artists.

Circa Early 1900s, $2-4 (left)
Cancelled 1946, $2-4 (right)

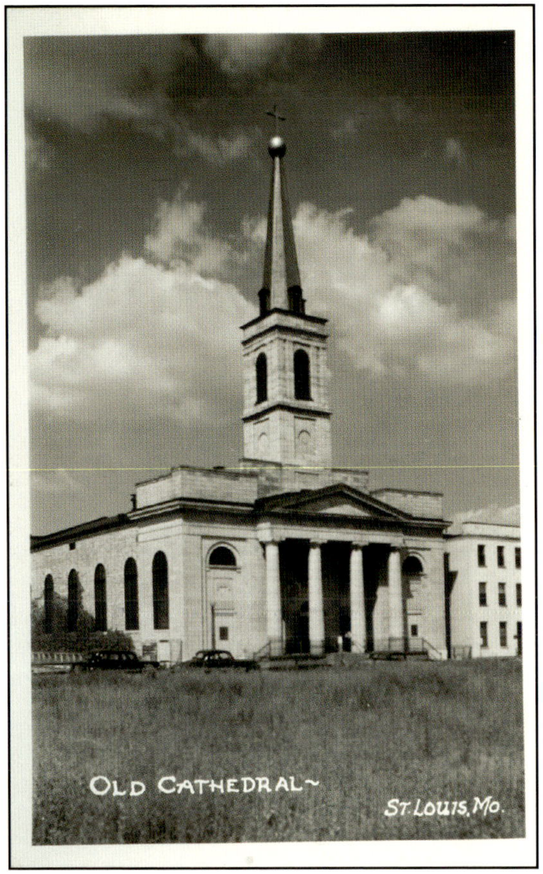

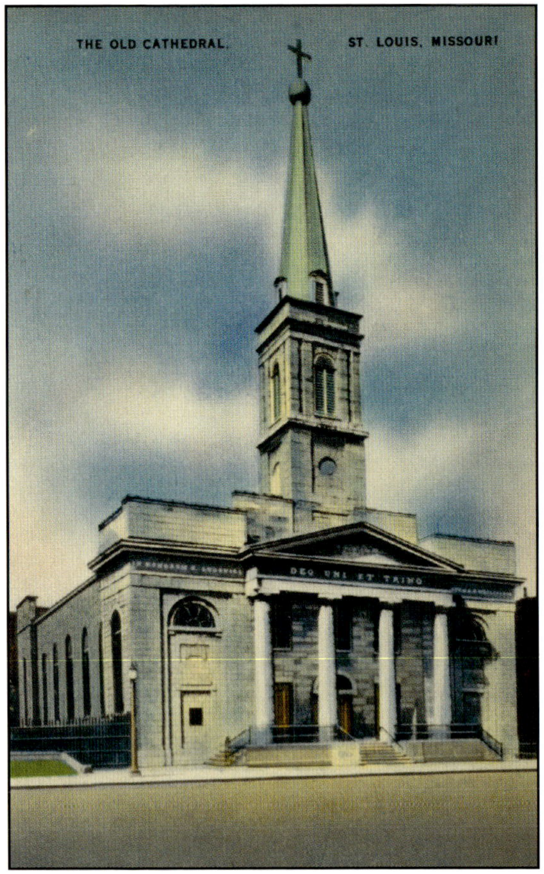

The Old Cathedral is noted as the oldest cathedral church west of the Mississippi River. The construction began in 1831, and the church was dedicated in 1834. The St. Louis diocese was headquartered at the Old Cathedral from 1826 to 1843 and covered nearly half of America. When the New Cathedral opened in 1914, the Old Cathedral was renamed the Church of St. Louis IX, King of France.

Circa Early 1900s, $6-8 (left)
Cancelled 1948, $2-4 (right)

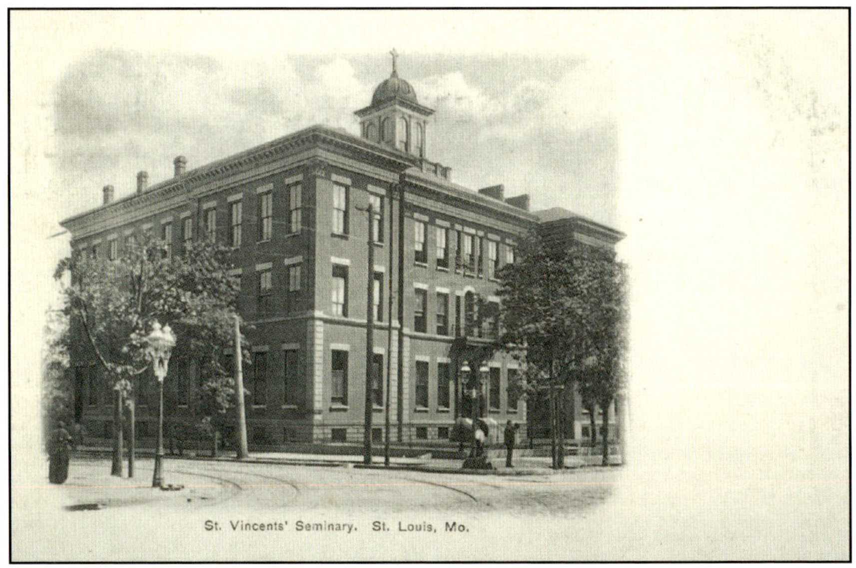

Occupying a three-story building at Grand and Lucas in 1875, St. Vincent's Seminary was initially originated at 10th and St. Charles Streets in 1843. The building was used in 1911 by the newly founded Catholic Free High School for Girls (also known as Rosati-Kain).

Early 1900s, $2-4

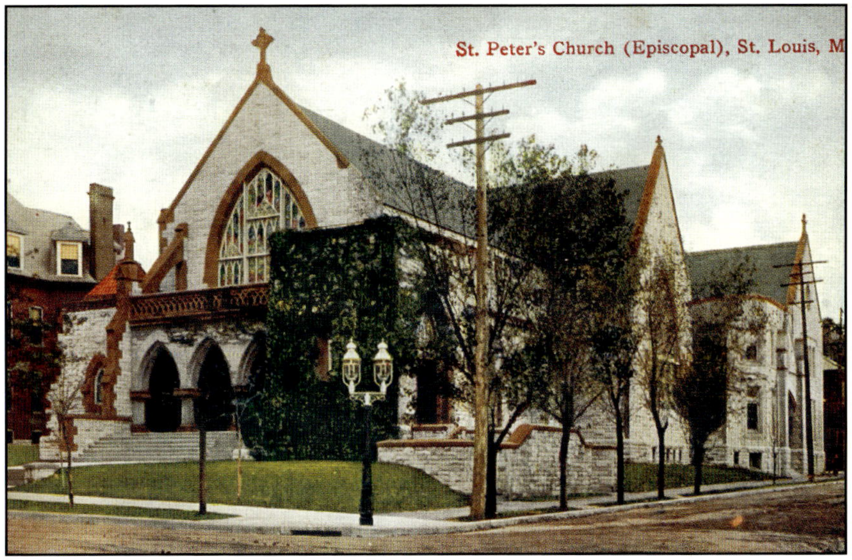

St. Peter's Episcopal Church was originally founded in 1868 as a mission of the Christ Church Cathedral. Also, it was a branch Sunday School for the western area of St. Louis.

Circa 1907, $2-4

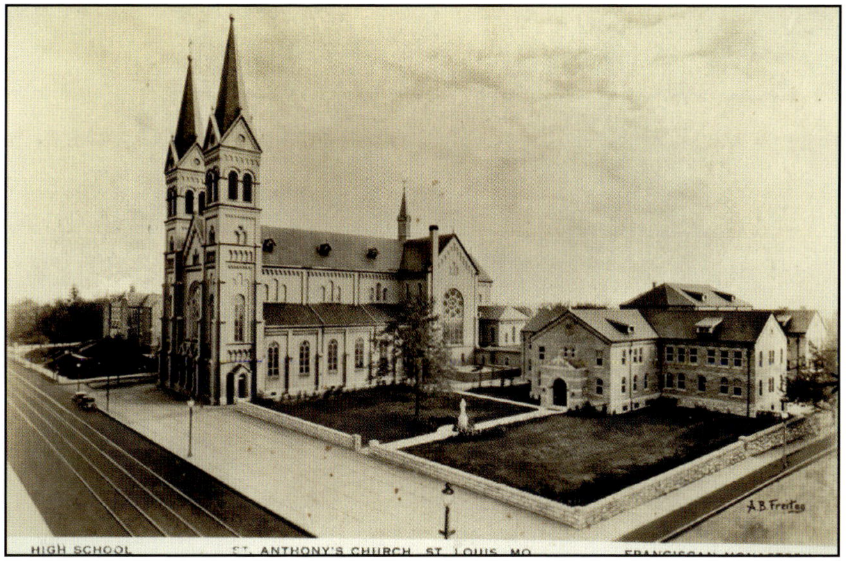

This photo of the St. Anthony's Church can often be found on tours of St. Louis today, and it's been heard that this church has more beautifully designed stained glass windows for its size than any other church in the U. S.

Circa Early 1900s, $6-8

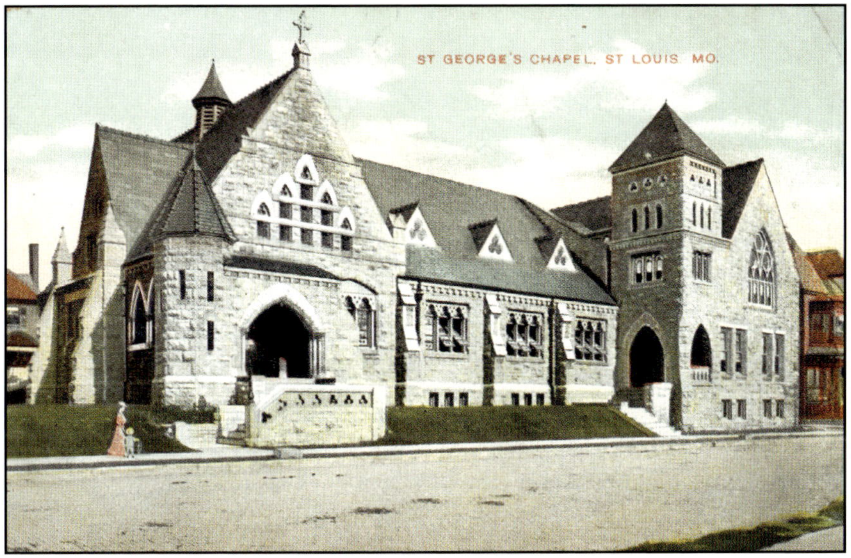

A large stone church was built in 1874 at this location, but was destroyed by fire in 1891. The new church, opened in 1892, was first known as St. George's Chapel because it had been built from the stones of the prior church. In 1928, after having been both a mission chapel and a separate parish, it merged with the St. Michael Church and All Angels Church, and is now known as St. Michael and St. George.

Circa 1907, $2-4

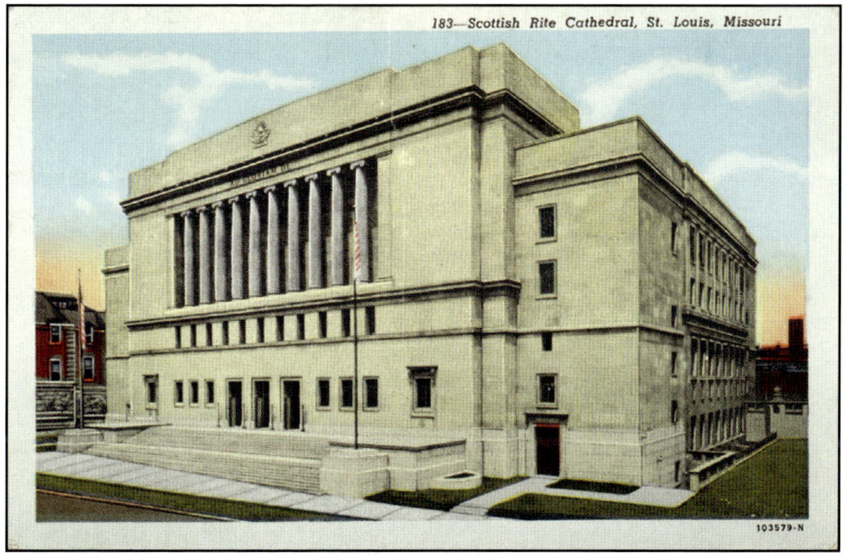

The Scottish Rite Freemasonry is an organization that provides services to St. Louis residents from Lindell Boulevard.

Cancelled 1950, $2-4

St. Stephen's Evangelical Lutheran Church was organized in 1930. It was formerly the St. George's Episcopal Church.

Cancelled 1948, $2-4

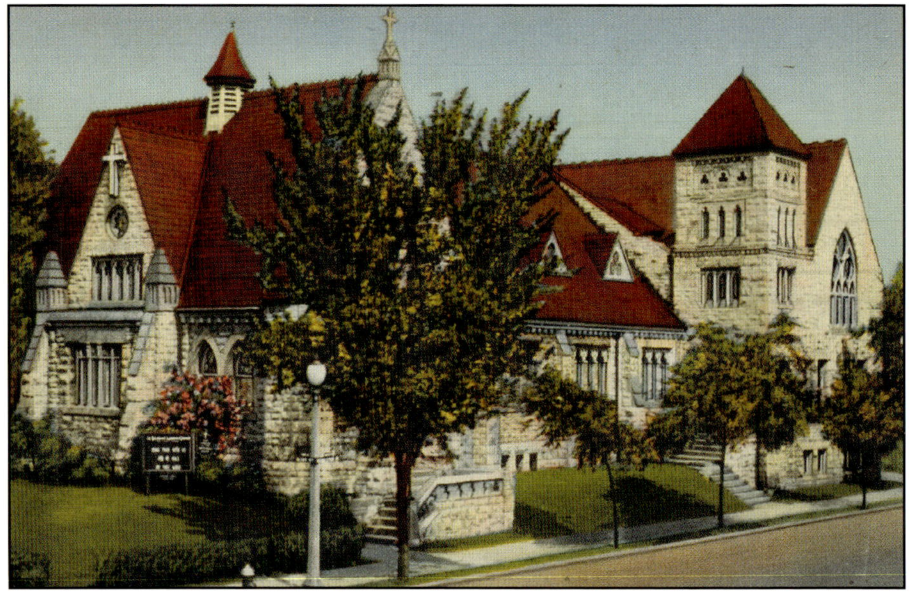

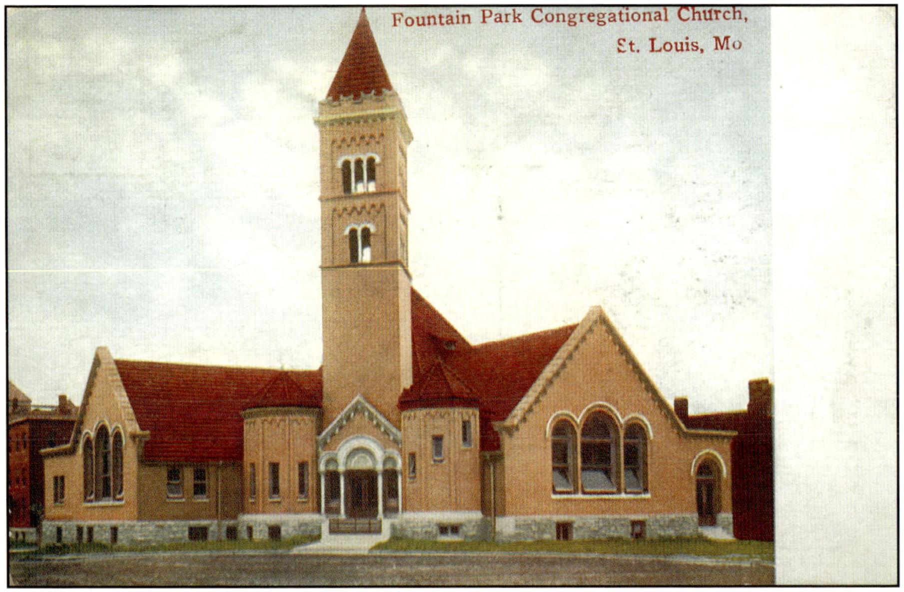

Fountain Park Congregational Church on Fountain Avenue (now the Centennial Christian Church) got its beginning as the Mayflower Mission Sabbath School at Grand Avenue and Lucky Street in 1867.

Circa 1907, $3-5

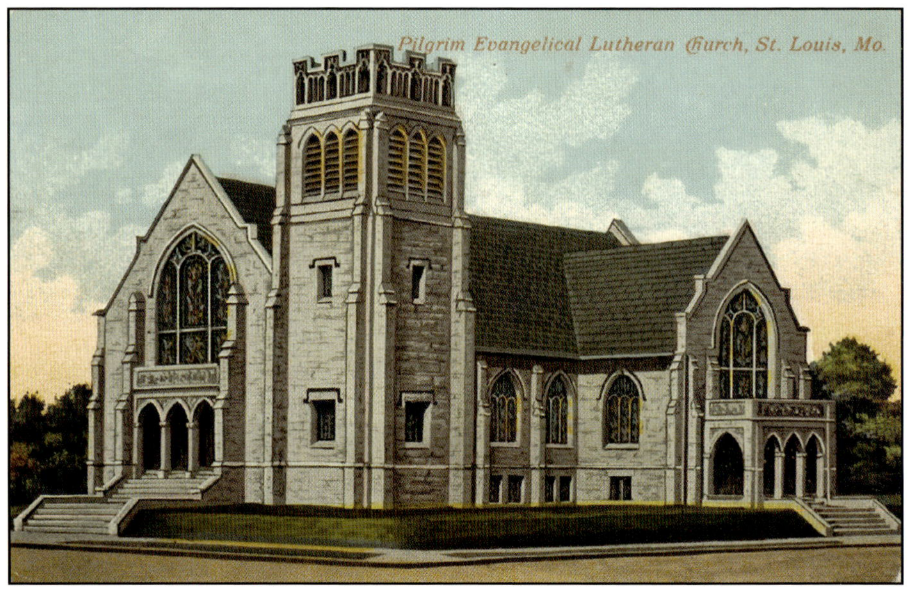

The Pilgrim Evangelical Lutheran Church, organized in 1912, was a member of the Lutheran Church-Missouri Synod. (In 1976, it left the Missouri Synod and joined the Association of Evangelical Lutheran Churches.)

Cancelled 1924, $2-4

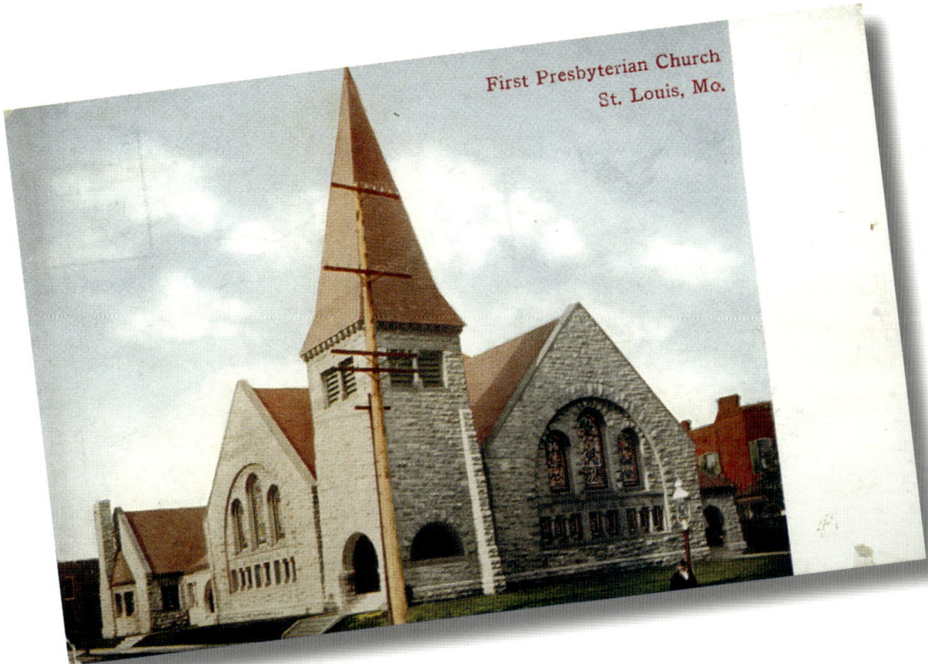

The First Presbyterian Church of St. Louis had it's first building completed on 4th Street in 1825, costing $8,000. The congregation enjoyed services in this building until 1855.

Circa 1907, $2-4

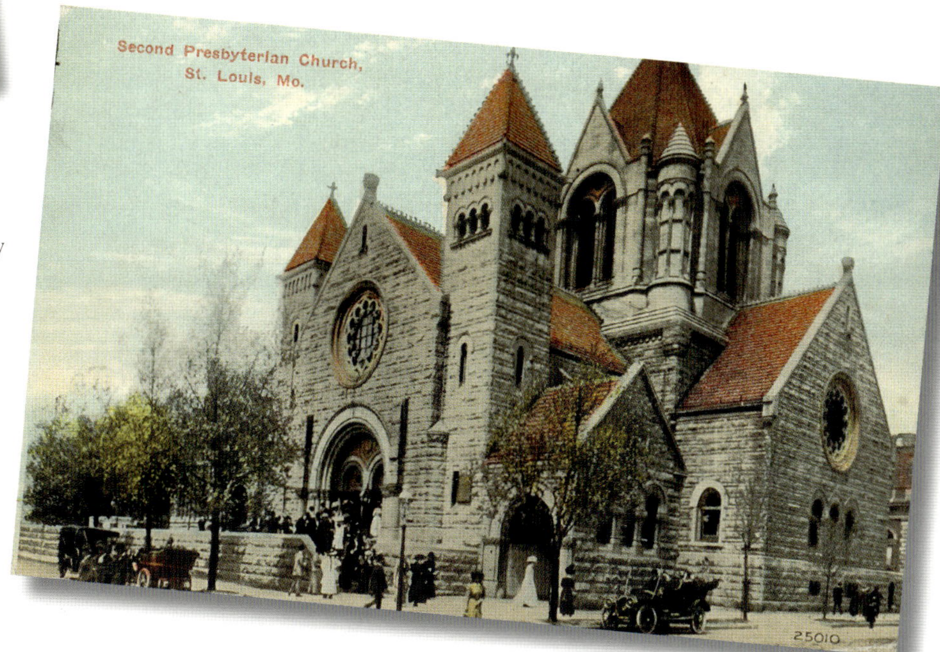

The Second Presbyterian Church, founded in 1838, was in a temporary location (at 5th and Pine) as a colony from the First Presbyterian Church.

Circa 1907, $2-4

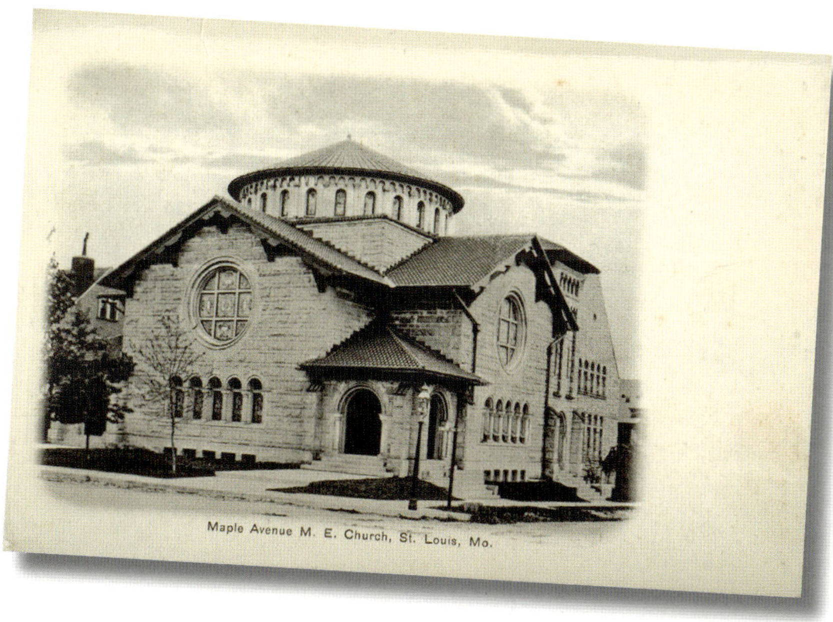

The Maple Avenue Methodist Episcopal Church was organized in 1892, and erected and dedicated in 1895, at the corner of Maple Avenue and Belt. Unfortunately, the church fell victim to fire in 1957.

Early 1900s, $2-4

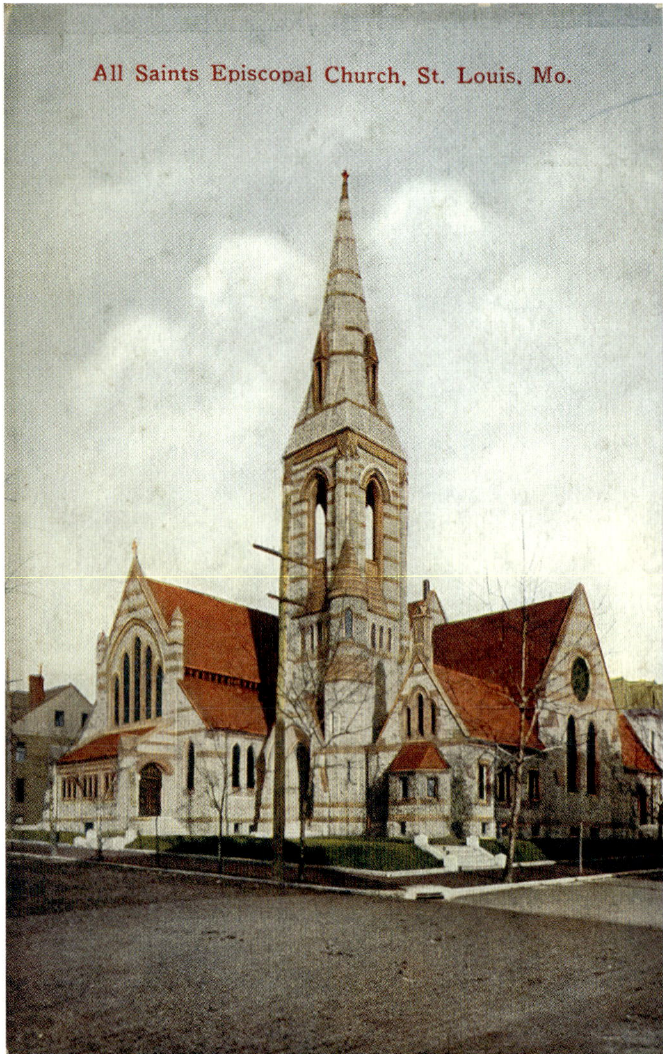

The All Saints Episcopal Church had the first and only black congregation within the Episcopal Diocese of Missouri. Organized at the Mission of Our Savior Sunday School in 1873, they moved into their first church one year later. A shared-space agreement in 1881 with the Trinity Episcopal Church (11th and Washington) allowed the mission to be nearer to the black community they served. They moved again in 1883, becoming All Saints Episcopal Church, to Washington and 22nd. Still another move would take them, in 1906, to Locust and Garrison, where they remained for fifty years.

Circa 1907, $2-4

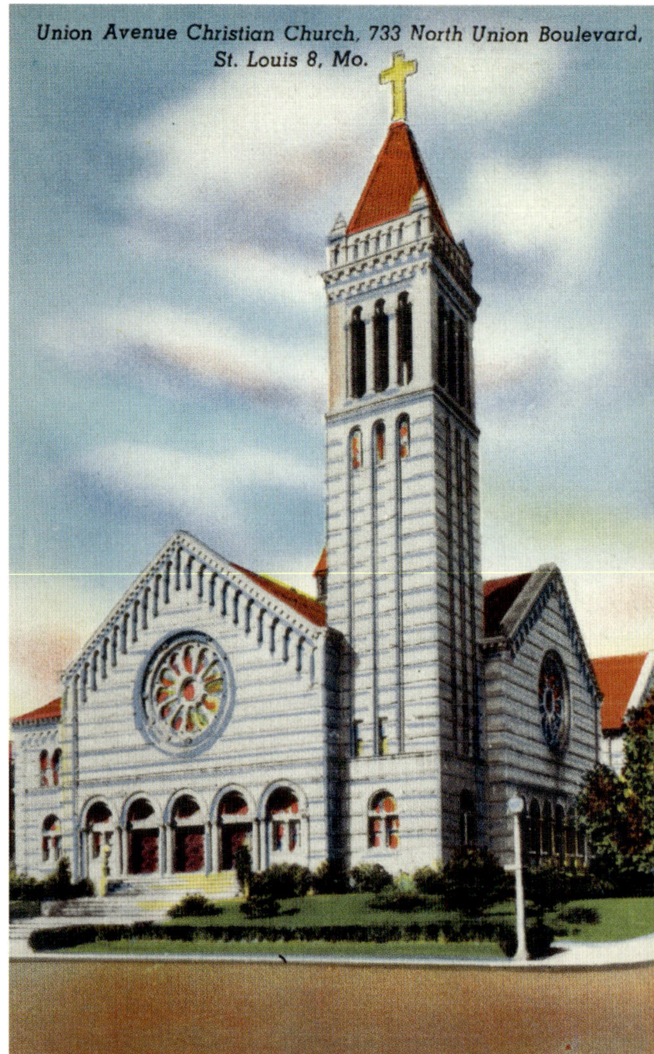

The Disciples of Christ first came to St. Louis in 1837, and soon founded the First Christian Church. The Central Christian Church and Mt. Cabanne Christian Church merged in 1902 to create the Union Avenue Christian Church.

Circa 1930s, $2-4

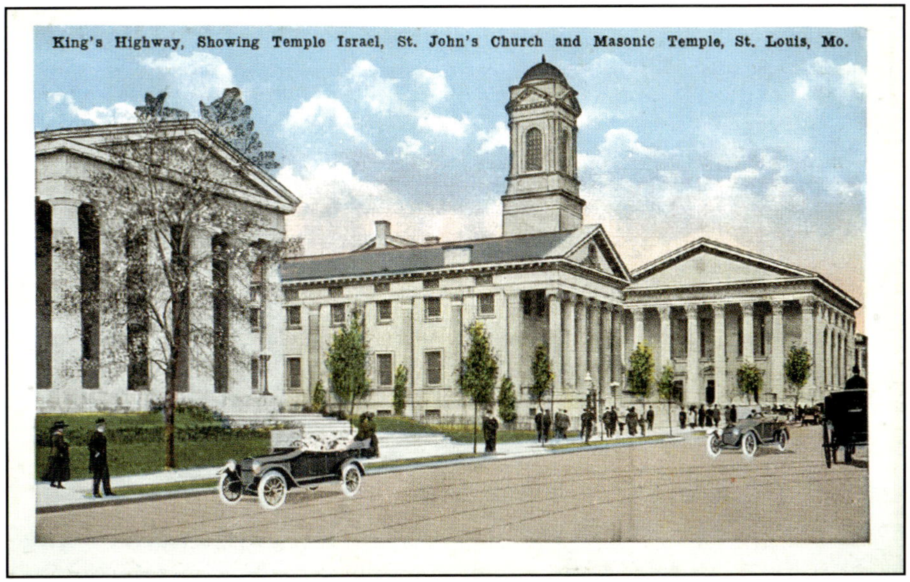

Circa 1920s, $3-5

This Kings Highway location at the central west end of St. Louis is known as "Holy Corners," due to the combination of religious facilities located here (intersecting with Washington, McPherson, and Westminster). St. John's Methodist Church, the Second Baptist Church, the Temple Israel (former), the First Church of Christ (built for the first Christian Science congregation west of the Mississippi), and the Tuscan Temple are all part of "Holy Corners."

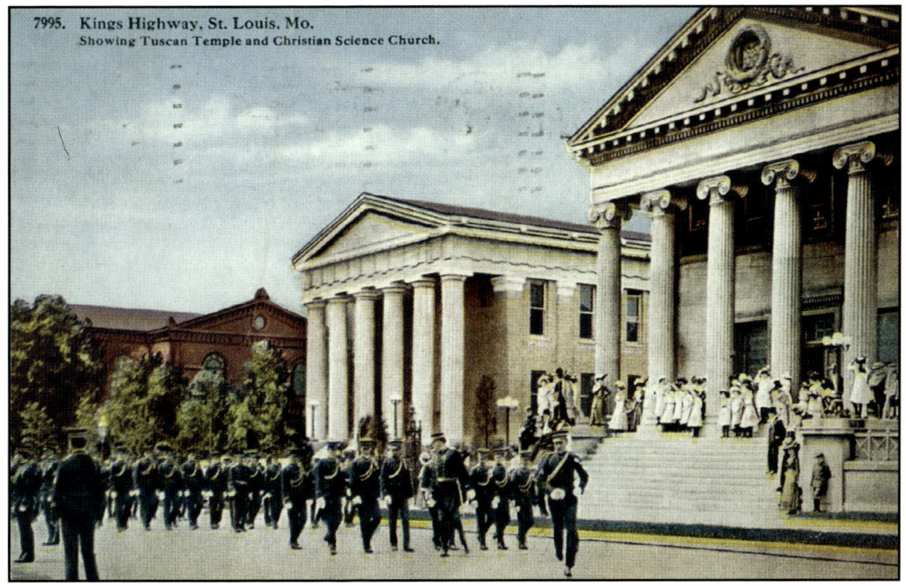

Cancelled 1917, $2-4

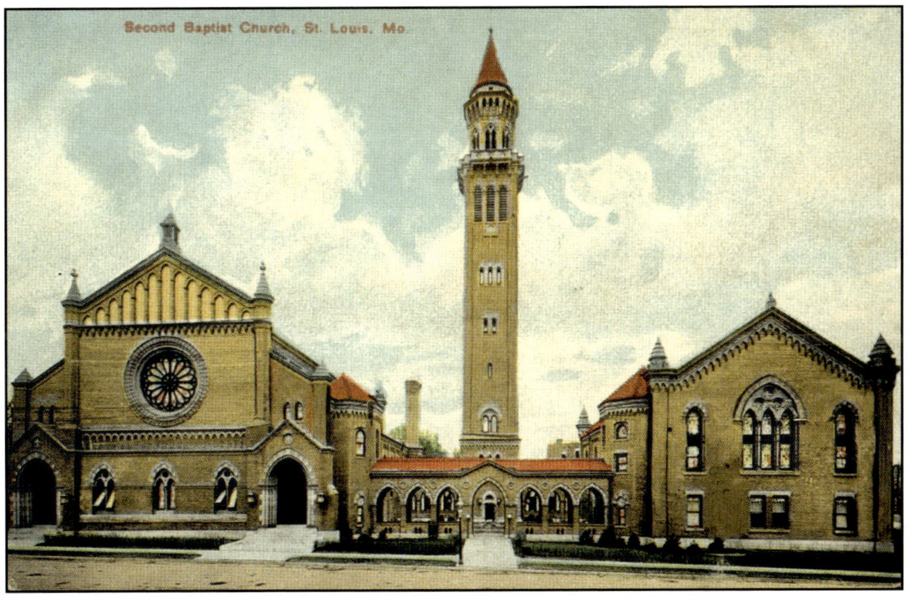

Circa 1907, $2-4

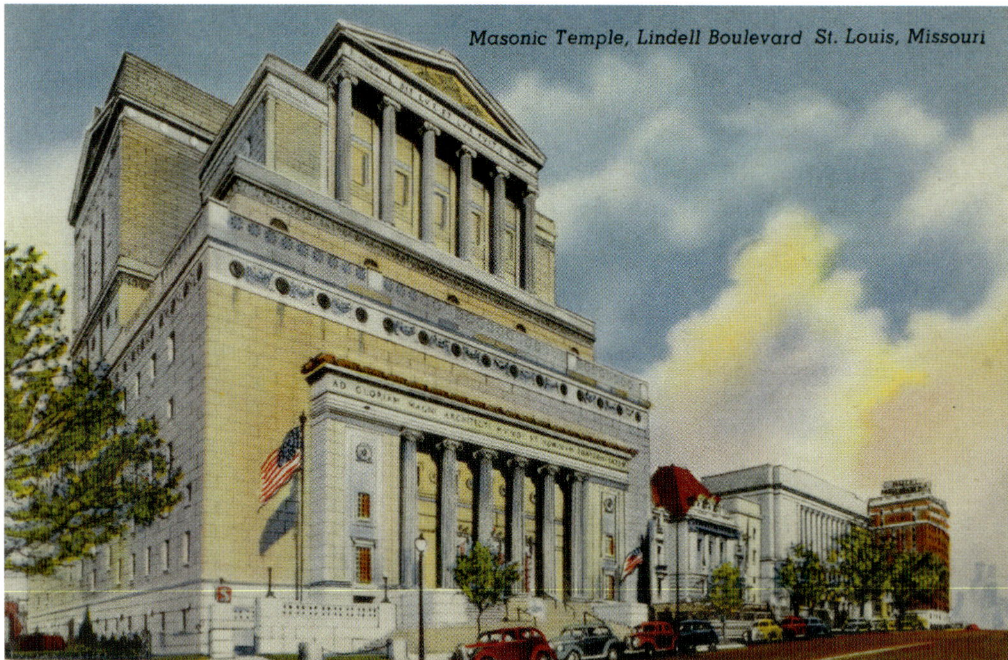

Cancelled 1944, $2-4

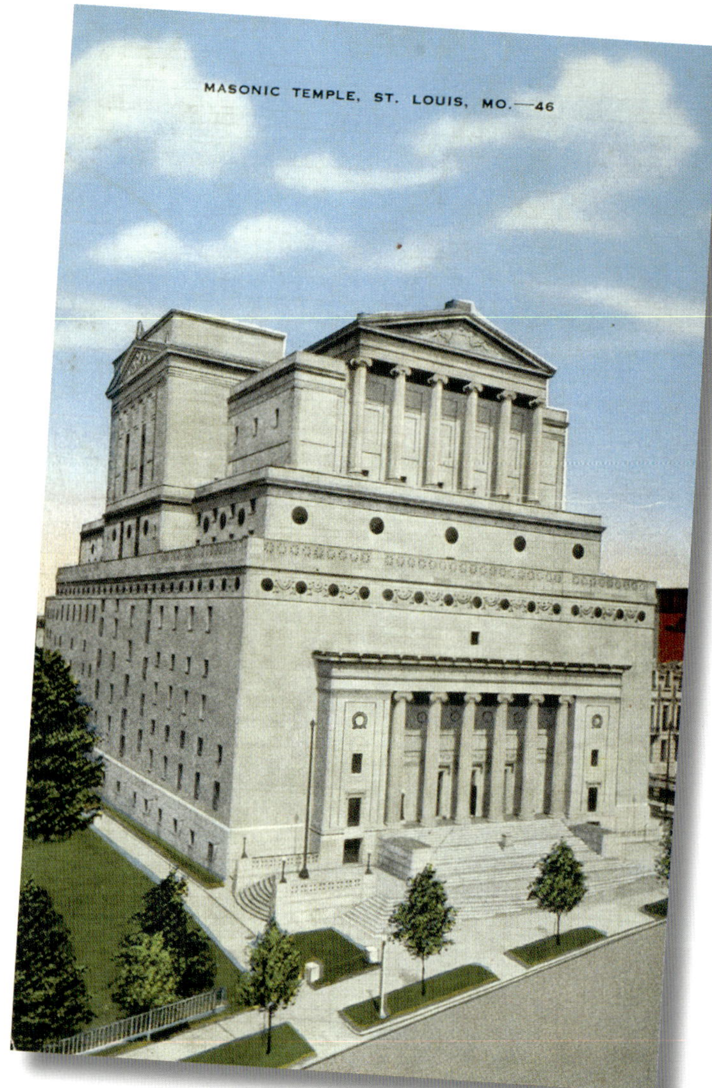

The Masonic Temple, located on Lindell Boulevard, is positioned just west of Grand Avenue. The building is twelve-stories high and was considered to be one of the most lovely the city had to offer.

Circa 1930s, $2-4

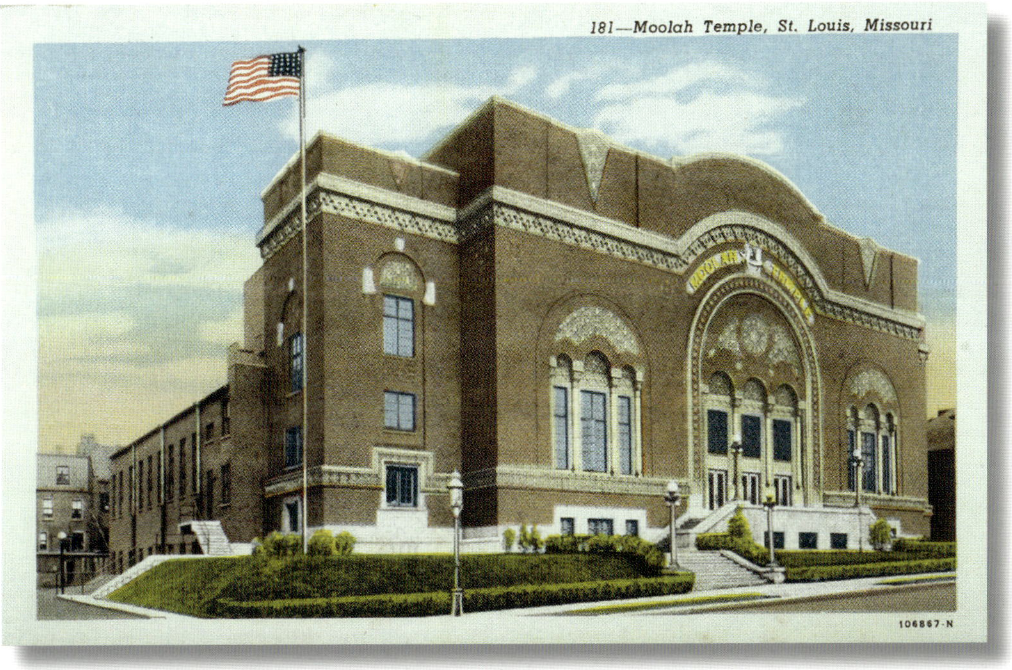

The cornerstone for the Moolah Temple was laid at midnight on October 21, 1913, and the first Moolah meeting was held in there on March 18, 1914.

Circa 1914, $2-4

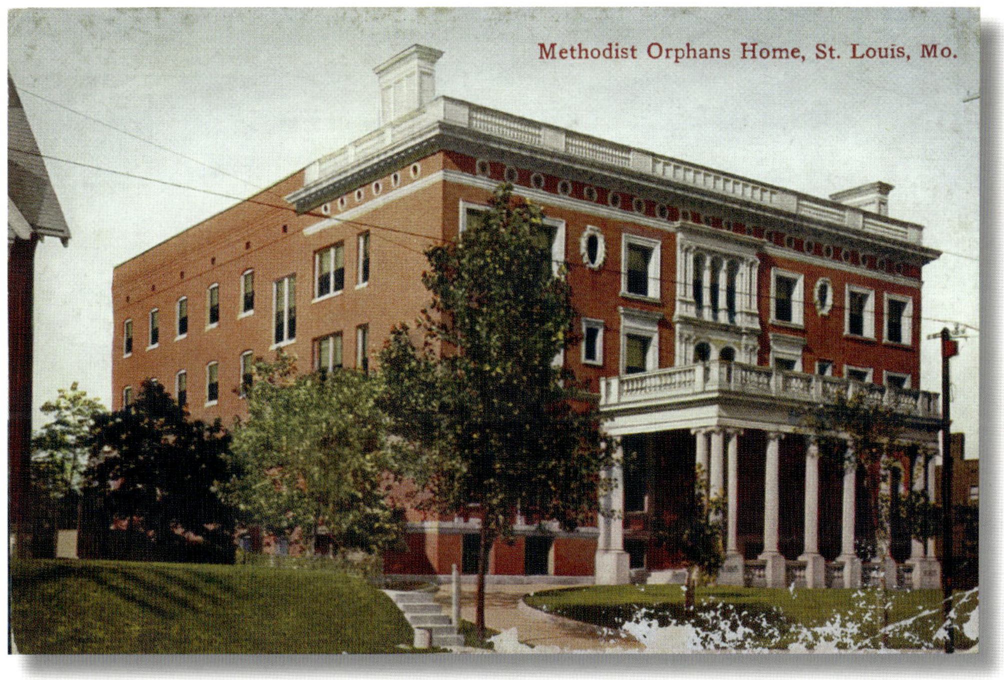

Chartered in 1879, the Methodist Children's Home accepted transferred children from the Central Wesleyan College and Central Wesleyan Orphan Home when those two institutions separated in 1884.

Circa 1907, $2-4

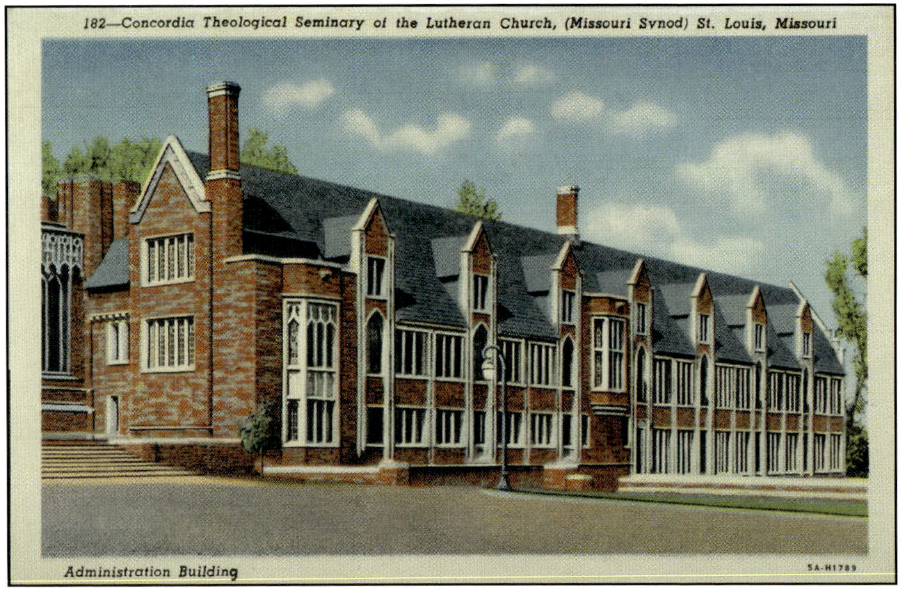

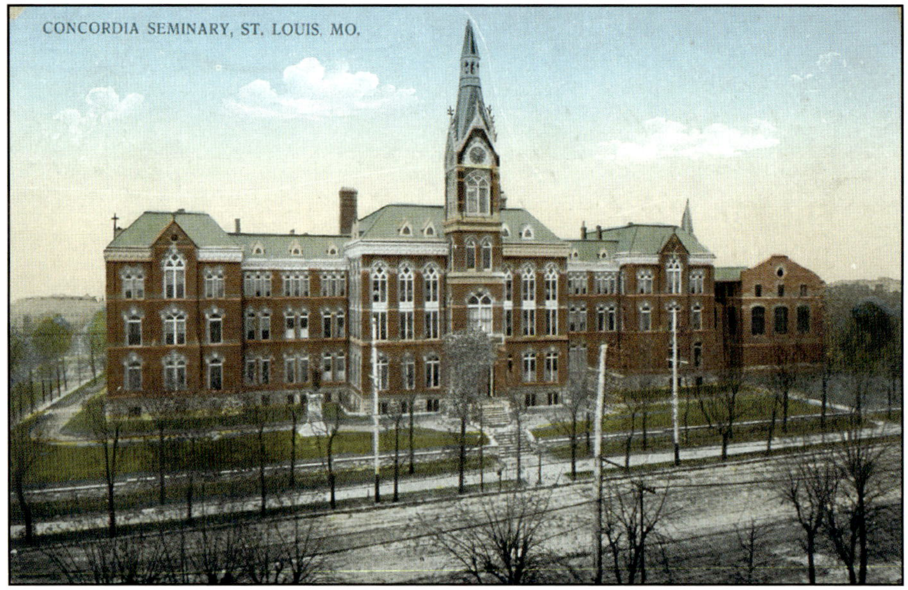

The Concordia Theological Seminary of the Lutheran Church is centered in the Gospel of Jesus Christ, valuing faithfulness to the scriptures and confessions, servant-hood to Christ and His church, responsiveness to the contemporary contest of the world, and excellence in all endeavors. The Seminary buildings were erected in Tudor Gothic style, including fifteen residences and a radio station, at a cost of nearly $3,000,000.

Circa 1930s, $2-4 (left)
Circa 1907, $3-5 (right)

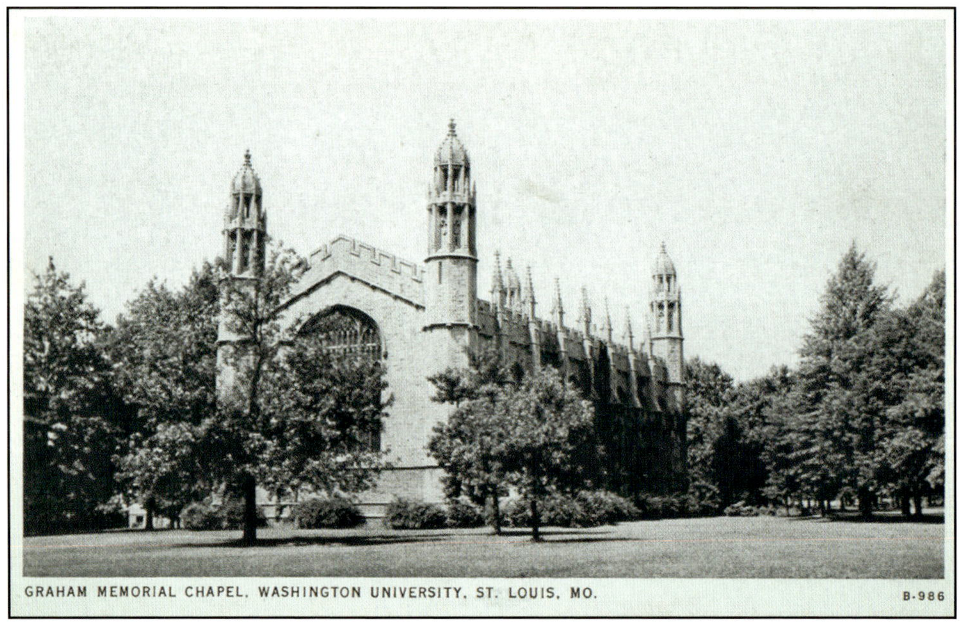

Dedicated in 1909 and named for Benjamin Brown Graham, the Chapel was given to the Washington University by Graham's widow, Christine, as a memorial.

Circa 1907, $6-8

Hotels

St. Louis has always been a fine hostess for the travelers of the world, whether it be the fur traders, people passing through to Oregon and points west, or the visitors flocking to see and experience the mighty Mississippi River. Here, see turn of the century hotel cards, depicting all the special features of the times, including the locations for night life, entertainment, and business accommodations.

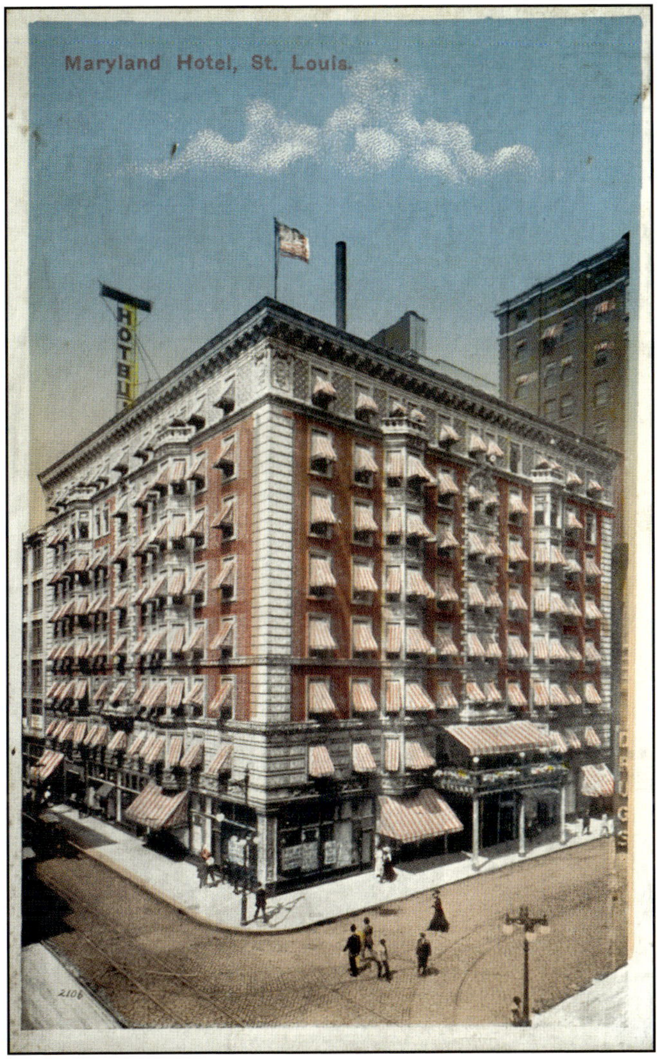

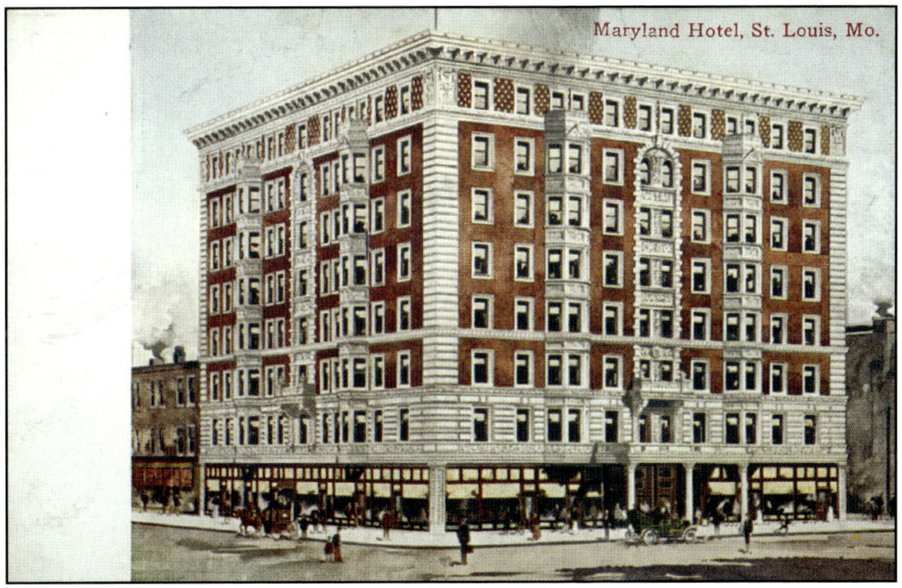

The Maryland Hotel was located at 9th and Pine and was noted as being one of the city's most beautiful hotels.

Circa 1914, $2-4 (left)
Circa 1907, $2-4 (right)

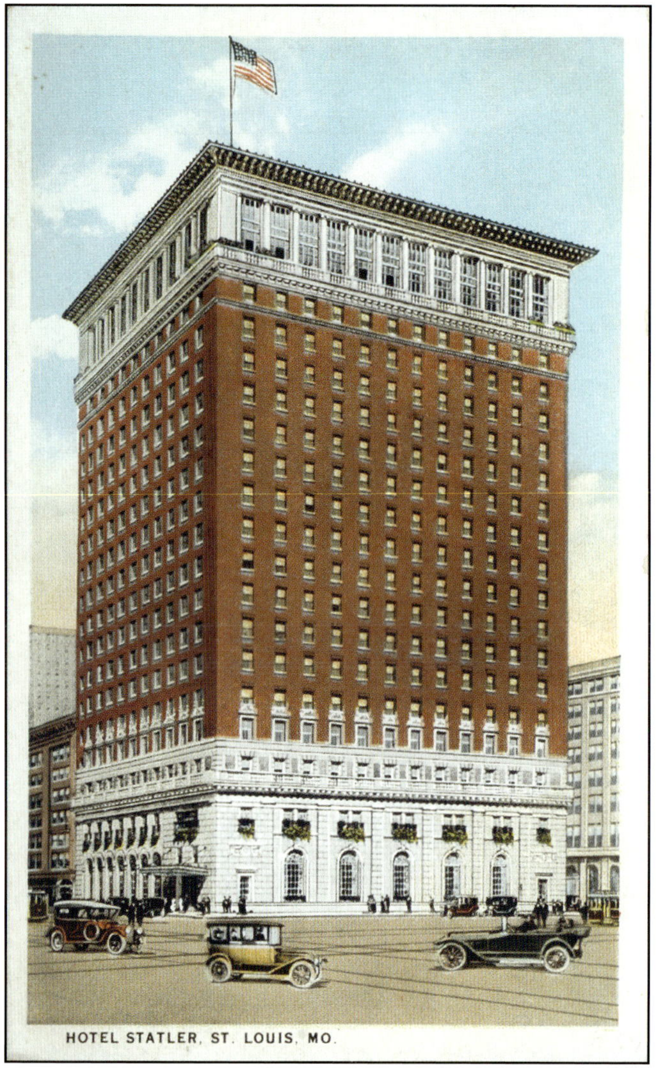

The Hotel Statler, one of Ellsworth Milton (E. M.) Statler's grand projects, was built in 1917. Each of his hotels was more spectacular and innovative than the one prior. Statler died in 1928, but the company stayed in the hotel business, until selling it to Conrad Hilton (Hilton Hotels) in 1954.

Circa 1920s, $2-4

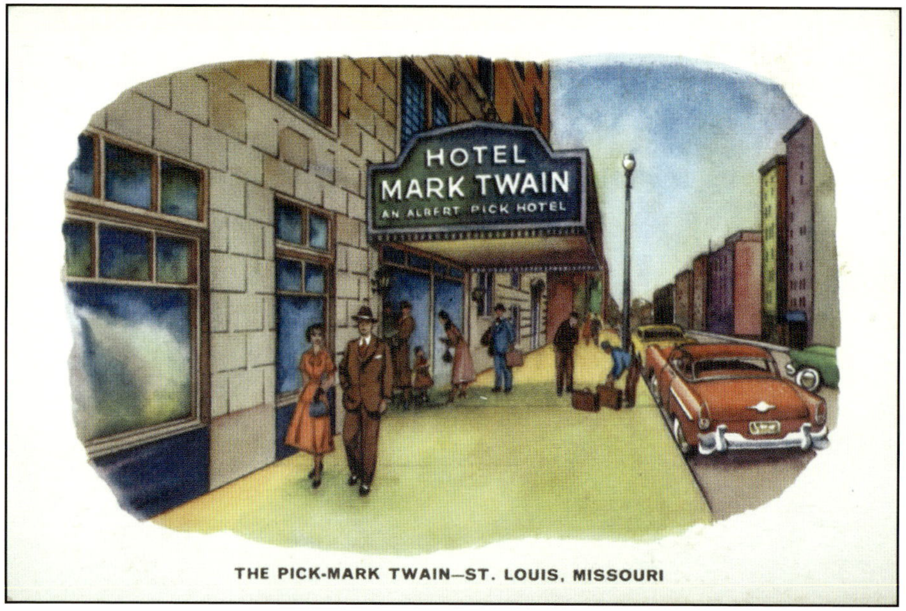

The 100-year-old Mark Twain Hotel was previously known as the Maryland Hotel shown prior. It was designed in 1907 by Albert Barleton Groves and characterizes the city's beautiful old architecture. The rear of the card advises that there are 300 rooms with bath available at the Mark Twain.

Circa 1950, $2-4

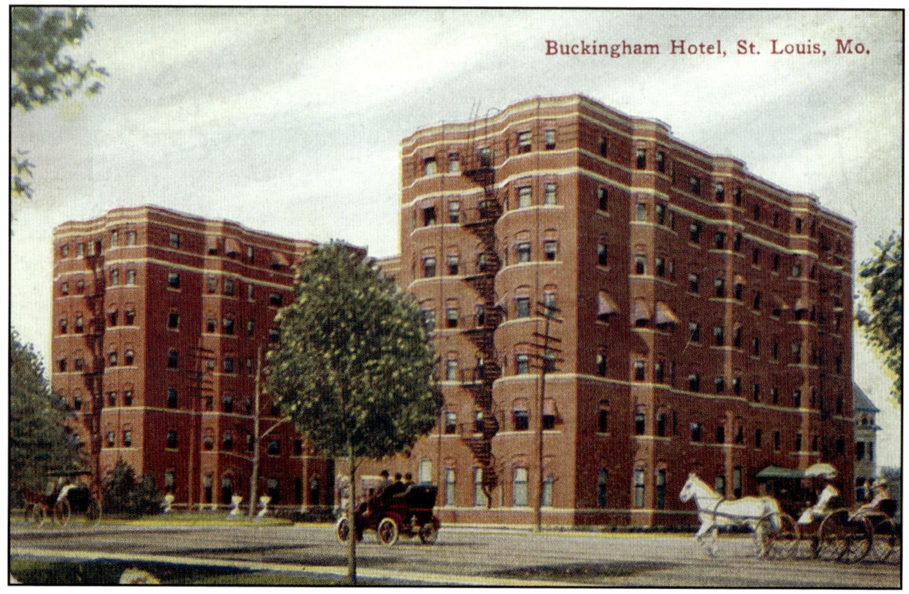

The Buckingham Hotel in St. Louis was known for holding varied important organizational meetings and lectures, including those conducted by the St. Louis Society of the Archaeological Institute of America (founded in 1906). These meetings, often accommodating 250 members and guests would gather in the Parlor.

Circa 1908, $3-5

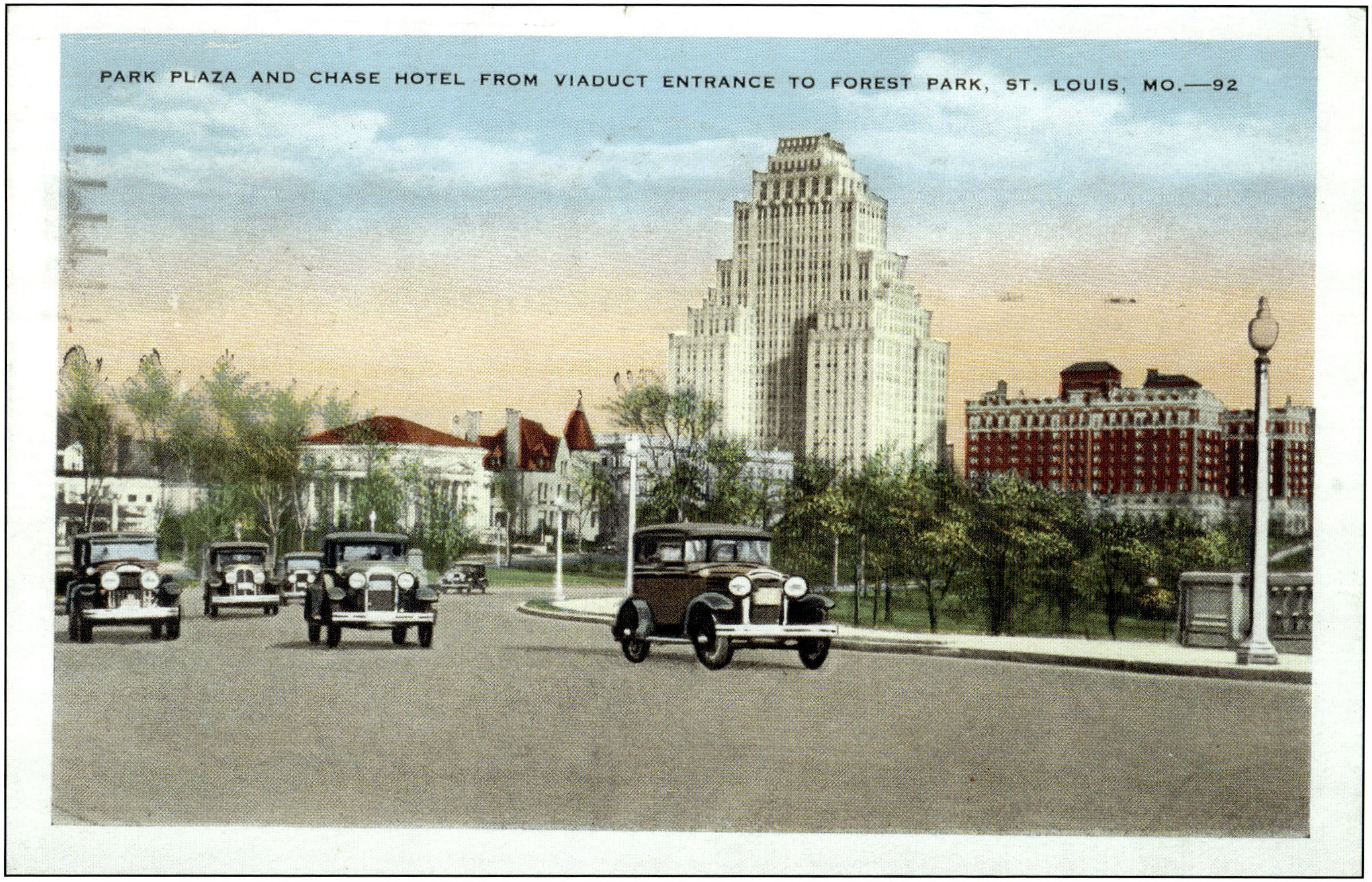

The Chase Hotel opened in 1922, and was built by and named after Chase Ullman. Construction on the Park Plaza began some seven years later and became the backdrop for high-end entertainment, including Frank Sinatra, Jerry Lewis, Dean Martin, and Bob Hope.

Cancelled 1932, $2-4

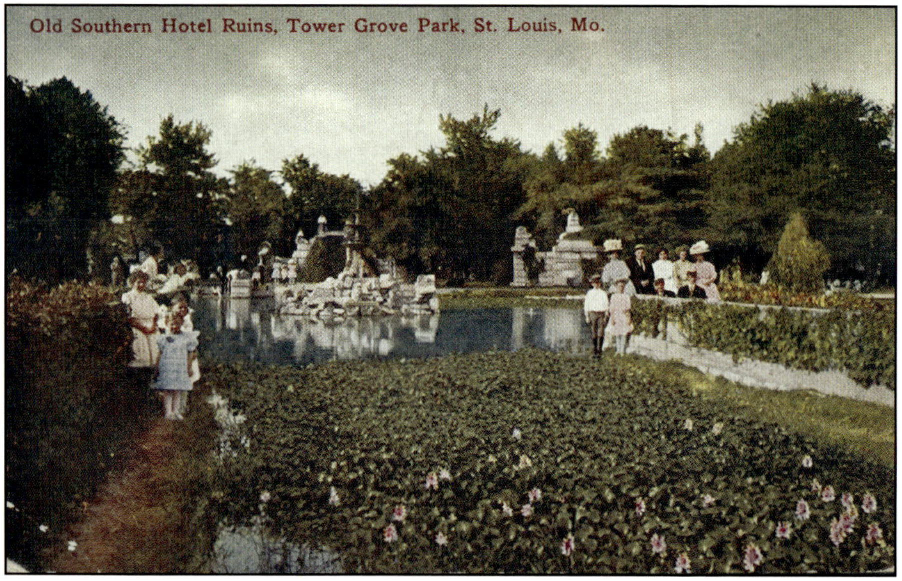

Circa 1907, $2-4

Circa 1907, $2-4

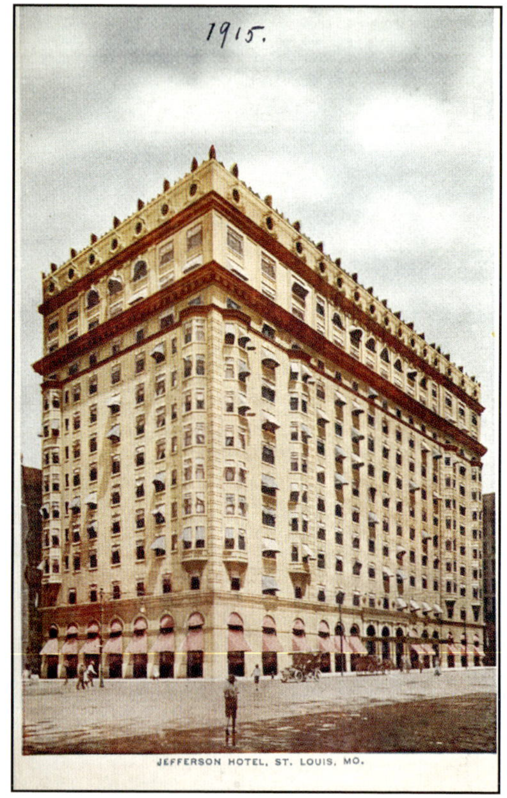

Unfortunately, as the business district, seeking new properties, moved to the west end of St. Louis, much of the hotel business was adversely affected. The Southern Hotel (shown here in ruins) closed in 1912, followed by the distinguished Planters Hotel in 1922. The Planters Hotel, once the city's largest hotel, lost that designation to the Hotel Jefferson (opened in 1904 in the west part of St. Louis). Note the view to the west.

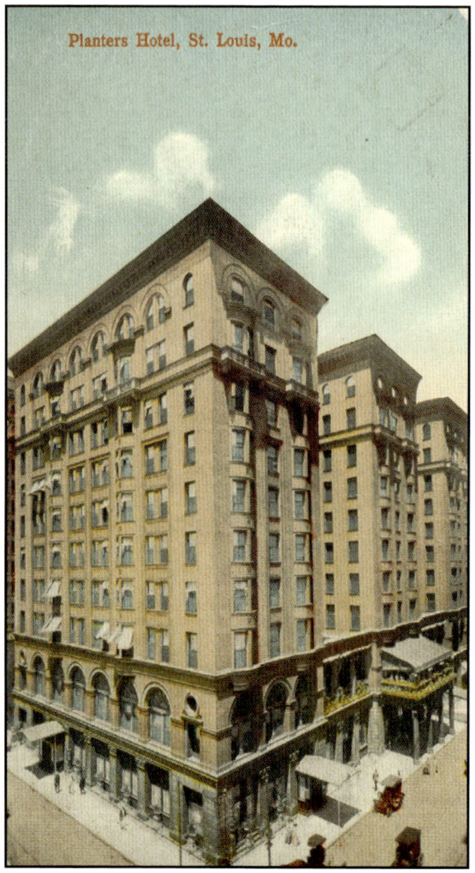

Circa 1907, $2-4

Cancelled 1908, $3-5

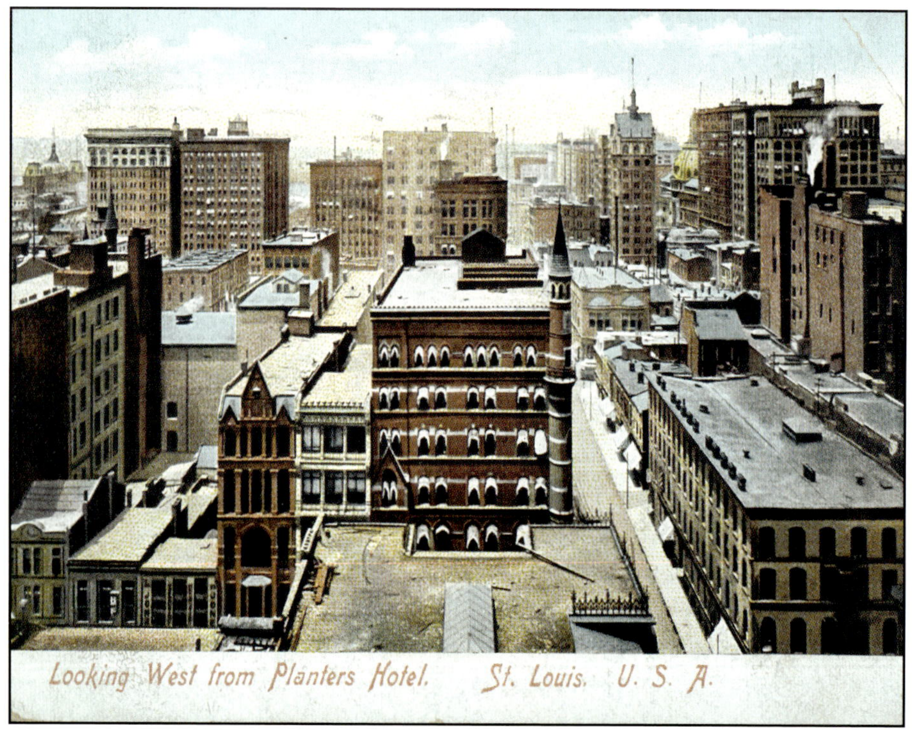

On the Water!

The major reason for such growth in St. Louis has been its proximity and usage of the vast water body at her disposal. With so much river travel, people working and visiting St. Louis required all the economic favors possible for a successful lifestyle.

And if the masses were not traveling through the water to their desired destinations, then they were searching for ways to go over the waters of St. Louis.

Eads Bridge—An Era in Bridge Building

One of the most spectacular structures in St. Louis is the Eads Bridge, engineered by James Buchanan Eads—one of the marveled self-taught engineers of the time. This bridge was the first bridge across the Mississippi River and is still used today, testifying to the significant precision of its construction.

The project was not without issue, however, during the early conception phase in 1869. Eads specified that the bridge needed to be at least fifty feet above the surface of the water in order for smokestack clearance of the ships using the Mississippi River. Additionally, the central span requirement was 500 feet, something that scholarly engineers found impossible at the time.

The impact that such a bridge would have on the economic development of the city did not go unnoticed by those people *in the know*. Eads, at an 1867 convention dealing with improvements of the Mississippi and its tributaries, clearly defined how his plans for the bridge would bring St. Louis to the spotlight.

There were, of course, the financial issues that plagued any project of this nature, along with other suggestions/schemes that called for much less funding. It was estimated that the cost of the bridge would be $736,000—this would be cause for great delay. (The actual final cost was $10,000,000.)

Eads, though, would not be swayed from the task, despite financial issues, government authorizations, nor continued discussion about the possibility of success. He spent seven years creating this fantastic example of American ingenuity, opening the bridge for use on July 4, 1874. The images here show varied views of this famous bridge.

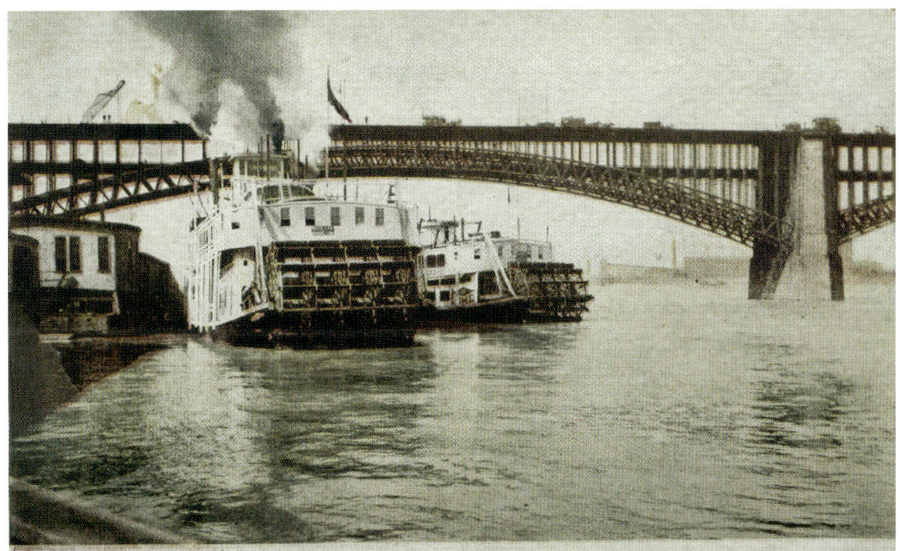
12007. Eads Bridge and River Scene, St. Louis, Mo.

Circa 1907, $3-5

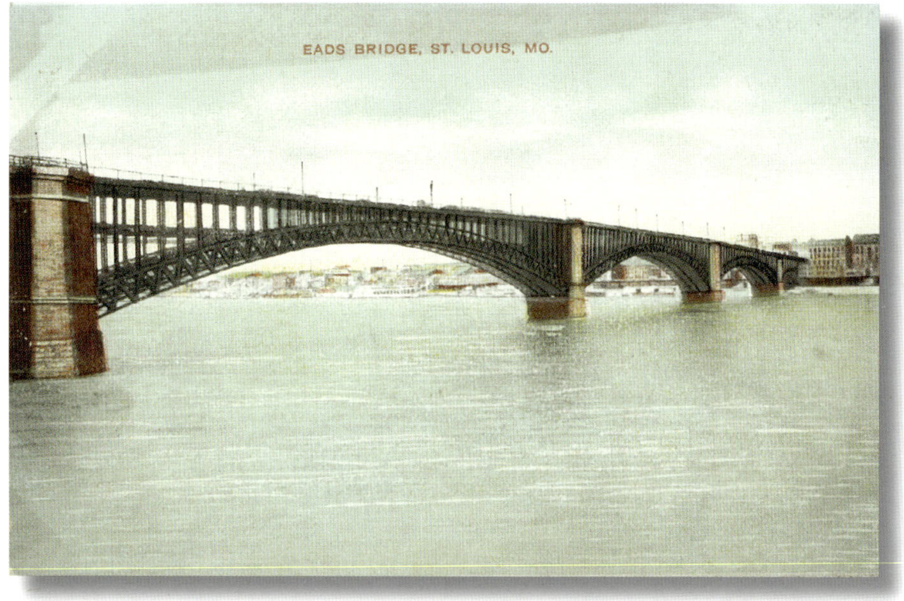

Circa 1907, $2-4

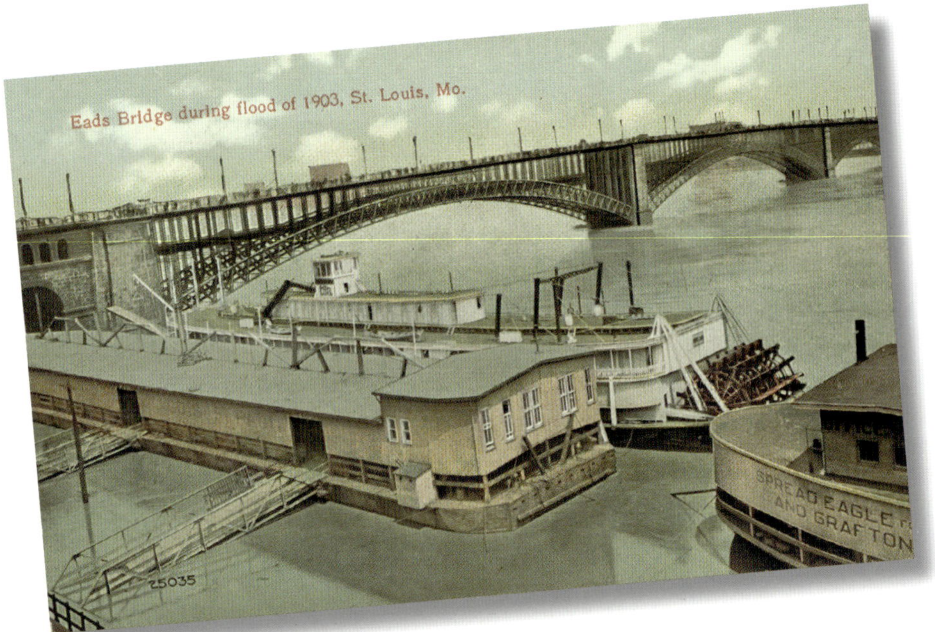

Circa 1907, $2-4

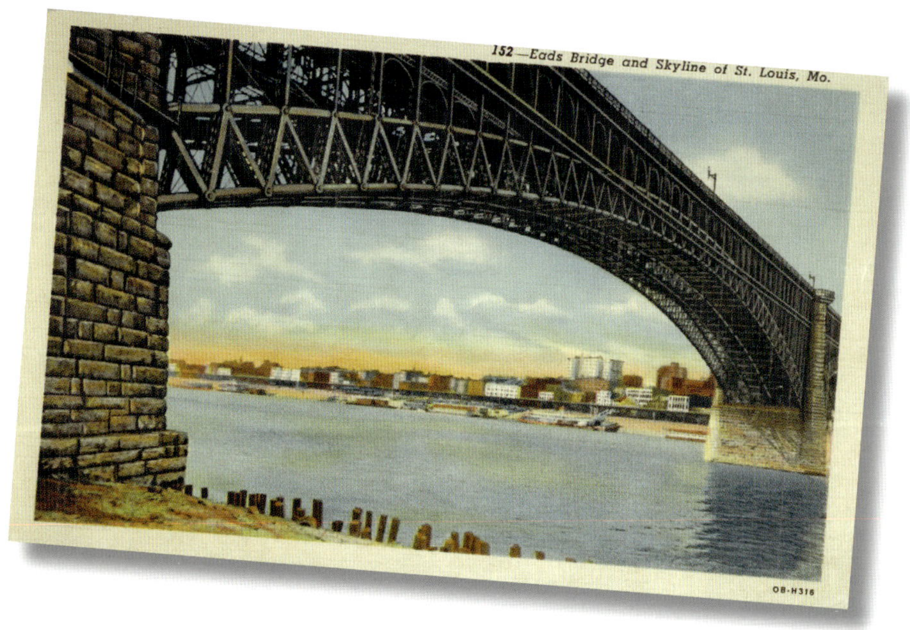

Circa 1907, $2-4

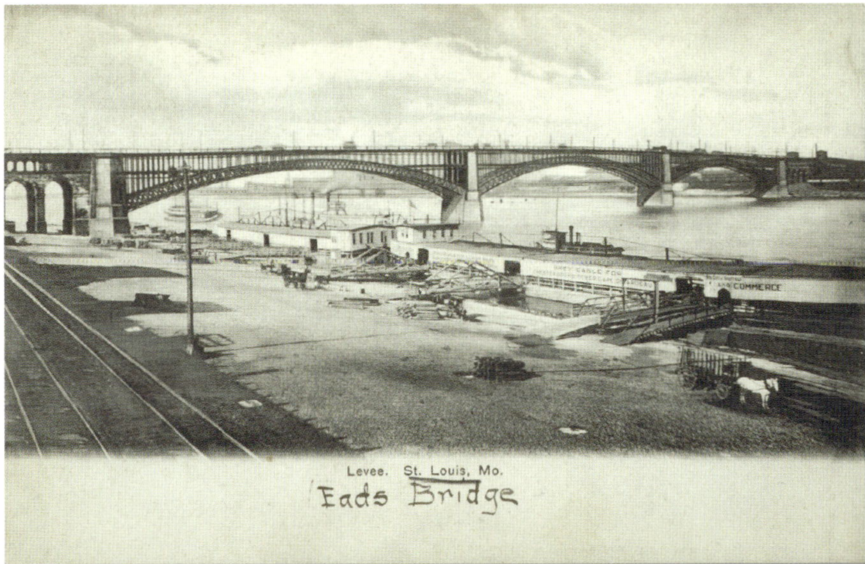

Circa Early 1900s, $3-5

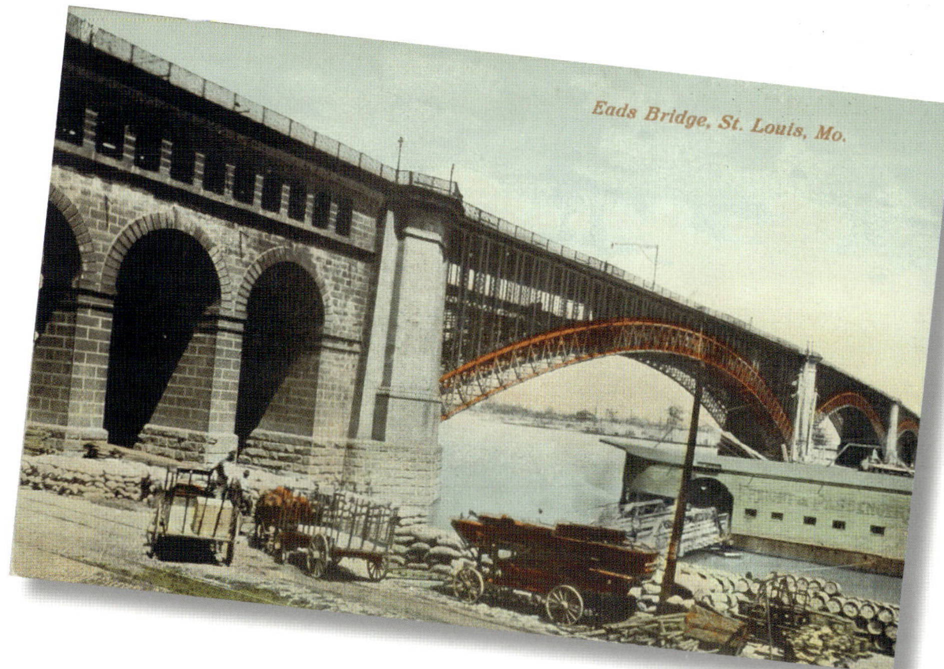

Circa 1907, $2-4

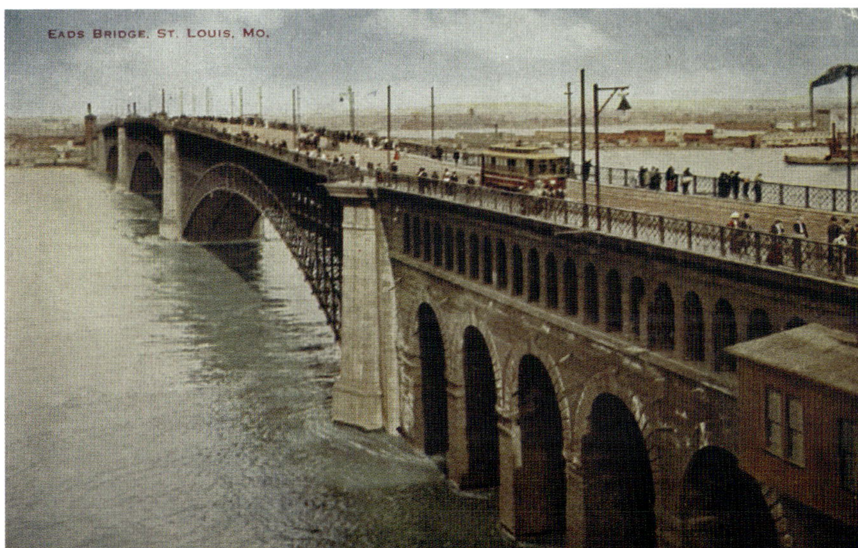

Circa 1907, $3-5

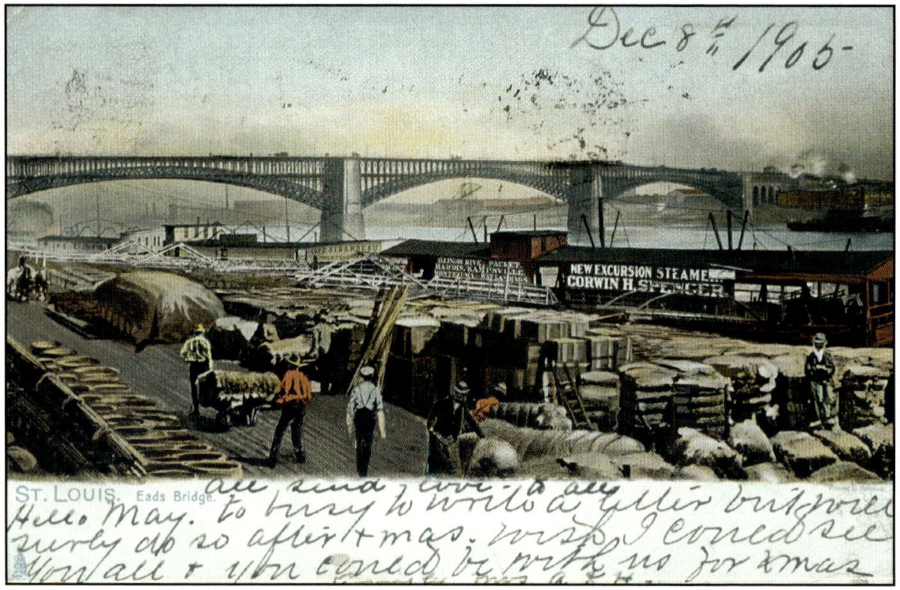

Cancelled 1905, $2-4

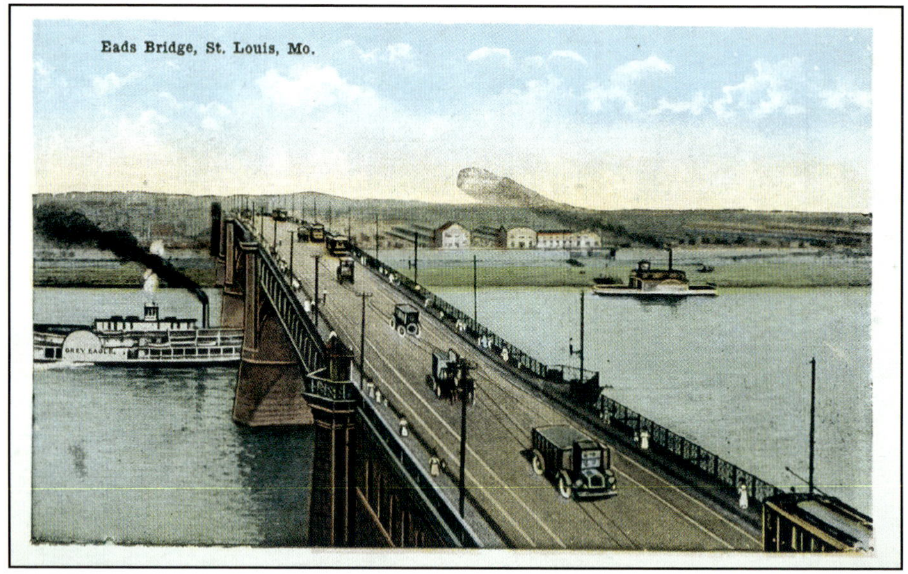

Circa 1920, $2-4

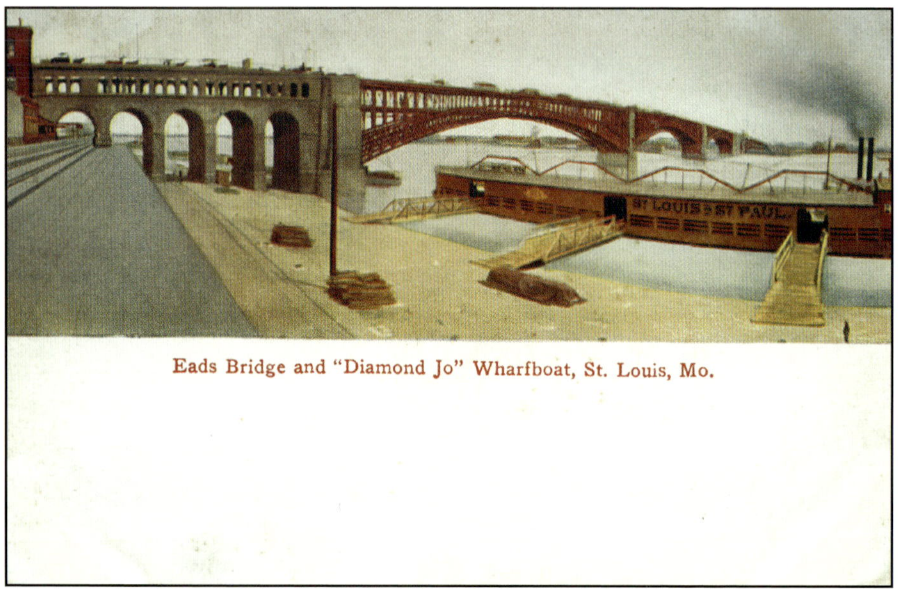

Circa 1907, $3-5

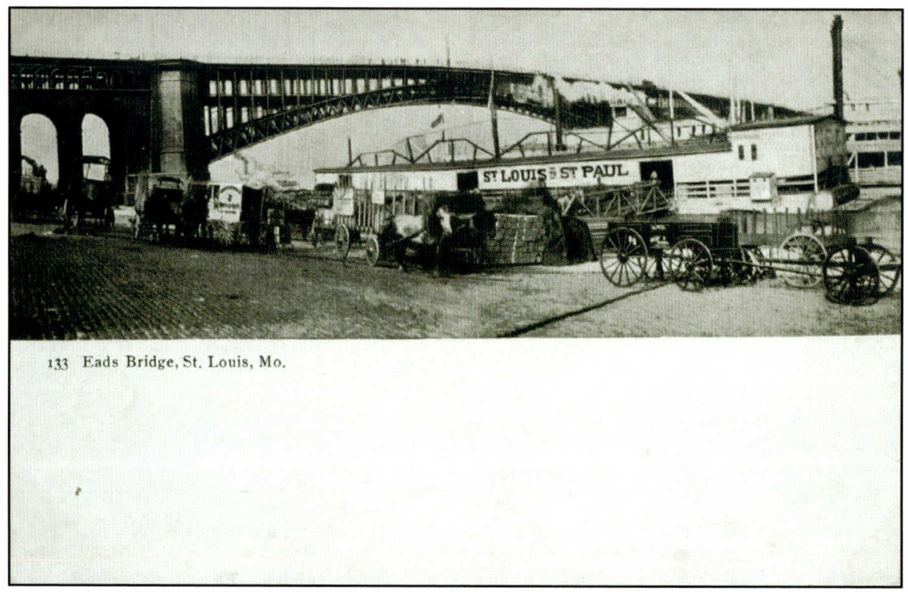

Circa Early 1900s, $6-8

Other Important Bridges

Other bridges also brought significant commerce and progress to St. Louis, including the Grand Avenue Bridge, The Merchants Bridge, The Municipal Free Bridge, The Chain of Rocks Bricdge, and the MacArthur Bridge.

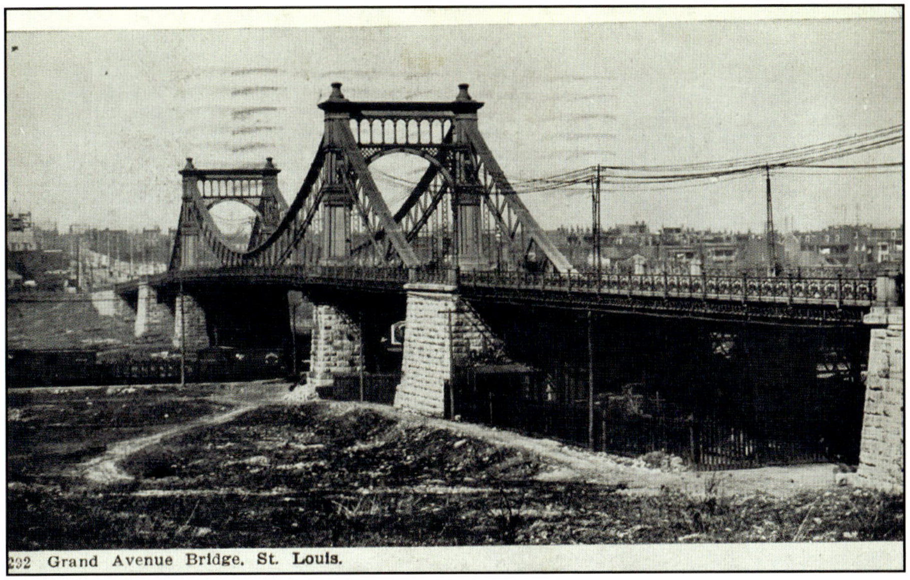

Cancelled 1910, $10-12

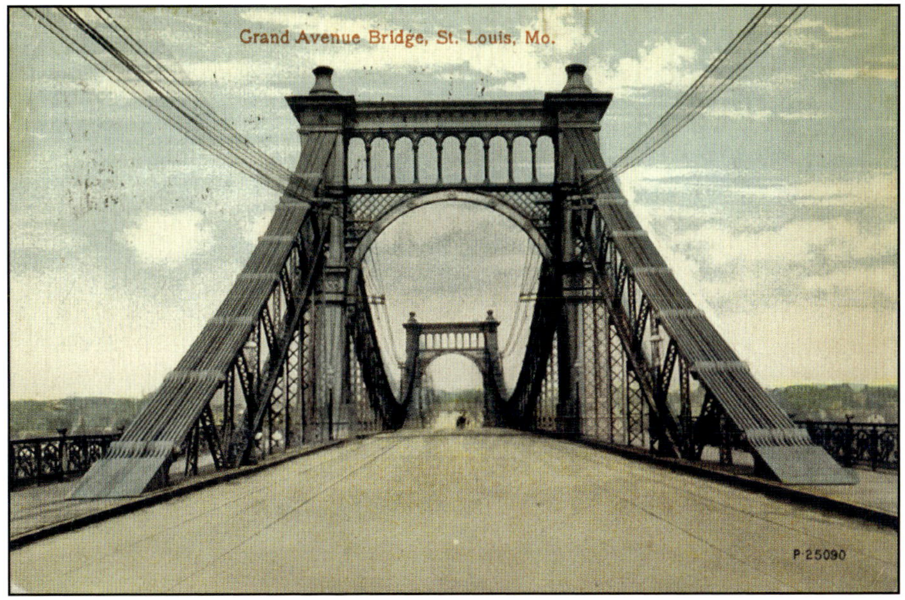

Cancelled 1913, $2-4

The Grand Avenue Bridge was a suspension bridge that was built in 1891 by the King Bridge Company. The total length of the bridge was 700 feet with its main span 400 feet. It was replaced in 1962 as part of urban renewal.

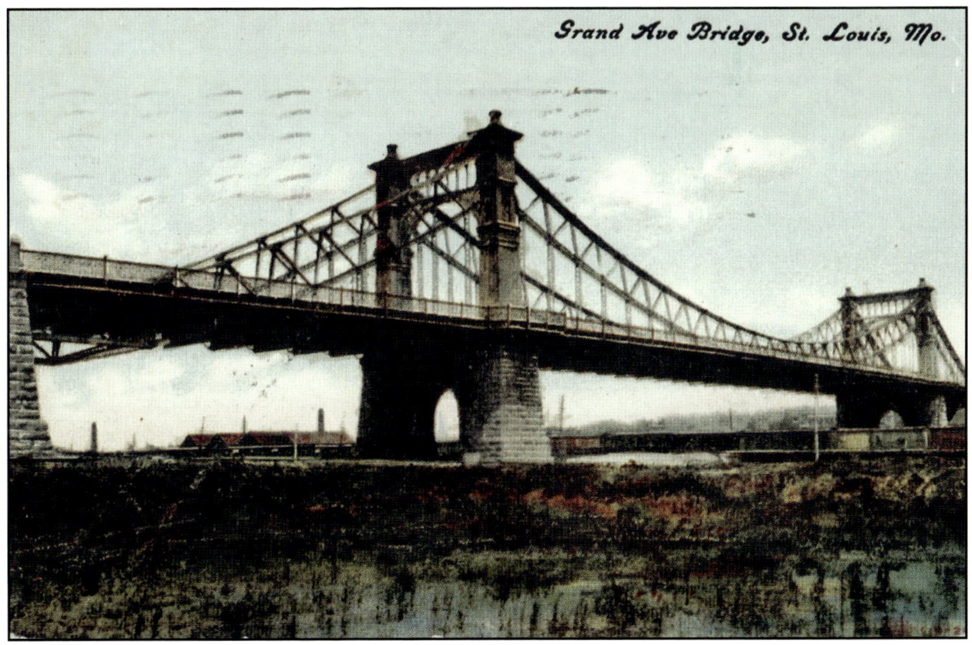

Cancelled 1912, $2-4

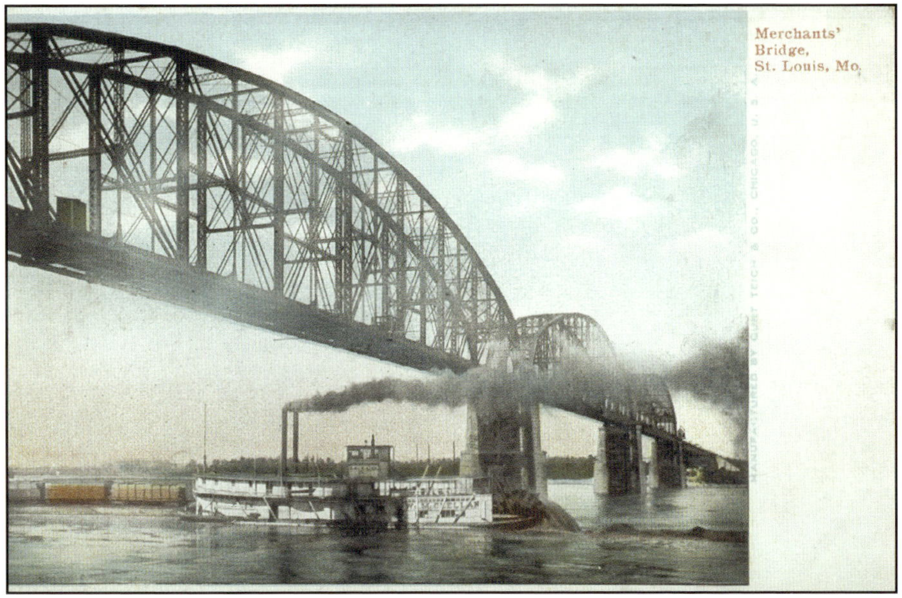

Circa Early 1900s, $2-4

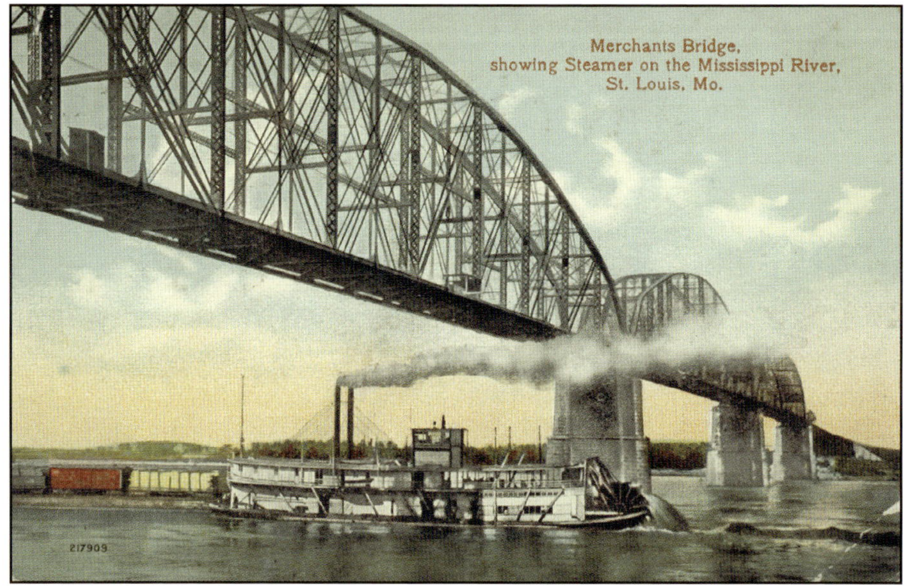

Cancelled 1914, $2-4

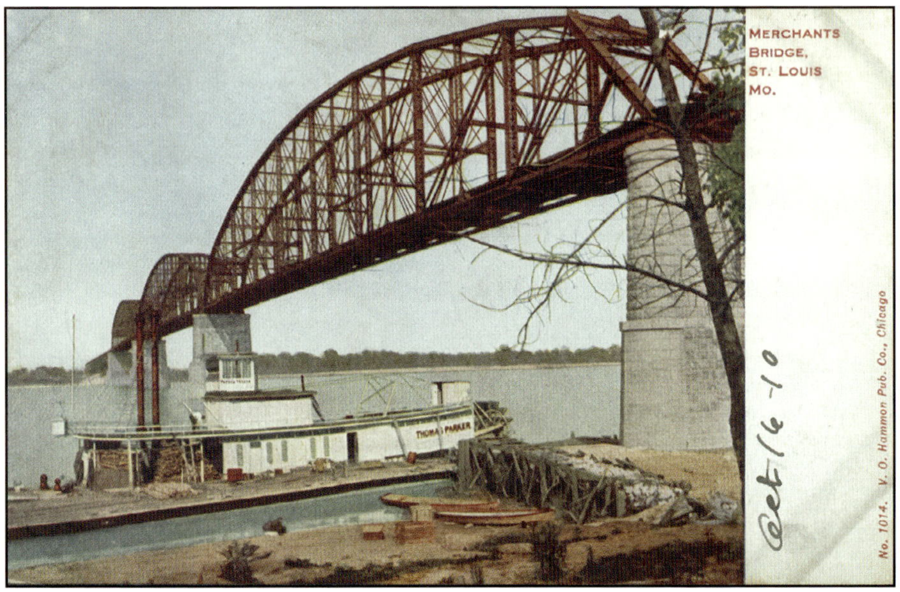

Cancelled 1910, $2-4

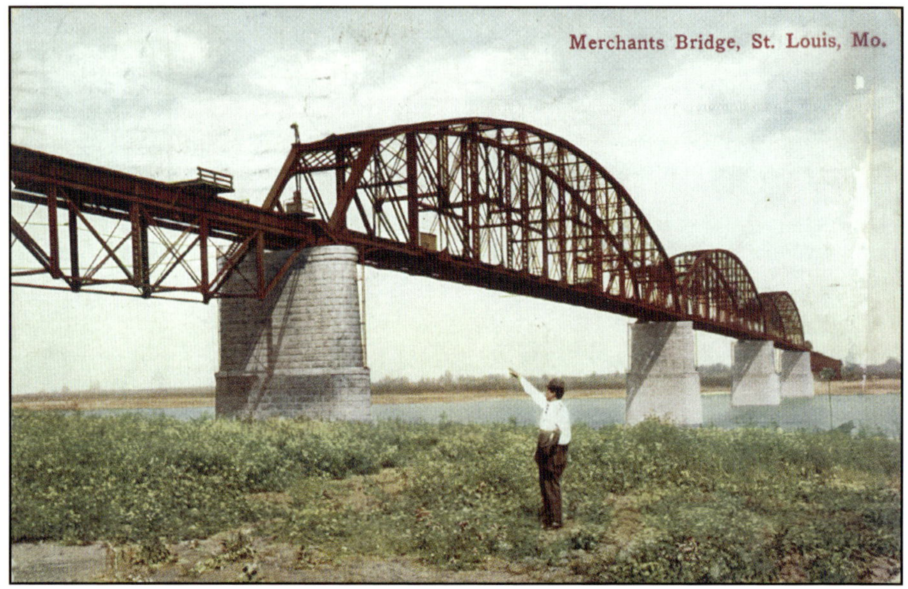

Cancelled 1911, $2-4

The Merchants Bridge connected St. Louis and Venice, Illinois by railroad. Completed in 1890, the three-span through truss railroad bridge was built by George S. Morison and E. L. Corthell (designers) and is now owned by the Terminal Railroad Association.

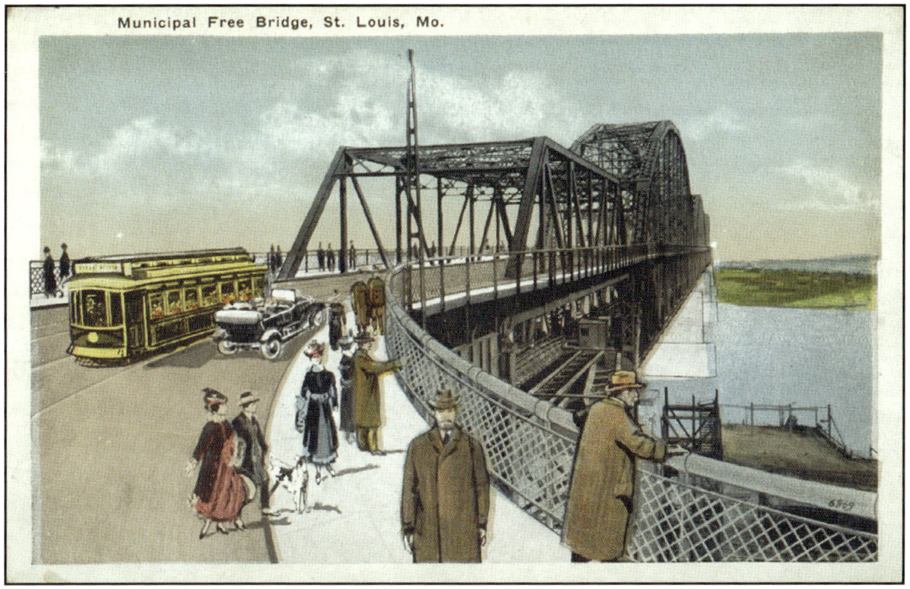

Circa 1907, $2-4

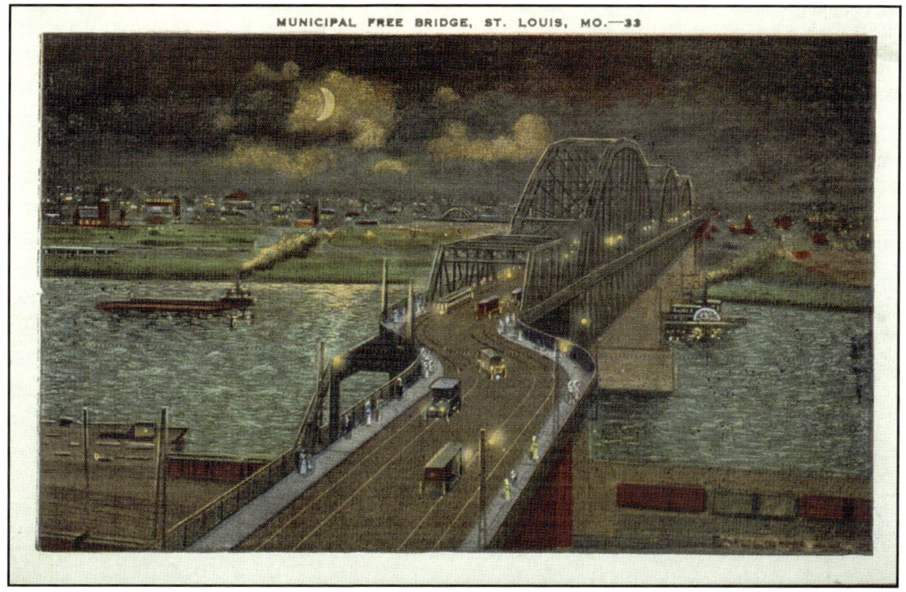

Circa 1920s, $2-4

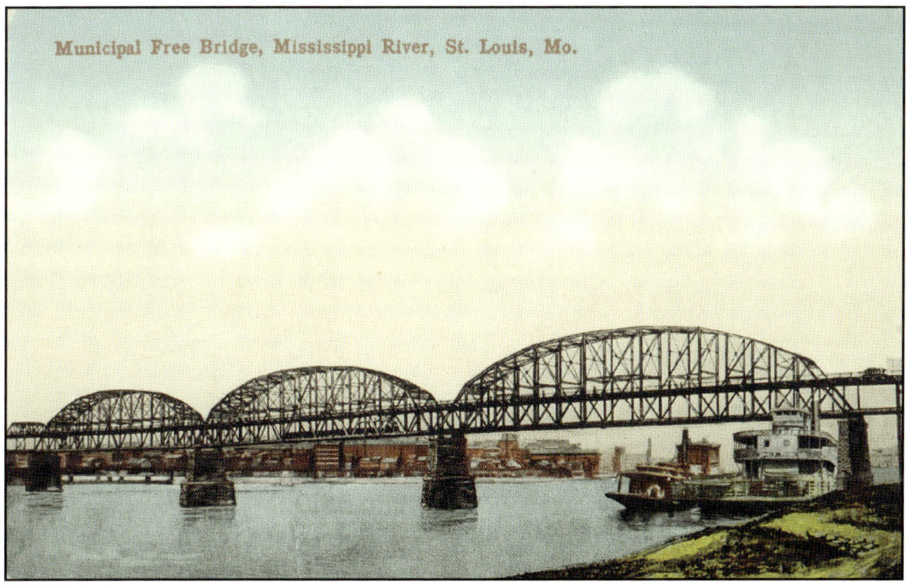

Circa 1907, $2-4

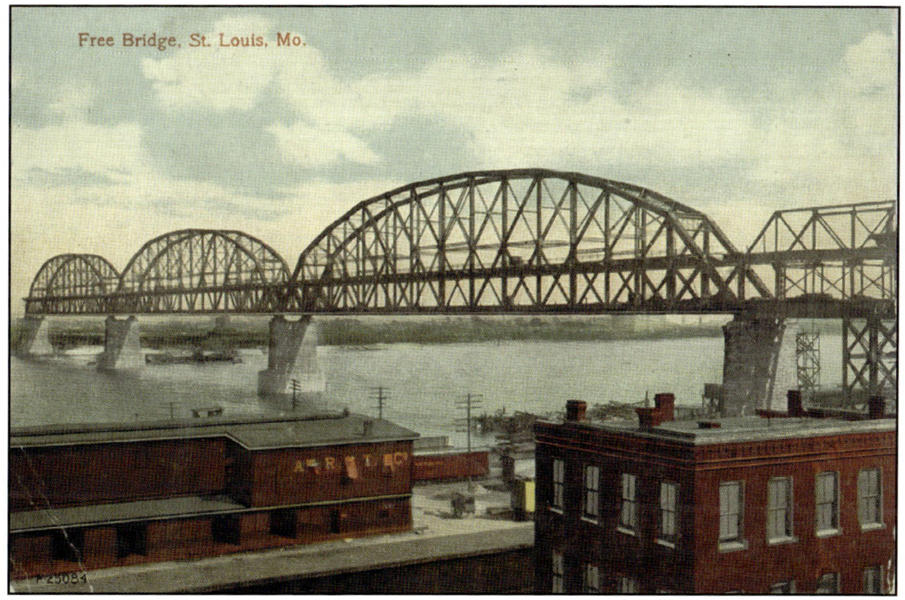

Circa 1907, $2-4

The Municipal Free Bridge began construction in 1907, although great financial difficulties caused delays. Both pedestrians and automobile traffic used the bridge, though the autos were charged a toll. The highway's upper deck was opened in 1917. Until the railway deck, on the lower level, was put into operation, trucks and horse-drawn vehicles used the bridge to transport goods free of toll. The cost of the bridge was $6,000,000.

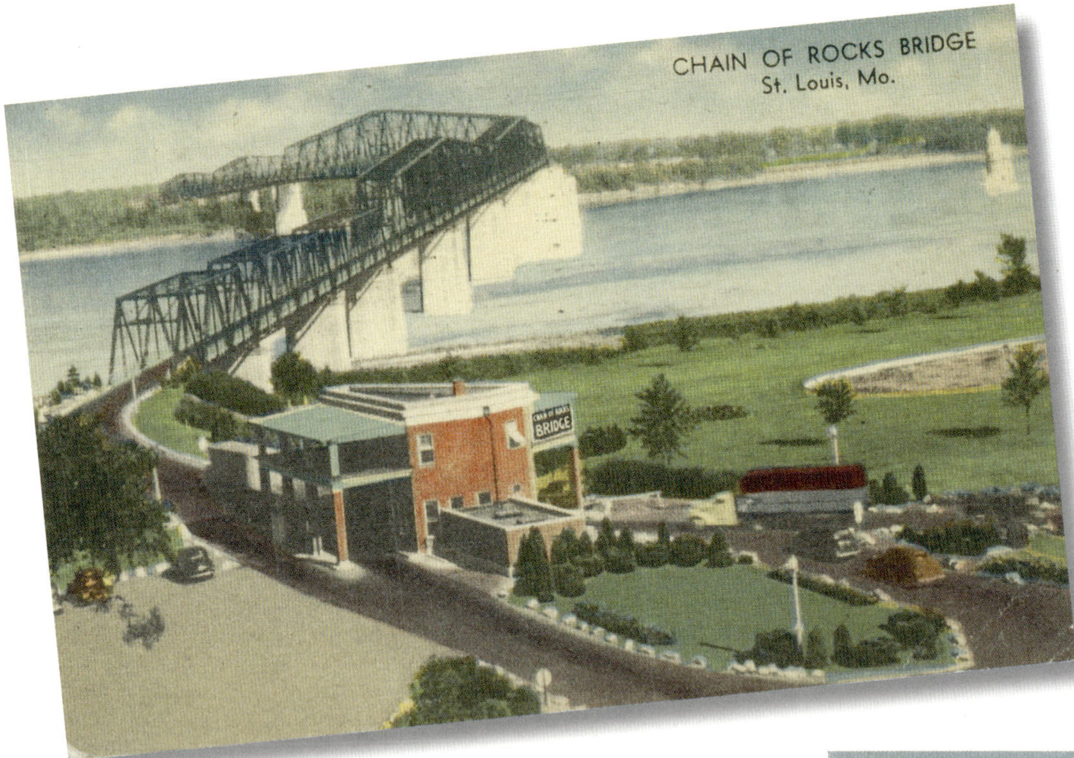

The Chain of Rocks Bridge crossed over the Mississippi using the Old U. S. Route 66. It was originally privately built in 1929 as a toll bridge, costing $3,000,000. Later, it was turned over to the city of Madison. The toll was removed when a law was established that made collecting tolls on U. S. highways illegal. The bridge was closed to traffic in 1968, but was reopened for pedestrians and bicyclists only in 1999.

Circa 1930s, $2-4

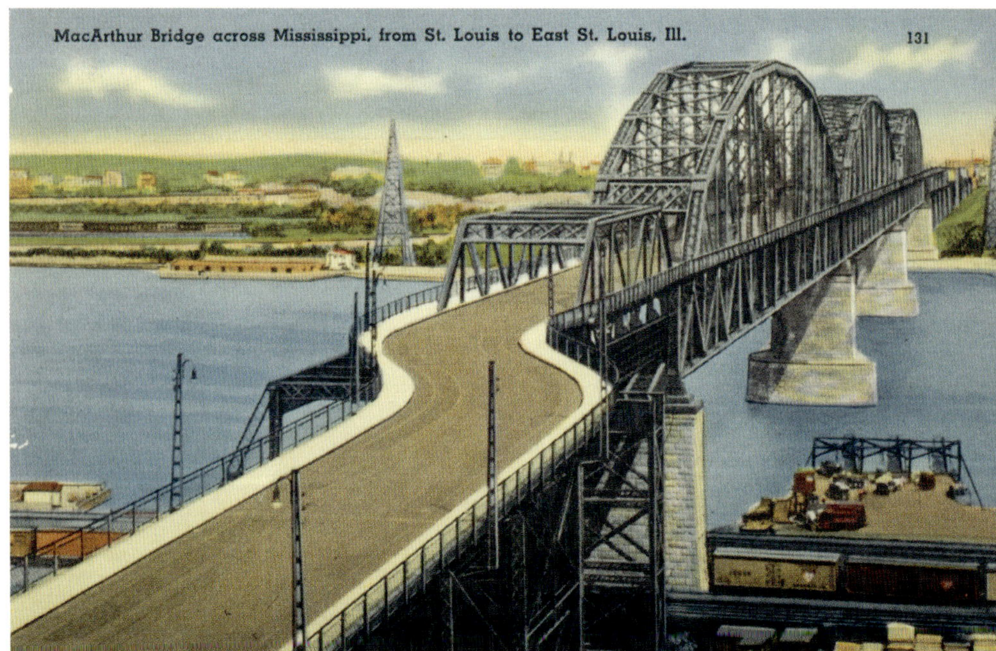

The three-span through truss MacArthur Bridge was built in 1907 and opened to highway traffic in 1917. The City of St. Louis had this bridge built to break a monopoly operated by the Terminal Railroad Association, who not only controlled two other bridges, but also charged unreasonable tolls. (Eventually, in 1989, St. Louis made a trade with the Terminal Railroad, trading this bridge for the Eads Bridge.)

Cancelled 1956, $2-4.

Levees

A levee can be a natural or artificial barrier that parallels the course of a river. Their primary purpose is to provide flood protection from high water, but there are other purposes, as well—depending upon urban, agricultural, or business needs. In St. Louis, the levees needed were mainline and tributary, and cover much territory.

The Mississippi River levee system is one of the largest in the world, stretching from Cape Girardeau, Missouri to the Mississippi Delta. So it's no surprise that levees were constructed on the Illinois side of the Mississippi to direct water to the Missouri side—thereby eliminating a second channel.

The following levee scenes in St. Louis show varied cargo and freight deliveries and loading practices.

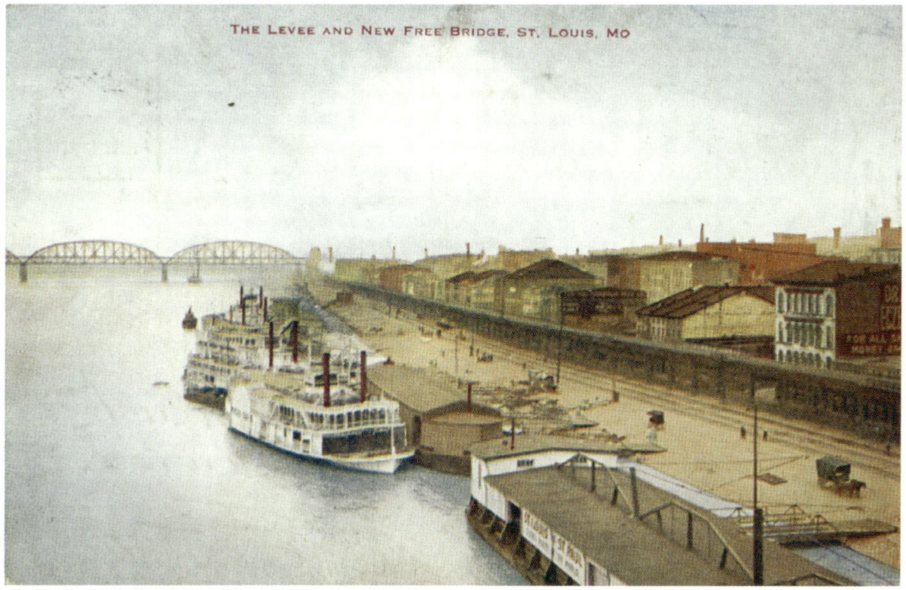

Cancelled 1919, $2-4

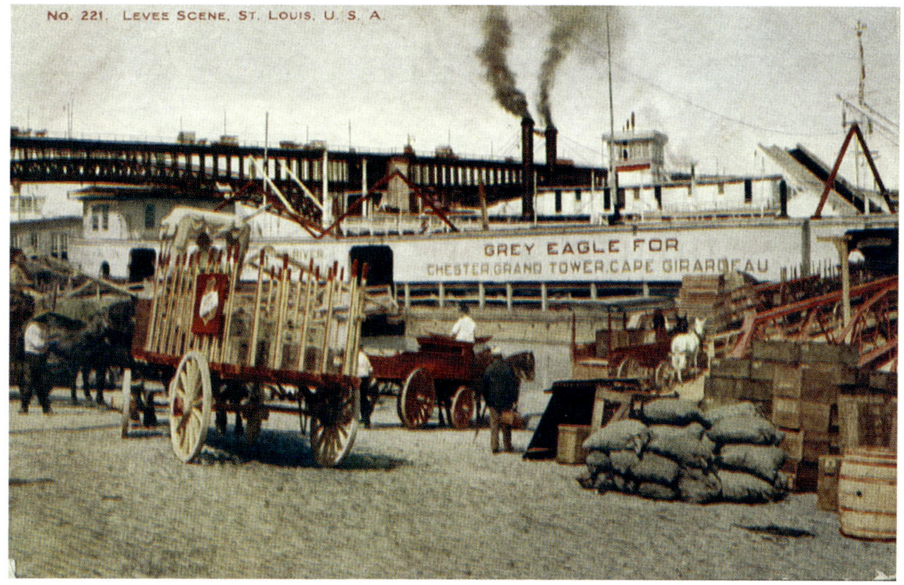

Circa Early 1900s, $3-5

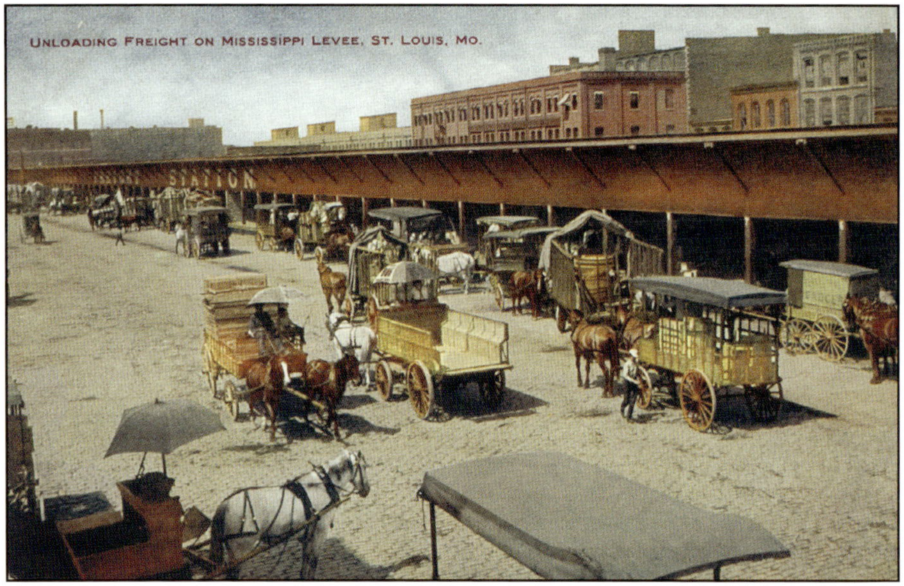

Circa 1907, $3-5

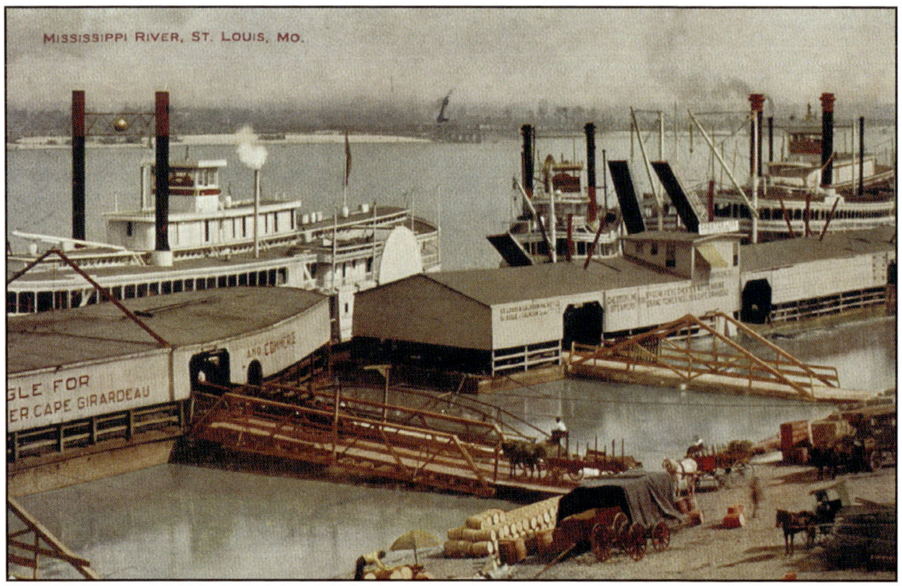

Circa 1907, $3-5

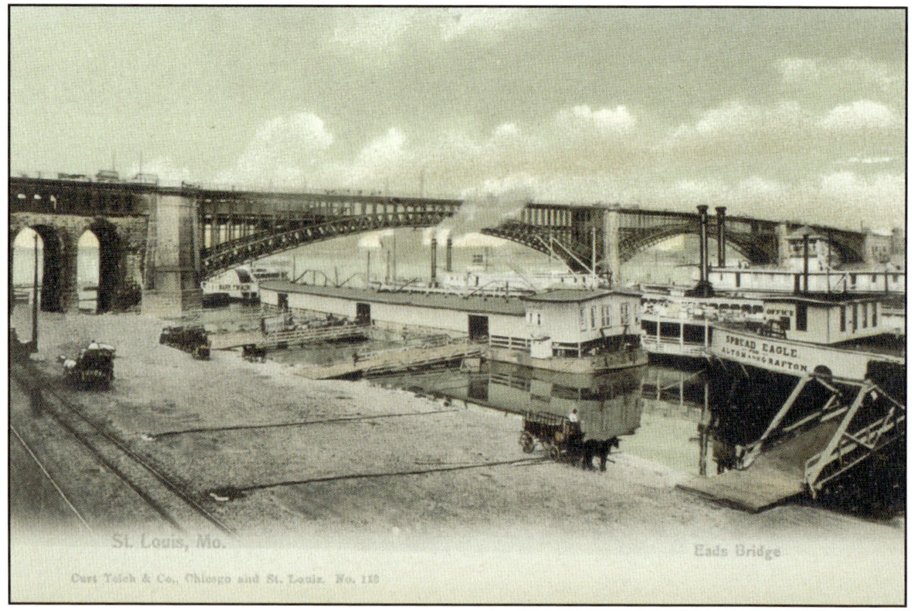

Circa Early 1900s, $3-5

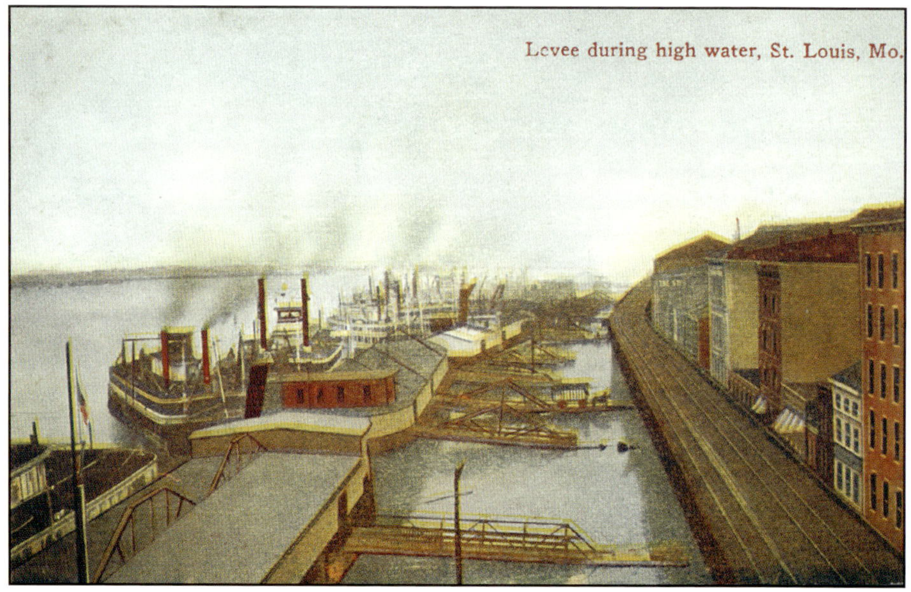

Circa 1907, $2-4

The Steamboat Era

In 1817, the steamboat era became an important part of the progress for both trade and reliable transportation. Boats powered by steam provided efficiency by allowing transportation up the river against currents, just as easily as down river. Barges and keel boats could not offer that luxury. When the 1830s arrived, steamboat traffic totaling as many as 150 boats at one time, could be seen at the St. Louis levee. This boom in transportantion was the catalyst that made St. Louis the second largest port in the country.

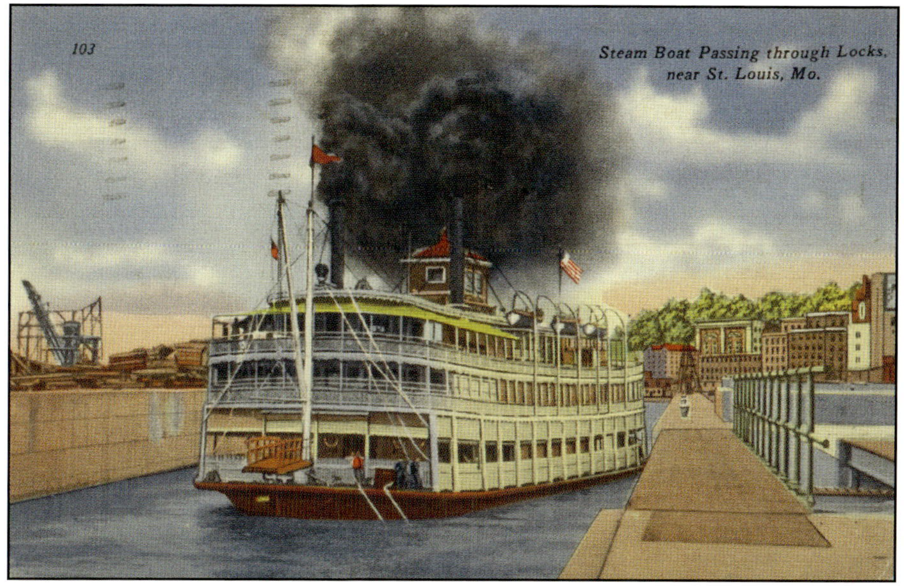

Circa 1930s, $3-5

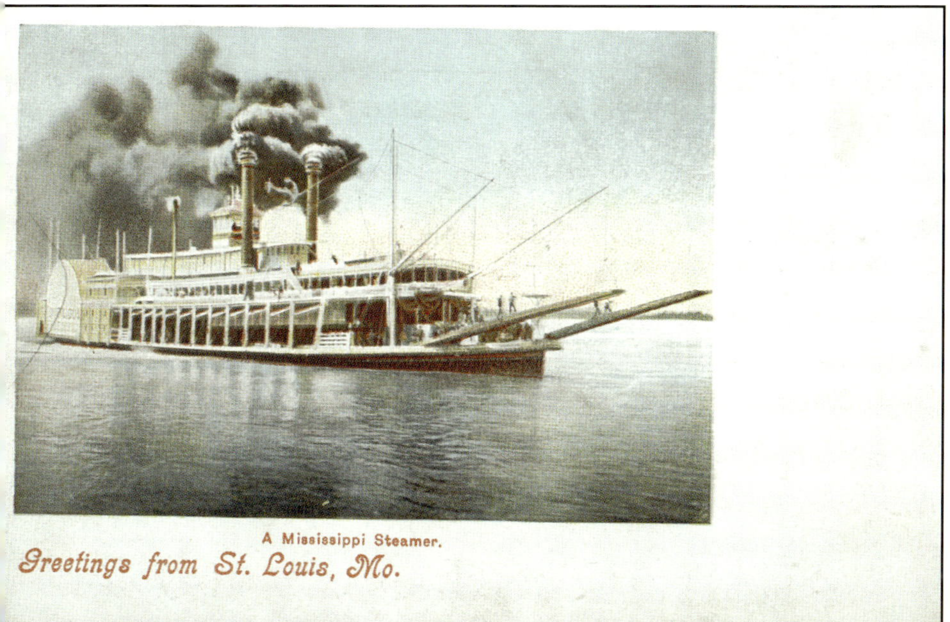

Circa Early 1900s, $3-5

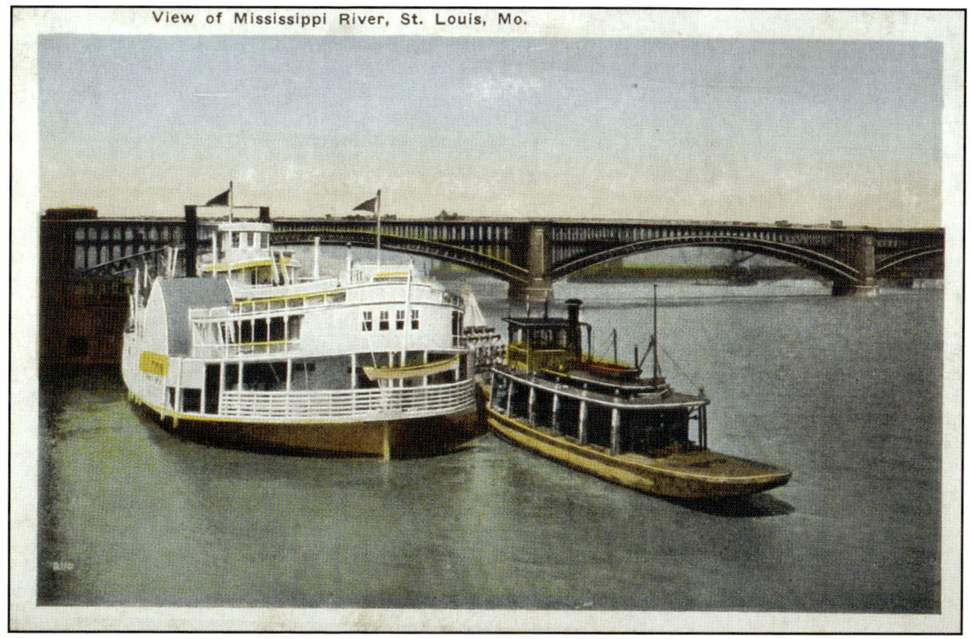

Pictured here, the excursion steamer *City of Alton*, with the Eads Bridge in the background. Some sources say that the *Alton* was used as a soldier transport in 1861.

Circa 1907, $2-4

The excursion steamer *Corwin H. Spencer* was a remodeled version of the *City of Monroe*, and *Hill City*. First named *City of Monroe,* it was damaged by the Great St. Louis Tornado in 1889, and was rebuilt and renamed *Hill City*. In 1900, it sank near Memphis, was raised, and remodeled again into the excursion boat you see here.

Circa 1907, $2-4

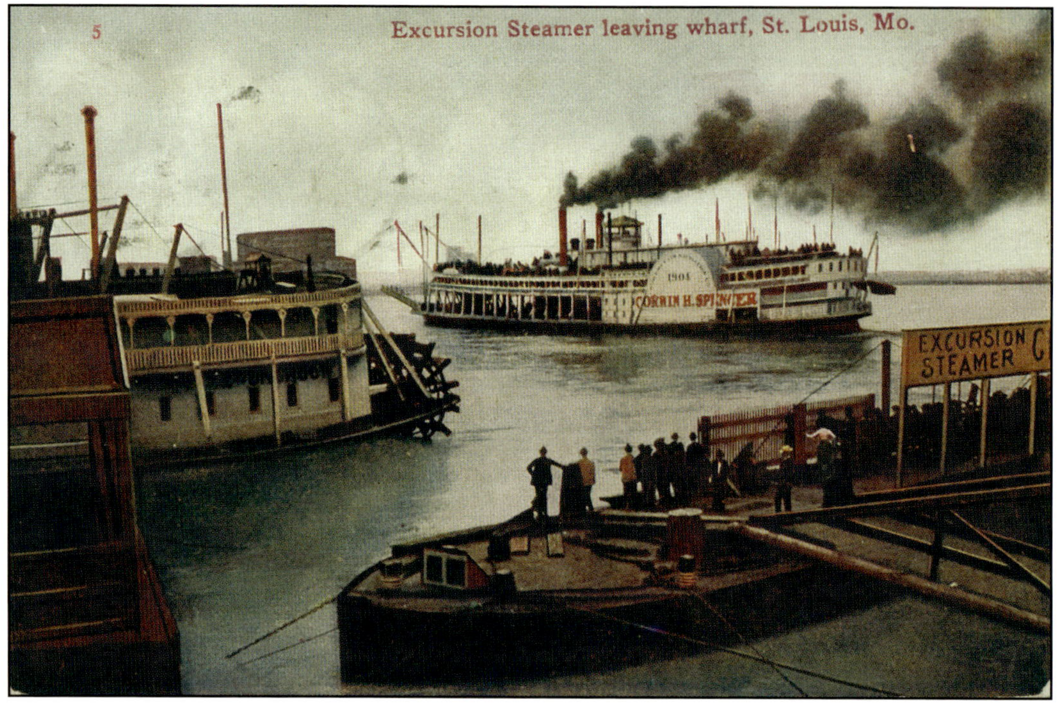

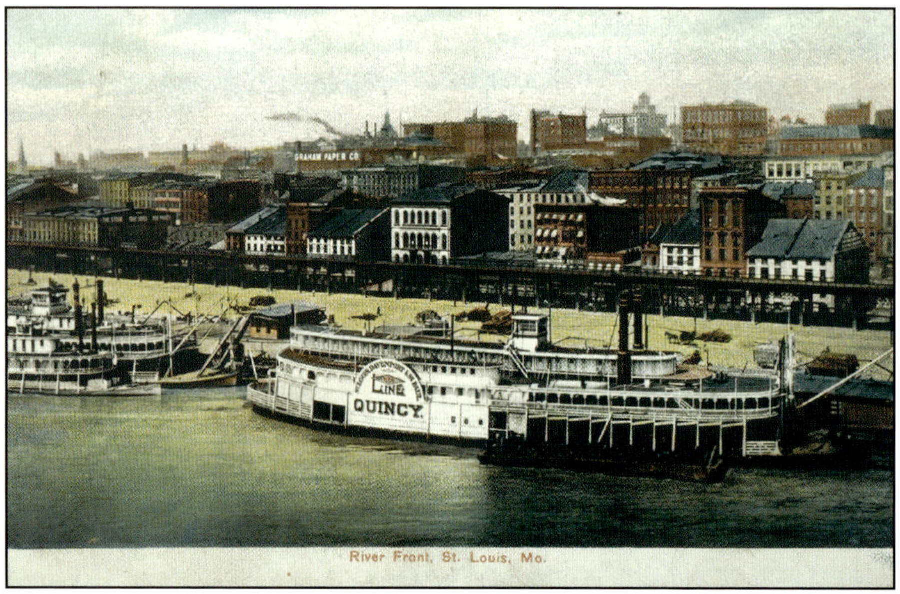

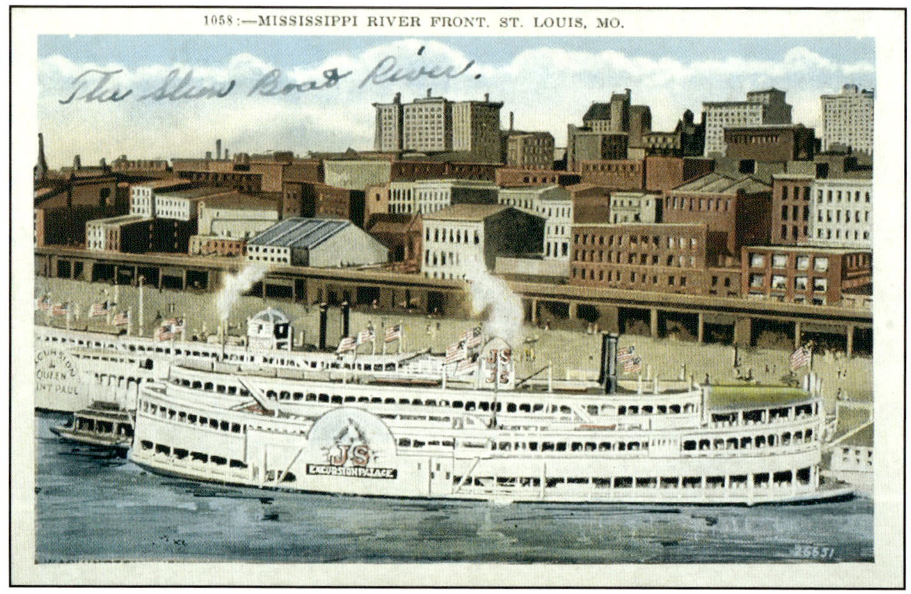

Research suggests that the *Quincy* was launched somewhere around 1896, and was renamed the *J. S.* after Captain John Streckfus, circa 1918-1919. It was dismantled in St. Louis circa 1938-1939.

Cancelled 1909, $3-5 (left)
Circa 1914, $2-4 (right)

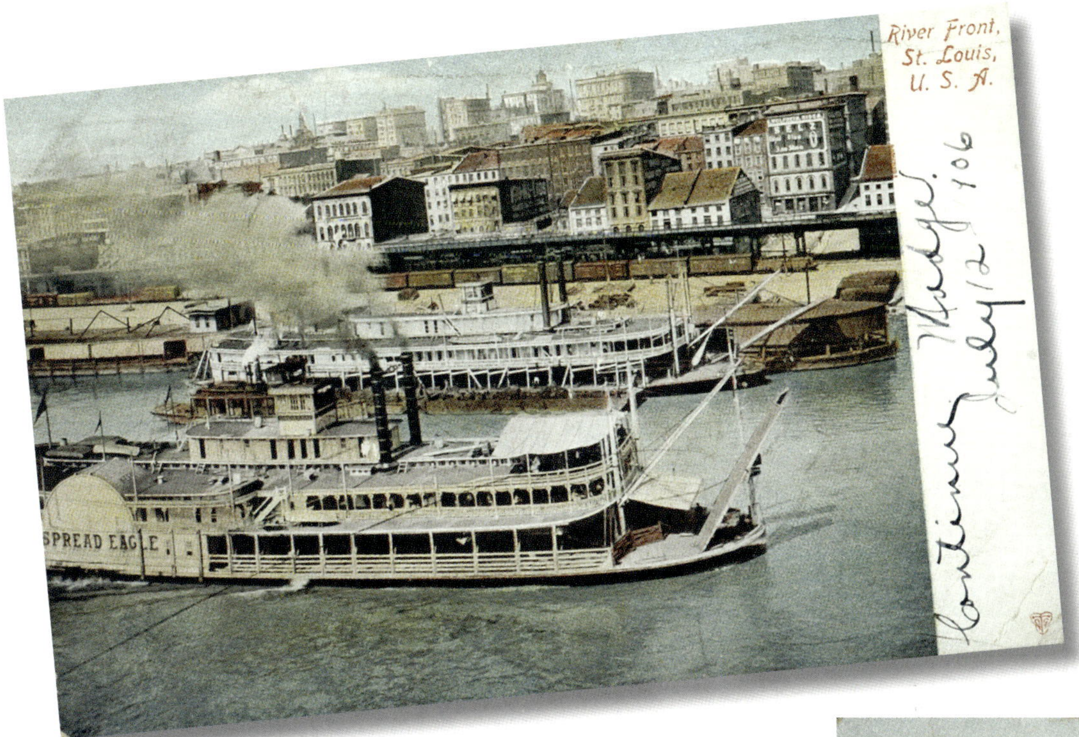

The steamer *Spread Eagle* was launched in 1857 in Brownsville, Pennsylvania, but managed to make her way to St. Louis from a sale to Captain Joseph LaBarge and the American Fur Company. In 1864, *Spread Eagle* sank near New Haven, Missouri, and the location where the boat went down was then called Spread Eagle Bend.

Cancelled 1906, $2-4

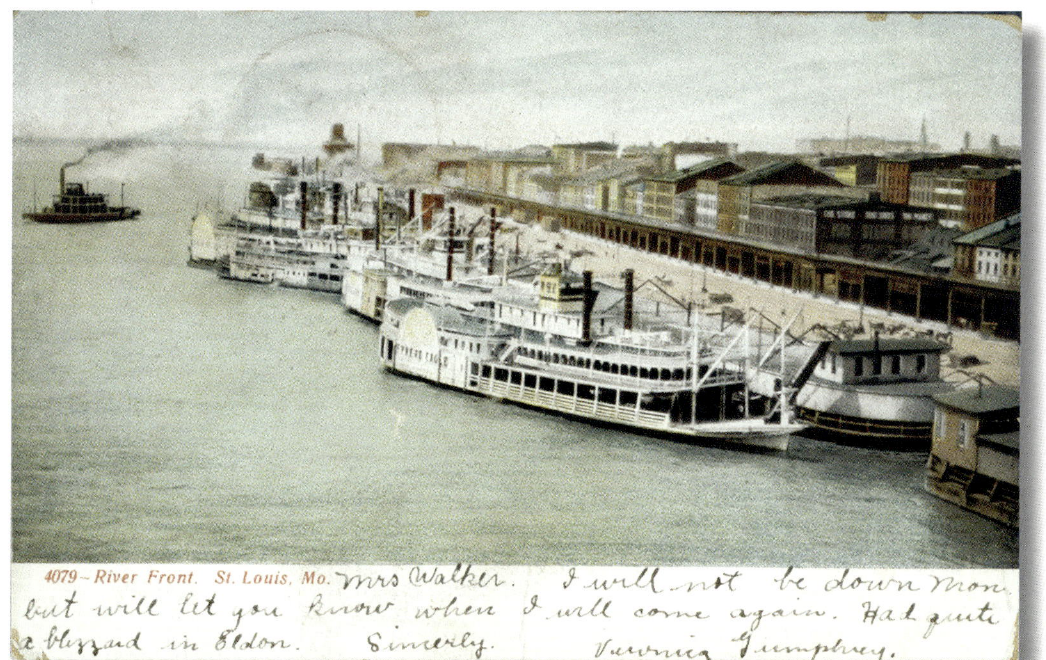

Circa 1907, $2-4

The *S. S. Admiral* was an especially notable steamer because all exterior decorative design was absent. The length of the boat was 375 feet, and the steel hull was divided into 74 water-tight compartments, constructed so that as many as 11 of those compartments could flood, while the boat still maintained the ability to stay afloat.

Circa 1907, $2-4

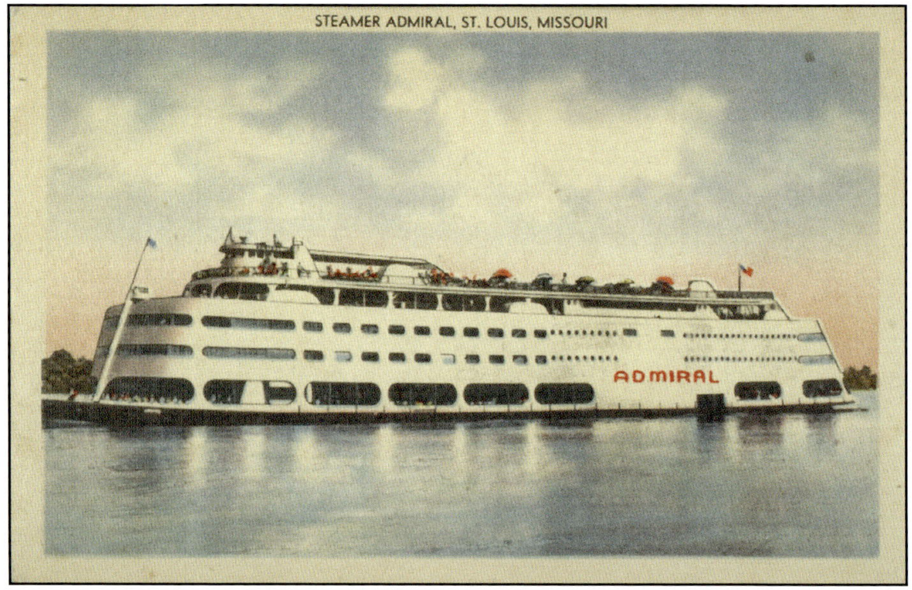

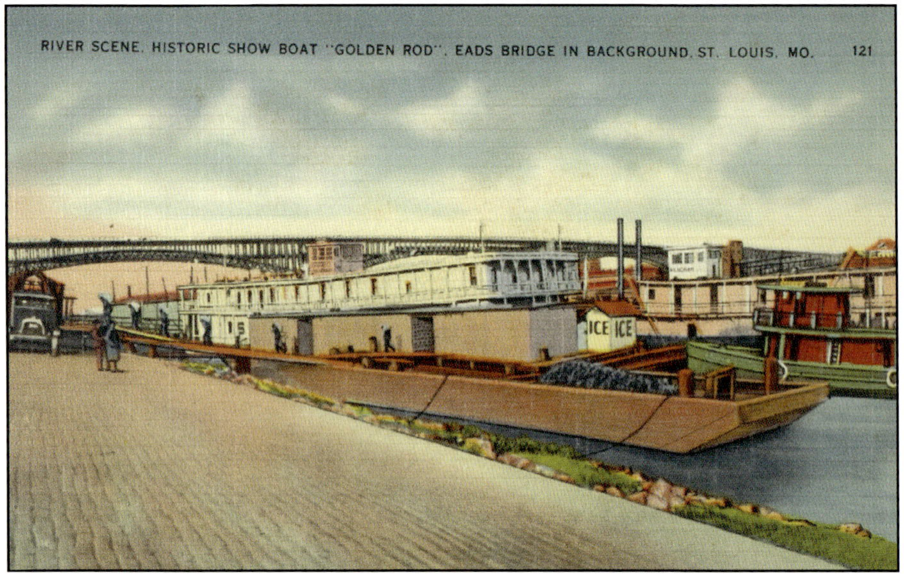

The Showboat, *Golden Rod,* built in 1908-1909, was noted as the largest showboat ever constructed. Though plain on the outside, she was considered to have the most highly decorated interiors of the time.

Circa 1907, $2-4

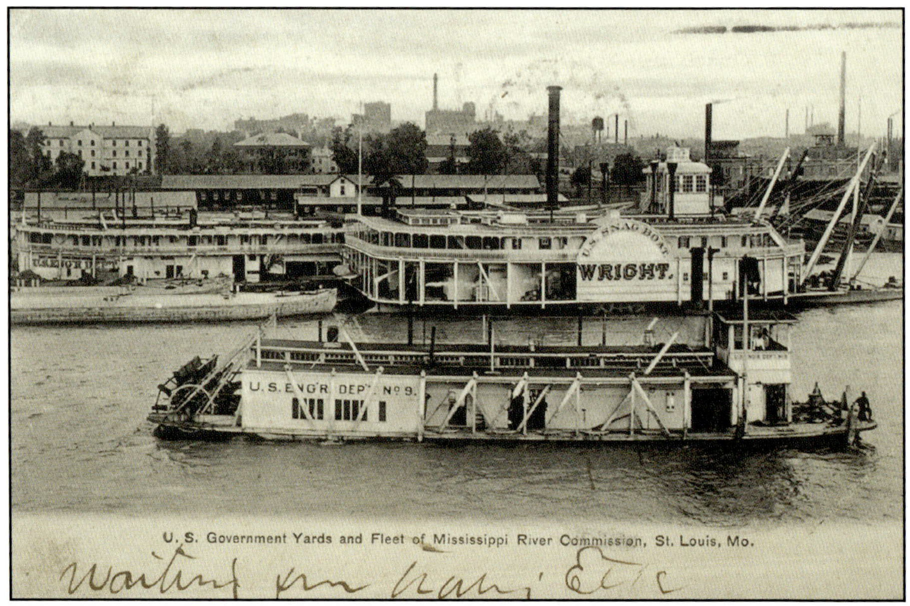

In 1879, the Mississippi Commission was established by Congress following the damage caused by heavy flooding. Its purpose was to recommend programs and policies, research potential flooding issues, inspect, and assist in flooding situations occurring along the Mississippi River.

Cancelled 1906, $8-10

Buildings

As the steamboat and railway traffic increased, and more people came to the city, the number of wonderful buildings of St. Louis grew—all filled with the necessities of living that complimented commerce. From the magnificent Coliseum to the St. Louis Arena, the architecture and prosperity are evident in the structures built. Following are views of these magnificent buildings.

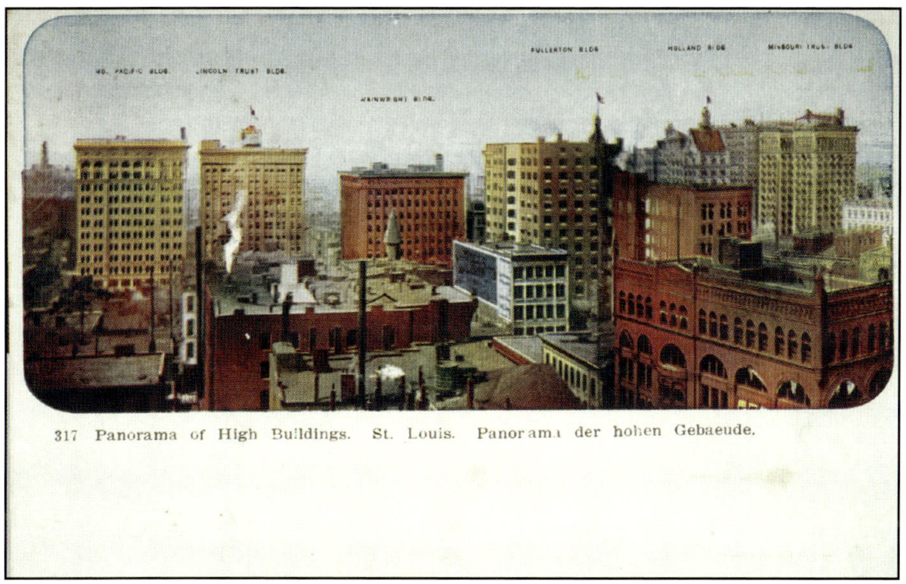

This panoramic view of downtown St. Louis shows such buildings as Missouri Pacific Building, Lincoln Trust Building, Wainwright Building, Fullerton Building, Holland Building, and Missouri Trust Building.

Circa Early 1900s, $2-4

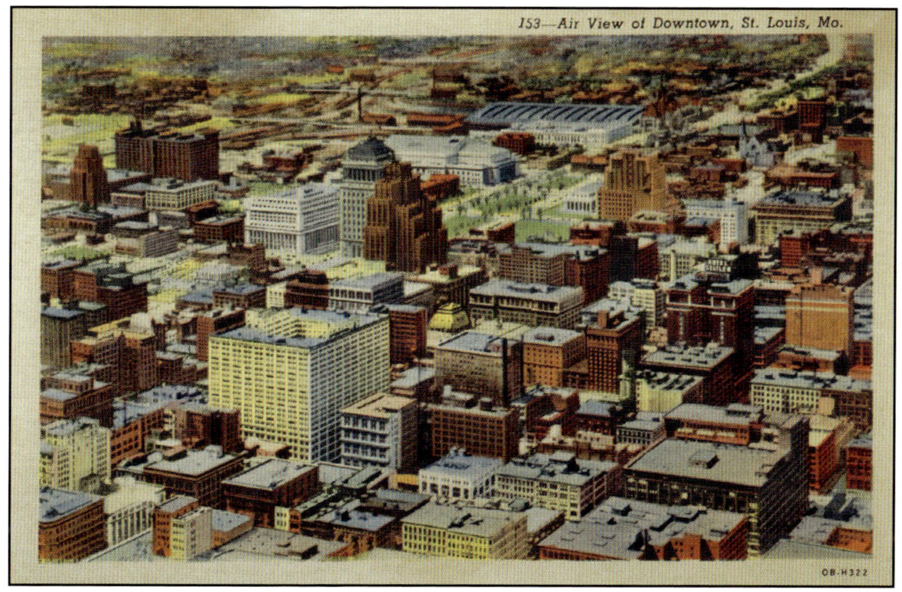

An aerial view shows downtown St. Louis featuring the Railway Exchange Building, which is the largest structure in the center foreground. Other buildings include; Southwestern Bell Telephone Company Building, the Municipal Auditorium, and the new United States Post Office.

Cancelled 1953, $2-4

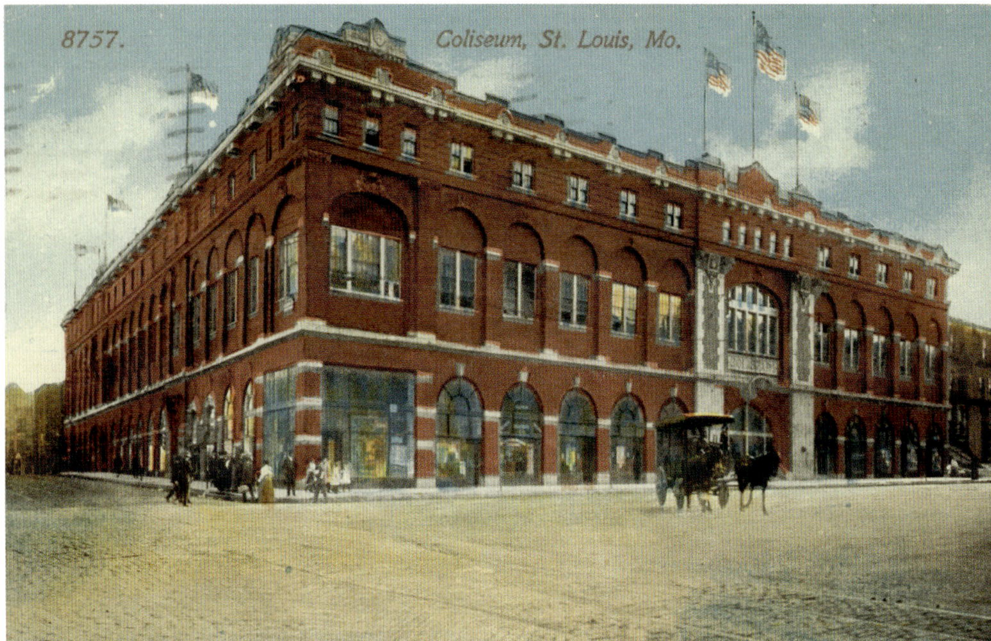

Located at the corner of Jefferson and Washington Avenues, the Coliseum was constructed in 1908, and was built over Uhrig's Cave. It cost $300,000 to build and can seat 14,000 people. Uhrig's Cave, built underground, was associated with a brewery and was the most elaborate of the St. Louis commercial caves. It featured a beer garden and a theater that seated 300. The American premiere of Gilbert and Sullivan's "*H.M.S. Pinafore*" was held here.

Cancelled 1915, $2-4

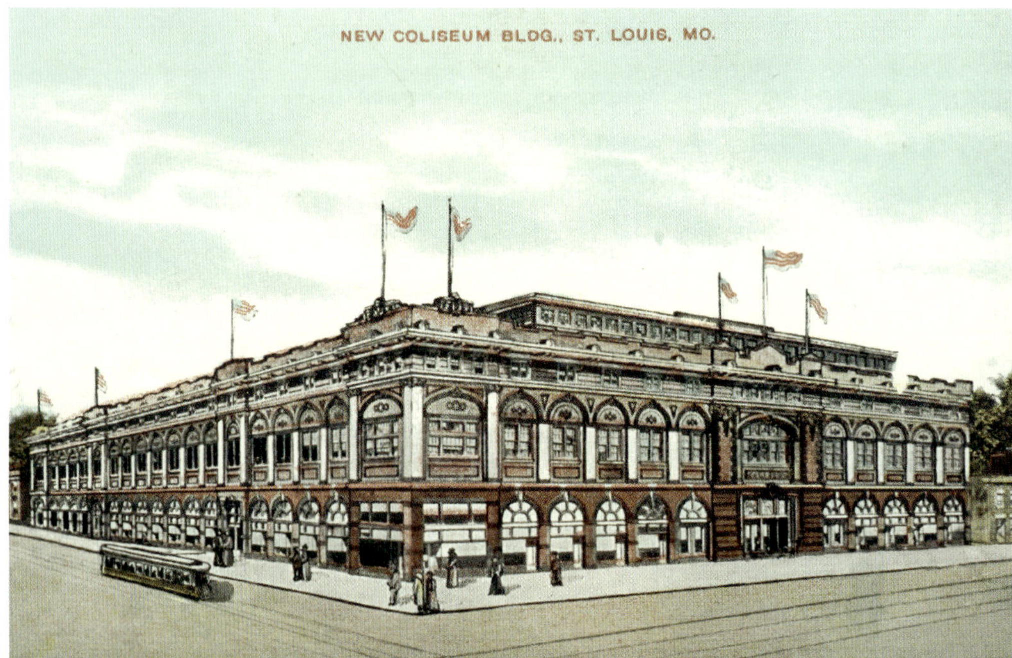

Circa 1907, $2-4

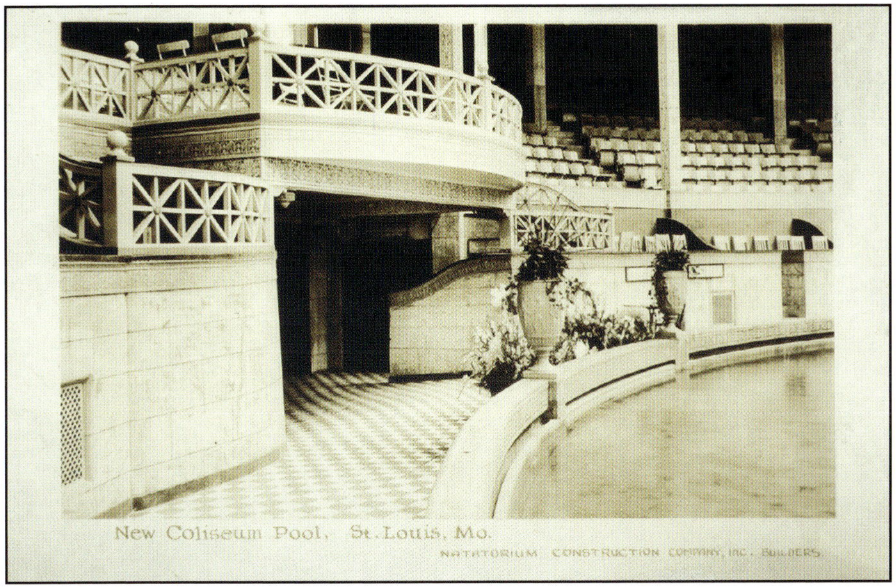

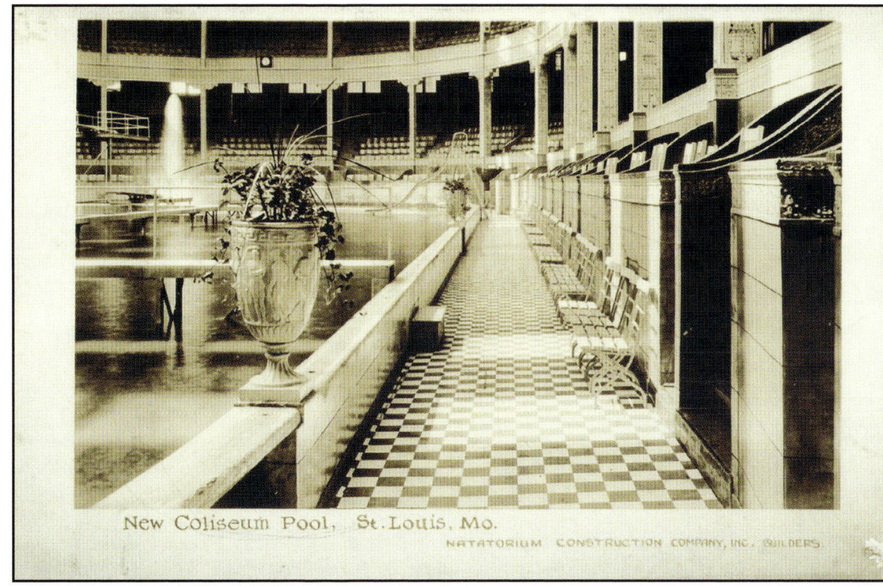

A look at the pool inside the Coliseum.

Circa Early 1900s, $6-8 (left)
Circa Early 1900s, $6-8 (right)

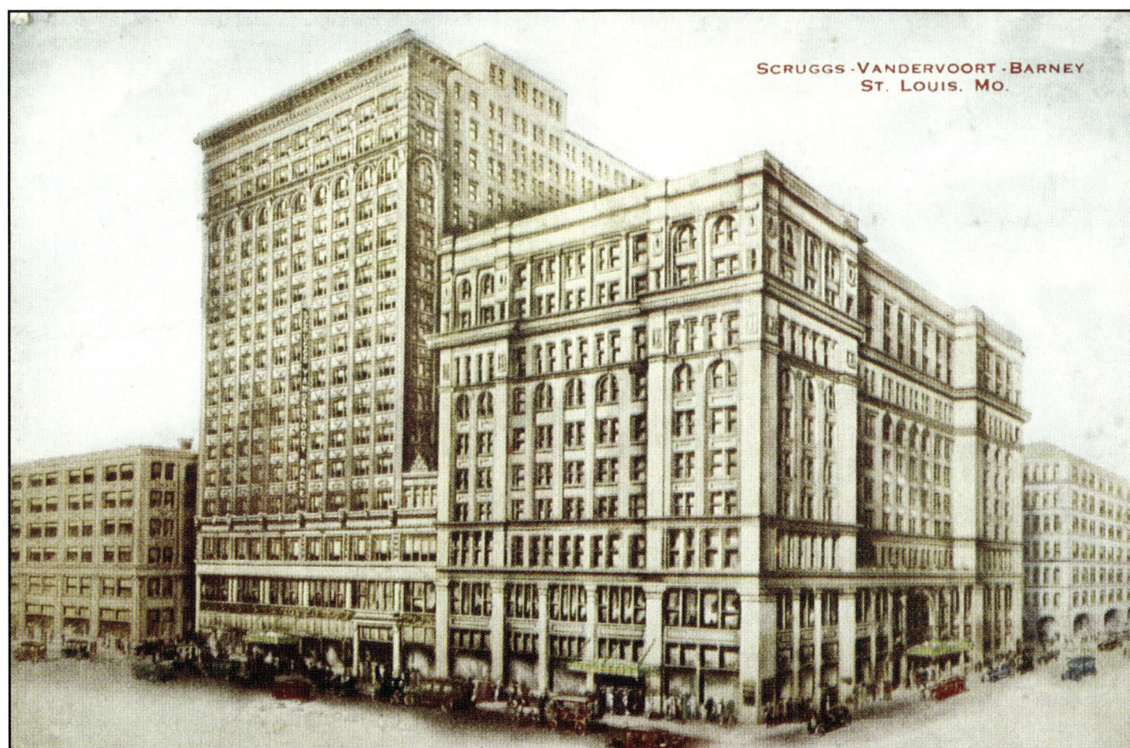

Scruggs-Vandervoort-Barney's, originally occupied in 1913 as a department store, then housed offices and galleries, including Landmarks Association of St. Louis. Also called the Century/Syndicate Trust Building, it was torn down in 2004.

Circa 1920, $2-4

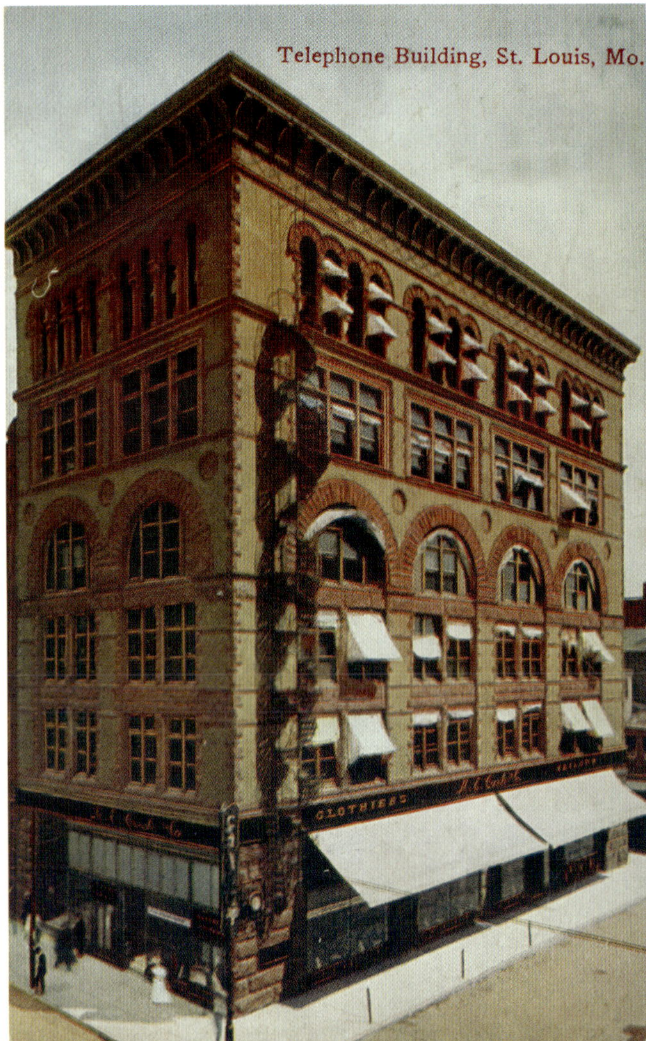

Now called the Bell Lofts Building, which includes City Grocers, offices, and fifteen loft-style apartments, the Bell Telephone Company's first three floors were built in 1889. An addition in 1919 added the rest of the seven stories.

Cancelled 1910, $2-4

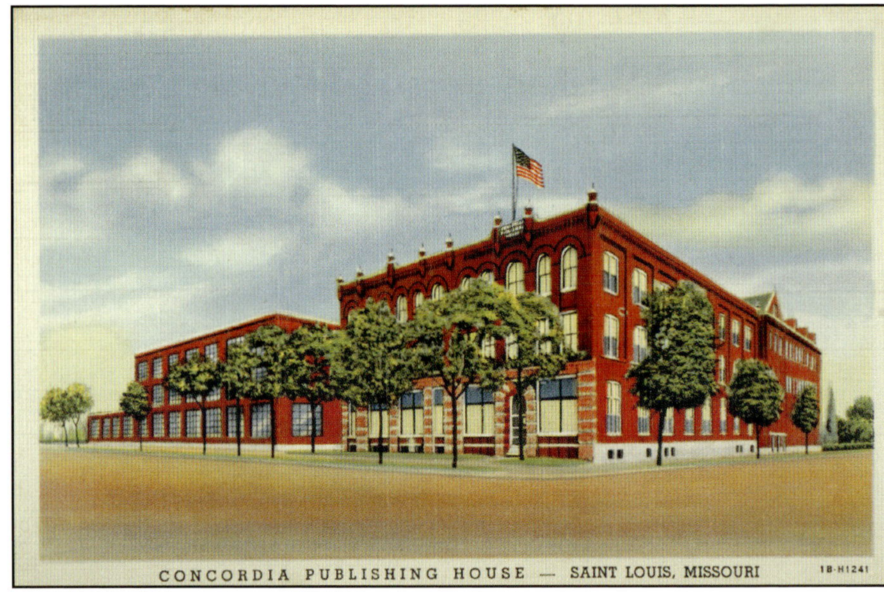

Concordia Publishing House was founded on September 11, 1869, as a way to reach out to and preserve the heritage of German Lutherans in their new world. The word "Concordia" is Latin for harmony.

Circa 1930s, $2-4

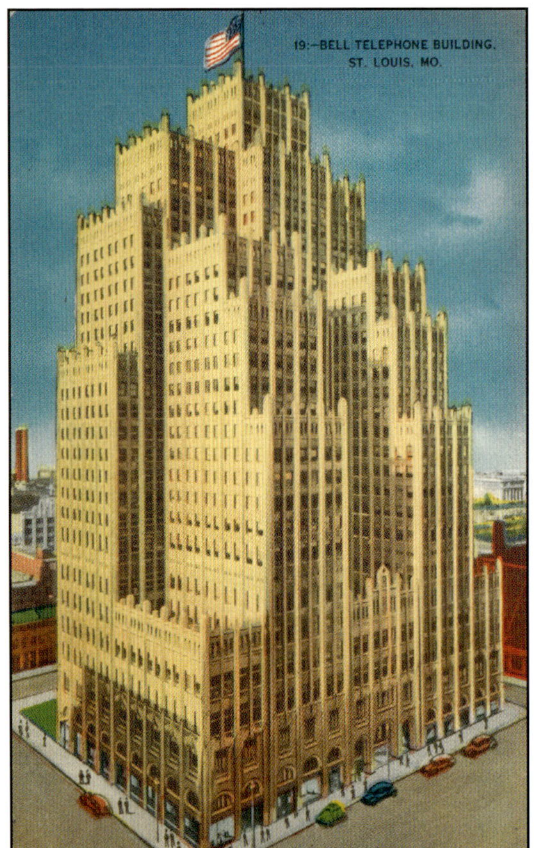

At 399 feet high, the Southwestern Bell Telephone Building was the tallest building in St. Louis at the time it was constructed. Built in 1925, it was also one of the last buildings built before the Depression and stands across the street from Soldiers' Memorial, City Hall, and the Municipal Courts Buildings.

Circa 1930s, $3-5

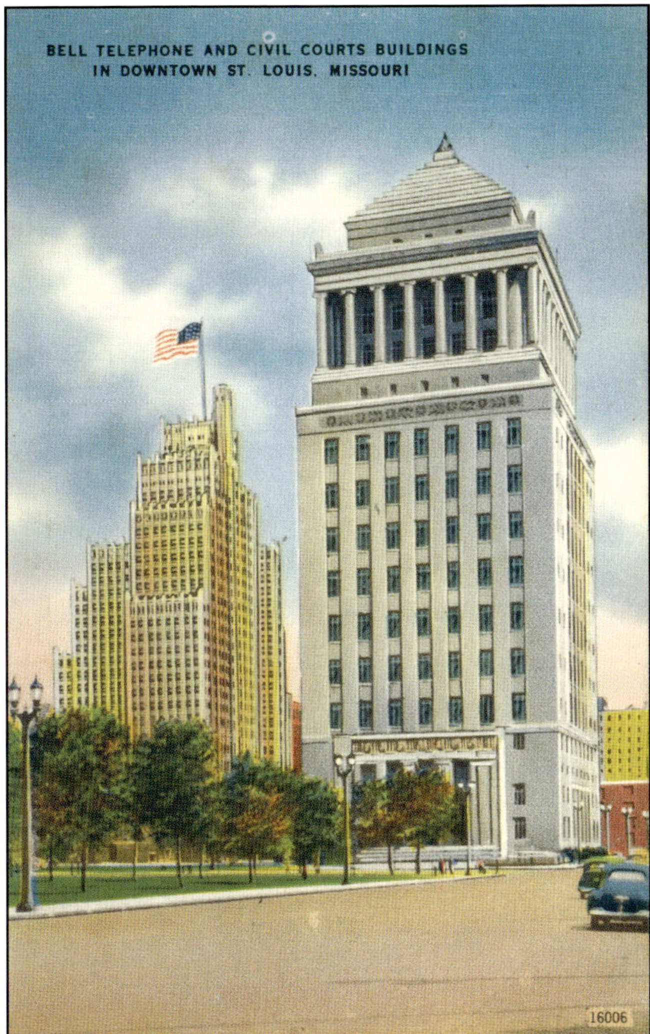

This alternate view of the Southwestern Bell Telephone Building shows the Civil Courts Building in Downtown St. Louis.

Circa 1930s, $6-8

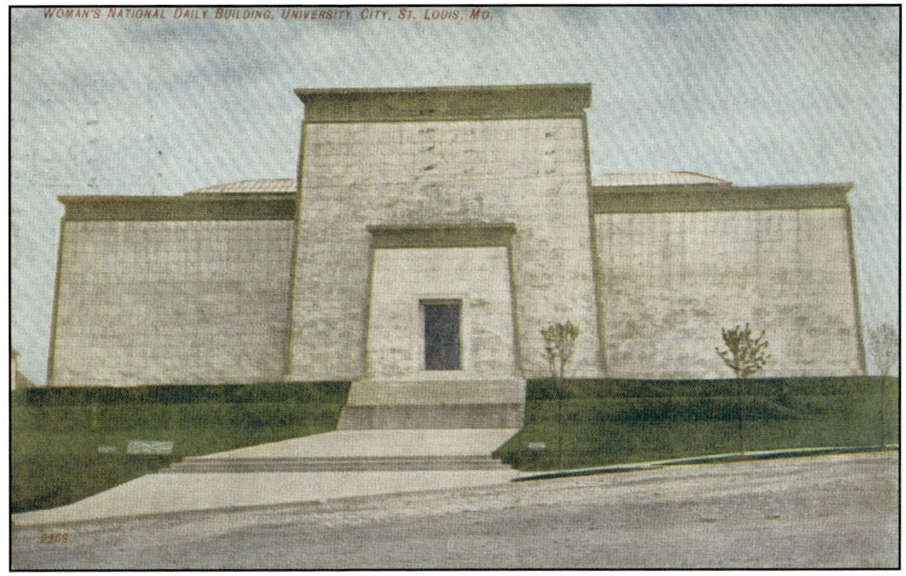

The *Woman's National Daily* Building is the original site of Edward Gardner Lewis's newspaper, *Woman's National Daily*.

Cancelled 1910, $2-4

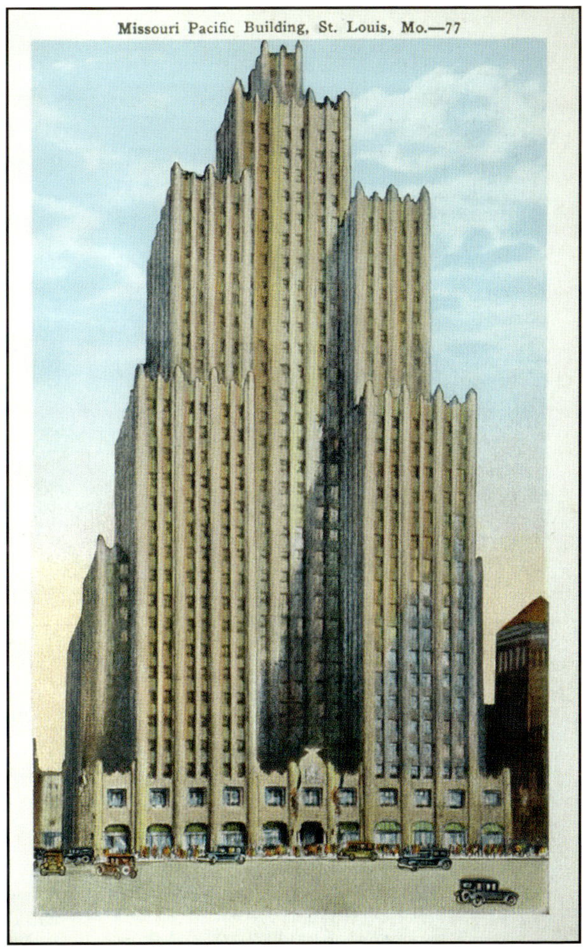

This postcard shows a wonderful view of the Missouri Pacific Building, now called Park Pacific. It was originally meant to be thirty-five stories, which would have made it the tallest building in the city, but due to the Depression, only twenty-three stories were completed.

Circa 1914, $2-4

At the time of this postcard, this building belonged to the Order of Railroad Telegraphers. Built in 1888, this forty-three-room house was originally owned by Samuel H. Cupples, who paid $500,000 to have it built. In 1940, it was acquired by St. Louis University, but is now a museum.

Circa 1914, $2-4

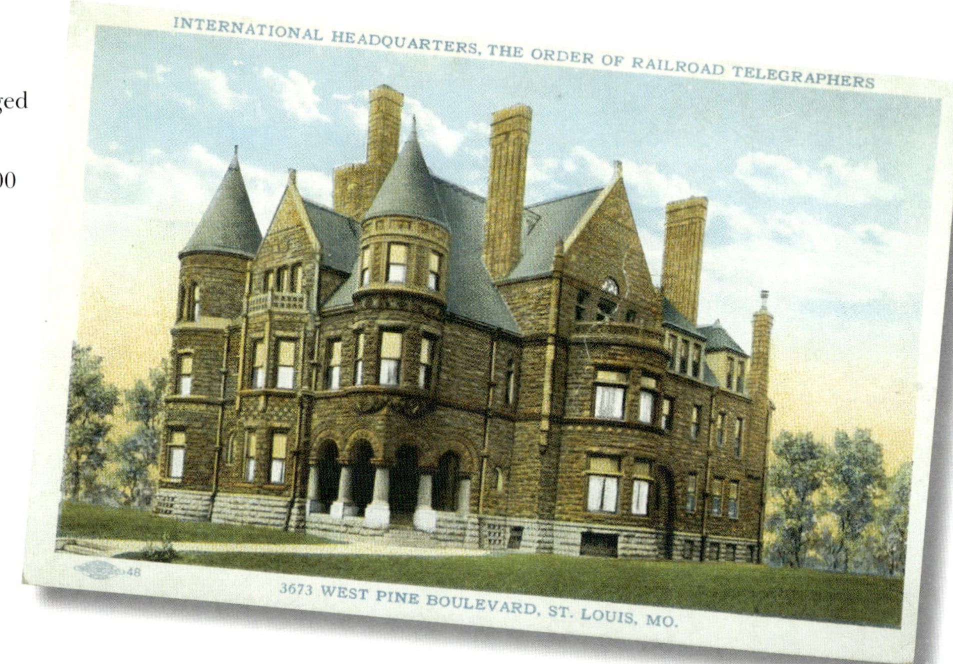

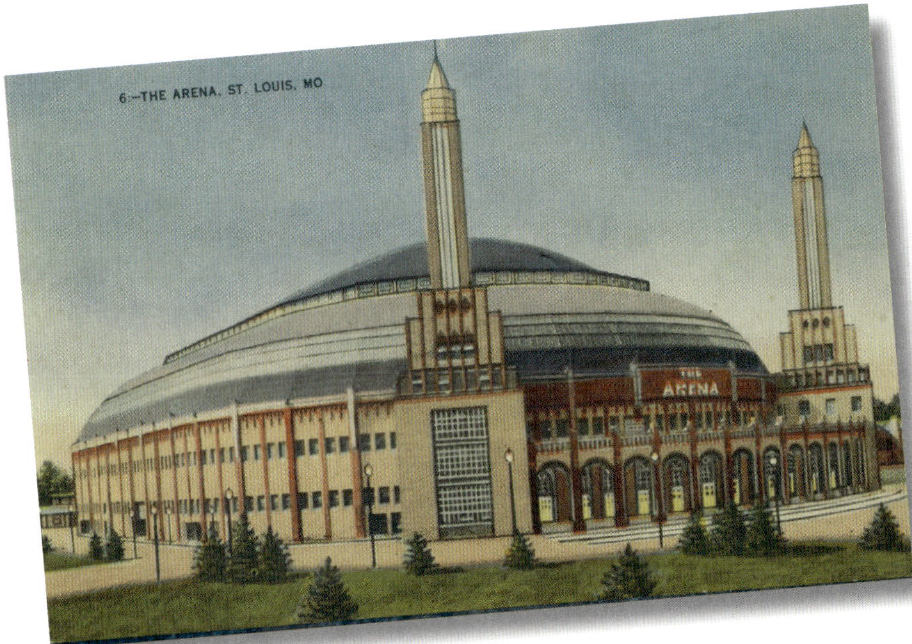

The St. Louis Arena, also known as the Checkerdome, was originally home to the St. Louis Blues. Seating 20,000, it was also used for conventions, horse shows, indoor circuses, etc. The building has since been torn down.

Circa 1930s, $2-4

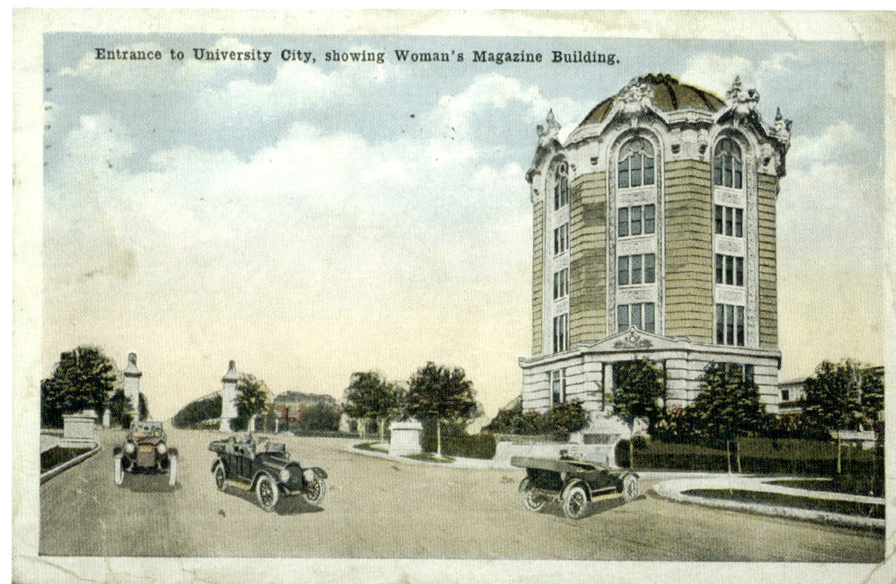

The entrance to University City, this postcard shows the original headquarters for the *Woman's Magazine*. This fireproof structure features hardwoods, mural paintings, and an elaborate central staircase made of marble and wood. It is now the city's City Hall.

Cancelled 1918, $2-4

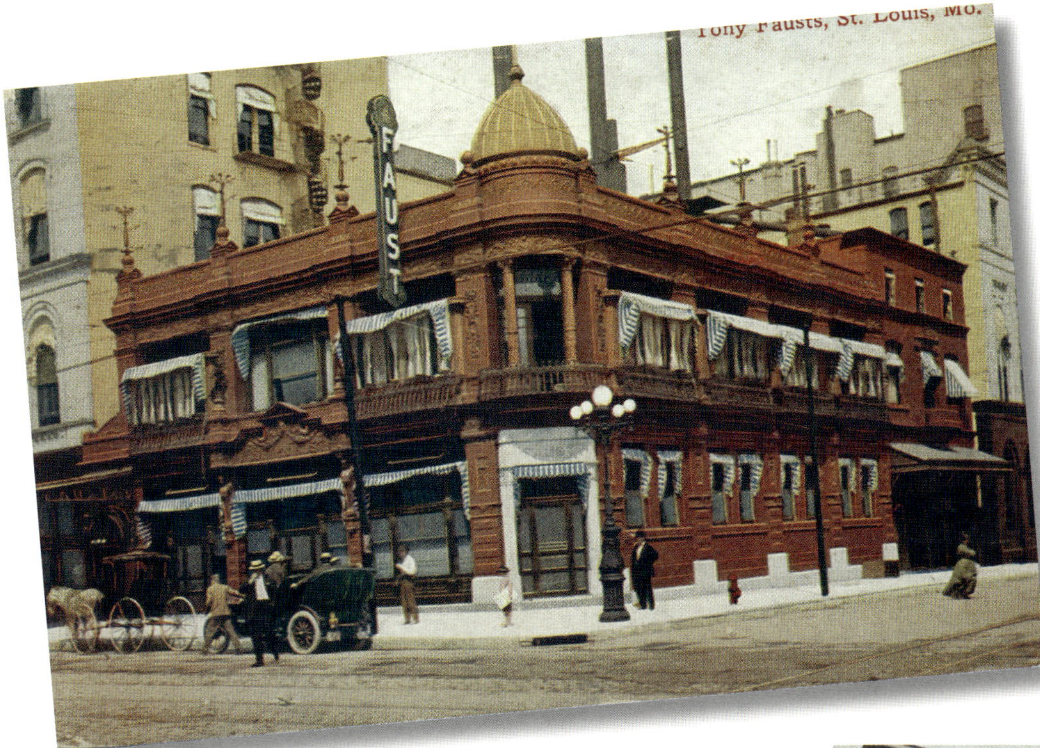

A corner view of Tony Faust's Restaurant, showing what was once the center of activity in St. Louis. Established in 1871, it remained a popular place to eat until it was closed in 1916, despite the best efforts of the citizens.

Cancelled 1908, $3-5

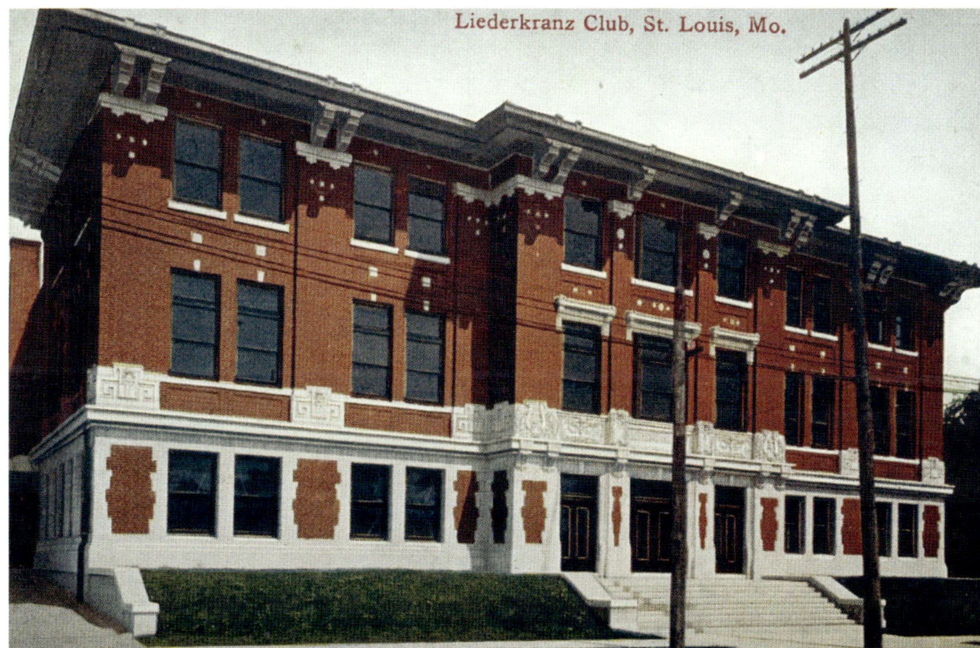

The 1850s brought to St. Louis a large number of Germans fleeing their mother country due to political harassment making the descendants of these settlers a large portion of ongoing population through the years. A front view of the Liederkranz Club is shown here, established for the most wealthy German-Americans who wanted to keep ties with community.

Circa 1907, $2-4

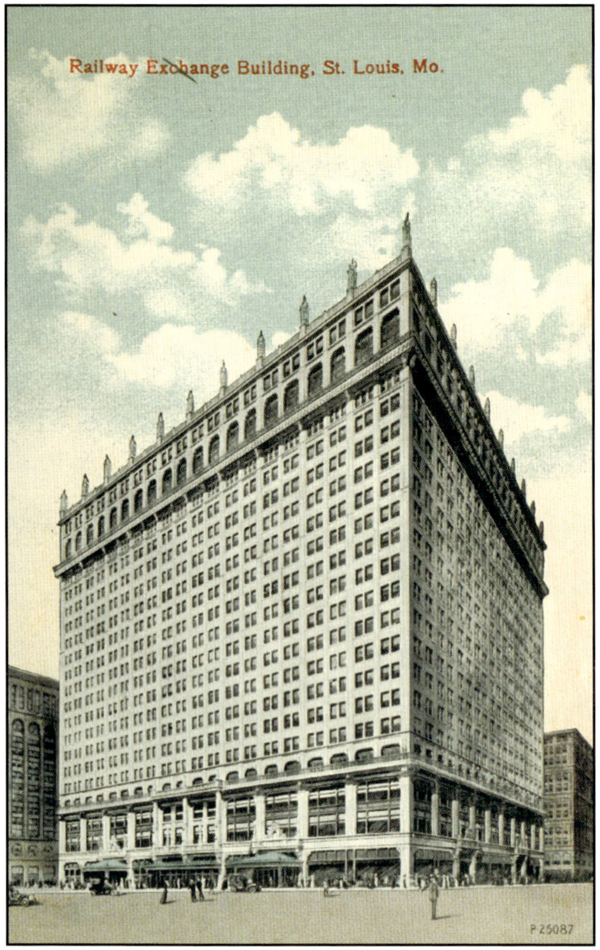

Once the largest office building in the world, the Railway Exchange Building also had one of the world's earliest fire sprinkler systems.

Circa 1907, $2-4

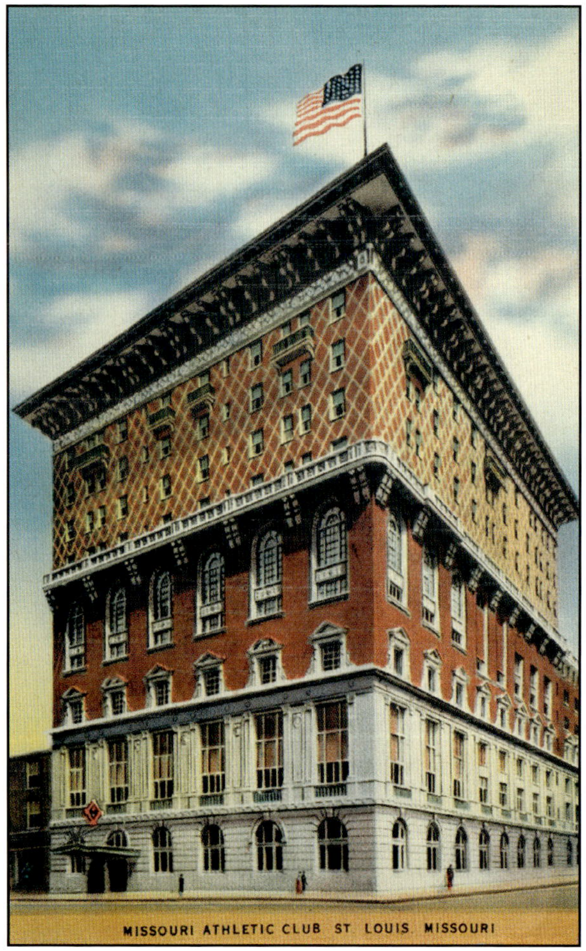

A view of the Athletic Club. Originally built in 1903, the first clubhouse was destroyed by a fire in 1914. The current clubhouse, re-opened in 1916, has hand ball courts, badminton, squash, mechanical exercise, a merchandise shop, Solarium, and is even air conditioned. Although the club has been through several names, including St. Louis Athletic Club and the Missouri Athletic Association, athletics has always been their main focus.

Circa 1930s, $2-4

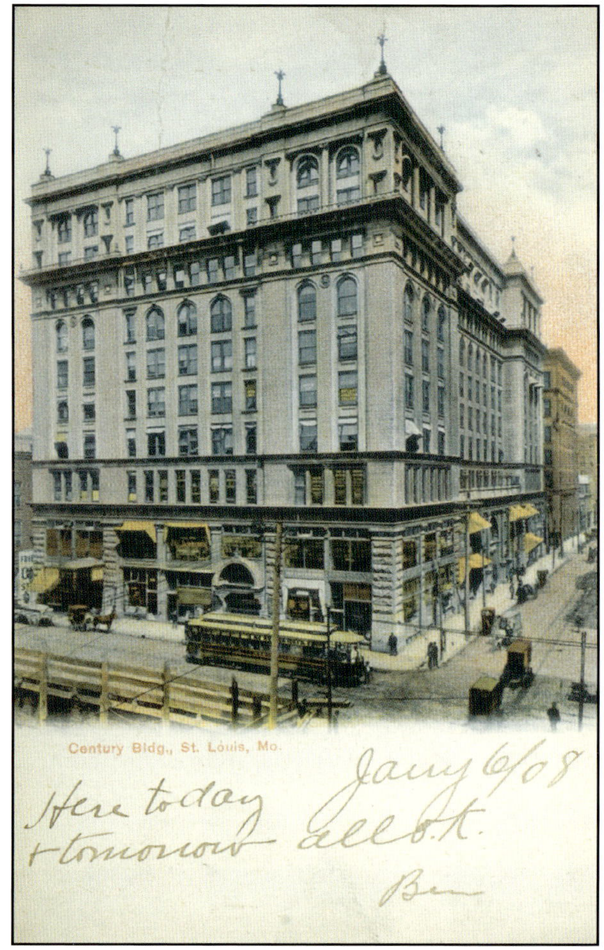

The Century Building, which is conjoined with the Syndicate Trust Tower, was once home to Scruggs-Vandervoort-Barney Department Store and the Landmarks Association of St. Louis. Before being demolished in 2004 and becoming a parking garage, it was one of the city's largest buildings, and arguably one of the most beautiful.

Cancelled 1908, $3-5

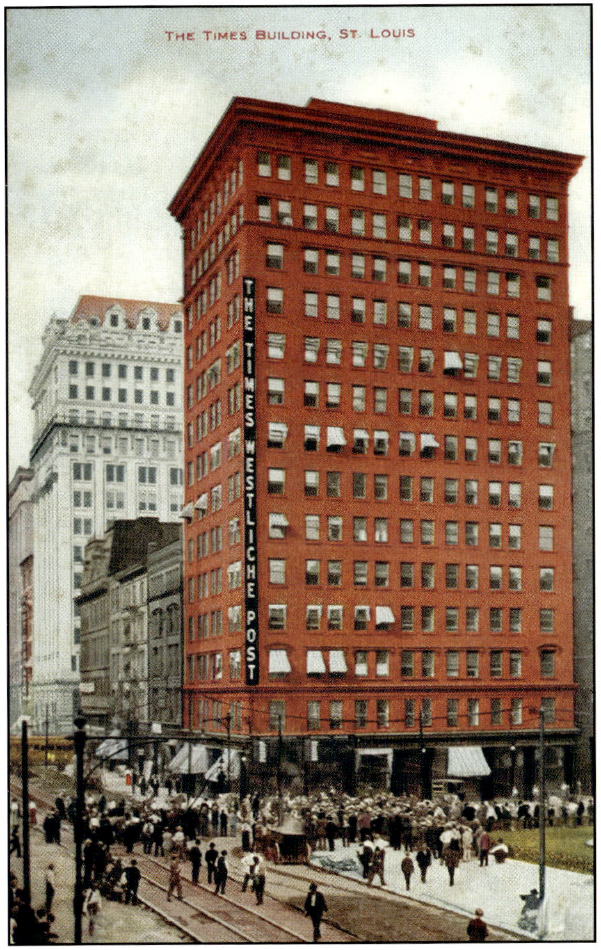

Once home to the *Westliche Post*, the *Times* Building is clearly shown here. A daily German-language newspaper, the *Westliche Post* attacked such issues as slavery and religious oppression. Surviving until 1939 and one of two German newspapers in the city, it also produced a magazine, *The Mississippi Blaetter.*

Circa 1907, $2-4

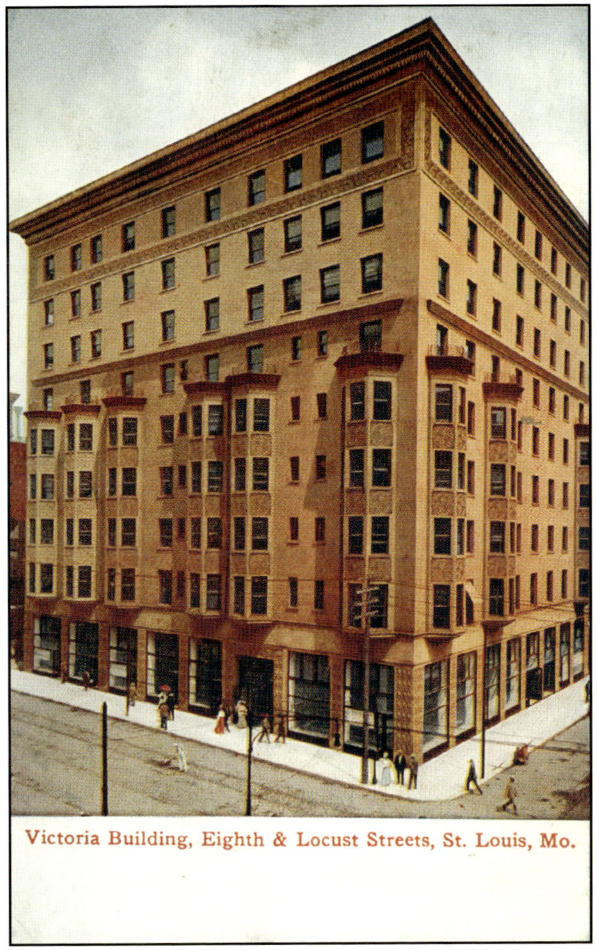

The Victoria Building, which was originally the St. Nicholas Hotel. Built in 1893 and severely damaged by a fire at the turn of the twentieth century, the hotel was rebuilt as an office building and named the Victoria Building. It remained there until 1971, when it was demolished.

Circa 1907, $2-4

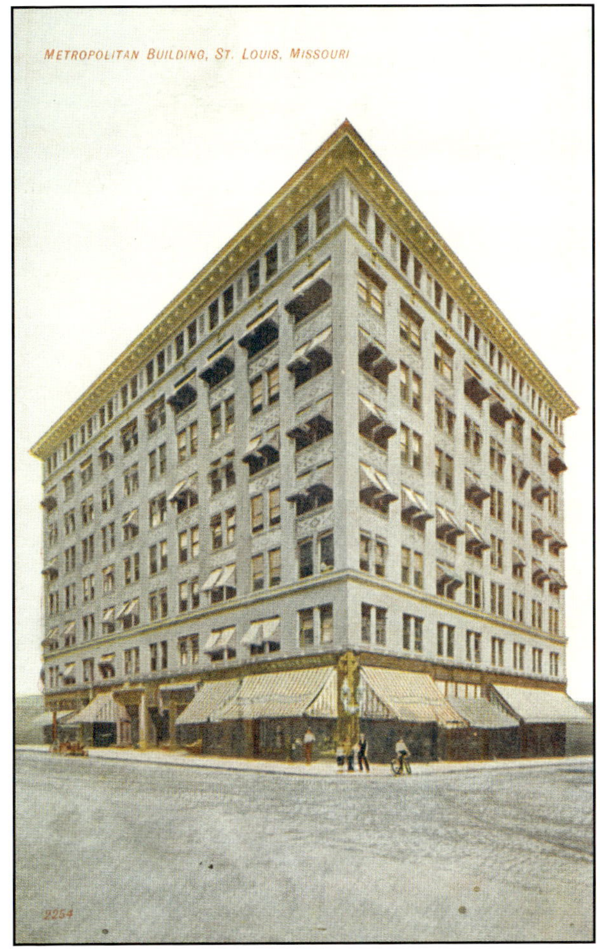

Once part of the Grand Center arts and entertainment district, the Metropolitan Building is now a hotel.

Circa 1907, $2-4

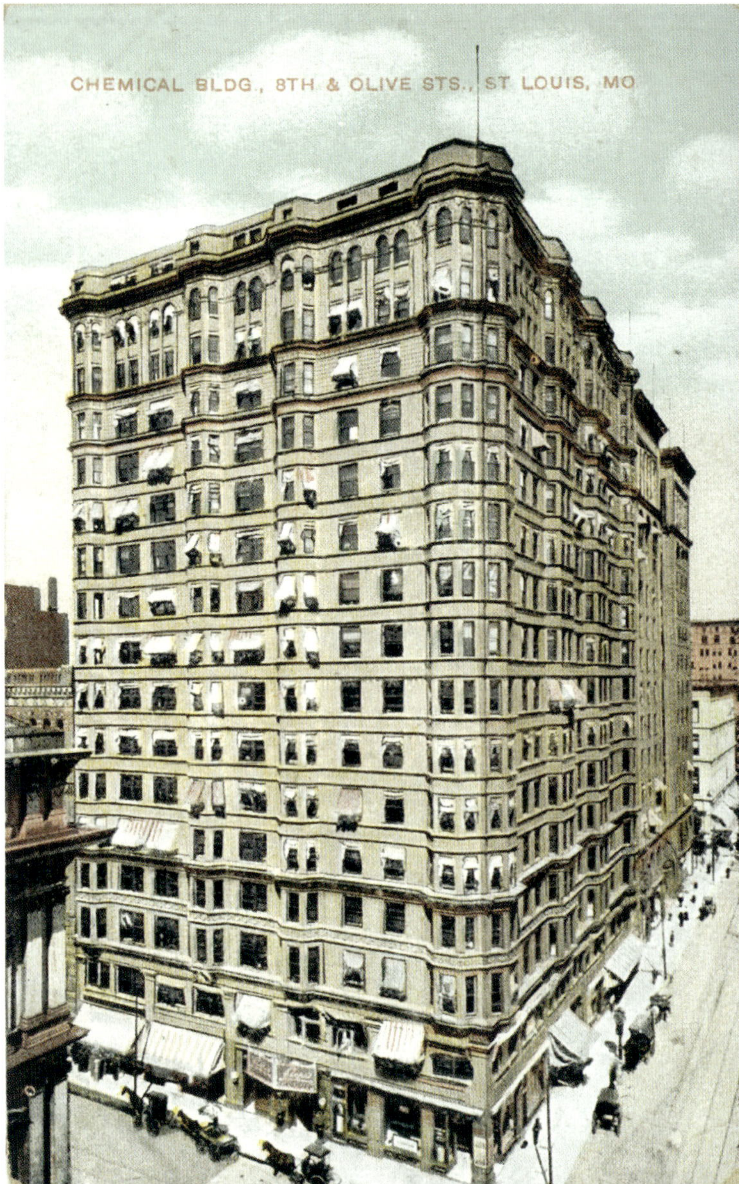

Here we see the Chemical Building, once called the Missouri Pacific Building. Built in 1896, this seventeen-story office building is being remodeled into an apartment building.

Cancelled 1908, $2-4

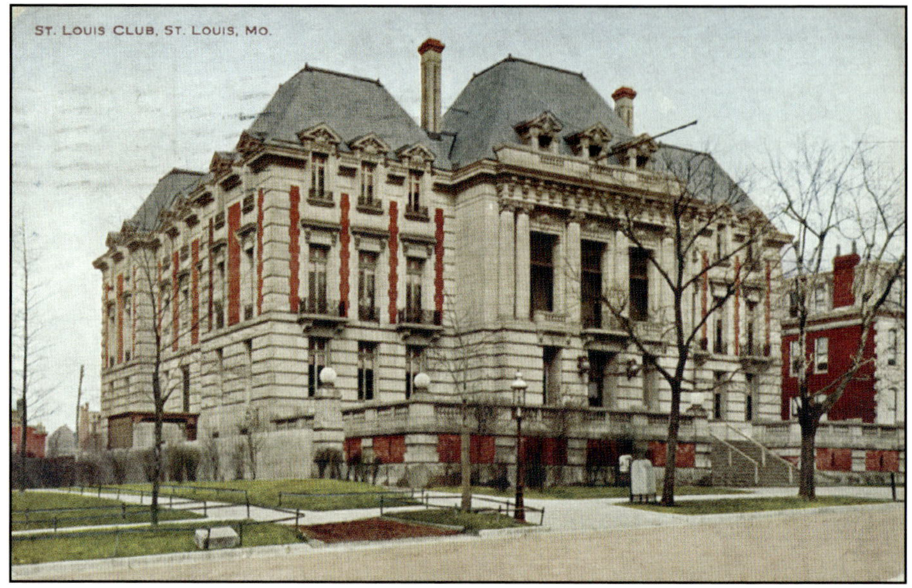

A view of the beautiful St. Louis Club, the most exclusive club of its time. Located at 3663 Lindell Boulevard, the interior of the building was destroyed by a fire in 1925. It was rebuilt as an office building and is now the district offices of the F. W. Woolworth Company.

Cancelled 1910, $2-4

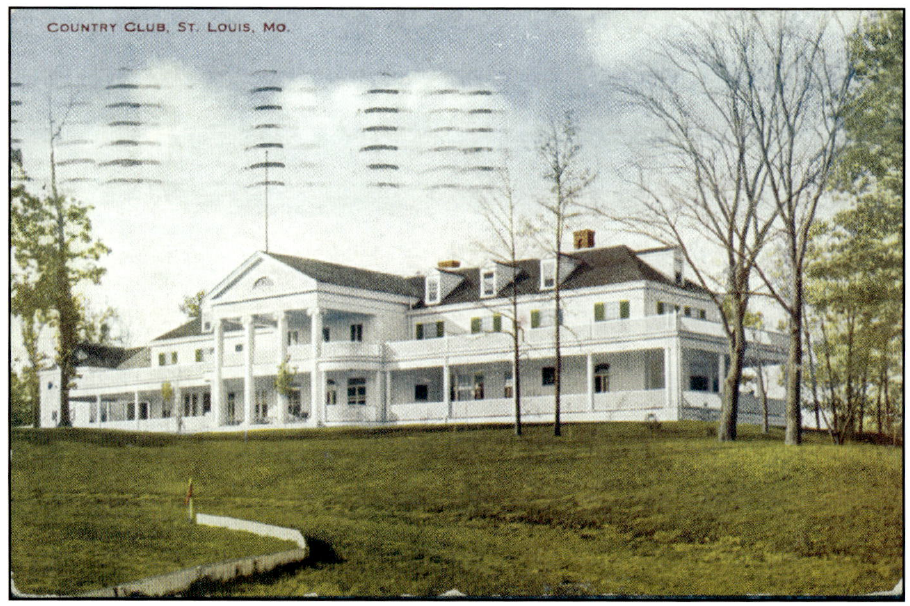

A view of the front yard of this gorgeous country club in St. Louis. This was just one of many of its kind in the city at this time.

Cancelled 1909, $2-4

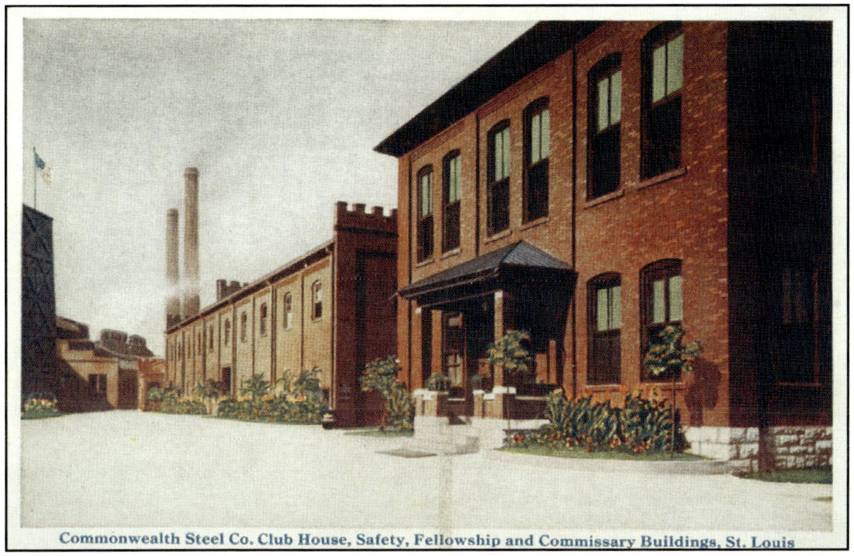

The Clubhouse, Safety, Fellowship, and Commissary Buildings of the Commonwealth Steel Company. This company was established by the Niedringhaus brothers in St. Louis in the late 1800s.

Circa 1907, $2-4

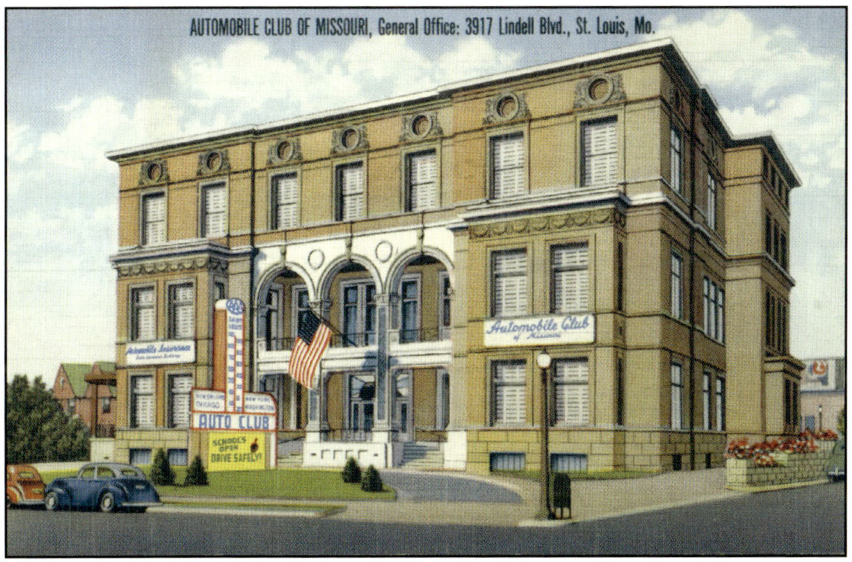

The Automobile Club. As the back of the postcard says: "When in St. Louis, visit the Auto Club's New Air Conditioned Home at 3917 Lindell Boulevard."

Circa 1930s, $2-4

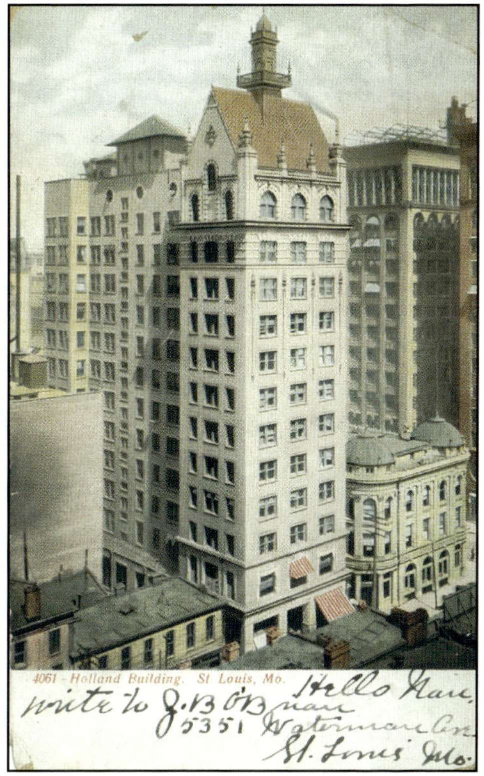

A nice full view of the old Holland Building in St. Louis, that has since been demolished.

Cancelled 1907, $3-5

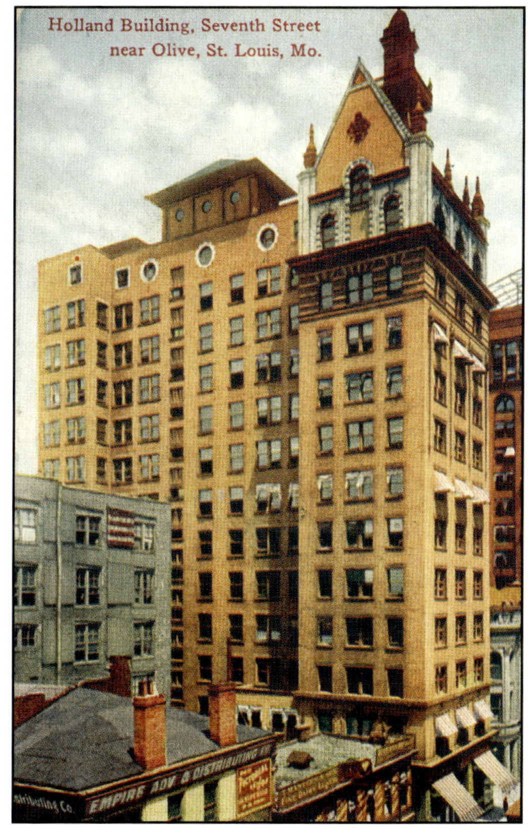

This later postcard allows you to see a fuller side view of the Holland Building, located on Seventh Street, near Olive Street.

Circa 1907, $2-4

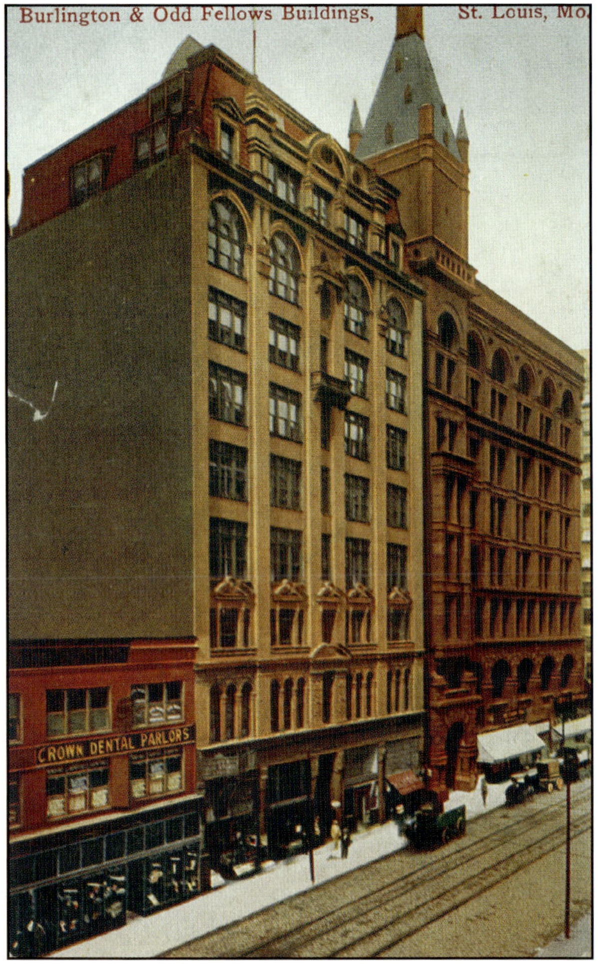

Here we see a view of the Burlington and Odd Fellows Buildings. The Odd Fellows Building was constructed in 1888, using brick and granite. A clock tower on the corner separates it from the Burlington Building.

Circa 1907, $3-5

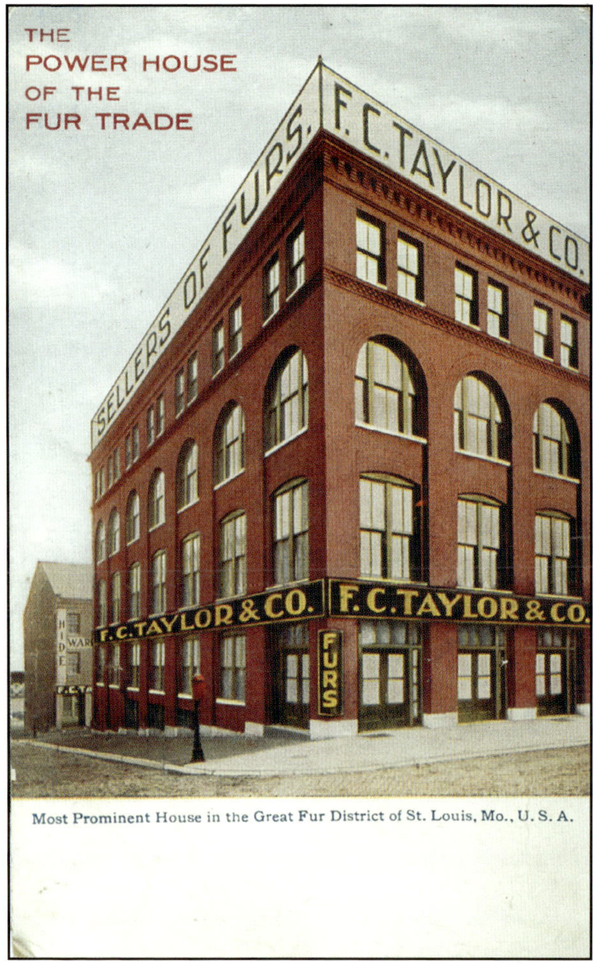

F. C. Taylor & Co., the powerhouse of the fur trade. As the advertising postcard reads, this was the most prominent house in the Great Fur District of St. Louis.

Circa 1907, $2-4

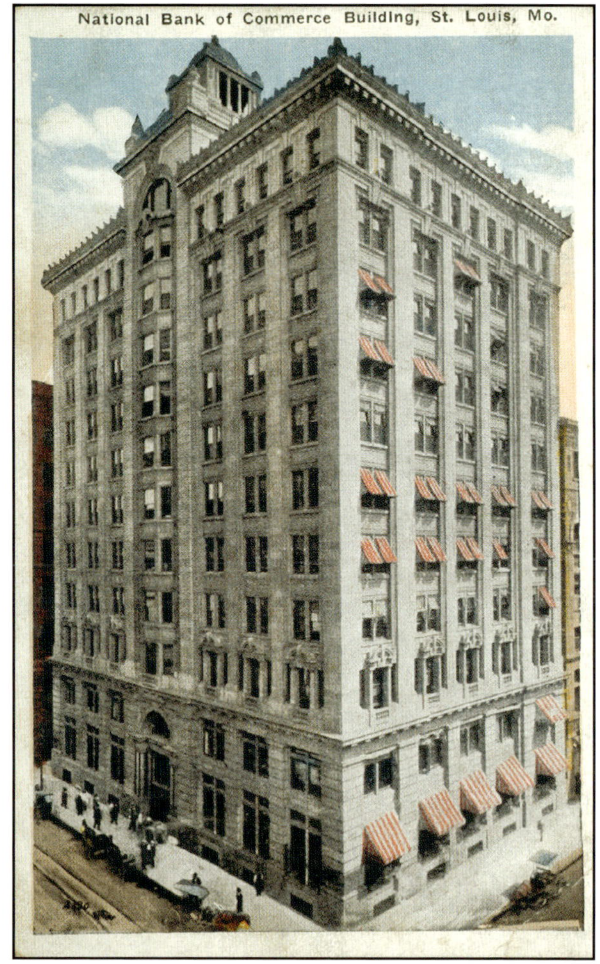

At the time, the National Bank of Commerce was the "most modern office and banking building in the city." Now called Commerce Bank, the company is still going strong throughout the country.

Cancelled 1918, $2-4

Parks

Providing recreational pursuits and lush garden scenes for visitors and residents alike, the parks of St. Louis have gone through history displaying a spectacular array of visual splendor.

Forest Park

Opening in 1876, Forest Park was designed to mimic the famous New York Central Park (although larger by about 500 acres), and is known as one of the largest urban landscape parks created in the late nineteenth century. It is located on the west side of St. Louis in the middle of the urban area and is best known as the site for the famous World's Fair (called the Louisiana Purchase Exposition of 1904).

Whether it be historic bridges, scenic lake views, or wandering paths, Forest Park held something, through the ages, for the families and visitors of St. Louis.

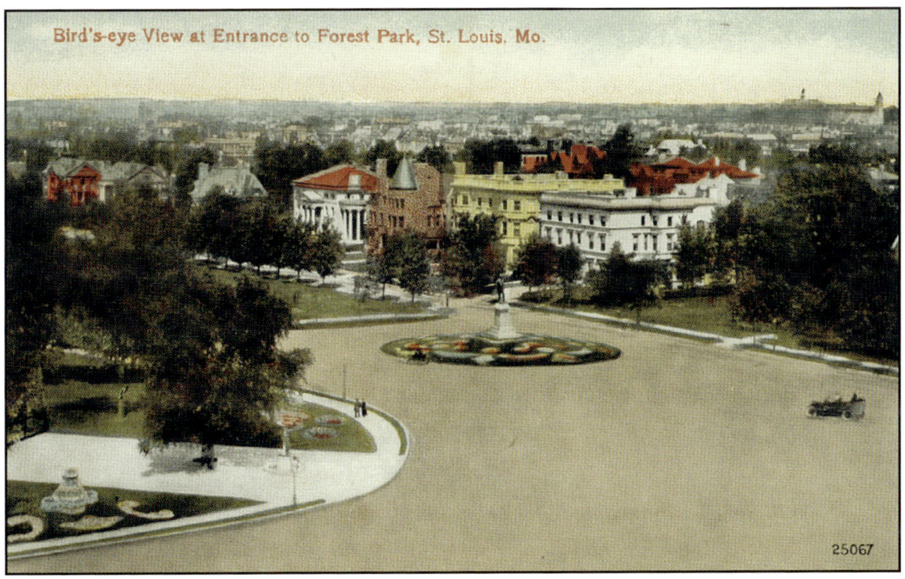

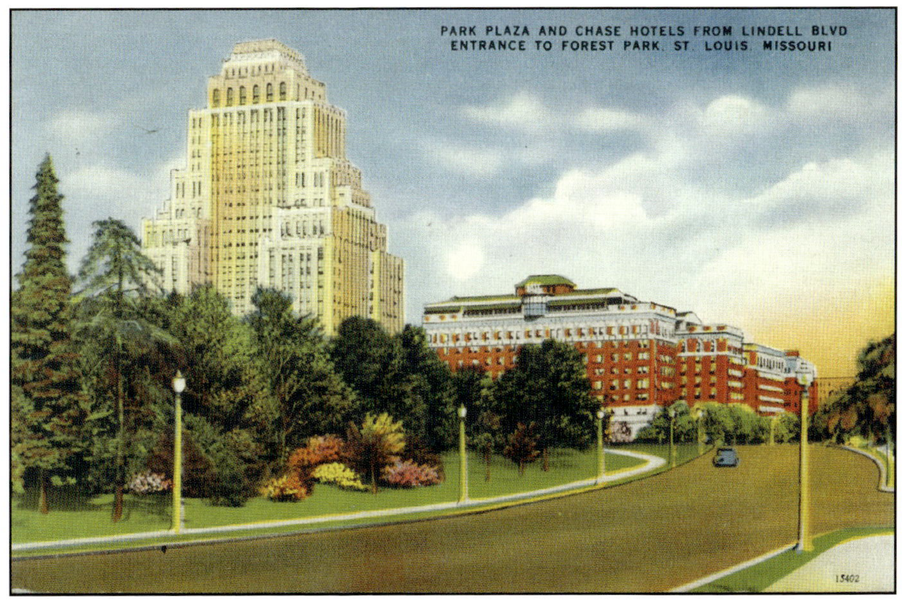

There were many entrances to Forest Park since it took up quite a bit of land—1,293 acres! Borders include Skinker Boulevard and Washington University (west), Highway 64/40 and Oakland Avenue (south), Kings Highway and the Barnes Hospital (East), and Lindell Boulevard (north). Following are some varied entrance scenes to the park.

Circa 1907, $2-4 (left)
Cancelled 1948, $2-4 (right)

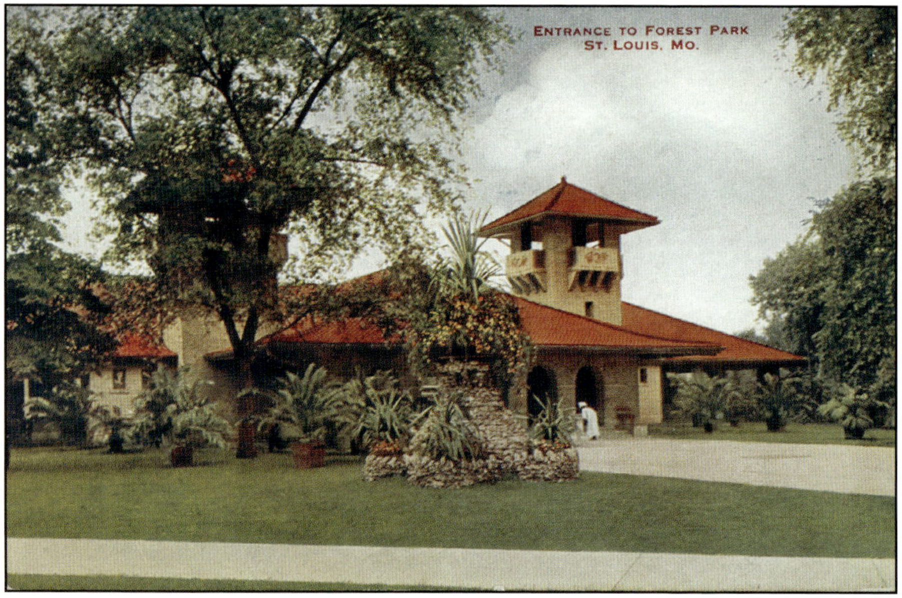

Circa 1907, $2-4

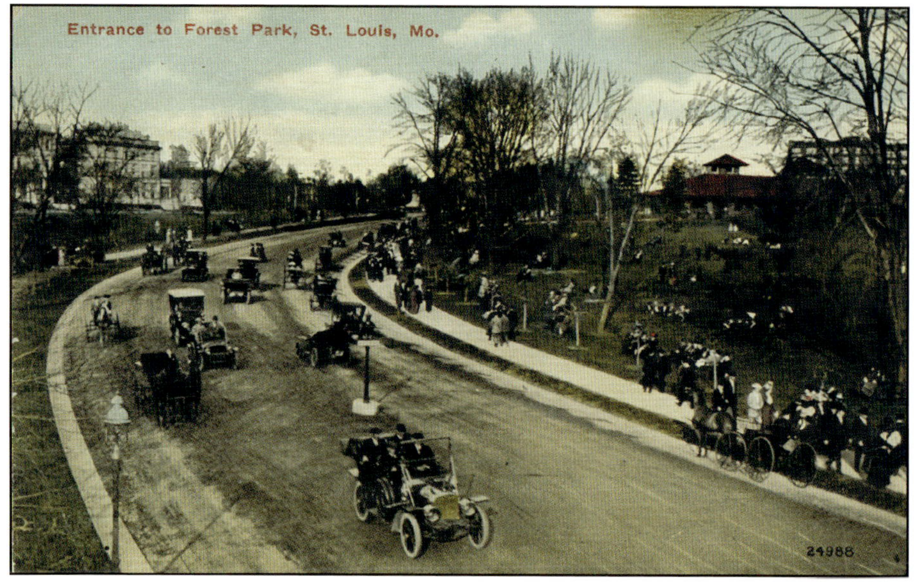

Circa 1907, $2-4

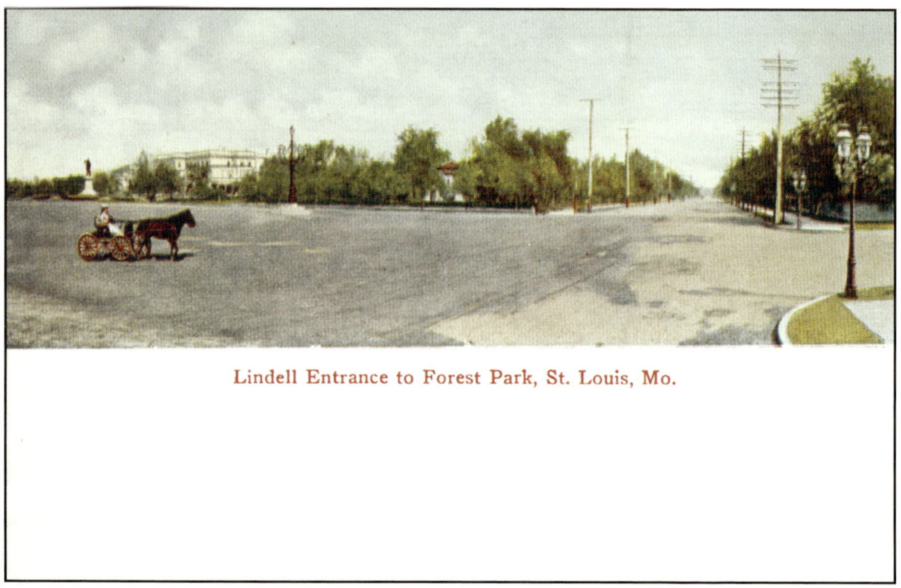

Circa 1907, $2-4

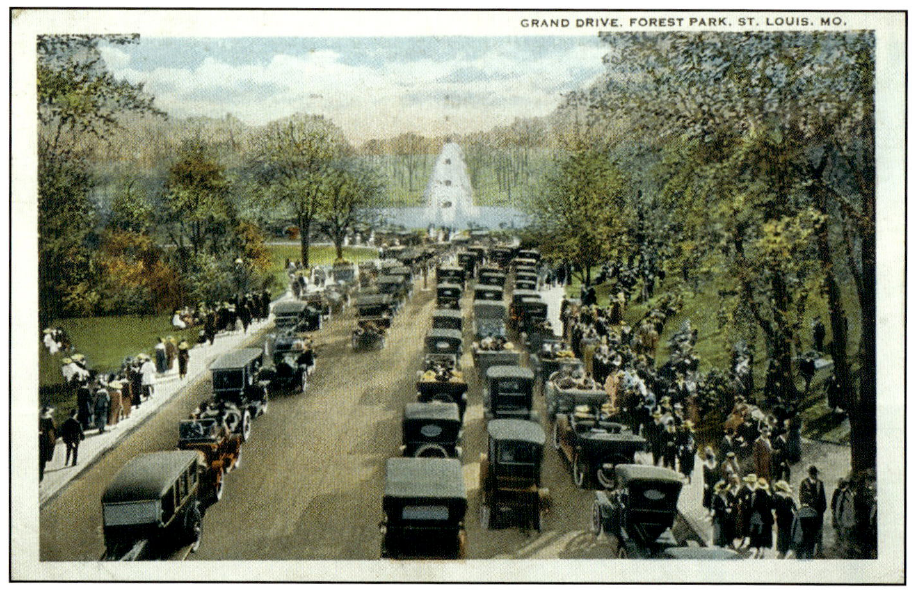

Circa 1914, $2-4

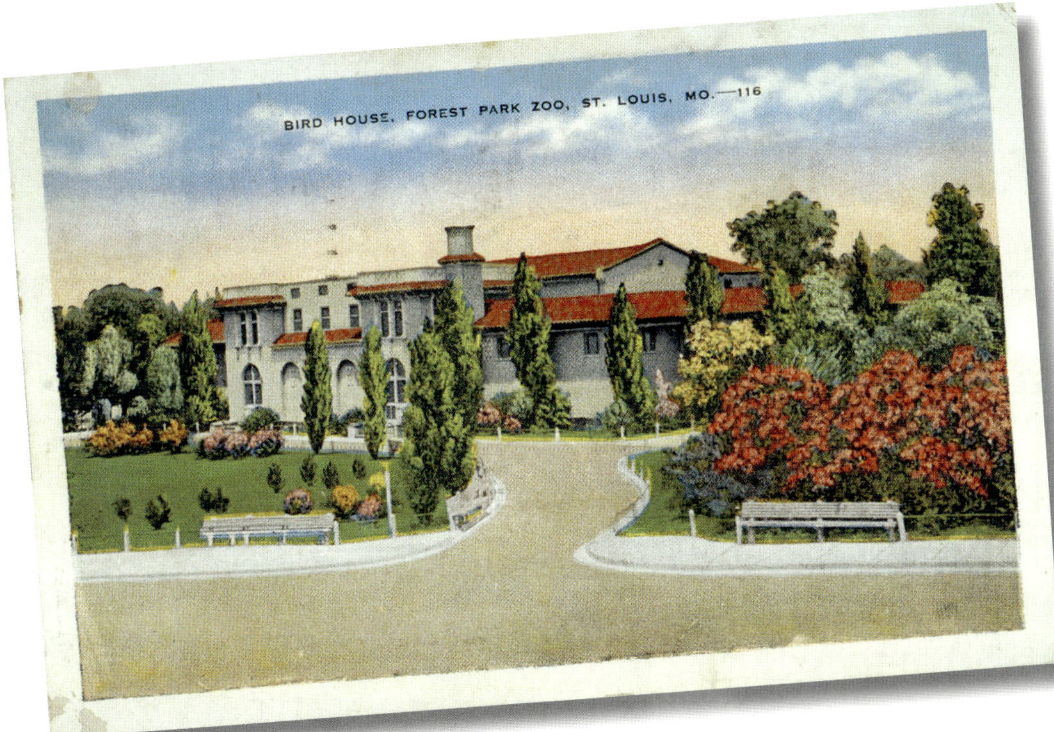

When the World's Fair closed, it left in its wake a wonderful bird cage—the largest walk-through Fair Flight Cage of the time. The citizens of St. Louis decided to buy the cage from the Smithsonian Institute in 1904 for $3,500 rather than see it dismantled and returned to the nation's capital. The St. Louis Zoo was born!

Cancelled 1937, $2-4

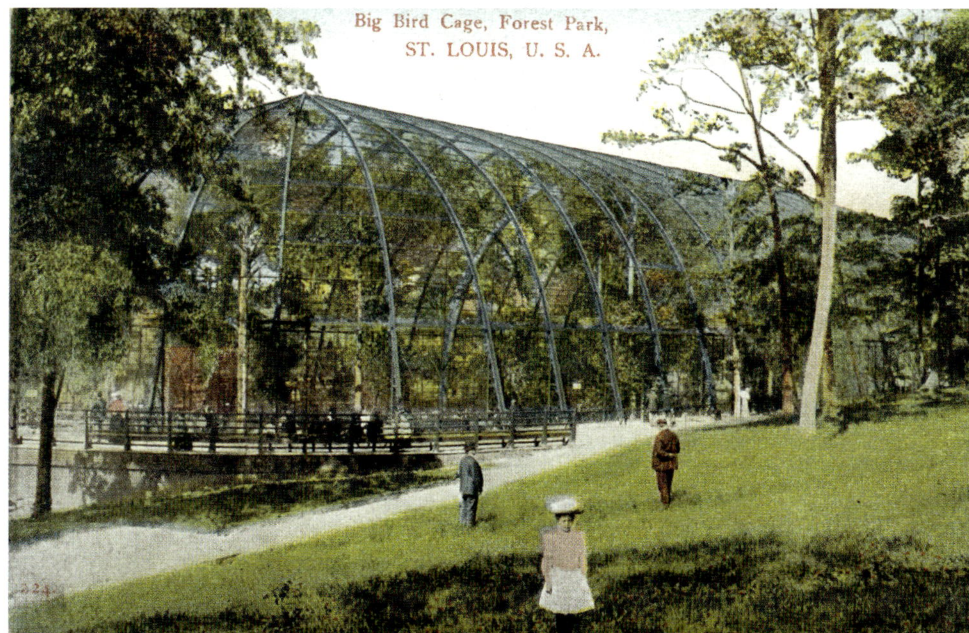

Circa 1907, $2-4

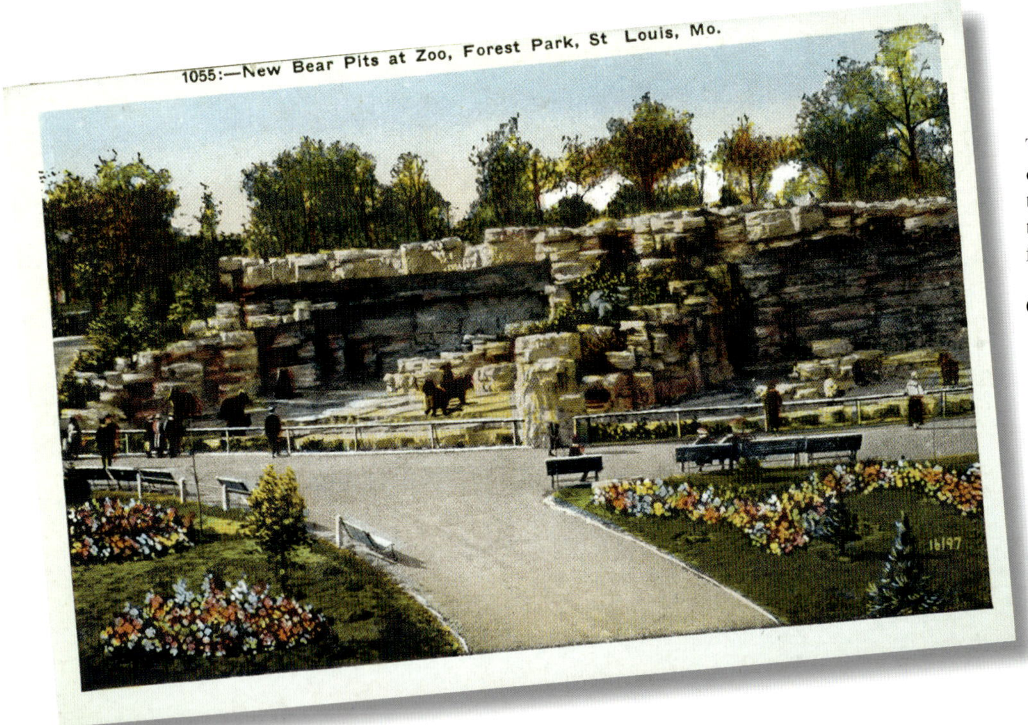

The St. Louis Bear Pit exhibit displays one of the first naturally-moated habitats of the time—no barred cages. In 1921, the first section of the completed pit, shown here, was finished.

Circa 1914, $2-4

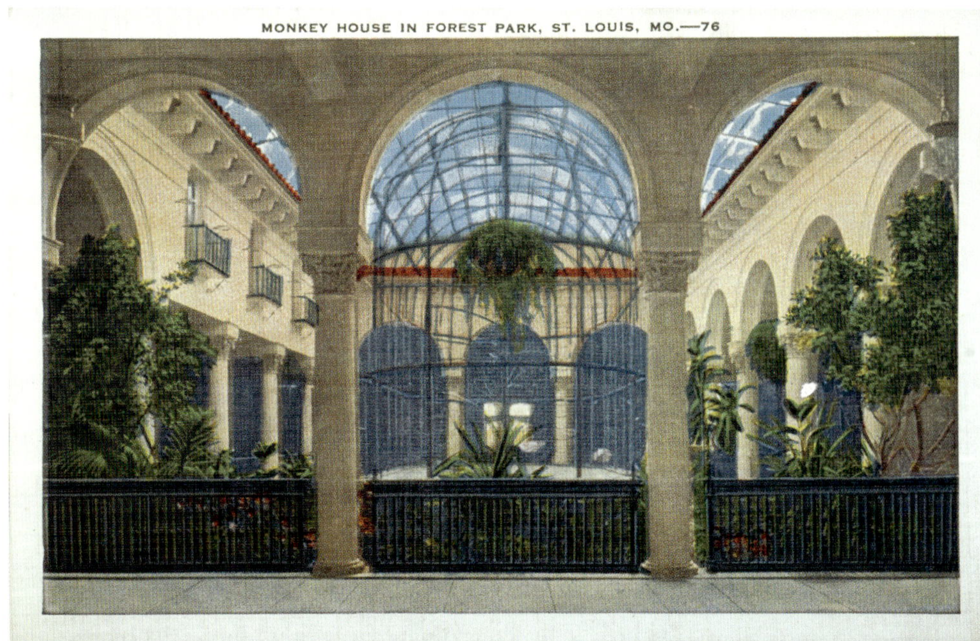

The Primate House was regarded as the finest monkey shelter in the U. S., costing $200,000 to build.

Circa 1930s, $2-4

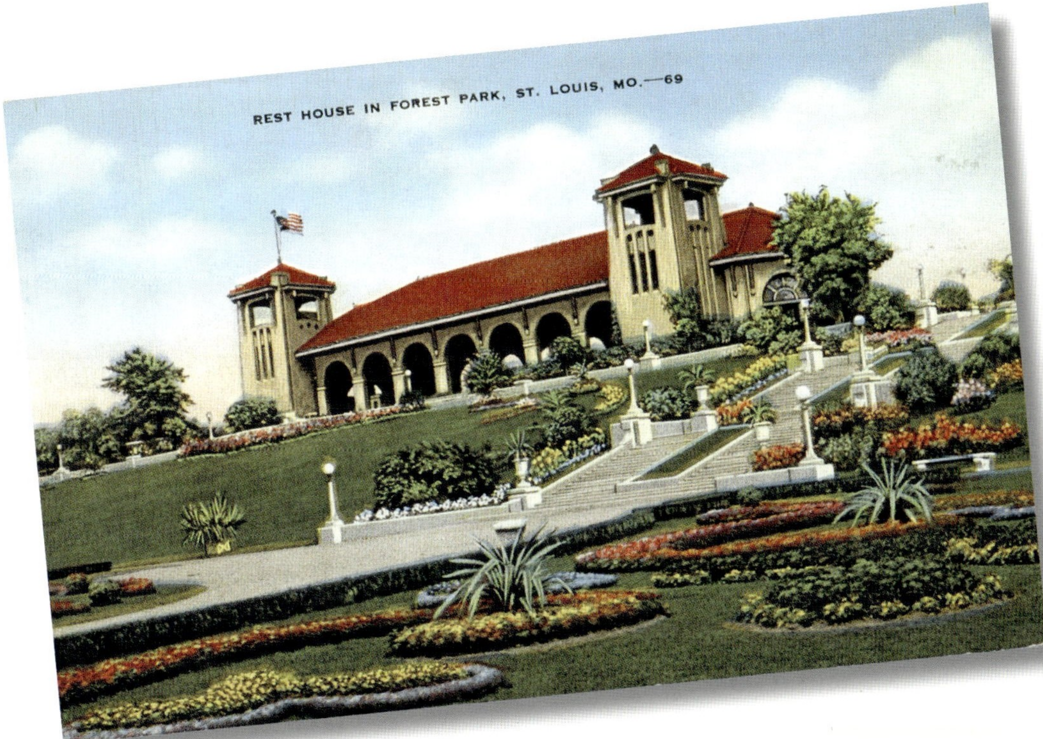

The World's Fair Pavilion, sitting on top of Government Hill, was built in 1909 from the proceeds of the Fair. People used this area extensively for varied entertainment venues—picnics, parties, receptions, events, etc. The pavilion sat approximately 500 people.

Circa 1930s, $2-4

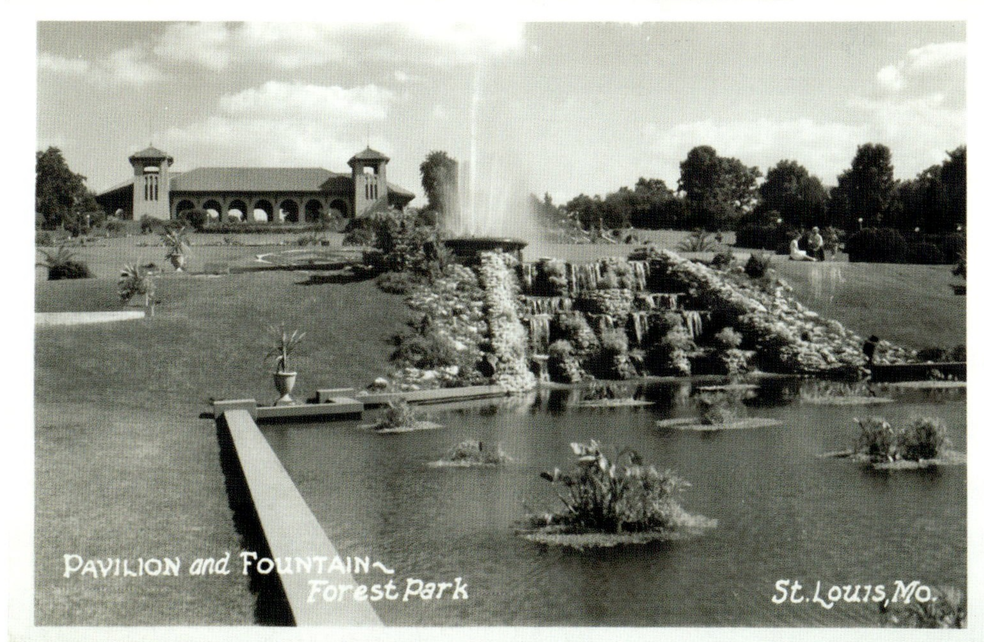

Cancelled 1953, $10-12

In 1916, the first outdoor theatre in St. Louis developed and played the classic, *As You Like It,* by the Margaret Anglin Shakespearean troupe. The Municipal Theatre (now called The Muny) came to being in 1917, taking a short 49 days to build—including a large stage, a 200-musician orchestra pit, and dressing rooms. At the time, tickets to the opera were set to be between twenty-five cents to one dollar, but 1,620 of the 9,000 seats were free of charge—and this is also true today. Text on varied postcards advise that the seating capacity is 10,000.

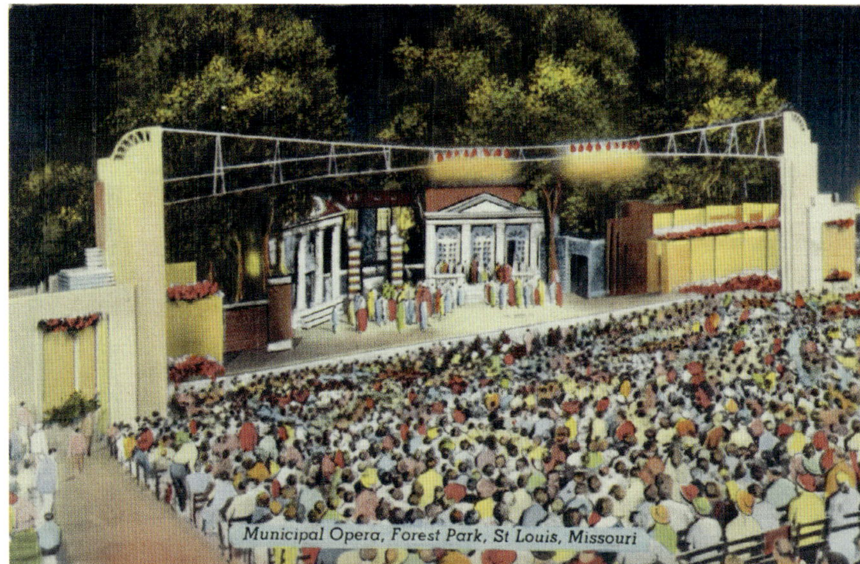

Cancelled 1948, $2-4

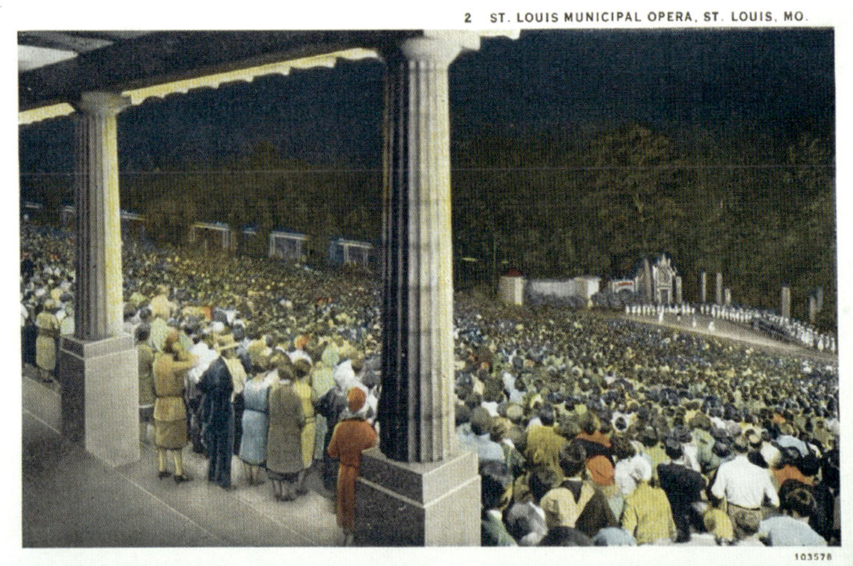

Cancelled 1931, $2-4

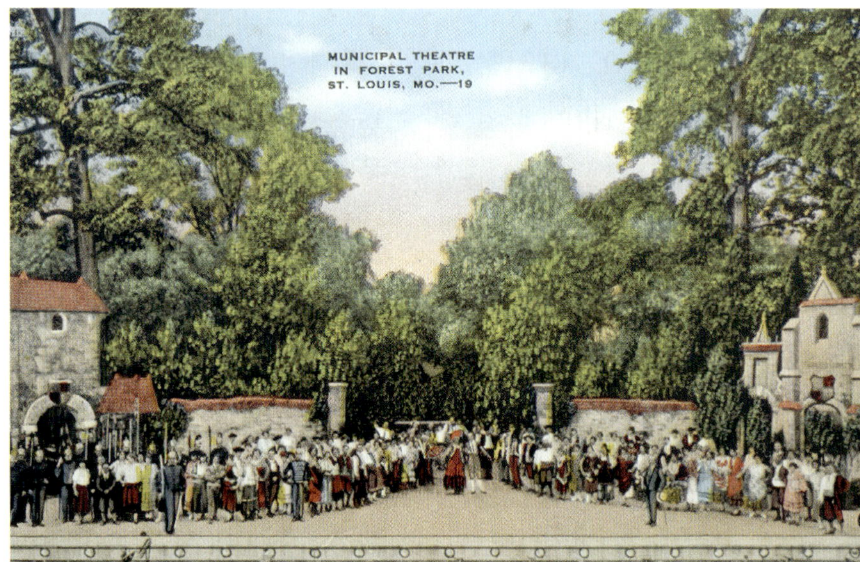

Circa 1930s, $2-4

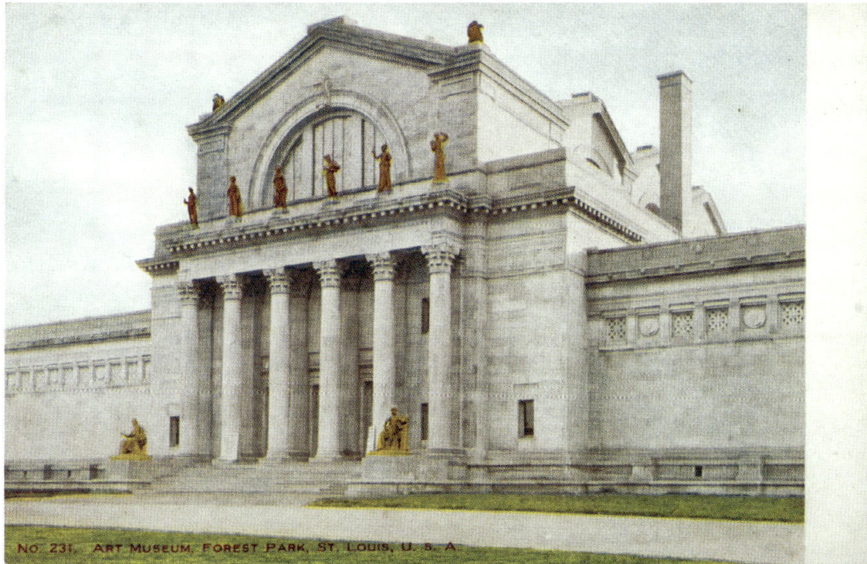

Circa Early 1900s, $2-4

Though the St. Louis Art Museum was found in 1879 (called the St. Louis School and Museum of Fine Arts, an independent part of Washington University), it was relocated to the World's Fair in 1904. The building in Forest Park is one of the few permanent structures still at the park.

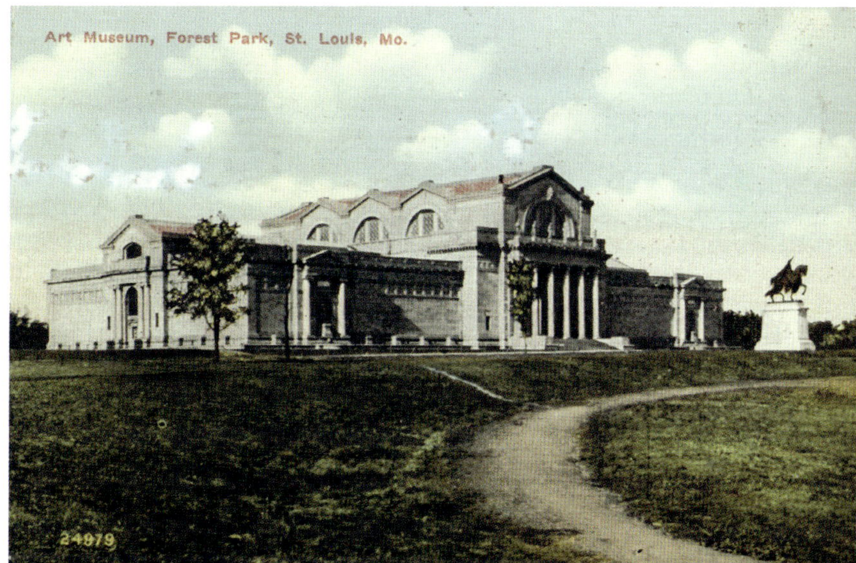

Cancelled 1911, $2-4

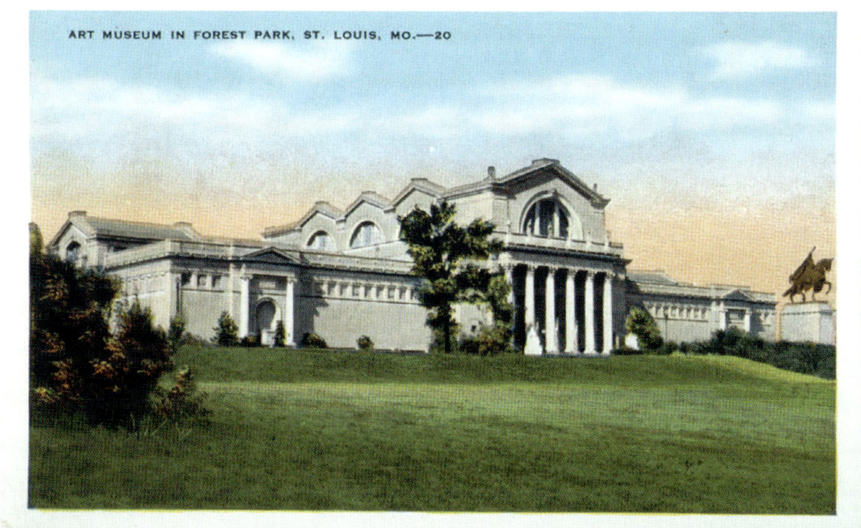

Circa 1930s, $2-4

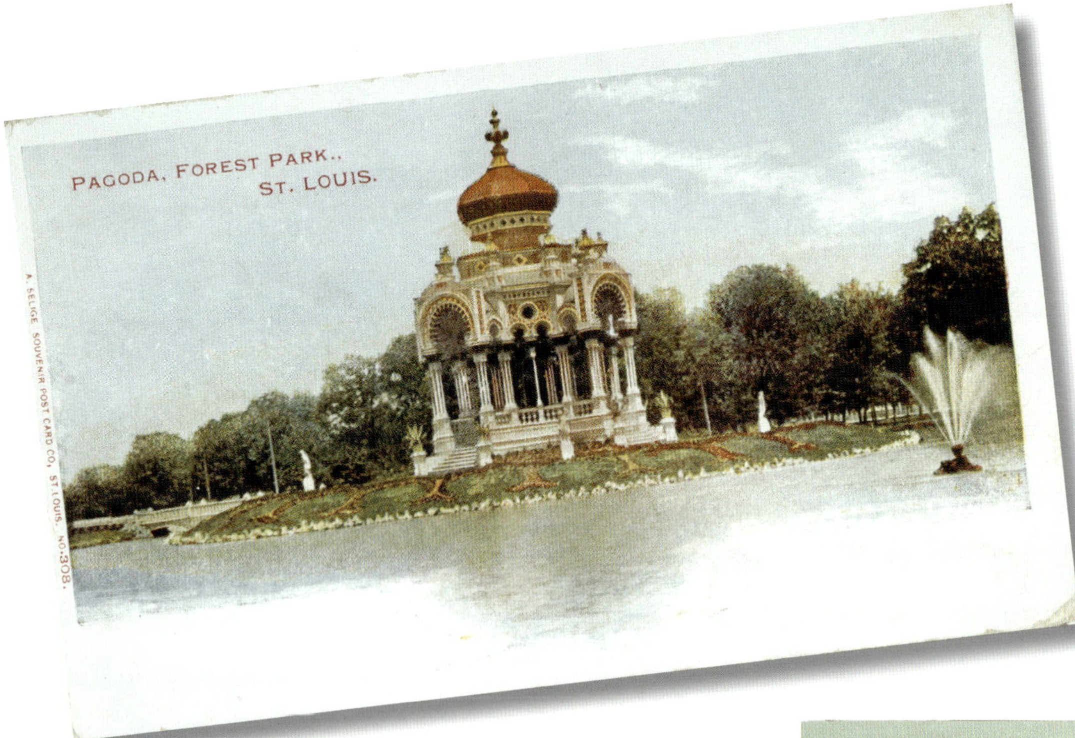

Shown here is the original bandstand pagoda of Forest Park. Standing on an island in the Pagoda Lake, it was dedicated in 1876, and renovated in time for the 1904 World's Fair. Unfortunately, it was deemed unsafe in 1911, and before it could be repaired, the structure was damaged *beyond* repair in a storm.

Circa Early 1900s, $3-5

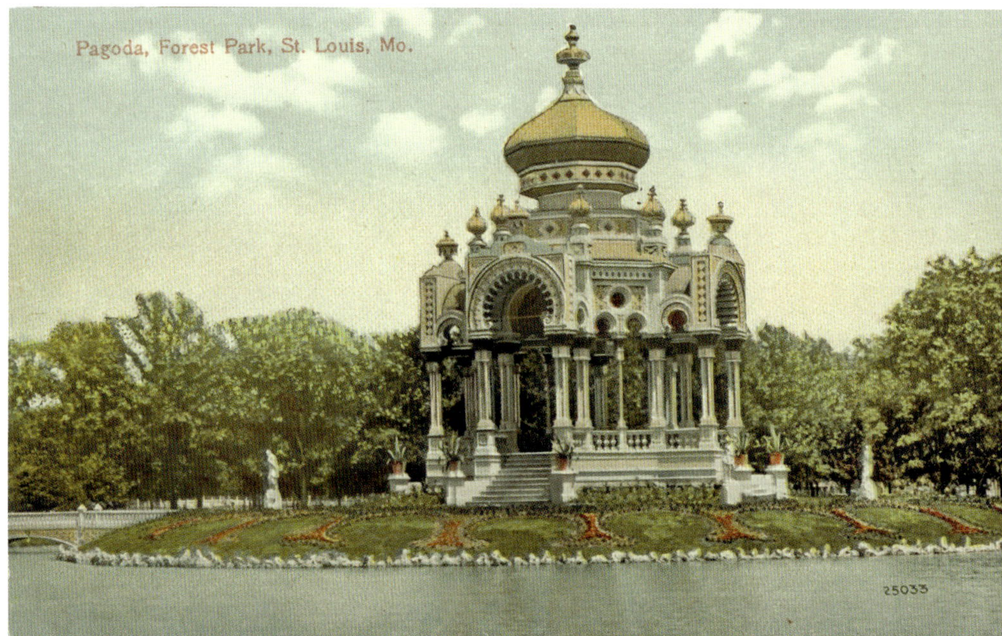

Circa 1907, $2-4

The Nathan Frank bandstand located on Pagoda Island outside the Municipal Theatre was built in a classic Renaissance design to replace the prior bandstand in 1924. Funds were donated by Frank.

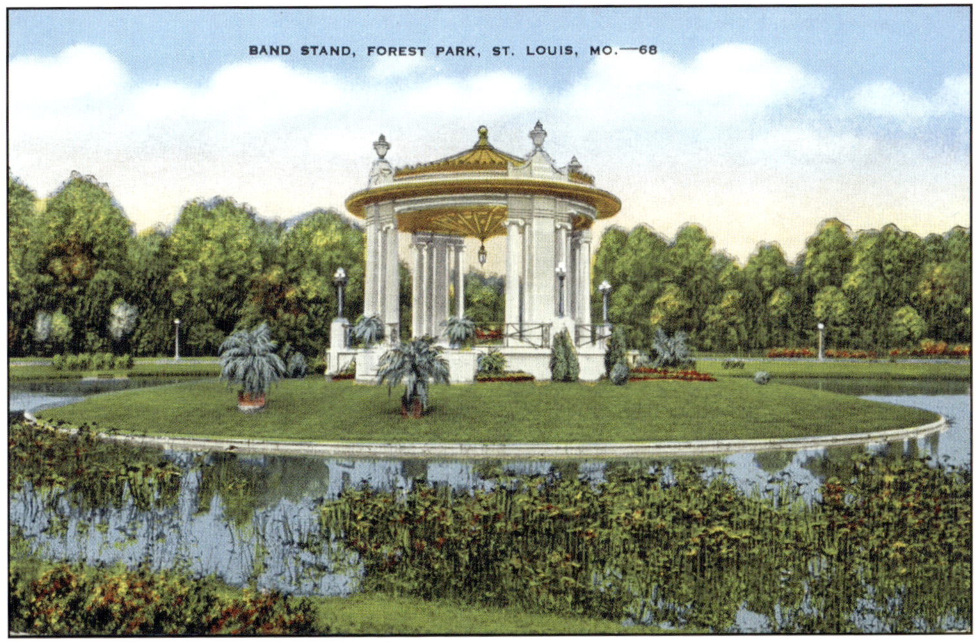

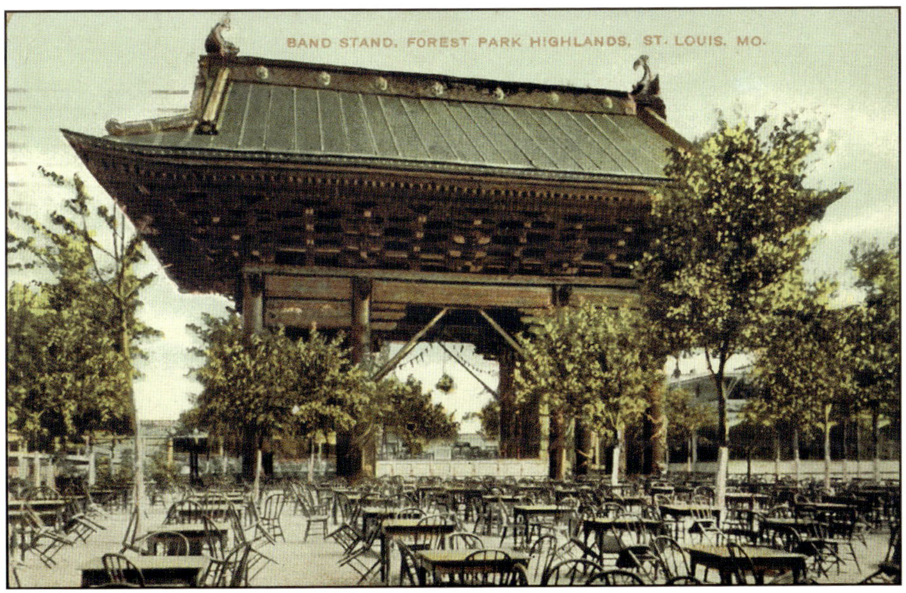

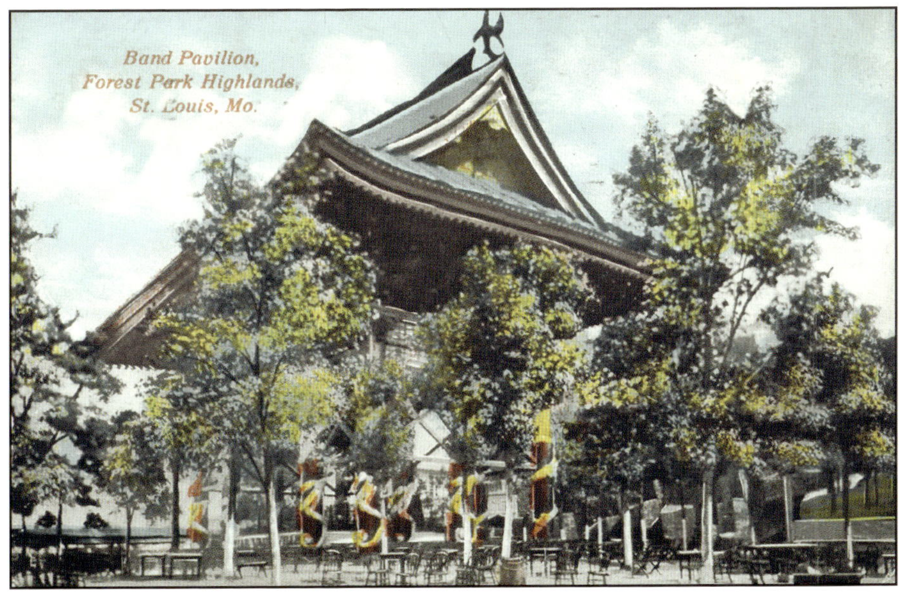

The bandstand in Forest Park Highlands was a recycled Japanese gate structure left over from the days of the World's Fair. The Highlands amusement park had roller coasters, a merry-go-round, galleries, swimming, and dancing. The Highlands was destroyed by fire in 1963.

Cancelled 1909, $2-4 (left)
Cancelled 1913, $2-4 (right)

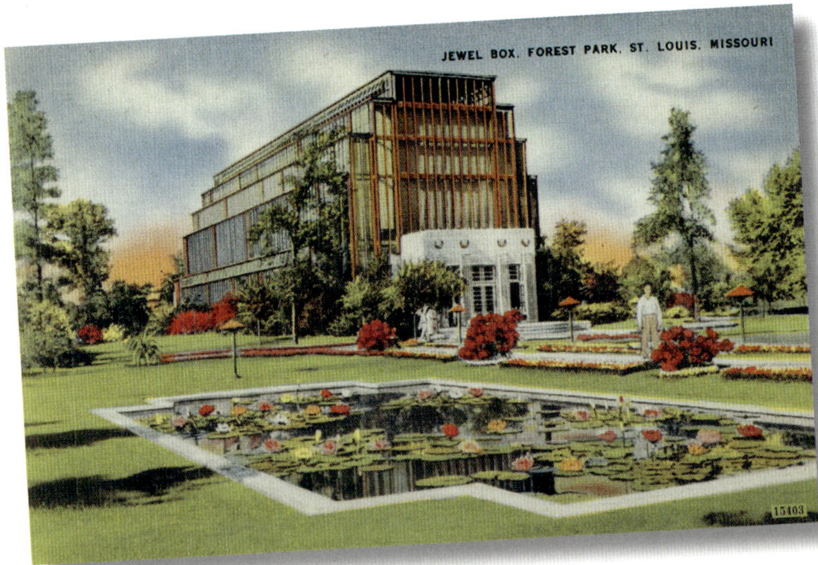

Circa 1930s, $2-4

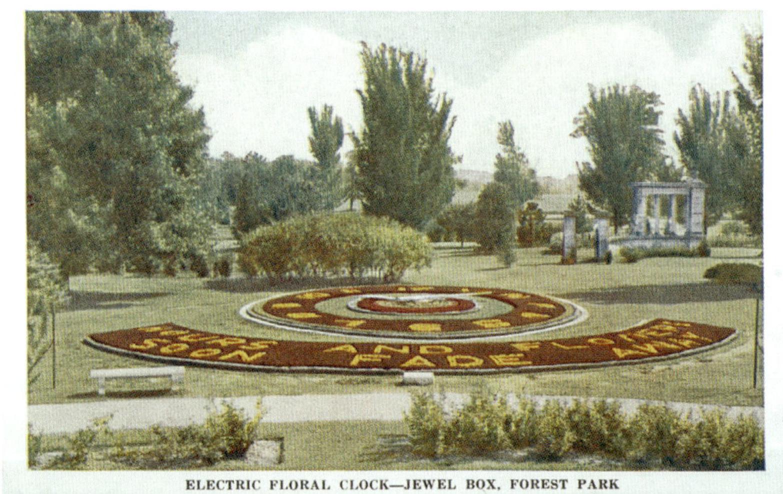

Circa 1930s (advertising card), $2-4

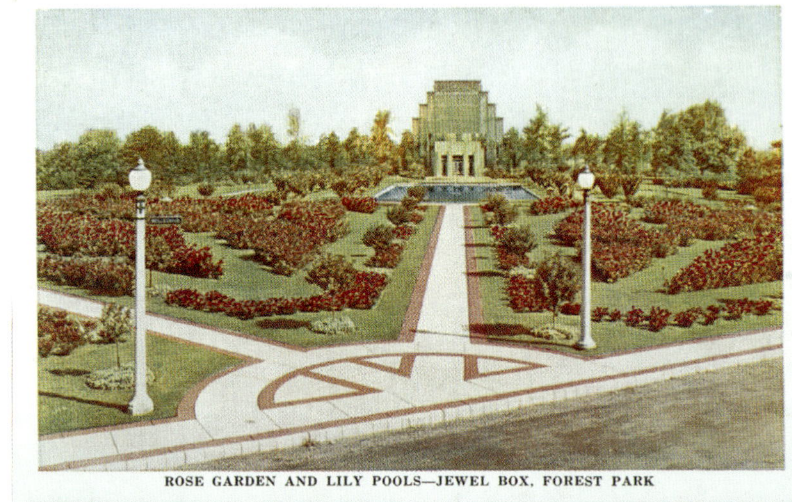

Circa 1930s (advertising card), $2-4

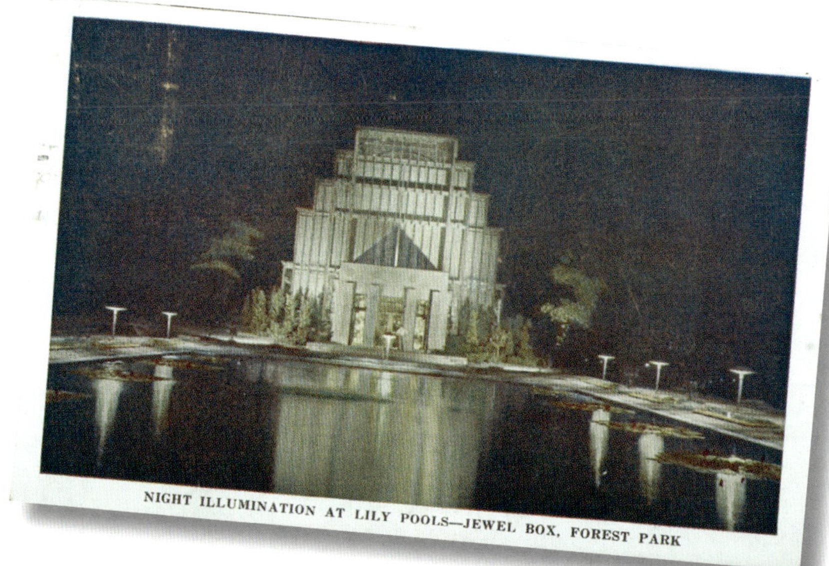

Cancelled 1954 (advertising card), $2-4

In 1916, the head gardener for Forest Park (John Moritz) prepared a greenhouse display, not only for visitors to see lovely flora, but to teach them about the varied plants that grow well in cityscapes. In 1926, because of gaining popularity, the displays were changed monthly and became know as the Jewel Box. The name came from a casual remark of a visitor describing the flower patterns and how they resembled a jewel box. When the press got hold of that tidbit, the name stuck. The Jewel Box was designed in an Art Deco style, constructed in practically all steel and glass, and is listed in the National Register of Historic Places.

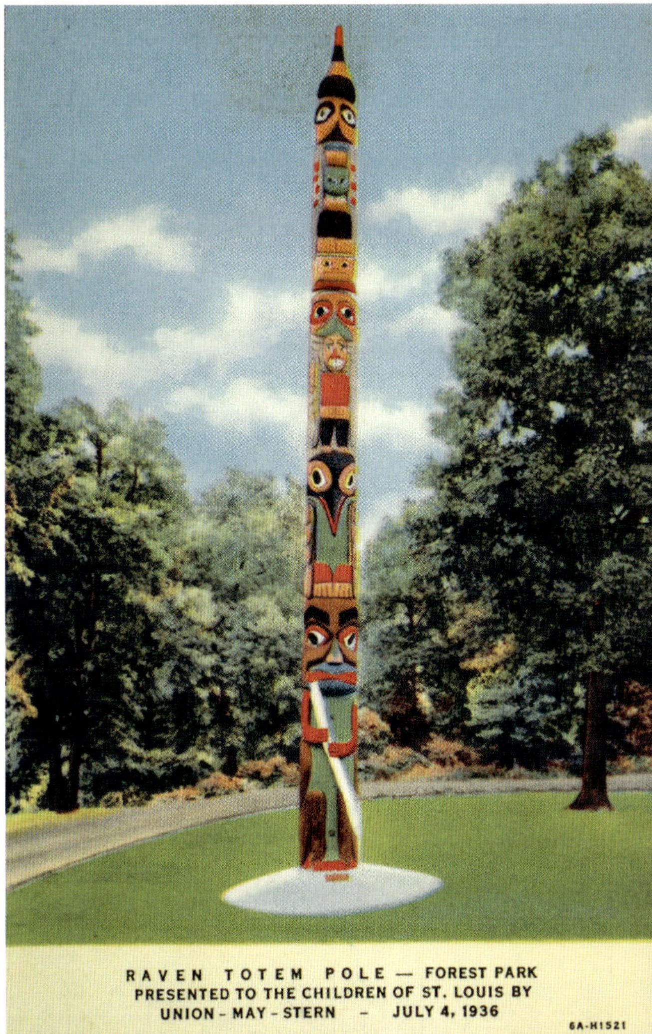

From the back of the card: *The Raven Totem Pole, Thirty-five Feet in Height. An original made by Alaskan Indians. The figures from the top to bottom are — The Raven, recognized as the creator of all, wearing his cap of authority and guarding a box containing the Sun, Moon, and Stars; The Young Raven, creator of Man and supporting all, Hi-Yi-Shon-A-Gu, the Indian Atlas.*

Circa 1930s, $2-4

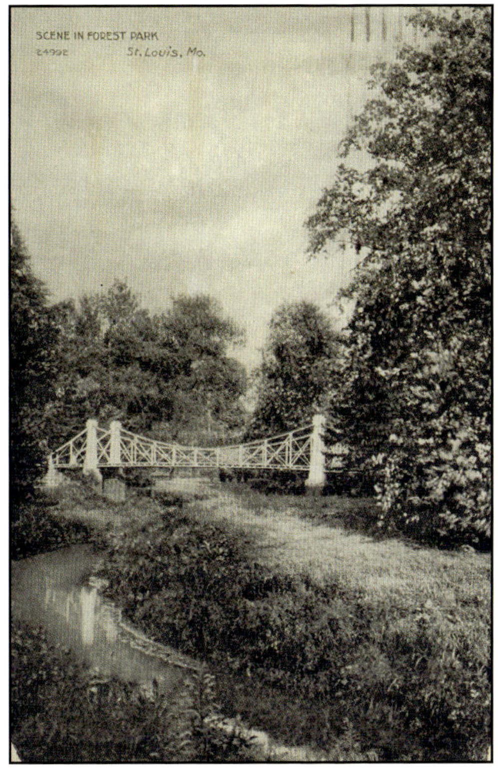

Cancelled 1909, $10-12

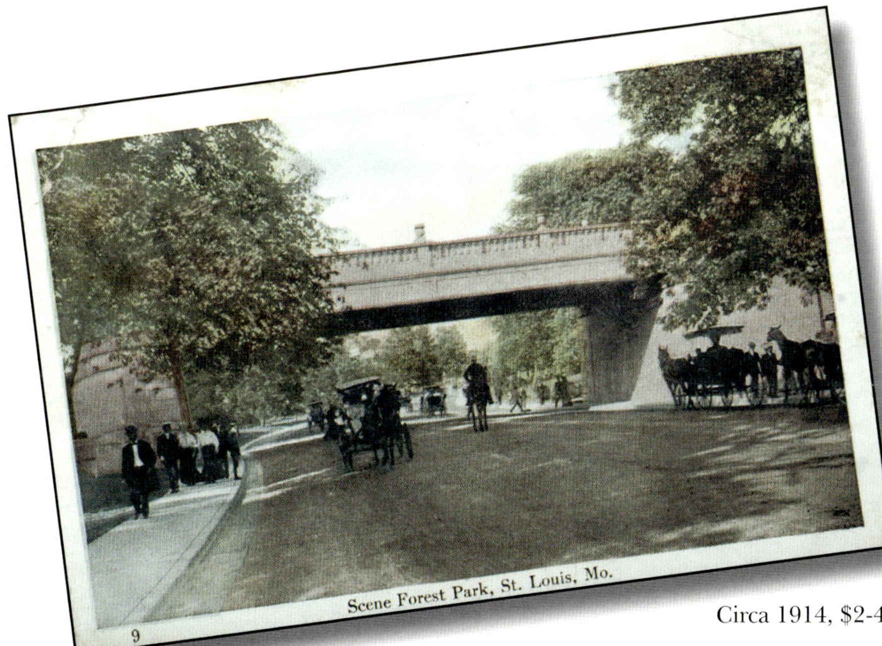

Circa 1914, $2-4

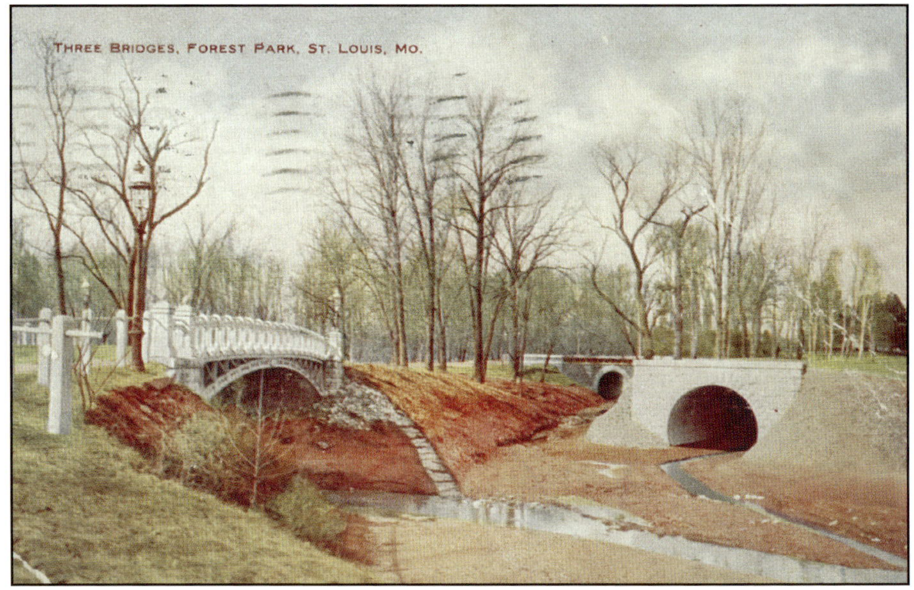

Cancelled 1909, $2-4

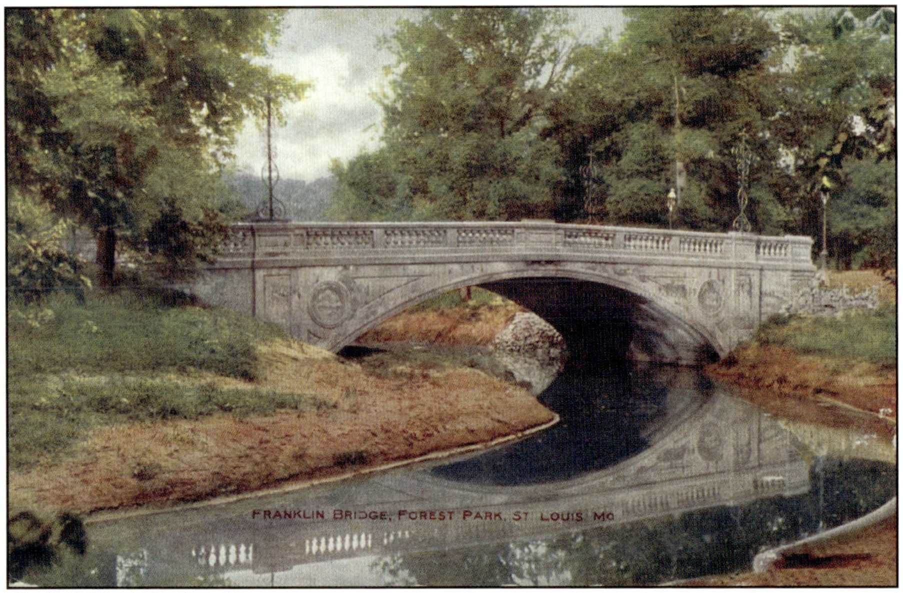

Circa 1907, $2-4

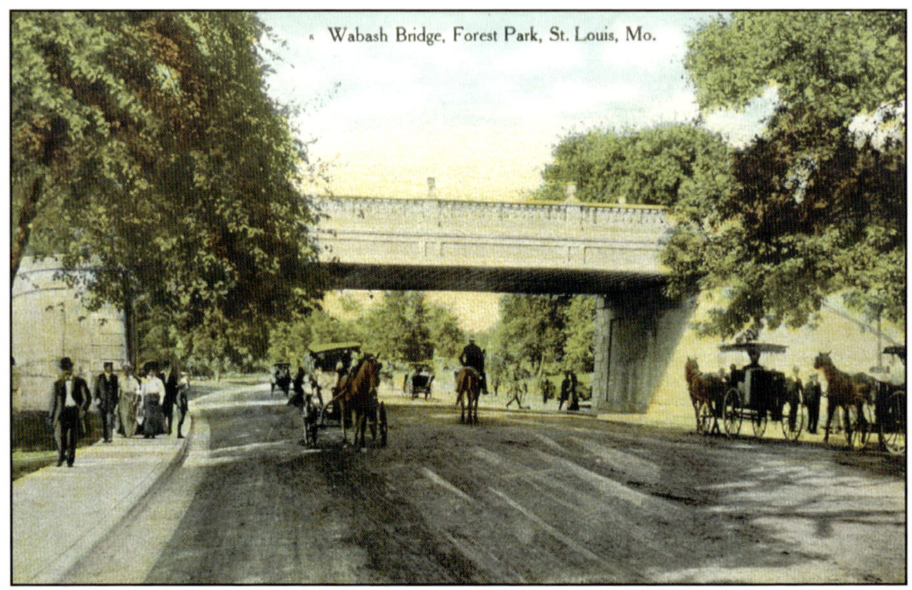

Circa 1907, $2-4

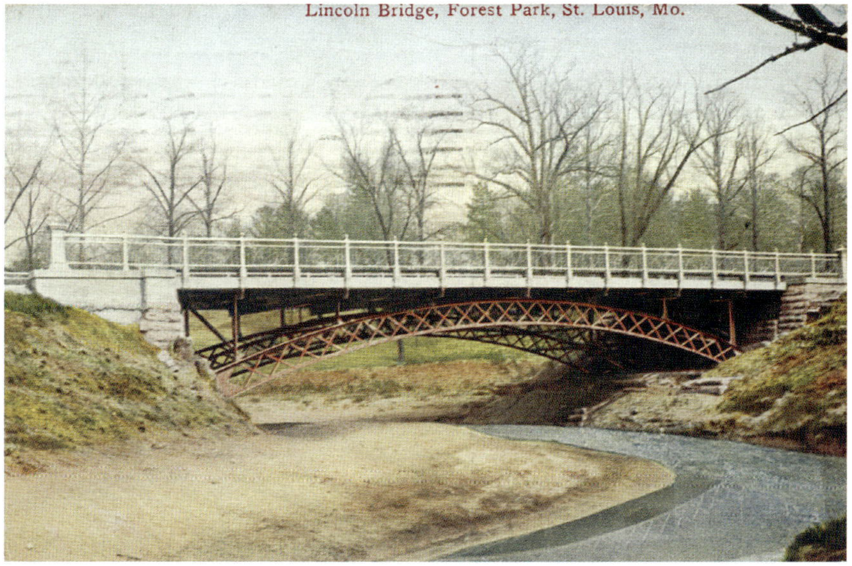

Cancelled 1908, $2-4

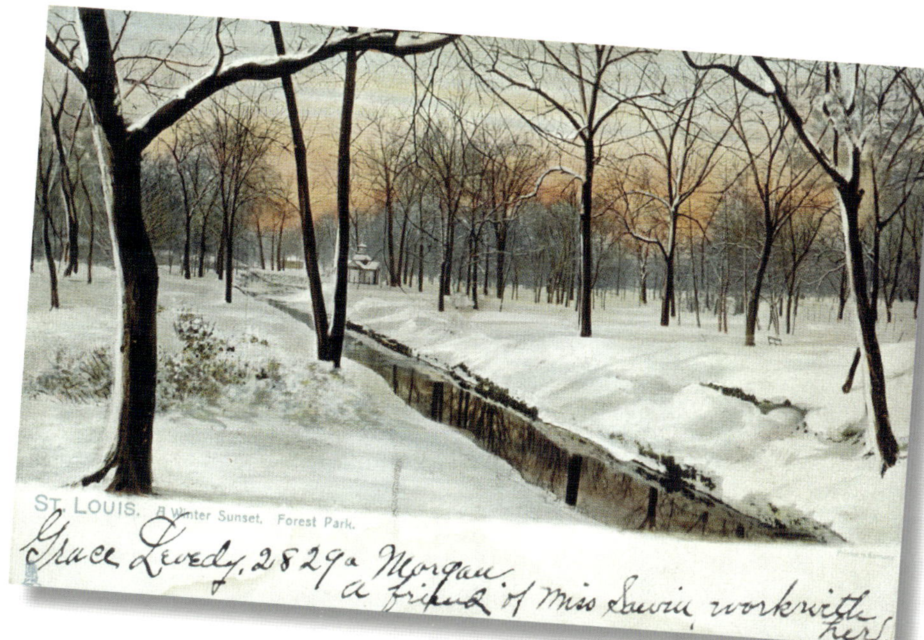

Cancelled 1906, $6-8

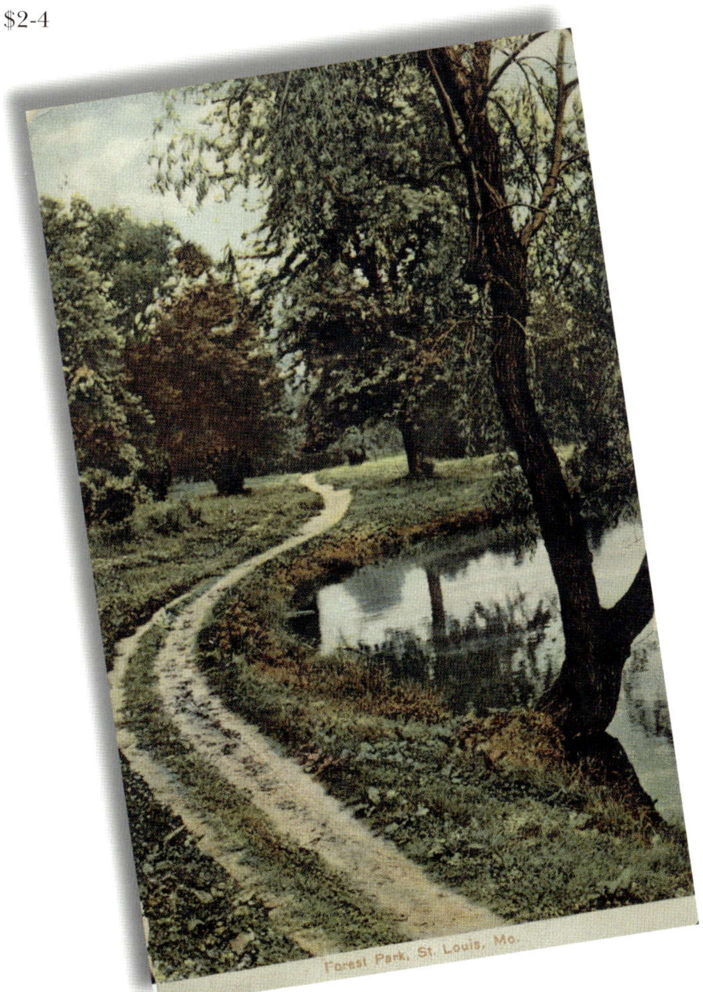

Cancelled 1909, $2-4

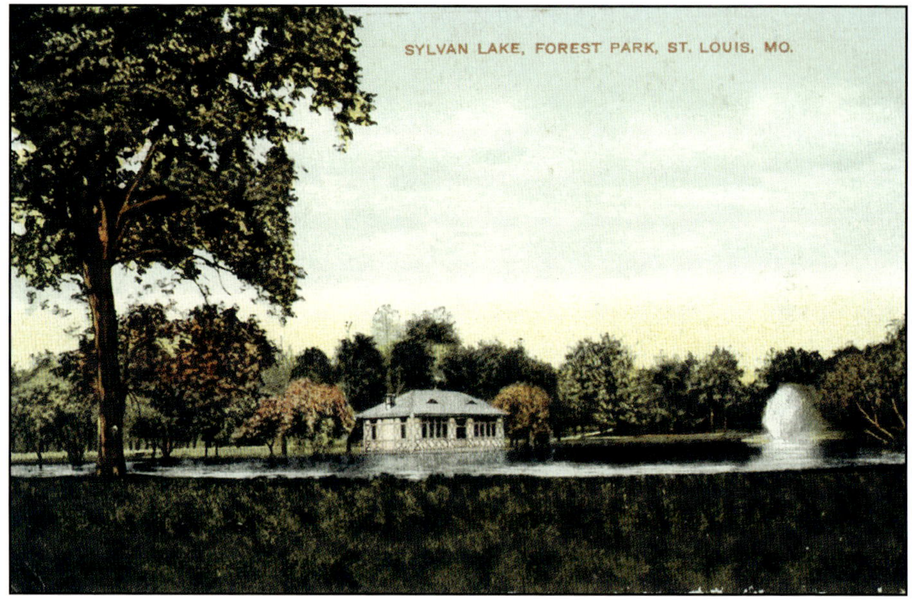

Circa 1907, $2-4

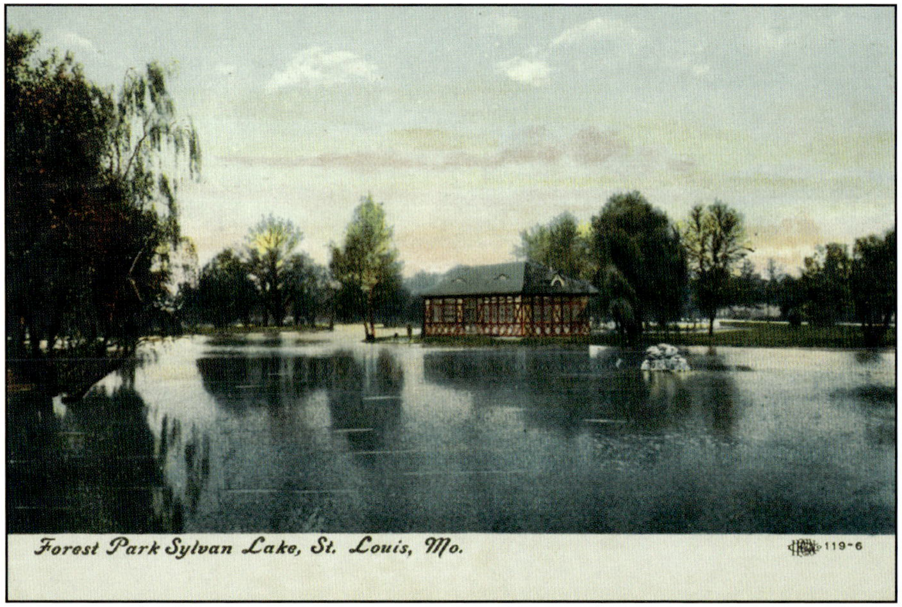

Circa 1907, $2-4

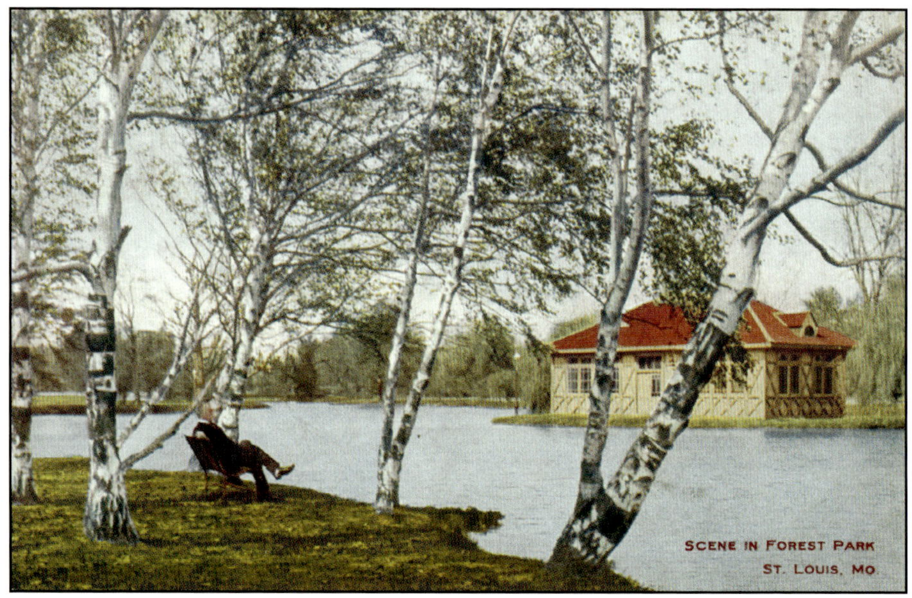

Cancelled (twice) 1907, $3-5

Other Scenic Parks

Forest Park wasn't the only scenic park in St. Louis. Hyde Park, Carondelet Park, Lafayette Park, and Compton Heights Reservoir Park were just a few of the wonderful places to relax and enjoy in St. Louis.

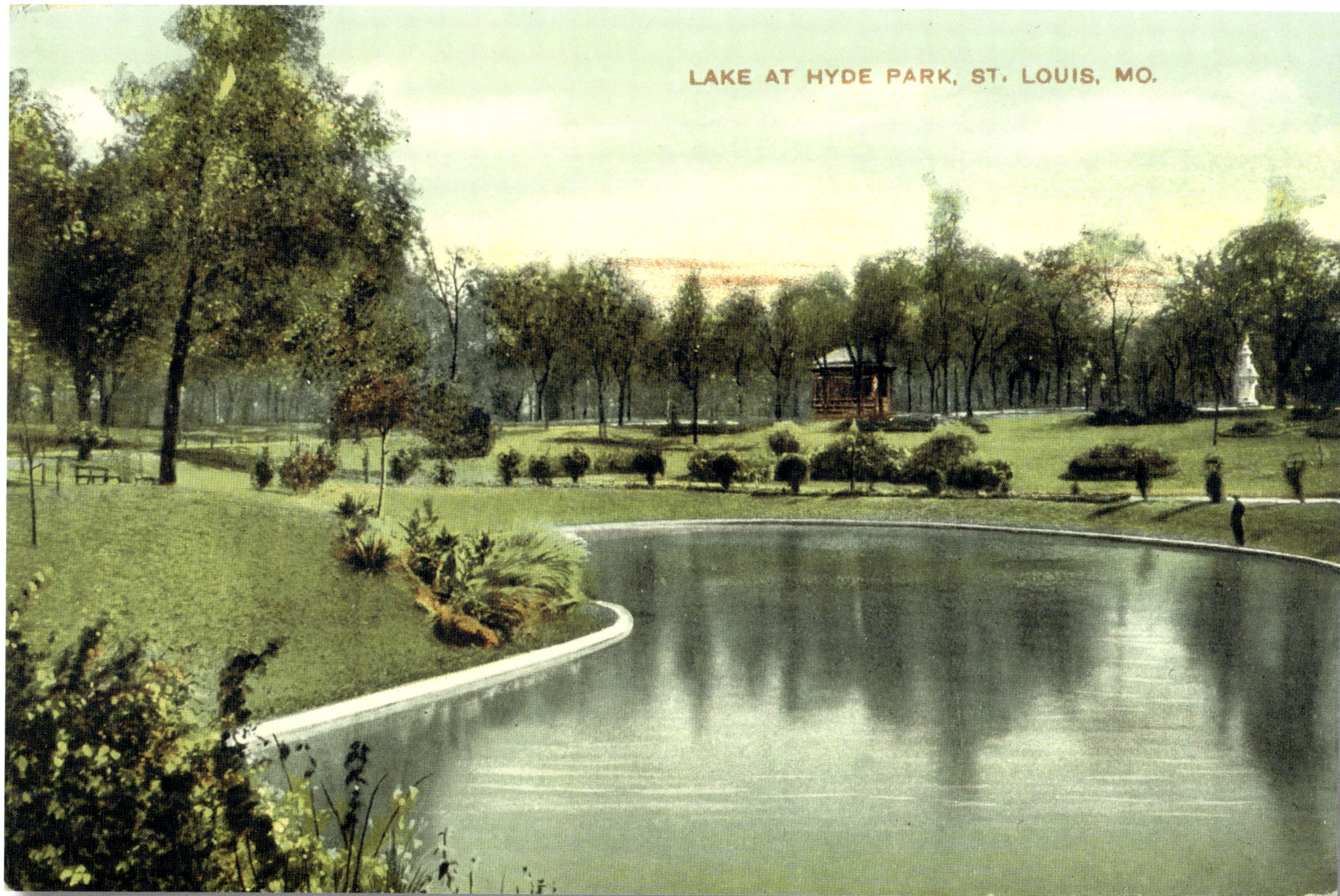

Originally, the property including Hyde Park was issued as a land grant. It was purchased by Dr. Bernard Farrar in 1842, and the doctor designated a part of the property for the park. (Dr. Farrar—in 1809 when he began his practice—was the first American doctor in St. Louis.) Farrar died of cholera in 1849, and his widow, in 1850, sold fourteen and one half acres to the city of St. Louis for $36,250 for the park.

Circa 1907, $2-4

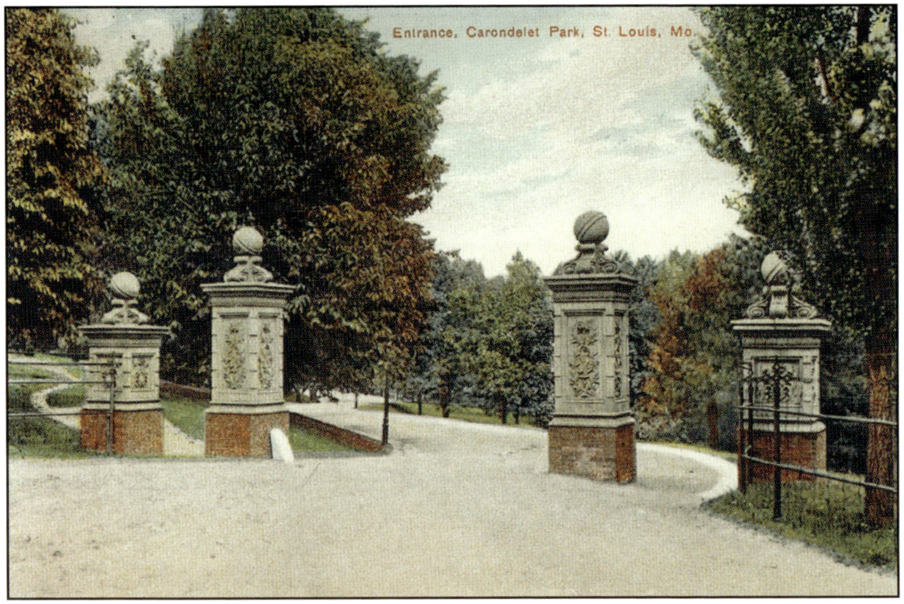

Circa 1907, $2-4

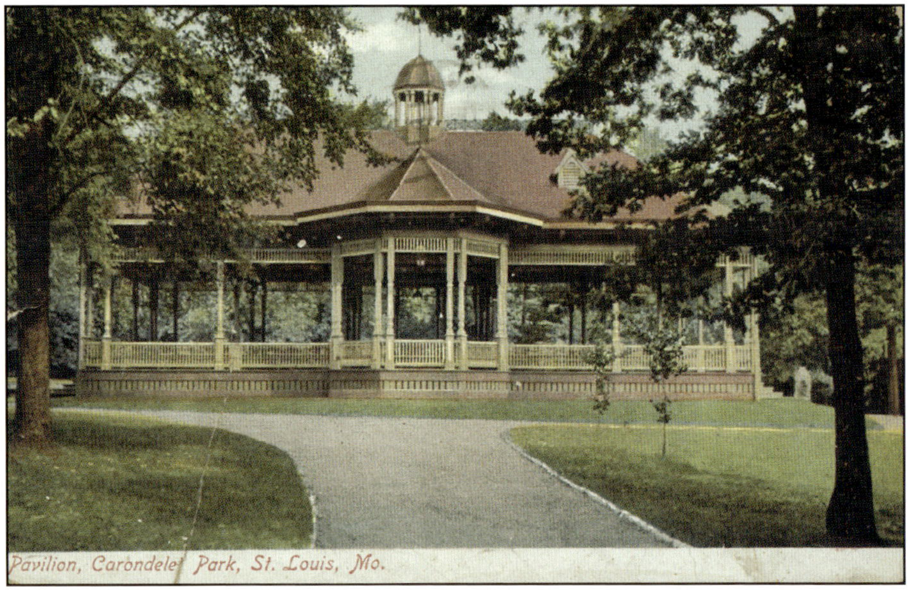

Cancelled 1915, $2-4

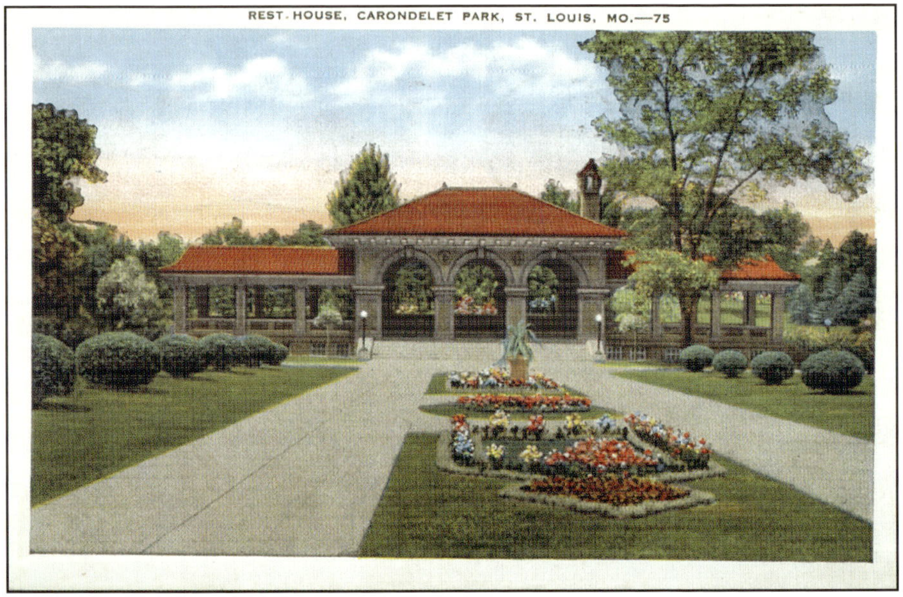

Cancelled 1941, $2-4

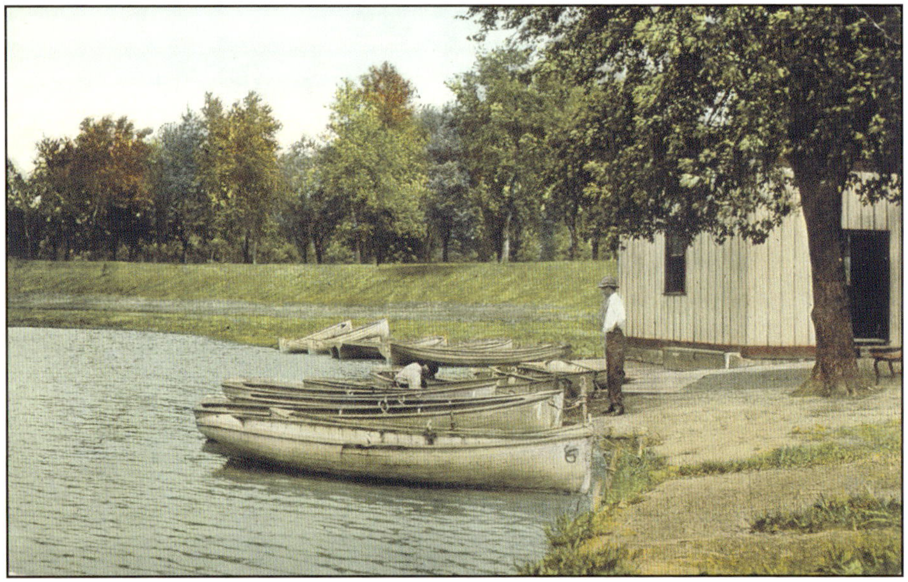

Circa 1907, $2-4

Ranking third in size for parks in St. Louis, Carondelet Park covers over 179 acres, with lakes, picnic grounds, playgrounds, athletic facilities, and beautiful scenery. Its bandstand was completed in 1898, and the boathouse in 1908. The park came about because St. Louis residents living in the far south of the city wanted a recreational area convenient to their homes. (Forest Park was too far away to travel for a visit in their opinions.) So, in 1875, the land was purchased by the city, and Carondelet Park was dedicated in 1876.

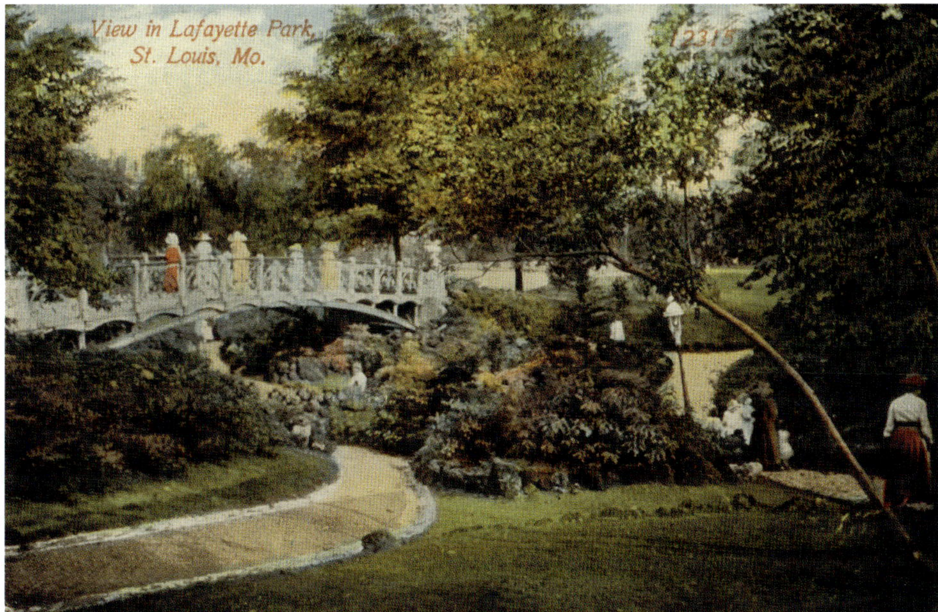

Named for the Marquis de Lafayette, the French patriot serving voluntarily under General George Washington during the American Revolution, the Lafayette Park is one of the oldest St. Louis parks. The park (with land originally preserved in 1836) was first used for the drilling of Grimsley's "Home Guard" and became know as "Grimsley's Folly."

Cancelled 1913, $2-4

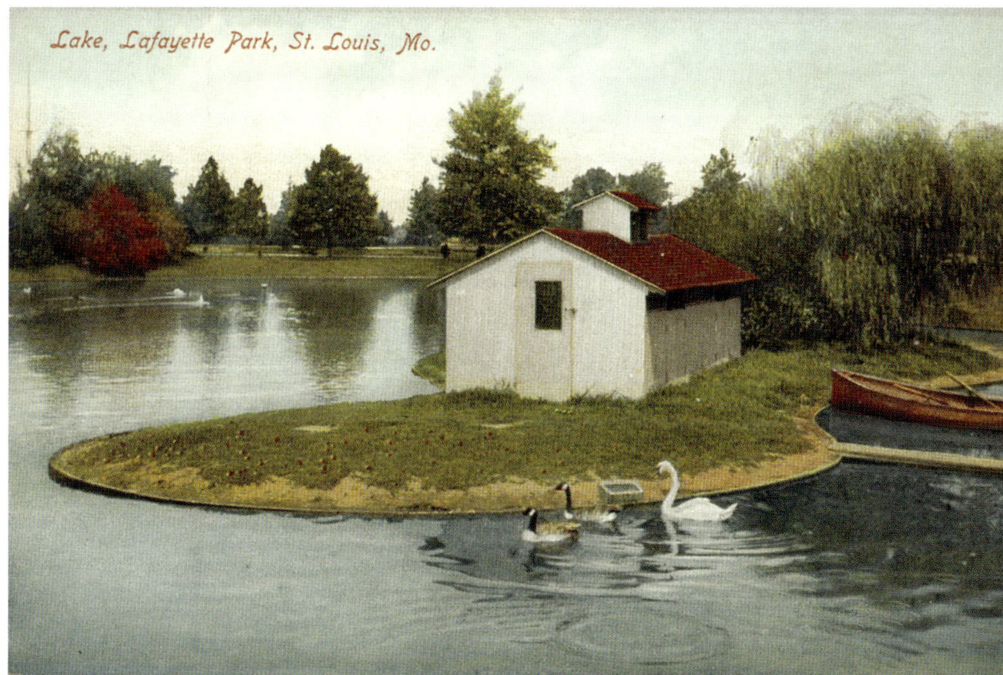

Circa 1907, $2-4

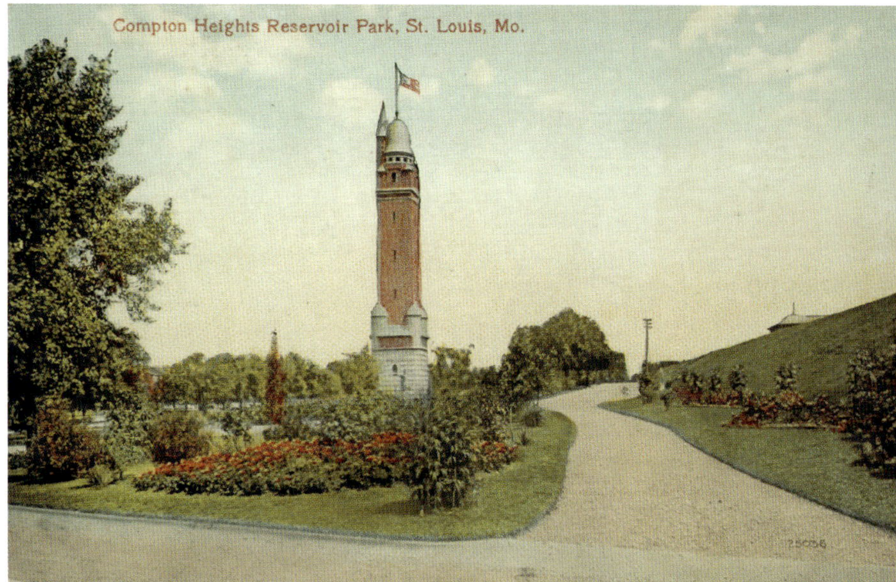

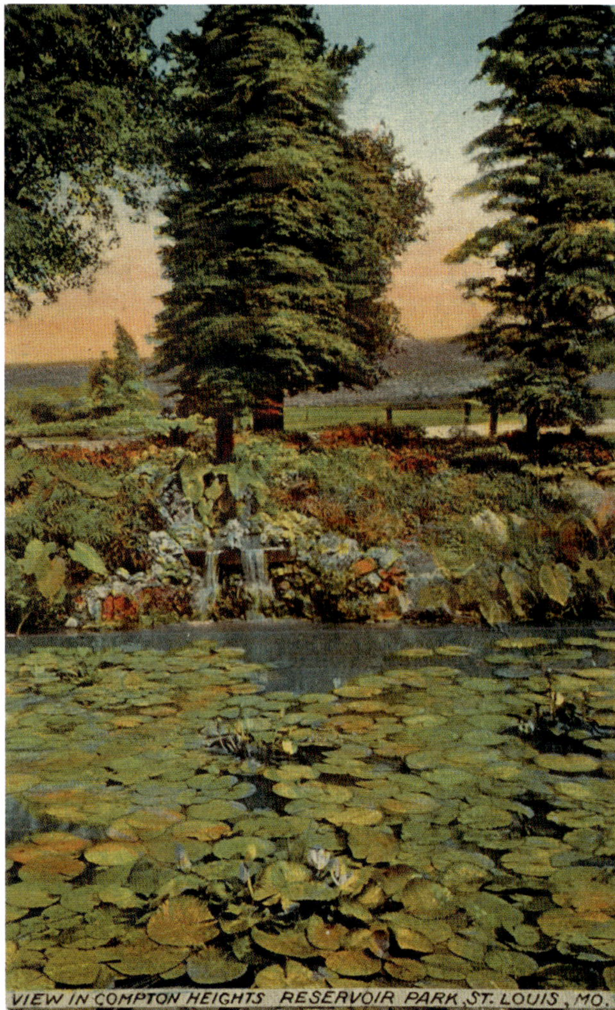

Compton Heights was noted, in 1855, as being one of the highest locations within St. Louis city limits and, therefore, was selected as the site for the main reservoir in 1867. The reservoir occupied about eighteen acres of a forty-acre property, so James Kirwood, chief engineer of the Water Department at that time, suggested that the remaining land be used as a park.

Cancelled 1915, $2-4

The water tower in the Compton Heights Reservoir Park, built in 1899 in Romanesque design by George Mann, is prominent as a St. Louis landmark. The stone base of its brick shaft cost $48,000.

Circa 1907, $2-4 (above)
Circa 1914, $2-4 (right)

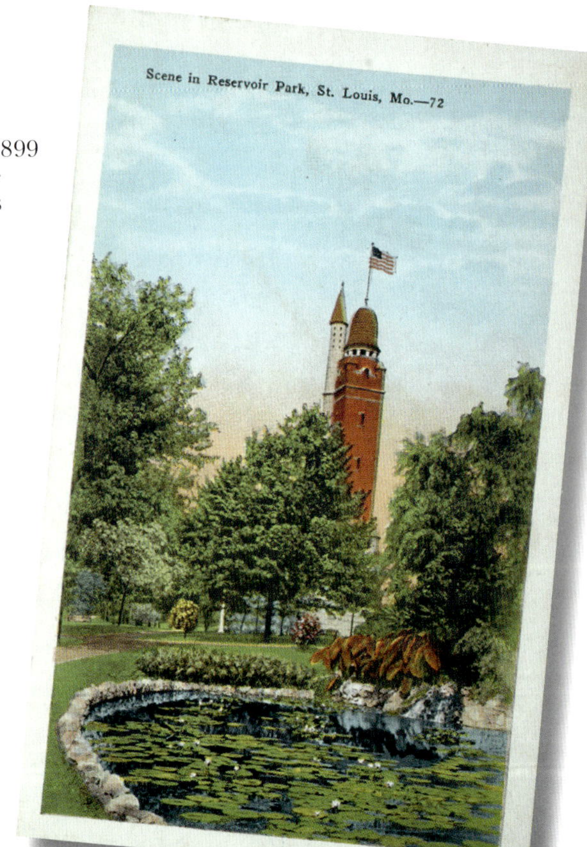

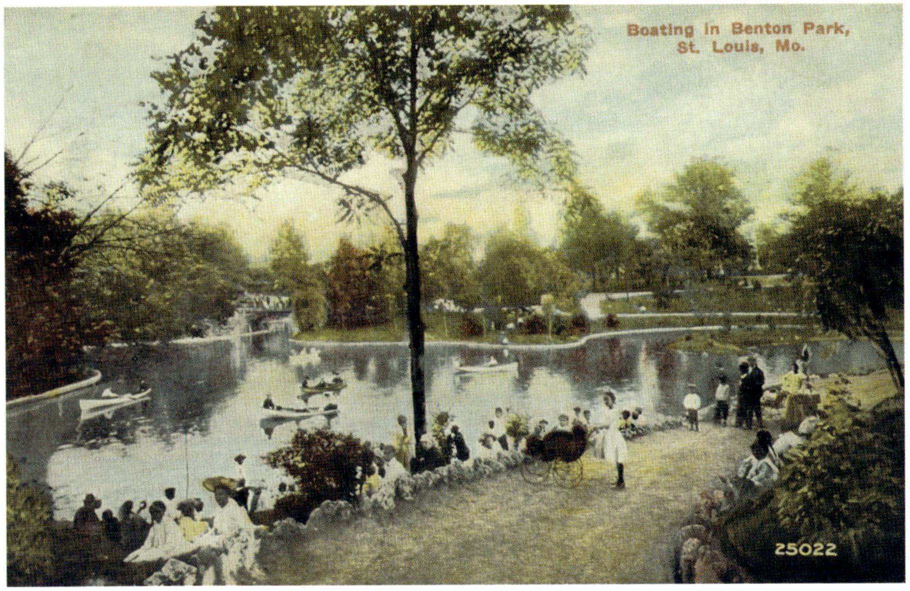

Circa 1907, $2-4

Initially, Benton Park was slated to be a cemetery, but in 1836, after the founding of Bellafontaine and Calvary Cemeteries, it was then turned into a lovely recreational area. Popular activities included boating on the artificial lake shown here and (in 1888) enjoying the greenhouse and landscaping. The rustic bridge was also a romantic draw for this lovely location.

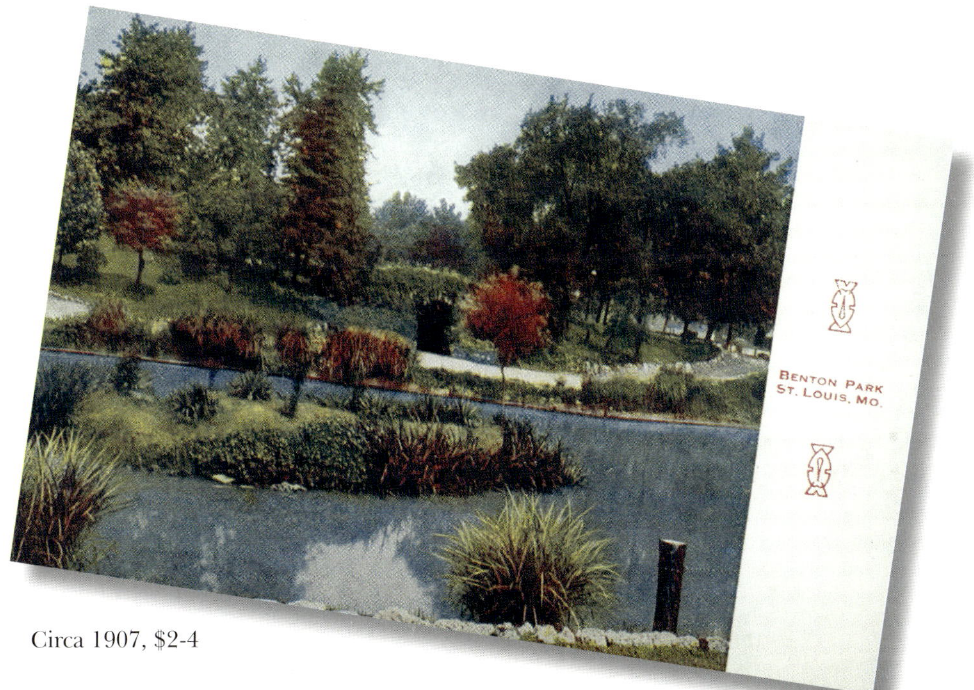

Circa 1907, $2-4

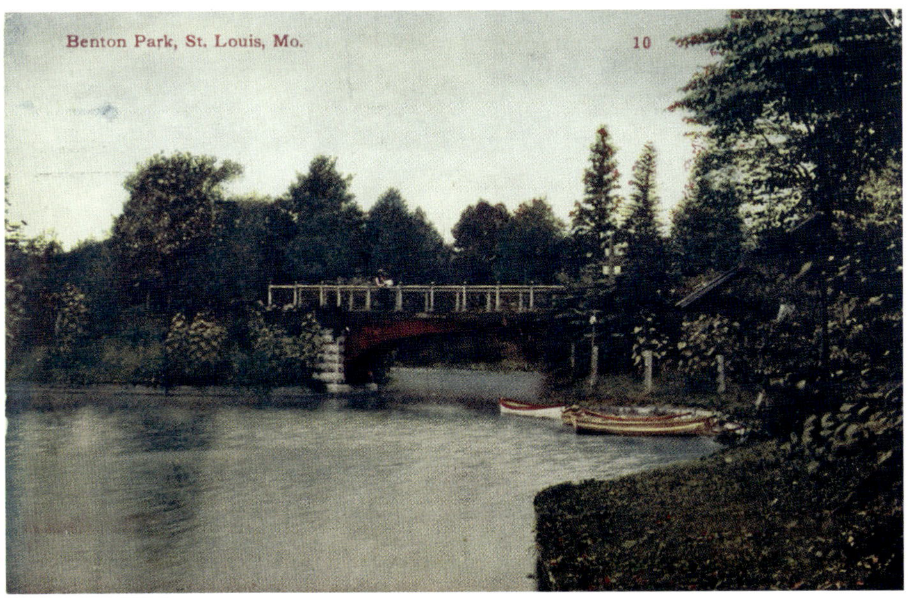

Circa 1907, $2-4

From part of the estate of Colonel John O'Fallon, the 160-acre O'Fallon Park was mainly used as a picnic area and driving park until the 1880s. In the 1890s, a bandstand, shelter with an observation tower, and lake were added. Unfortunately, the area of the park was reduced in 1954 to 127 acres to make way for Interstate Highway 70.

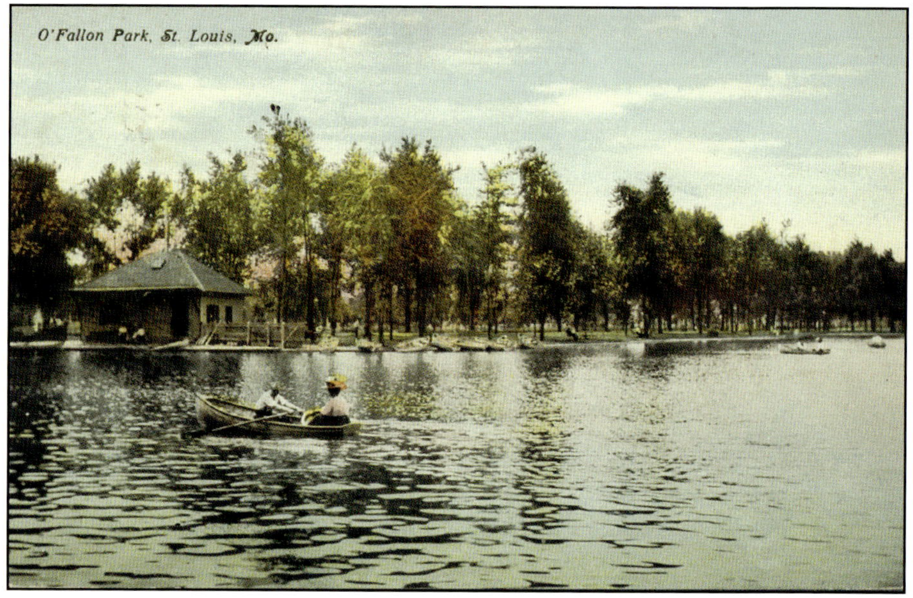

Cancelled 1911, $2-4

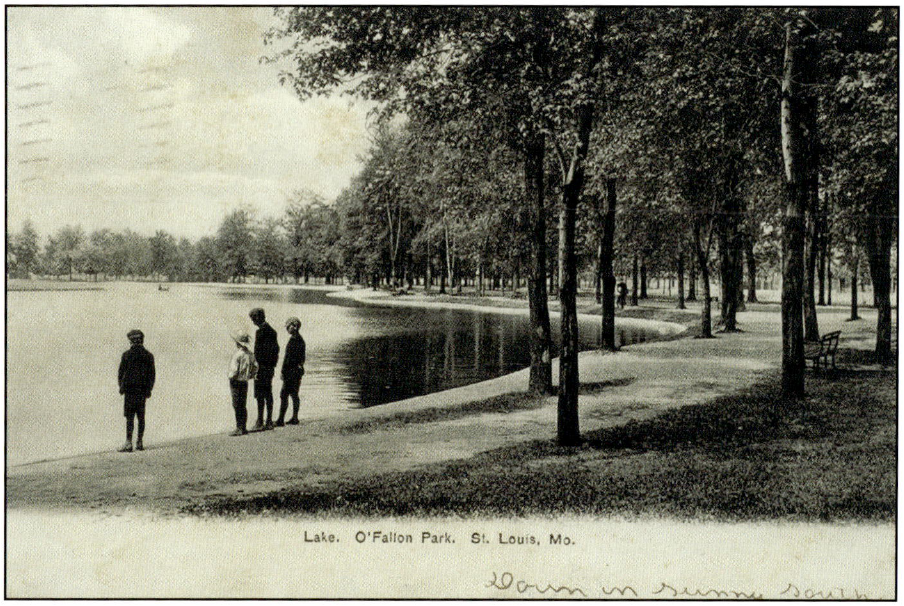

Cancelled 1907, $6-8

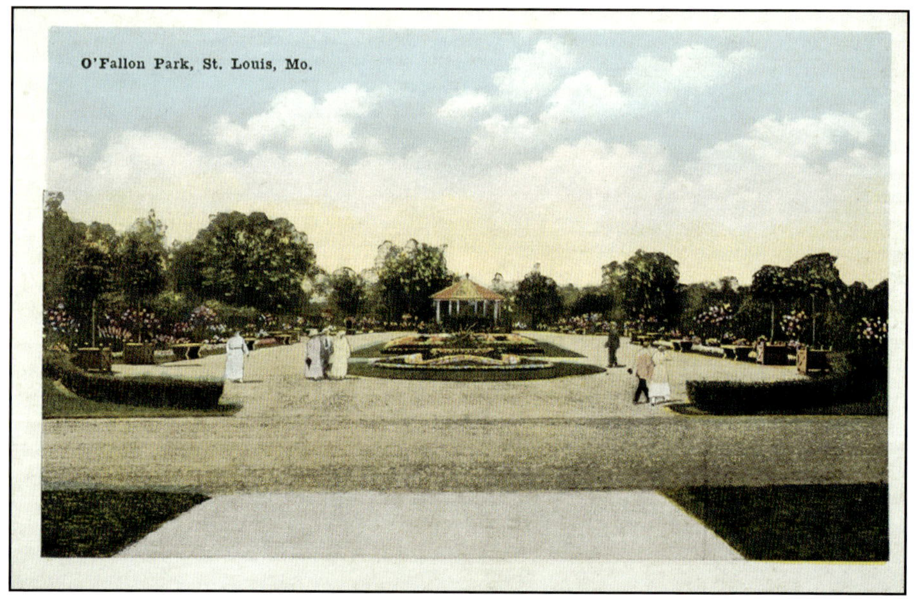

Circa 1914, $2-4

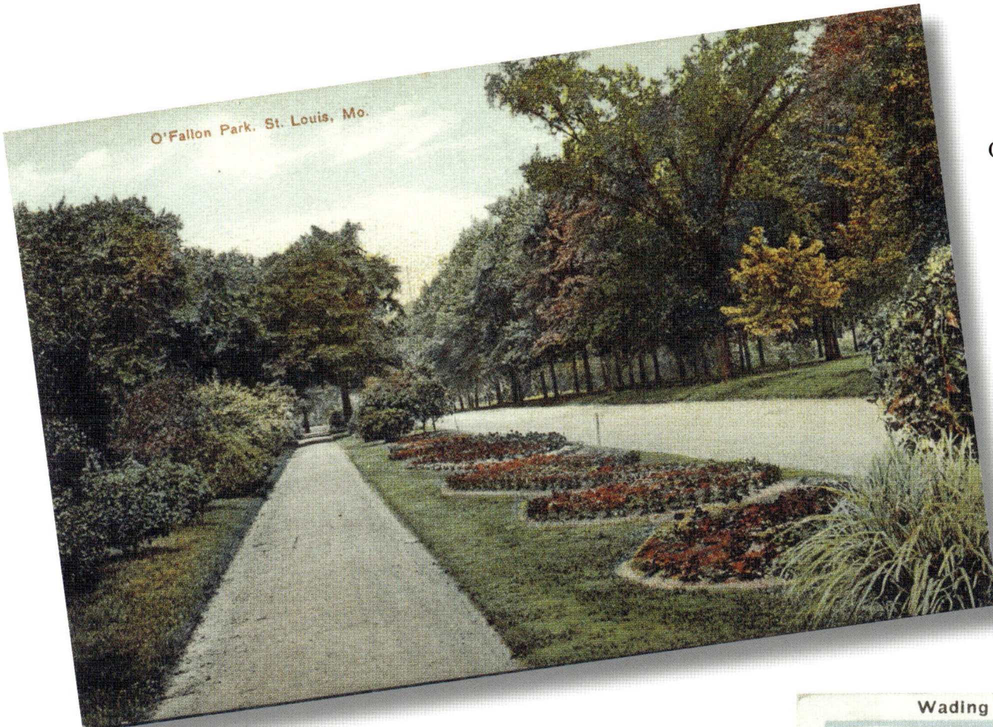

Circa 1907, $2-4

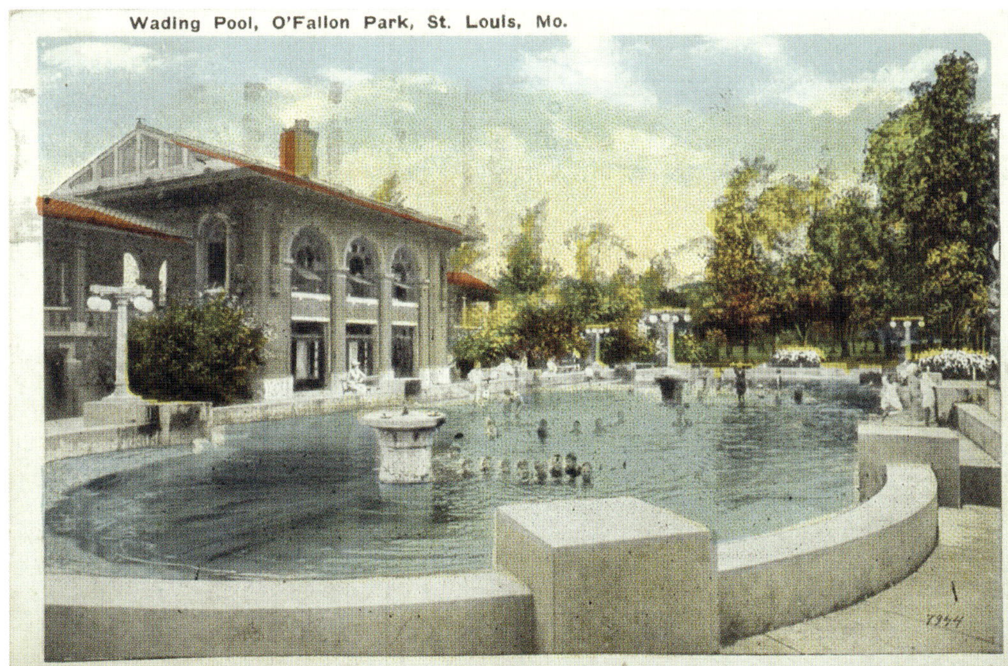

Cancelled 1920, $2-4

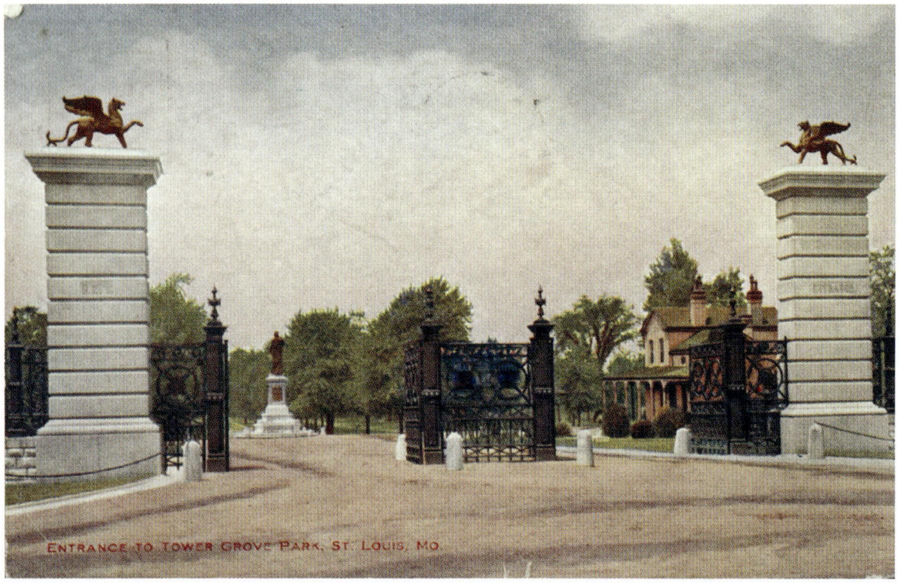

Cancelled 1908, $2-4

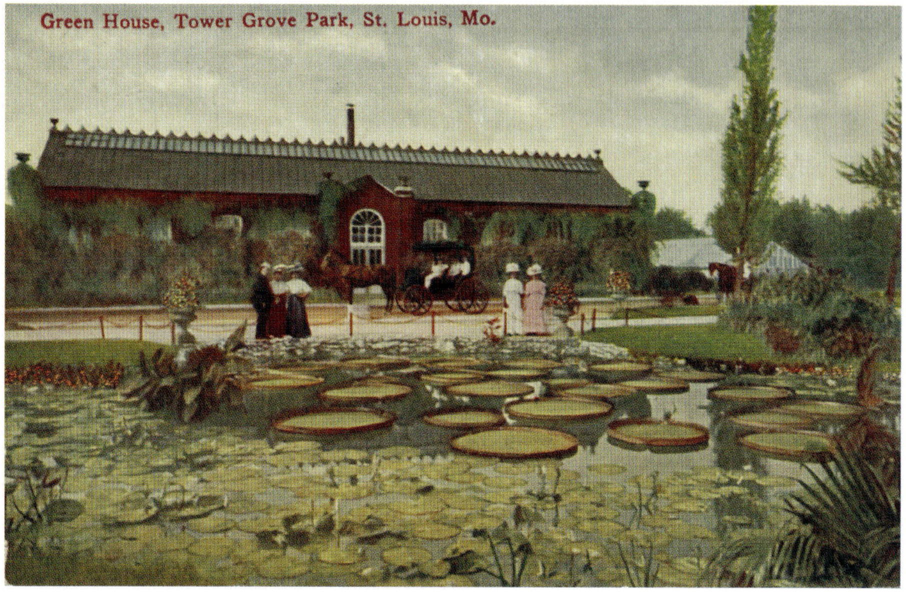

Circa 1907, $2-4

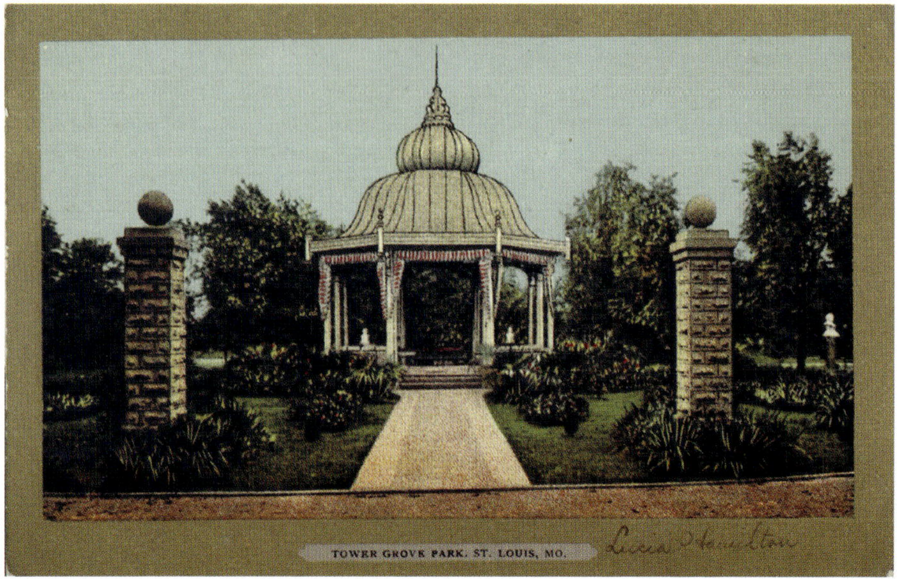

Cancelled 1907, $3-5

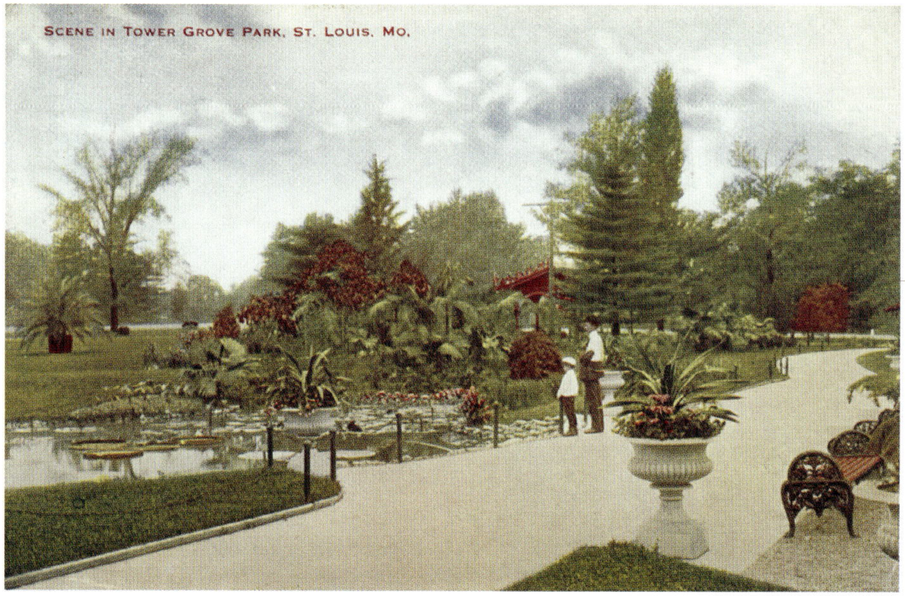

Cancelled 1913, $2-4

Henry Shaw (of Botanical Garden fame), in 1866, brought forth a proposition to use a part of the estate surrounding his villa as a park for the citizens of St. Louis. He believed that parks were "not only as ornaments to a great city, but as conducive to the health and happiness of its inhabitants and to the advancement of refinement and culture." Shaw was truly a person of devotion to St. Louis, for he spent twenty years improving park land and also donated three bronze statues (among other things) to the park. Here, view one of the Tower Grove pavilions and the greenhouse with a view of the lily pond.

Places to See!

Shaw Gardens

The Missouri Botanical Garden, or Shaw's Garden, was established in 1857 by Henry Shaw in the heart of St. Louis. Inspired by the Royal Botanical Gardens in England, it features exotic plants from around the world.

Before Shaw's death, he had a mausoleum built on the garden property and is still entombed there today. His will requested that his house, now known as Tower Grove House, be moved to the garden's property as well. The house was originally built for Shaw, and after the move, was remodeled to almost double its size.

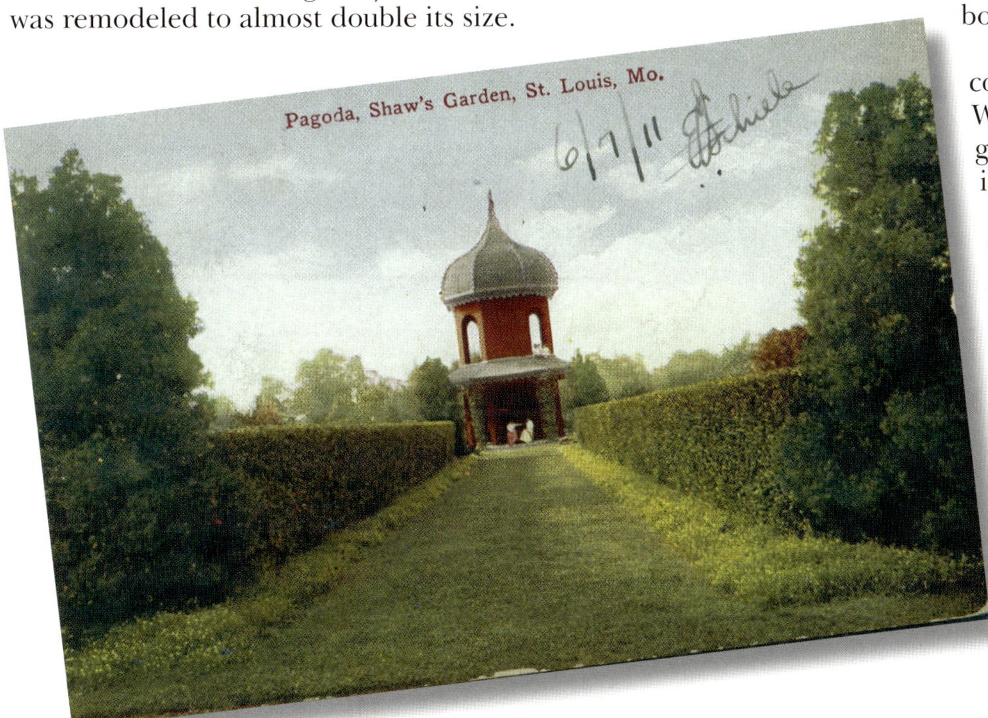

Guests enter the garden through the Ridgeway Center, which features the Garden Gate Café, the Garden Gate Shop, and the Spink Gallery, holding a collection of ceramics. The three main conservatory greenhouses are the Linnean House, Climatron, and the Schoenberg Temperate House.

The Linnean House is the oldest running greenhouse west of the Mississippi River. It was built in 1882 by Shaw and was named after Carl Linnaeus, who invented the current naming system for plant and animal species. Guests can enjoy busts of Linnaeus and other influential botanists while visiting this house.

Built in 1960, the Climatron is home to tropical plants. This climate-controlled dome allows for over a half acre of uninterrupted space. Winning the 1961 Reynolds Award for architecture and design, this greenhouse was named as one of the top architectural achievements in the country in 1976.

The Schoenberg Temperate House was built in 1990 to replace the Mediterranean House. This house features plants from Africa, Australia, Korea, China, Japan, South America, the California coast, and the Mediterranean Sea region in seven gardens. It also includes fruits such as pomegranates, figs, grapes, etc. These plants begin blooming in April and can be enjoyed throughout the summer.

Visitors can also visit The Kemper Center, an indoor and outdoor display for home gardeners. It features a library, demonstration room, and eight acres of gardens.

Cancelled 1911, $2-4

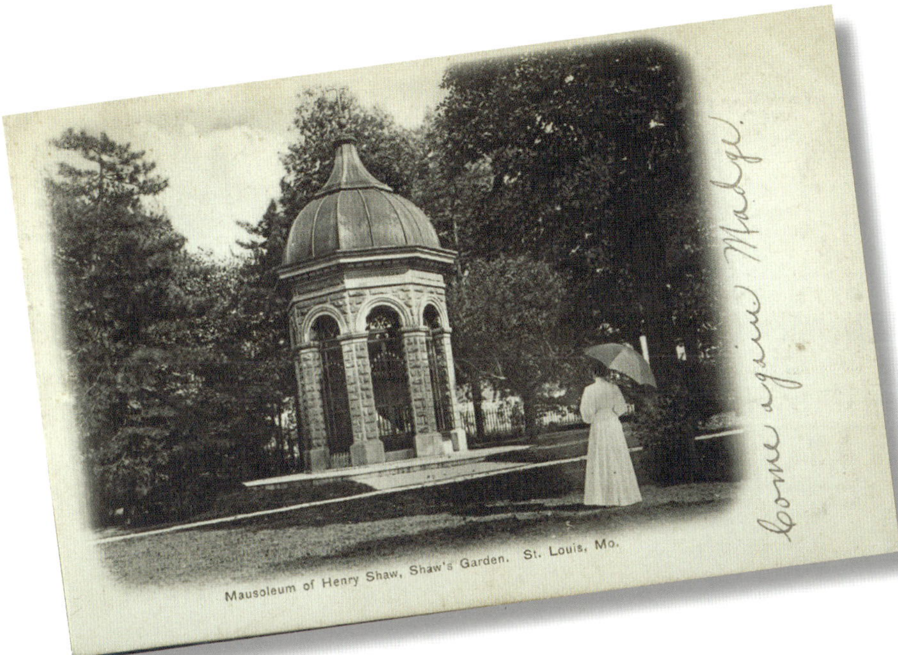

Cancelled 1906, $8-10

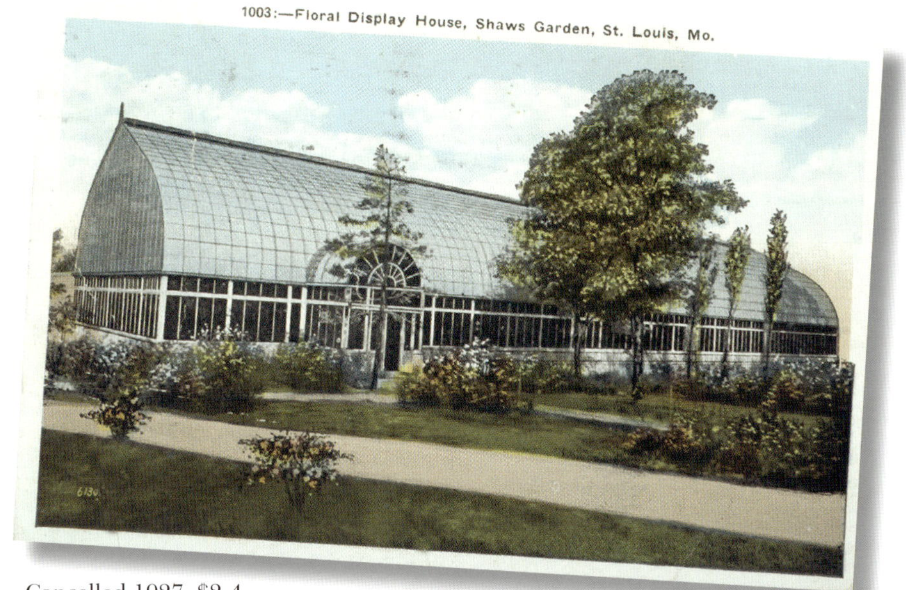

Cancelled 1927, $2-4

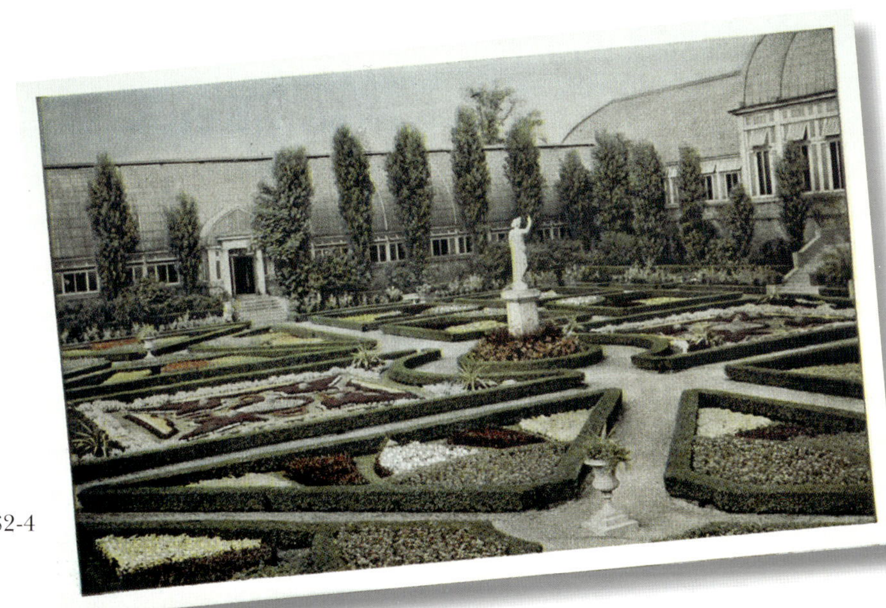
Circa 1914, $2-4

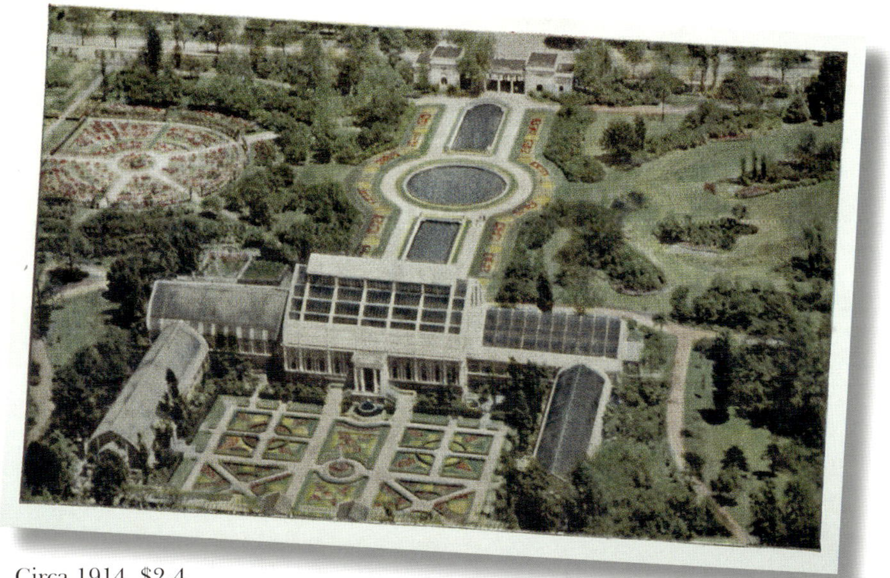

Circa 1914, $2-4

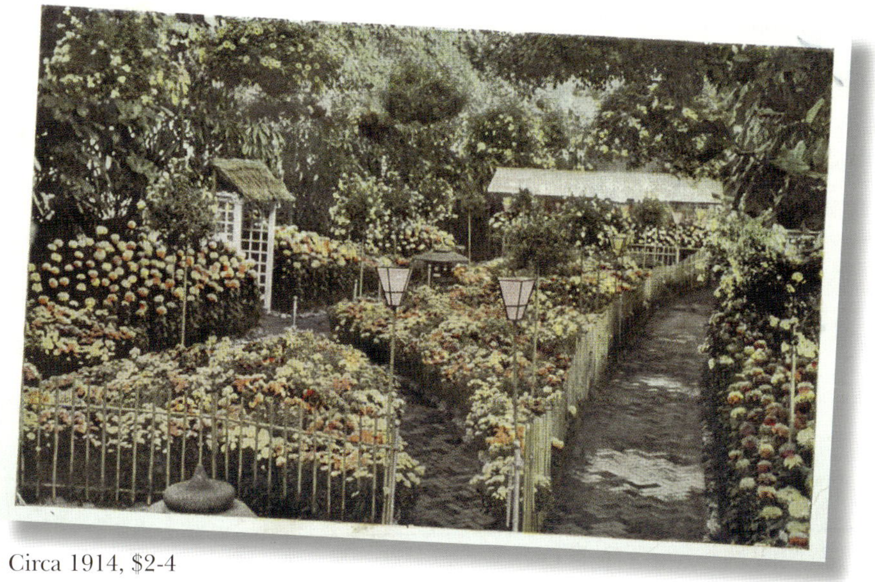

Circa 1914, $2-4

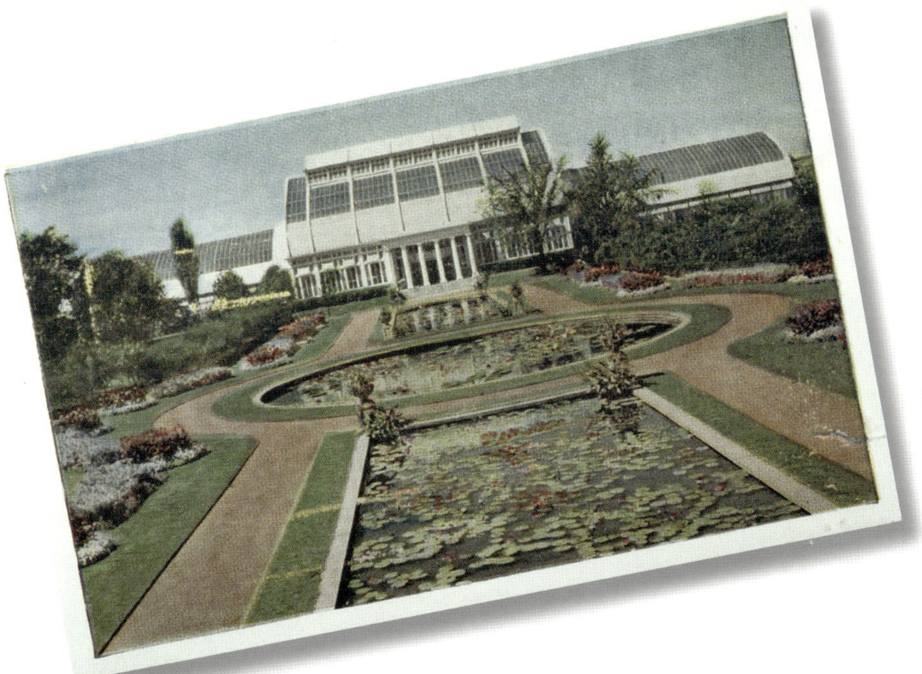

Circa 1914, $2-4

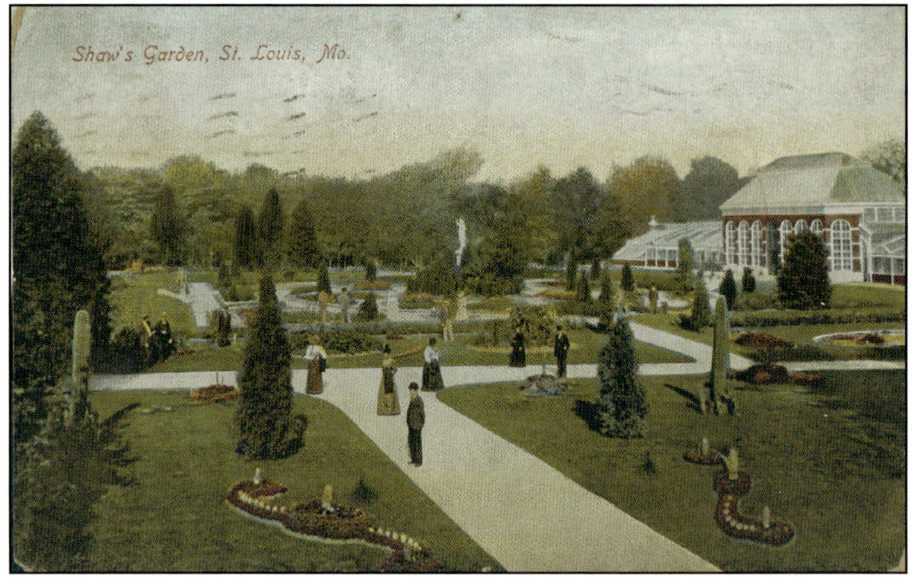

Cancelled 1907, $2-4

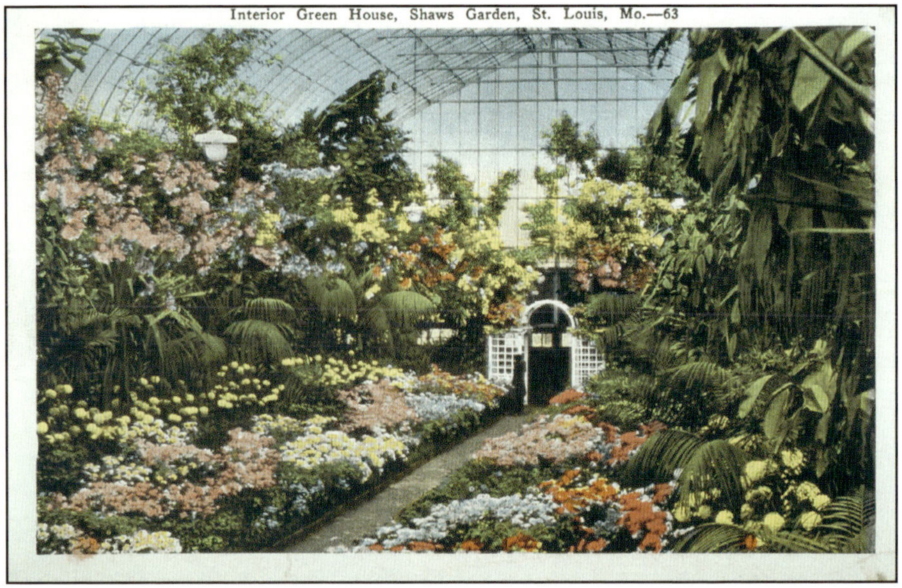

Cancelled 1929, $2-4

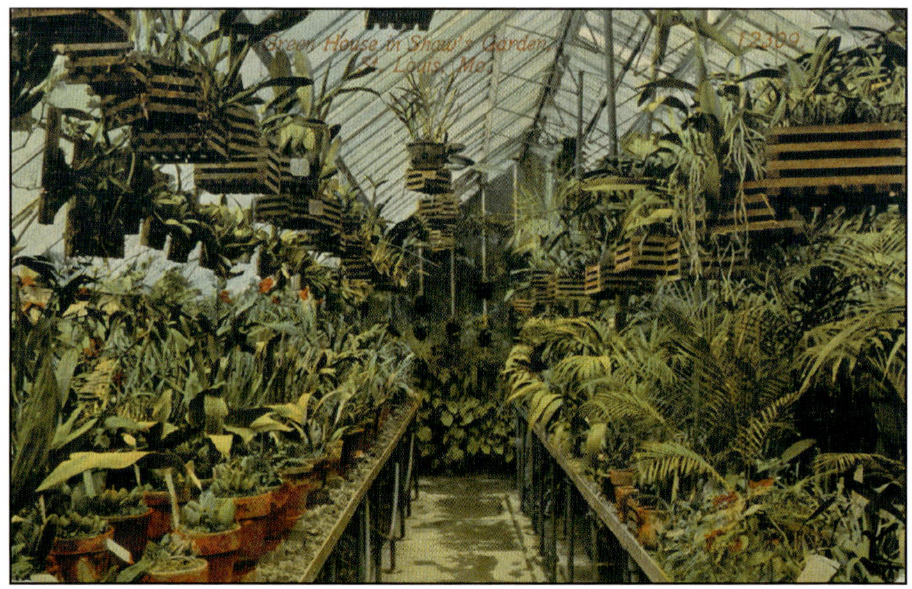

Cancelled 1914, $2-4

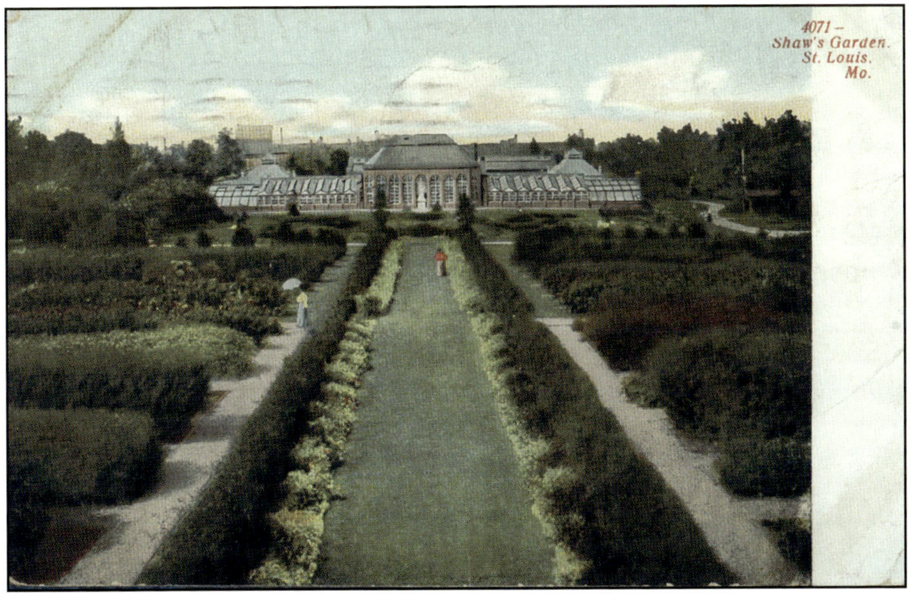

Circa Early 1900s, $8-10

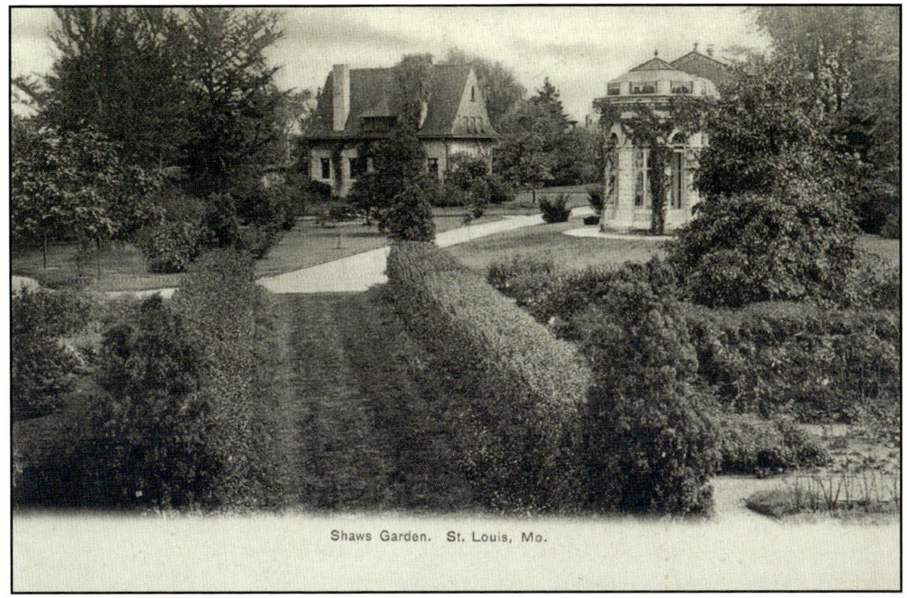

Cancelled 1909, $2-4

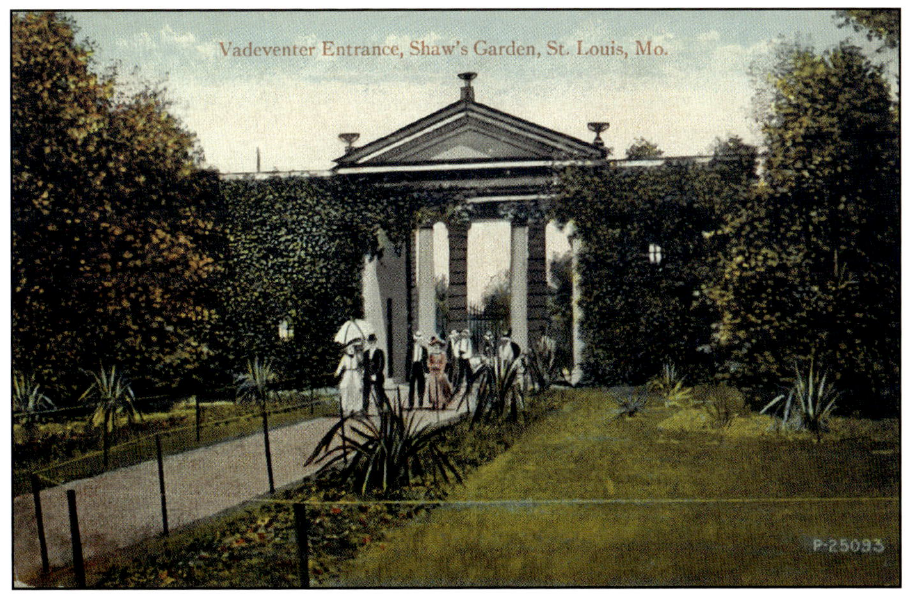

Circa 1907, $2-4

Cancelled 1912, $2-4

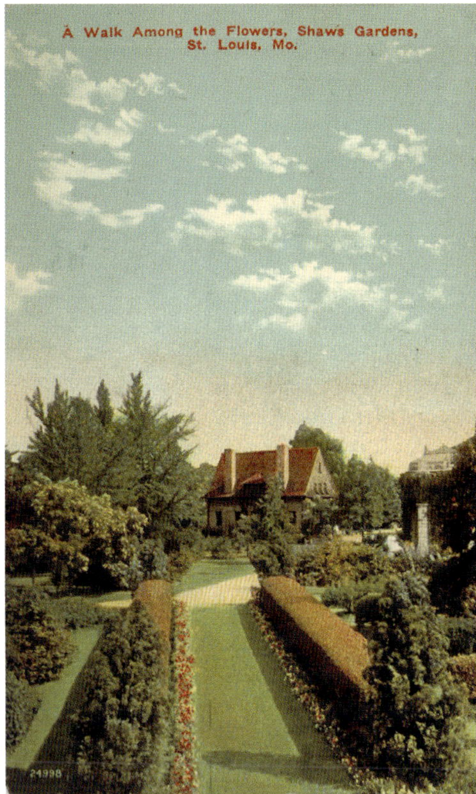

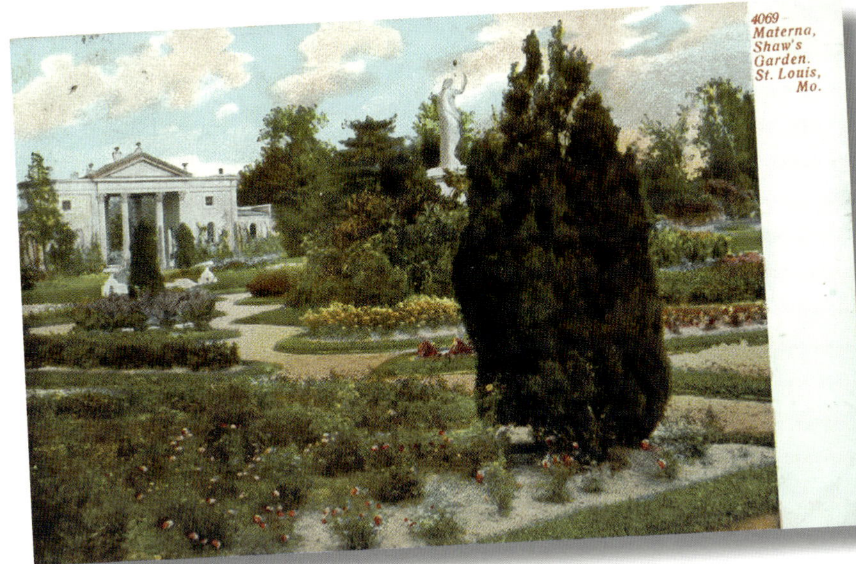

Cancelled 1909, $2-4

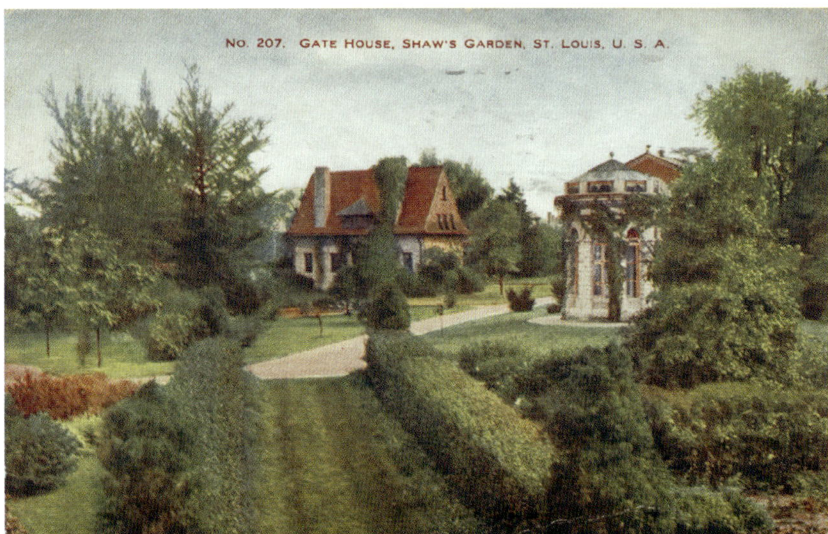

Cancelled 1907, $2-4

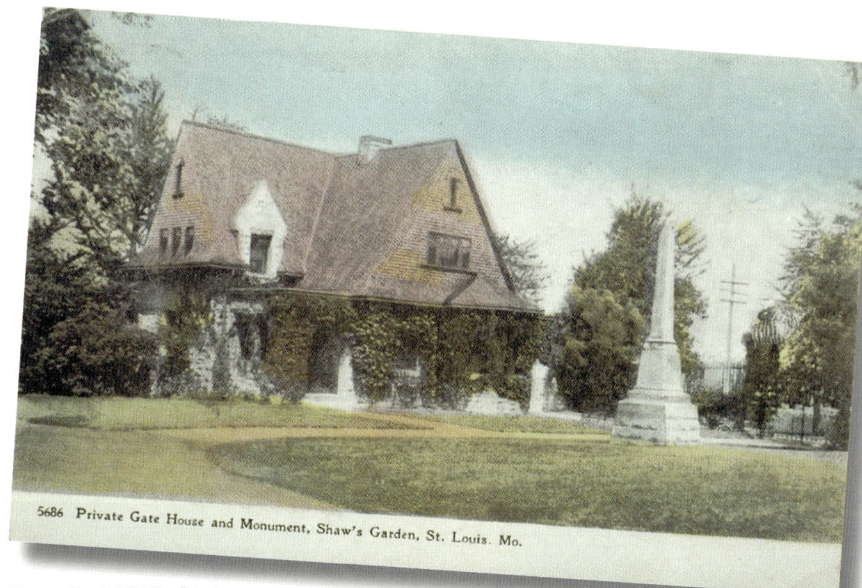

Cancelled 1908, $2-4

Other Great Places!

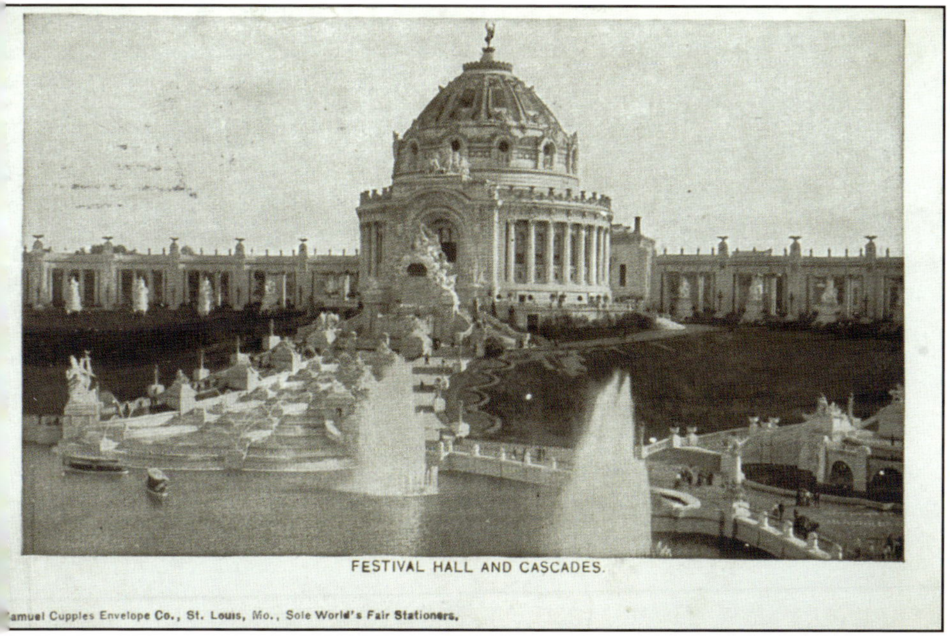

Festival Hall was designed in 1901 for the Louisiana Purchase Exposition (World's Fair), which was held in St. Louis in 1904. With it's 145-foot wide dome, it was the main focus of the fair and seated 4,000 guests. It featured an enormous stage that was able to support a full orchestra and was home to the world's largest pipe organ. Standing on a hill, which sat 200 feet below the top of the dome, the entrance to the hall was filled with fountains. These fountains were lined with colonnades, which ran into a lagoon. Three cascades poured out 90,000 gallons a minute, or 130,000,000 a day and could be illuminated at night.

Cancelled 1904 (twice), $8-10

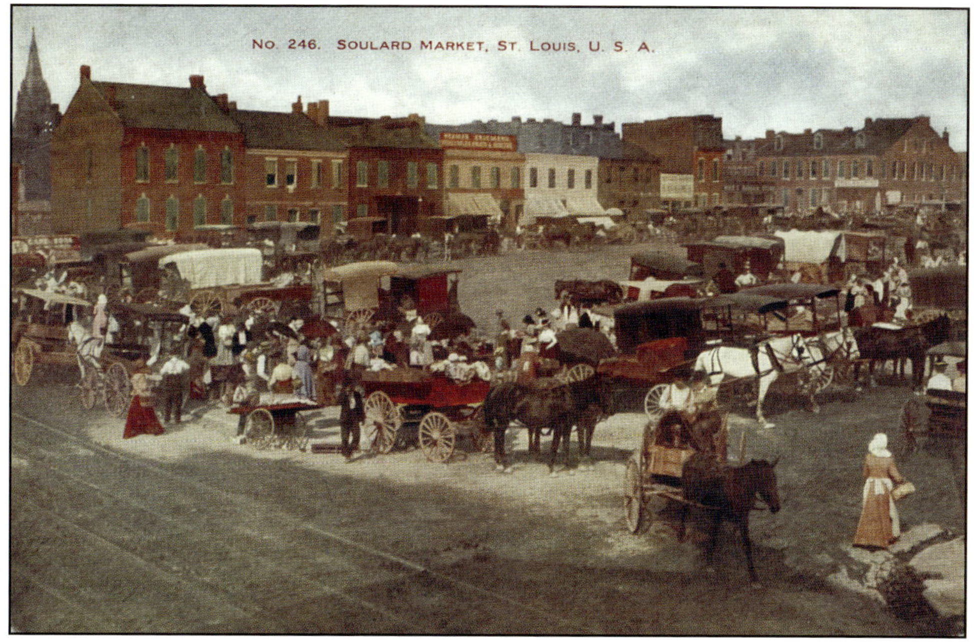

Resembling an old train terminal, Soulard Market is the oldest farmers market in the country. It is located less than five minutes south of downtown, St. Louis.

Circa Early 1900s, $3-5

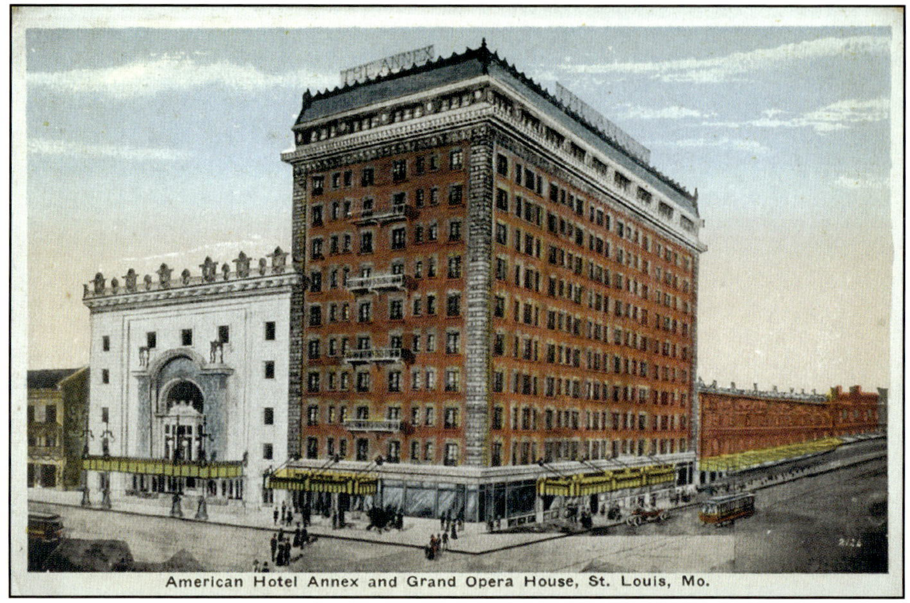

This view shows the American Hotel Annex and the Grand Opera House. The Grand Opera House, the building on the left, was once the city's oldest major theater. It started as the Varieties and was the only theater in St. Louis with floors that had interchangeable levels. Later, after it was sold to Benjamin DeBar, it was named DeBar's Opera House, and eventually became the Grand Opera House. It was destroyed by a fire in 1884, but rebuilt only to be demolished later. In its place now stands Busch Stadium.

Circa 1914, $2-4

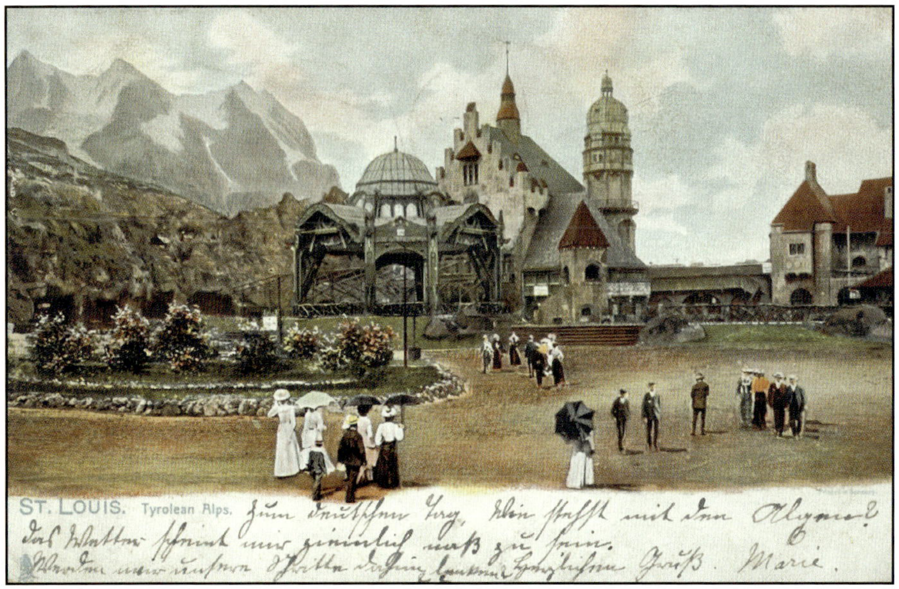

The Tyrolean Alps attraction; part of the World's Fair. Guests could enjoy beautiful scenery, delicious food and entertainment, such as comedians or concerts. The attraction featured castles, gabled homes, and churches as well.

Cancelled 1906, $3-5

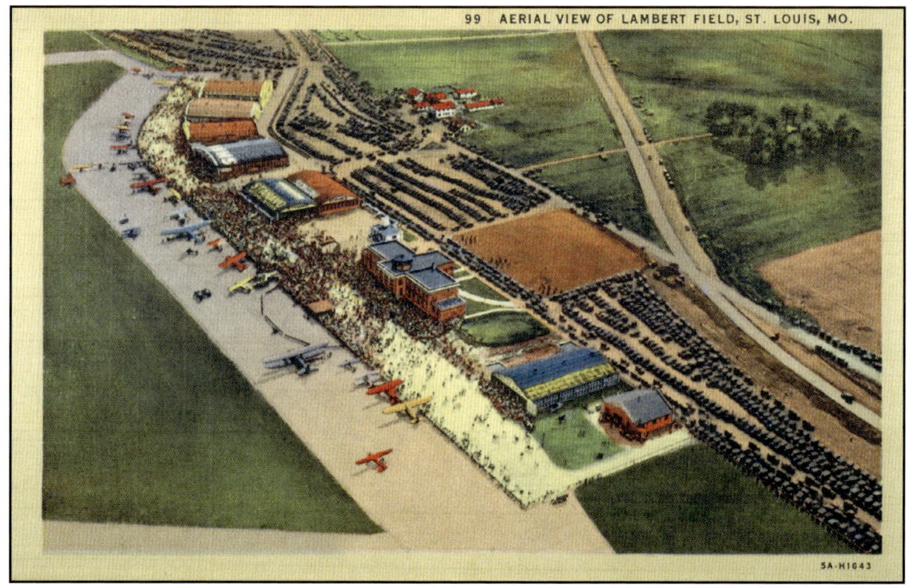

Lambert Field, which began as a balloon launch field is now one of the United States' largest airports. Spanning nearly 2,000 acres, it boasts four concourses and five runways.

Circa 1930s, $2-4

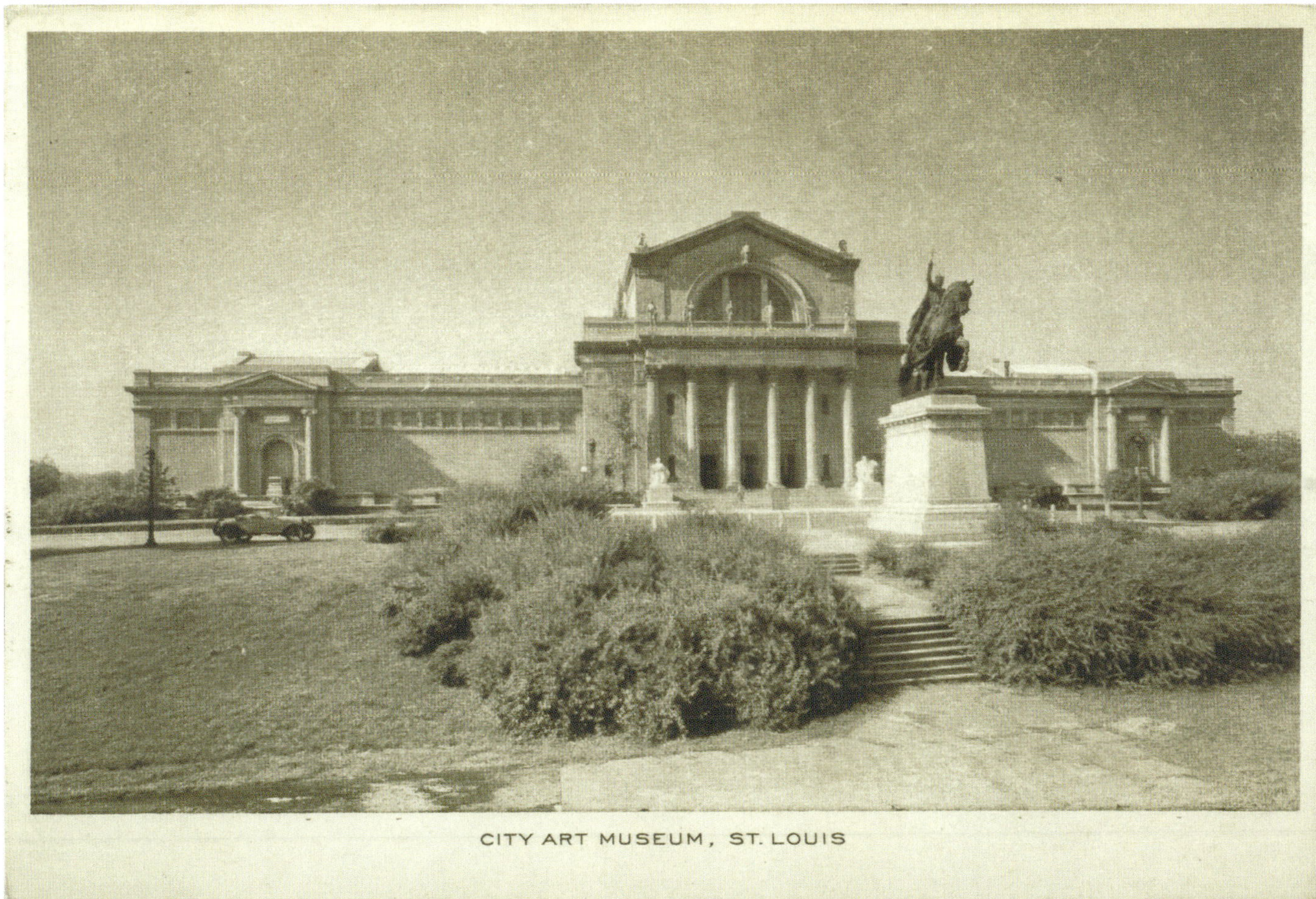

Circa 1907, $6-8

Originally located in downtown St. Louis and called the St. Louis School and Museum of Fine Arts, the St. Louis Art Museum was founded in 1879. After 1904's World Fair, the museum was demolished and rebuilt at its current location in Forest Park. The first meeting of the Ethical Society was held at the museum's Memorial Hall shown here. Priding itself on being a free museum, it has the largest collection of displayed artwork in the city.

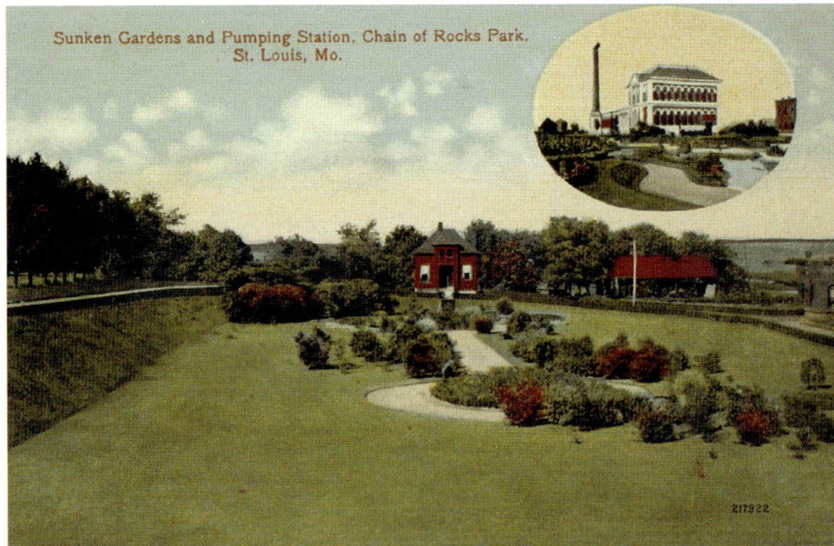

Beautiful sunken gardens with a view of the Public Library, and Christ Church Cathedral, the first Protestant Church founded west of the Mississippi River.

Circa 1907, $2-4

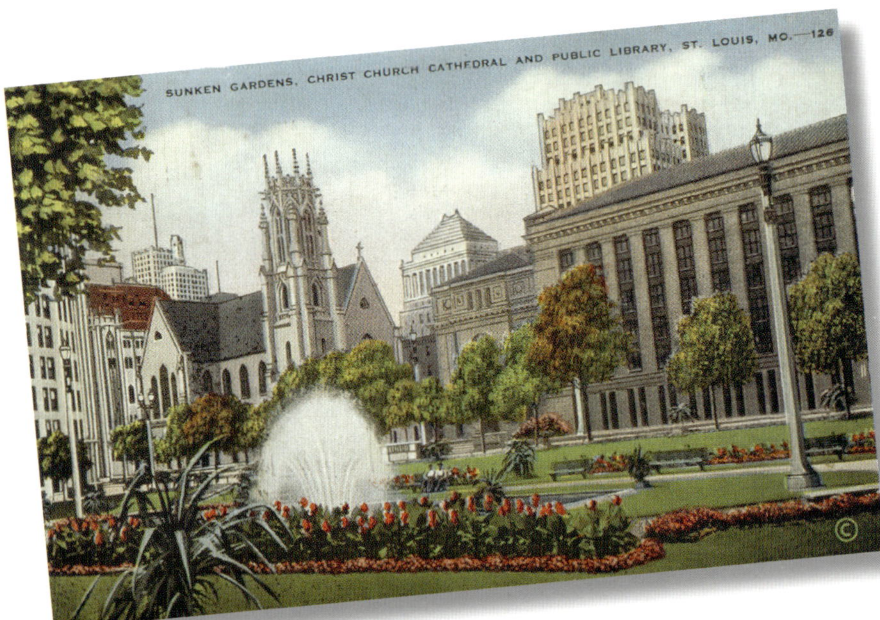

Circa 1914, $2-4

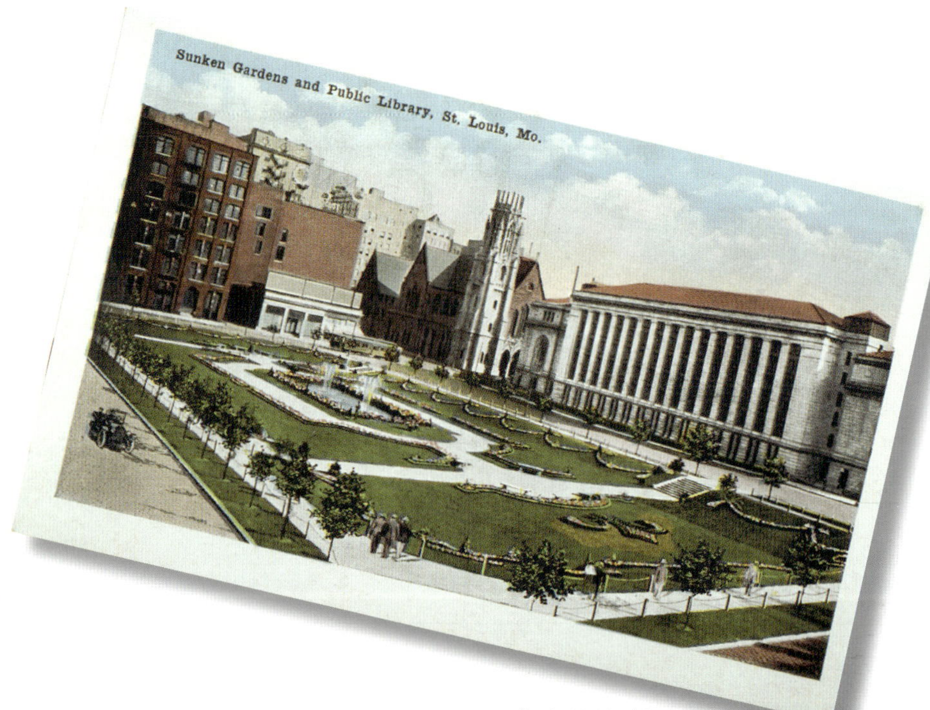

Cancelled 1941, $2-4

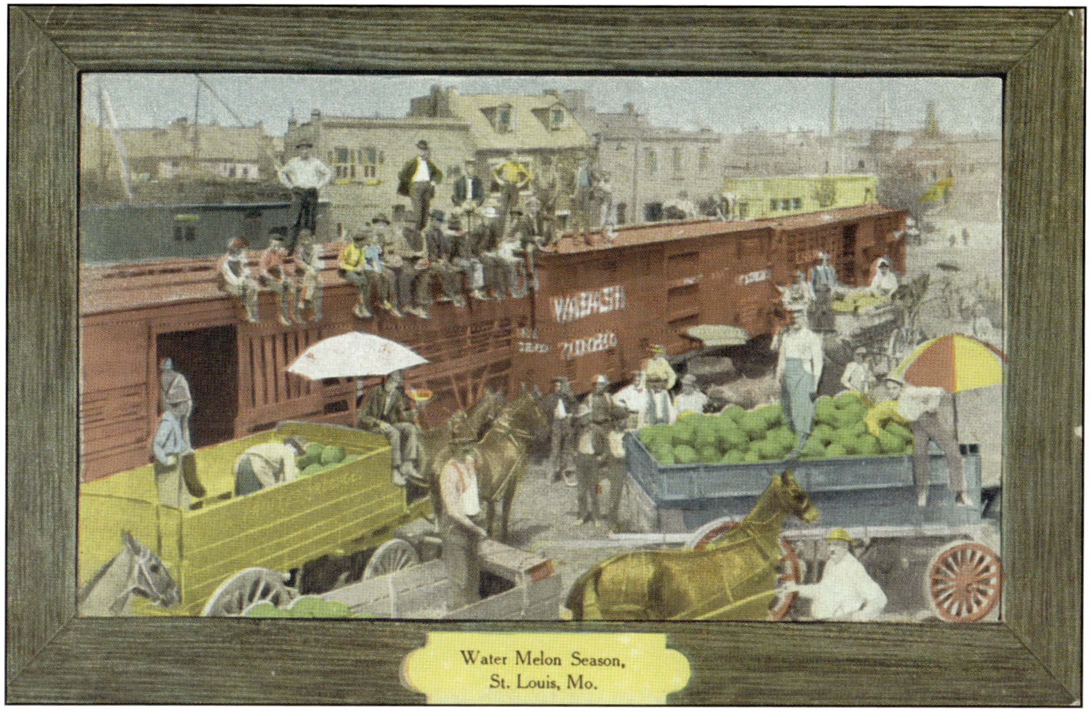

St. Louis natives enjoying the fine watermelon season at Wabash Station.

Circa 1907, $2-4

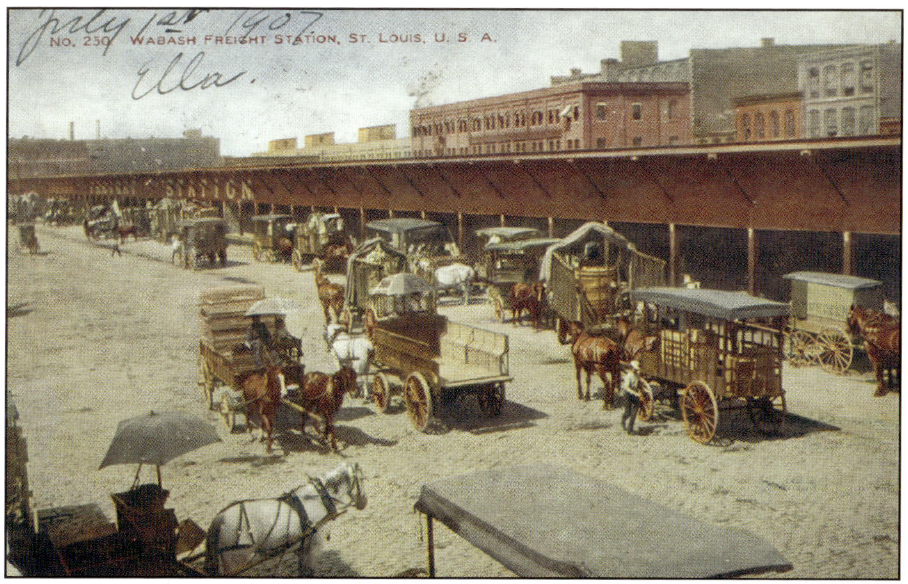

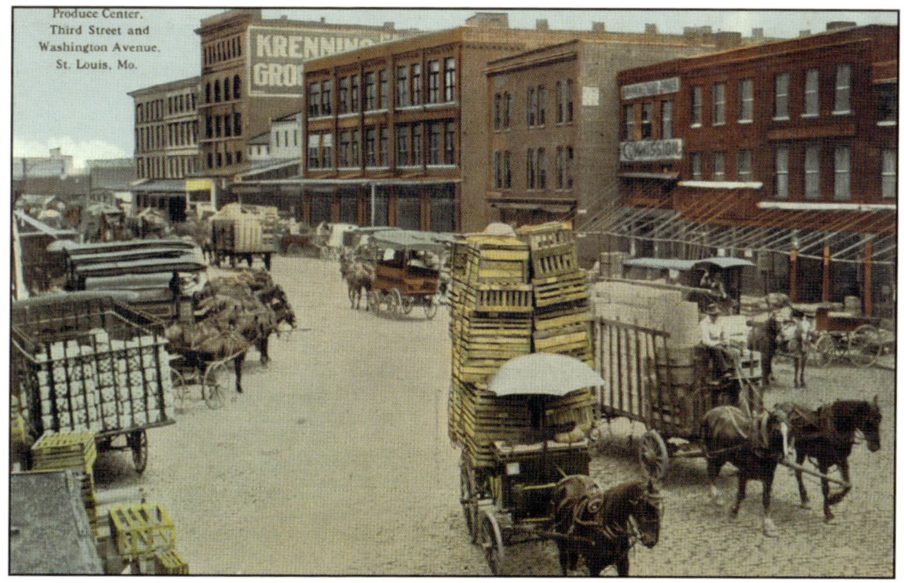

A view of the hustle and bustle of Wabash Station in St. Louis.

Cancelled 1907 (4 times), $3-5 (left)
Circa 1907, $2-4 (right)

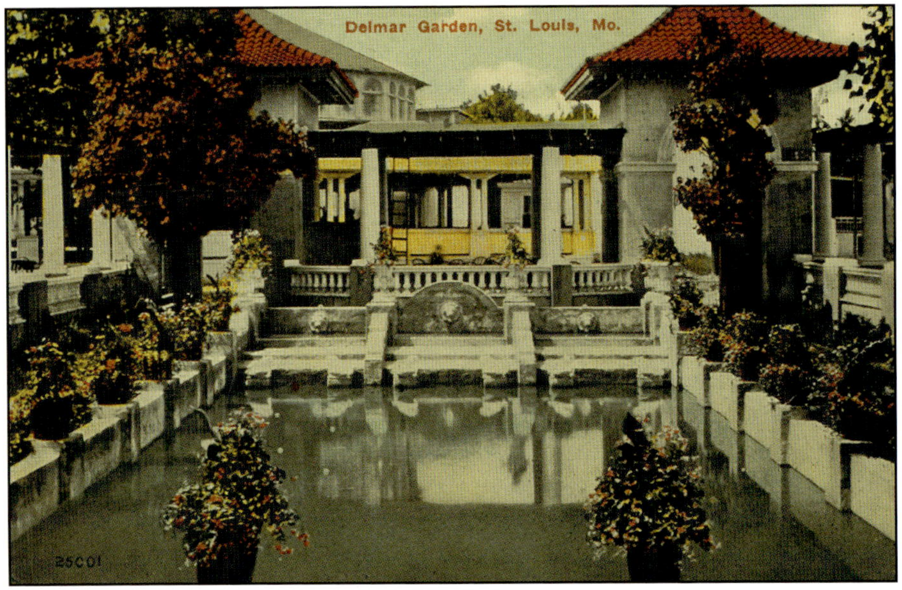

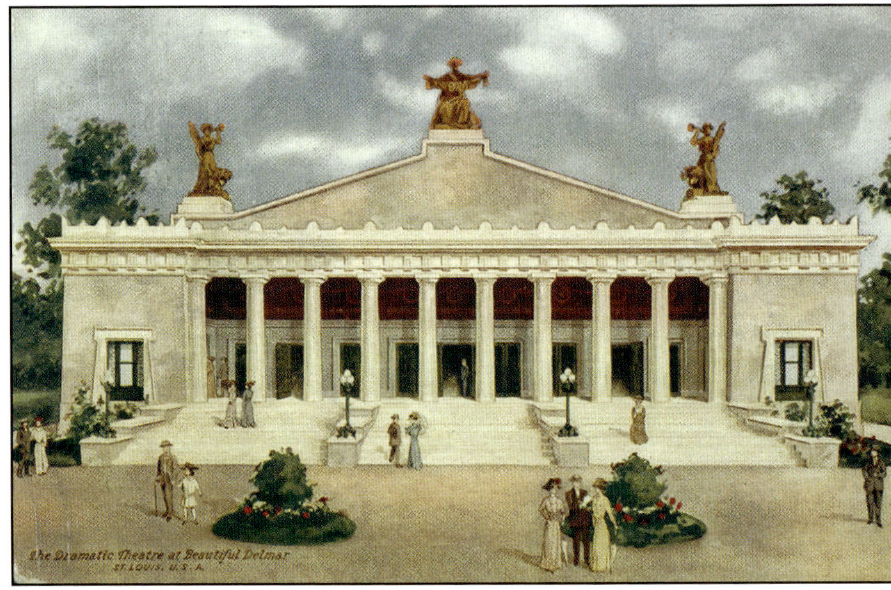

A beautiful view of the fountain outside Delmar Garden and the Dramatic Theatre, located on the grounds.

Cancelled 1913, $2-4 (left)
Cancelled 1909, $2-4 (right)

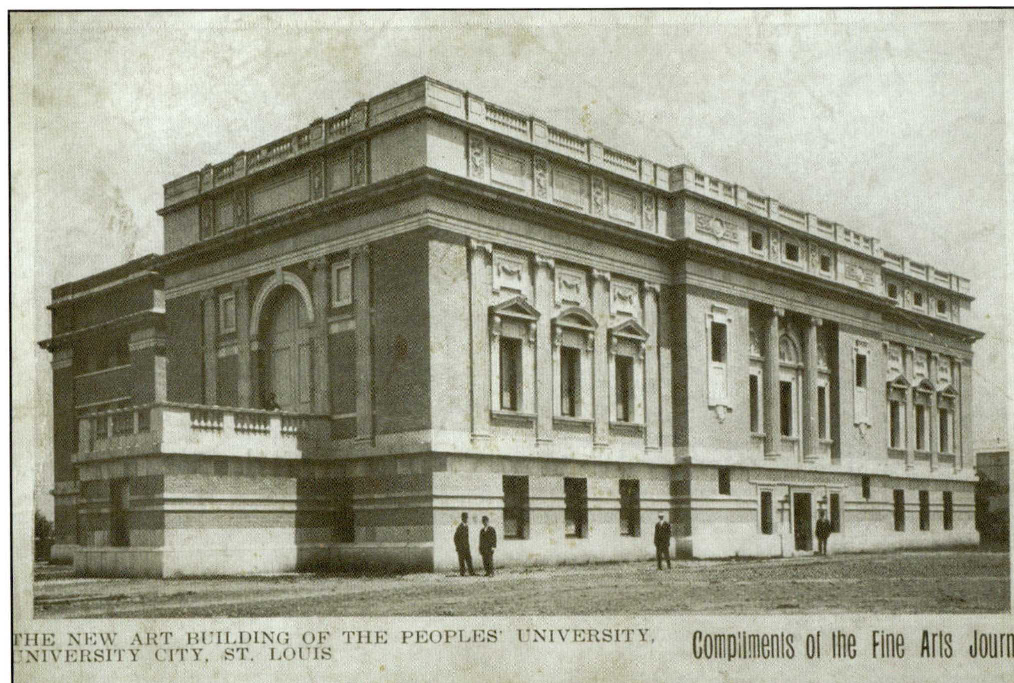

"The new art building of the Peoples' University" located in University City, St. Louis.

Circa Early 1900s, $6-8

The Streets of St. Louis

The city streets running through the busy metropolis of St. Louis have been bustling through the ages, as people moved to and fro—to work, to play, to grow. Though the streets on the following cards show different times and places, the charm of St. Louis shines through!

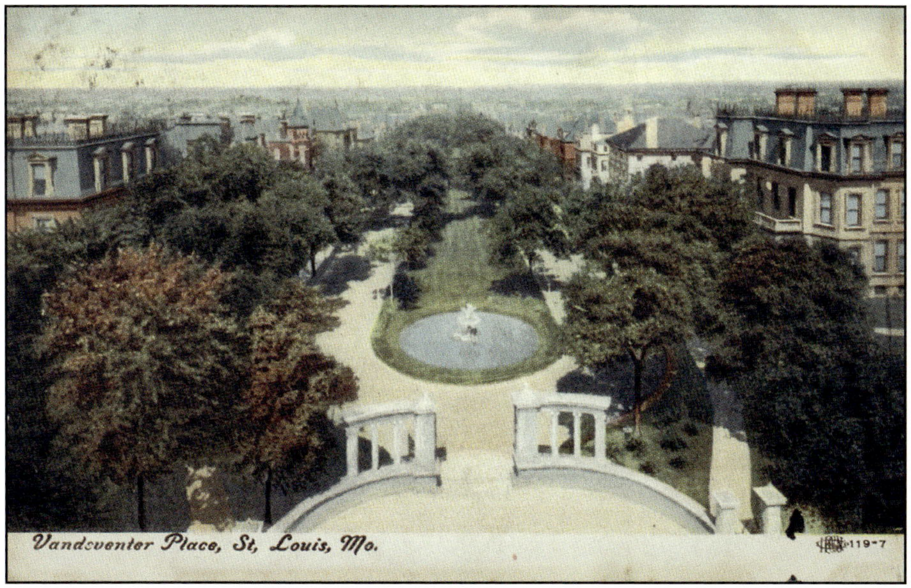

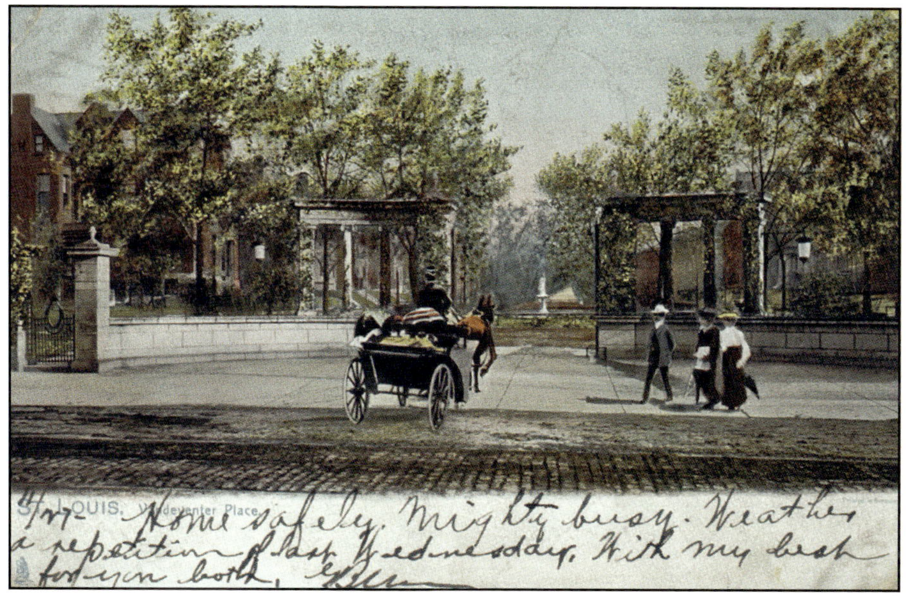

Vandeventer Place, designed in 1870 and named for Peter L. Vandeventer, who owned the tract where it was built. Vandeventer Place was designed as a private street with rigid restrictions for its occupants. This exquisite neighborhood, which was constructed to keep the noise and dirt from the city out, was known to house such wealthy residents as the mayor and president of the World's Fair, David R. Franci, and H. Clay Pierce, an oil magnate whose home is believed to have cost $800,000.

Cancelled 1908, $2-4 (left)
Circa 1907, $2-4 (right)

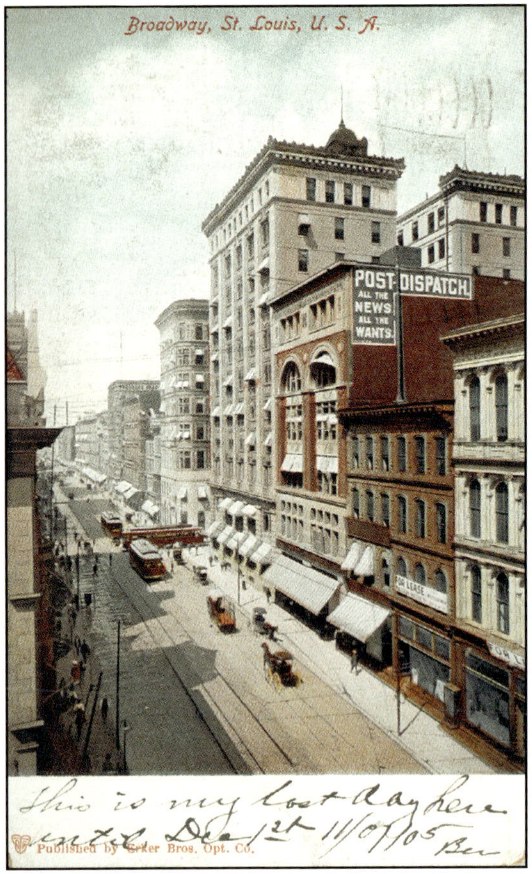

Cancelled 1905 (twice), $3-5

Several views of Broadway, North from Pine Street. Notice the Post-Dispatch building on the right of the first card shown here. The St. Louis Post-Dispatch is a daily newspaper covering local, national, and international news. It was founded in 1878, when Joseph Pulitzer merged the *St. Louis Dispatch* and *St. Louis Post*.

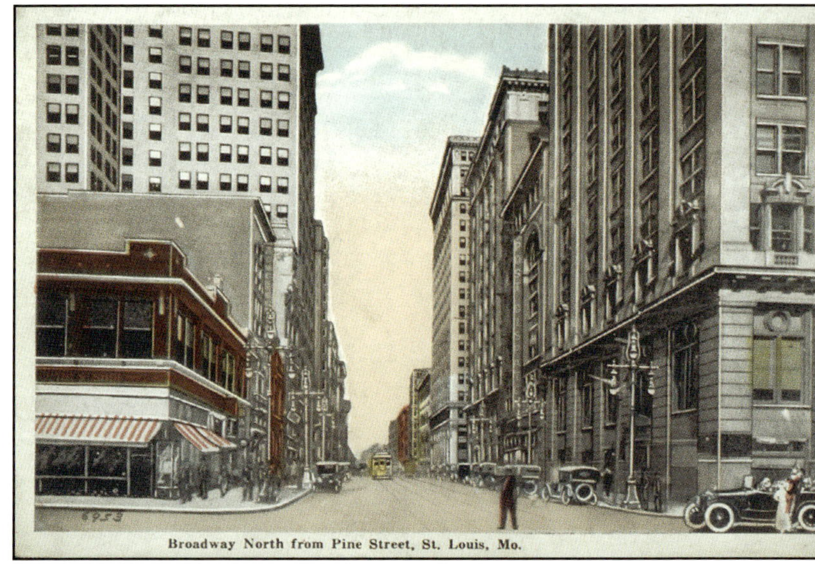

Circa 1907, $2-4

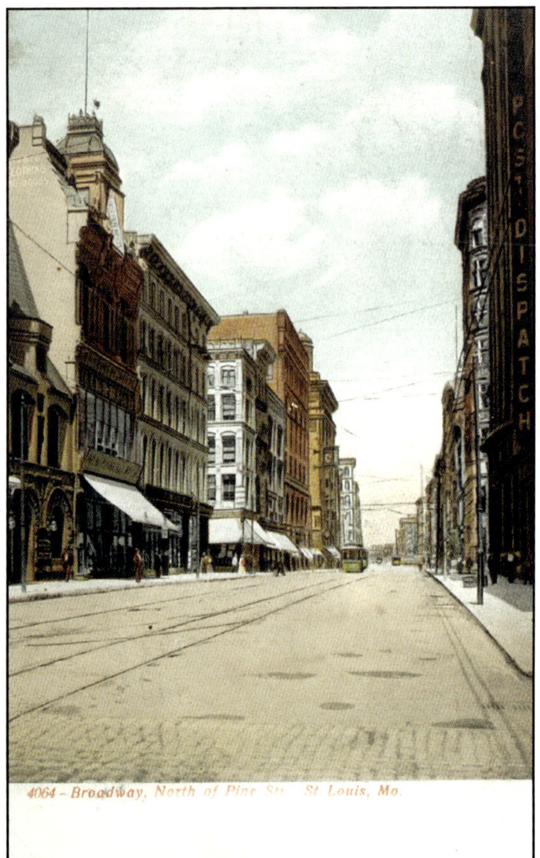

Cancelled 1908, $2-4

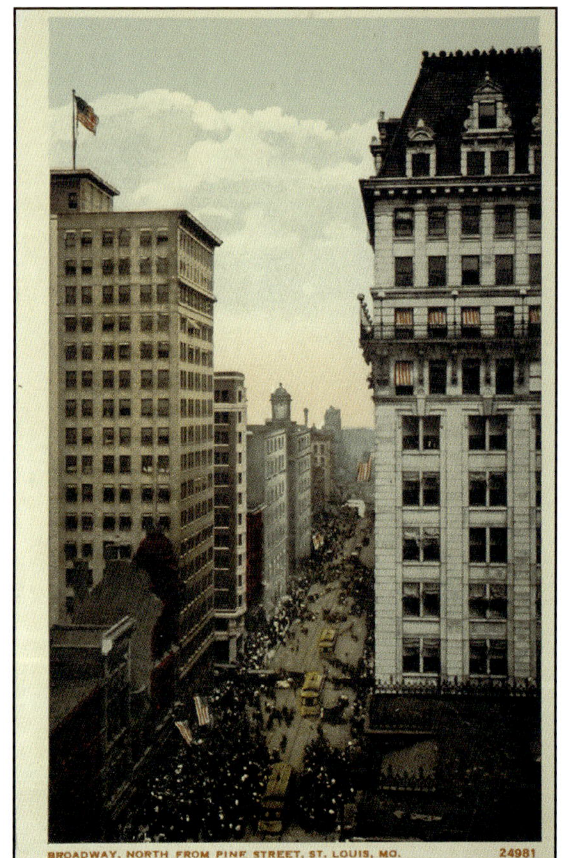

Circa 1907, $2-4

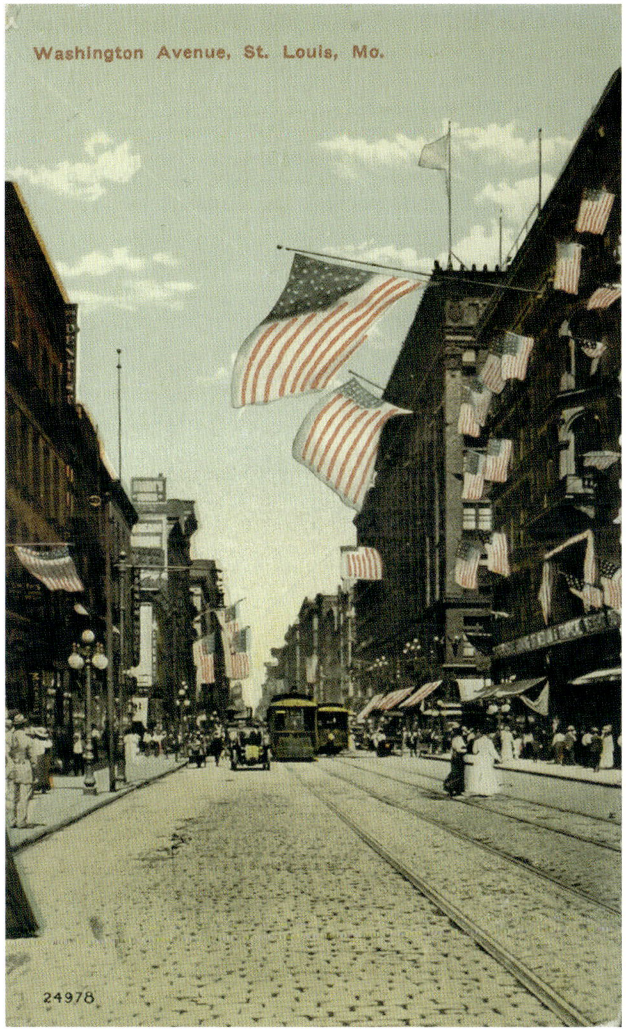

Circa 1907, $2-4

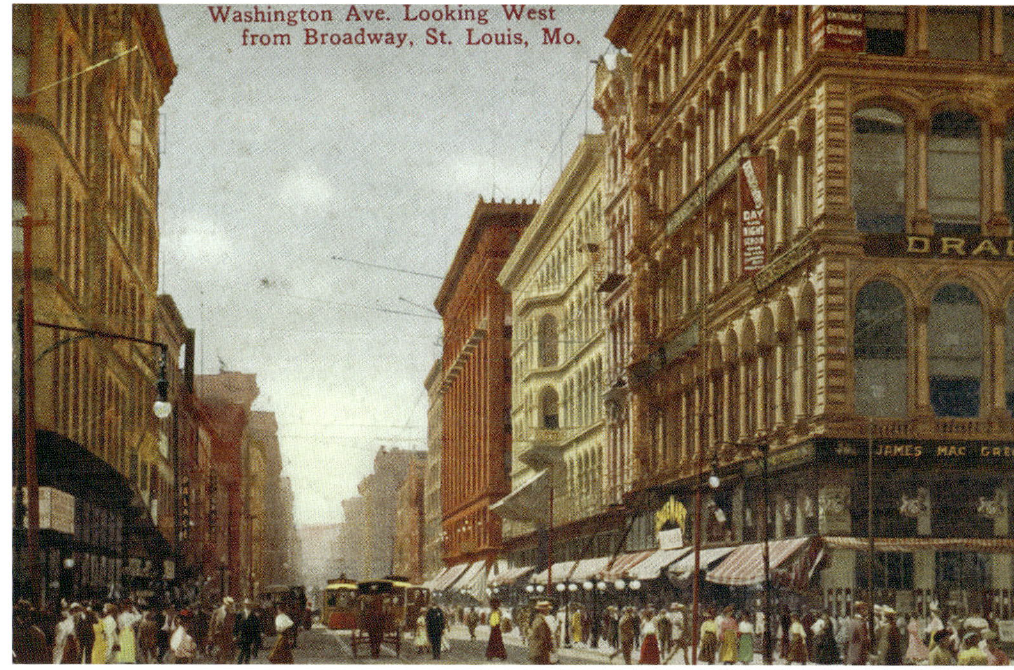

Circa 1907, $2-4

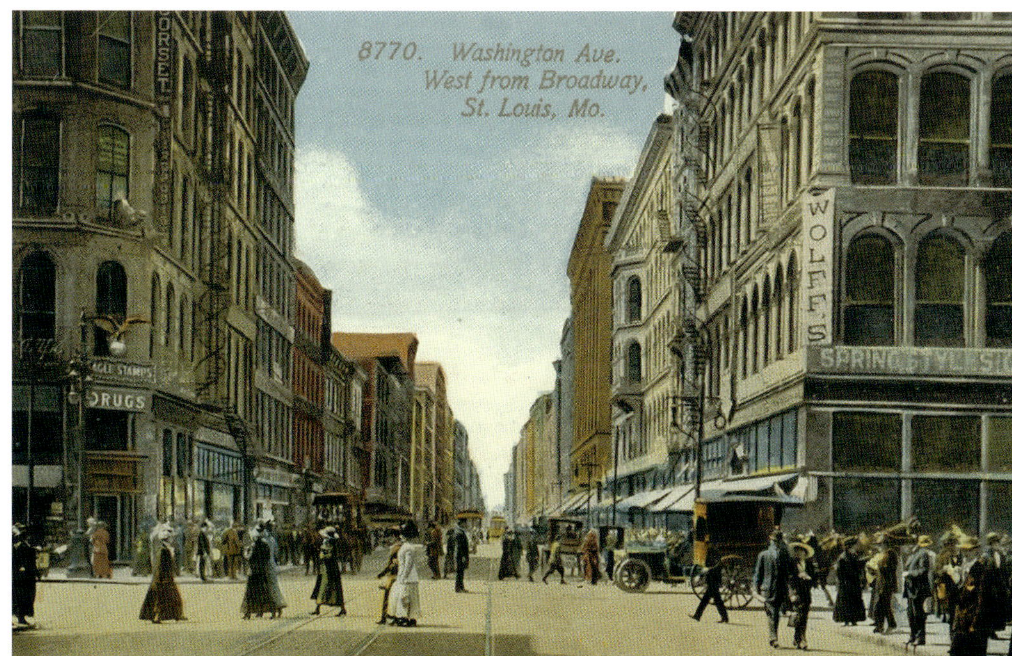

Circa 1907, $2-4

Washington Avenue, formerly a popular shopping district. Notice the vendors lining the streets. Plans have been set in motion to revive Washington Avenue to its former life with galleries, nightclubs, and other entertainment.

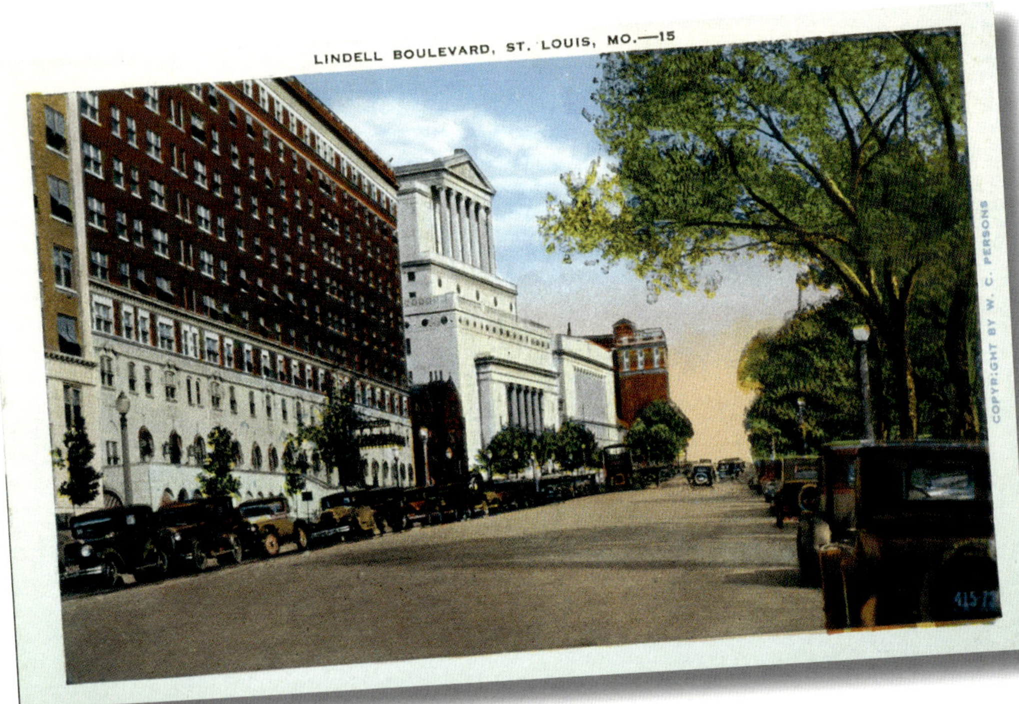

Lindell Boulevard, home of the St. Louis Club, The Automobile Club, and the Jefferson Memorial, which houses the Lindbergh collection. The western border leads into Washington University's campus. Notice the red building in both photos, giving us a view of the street from both directions.

Circa 1930s, $2-4

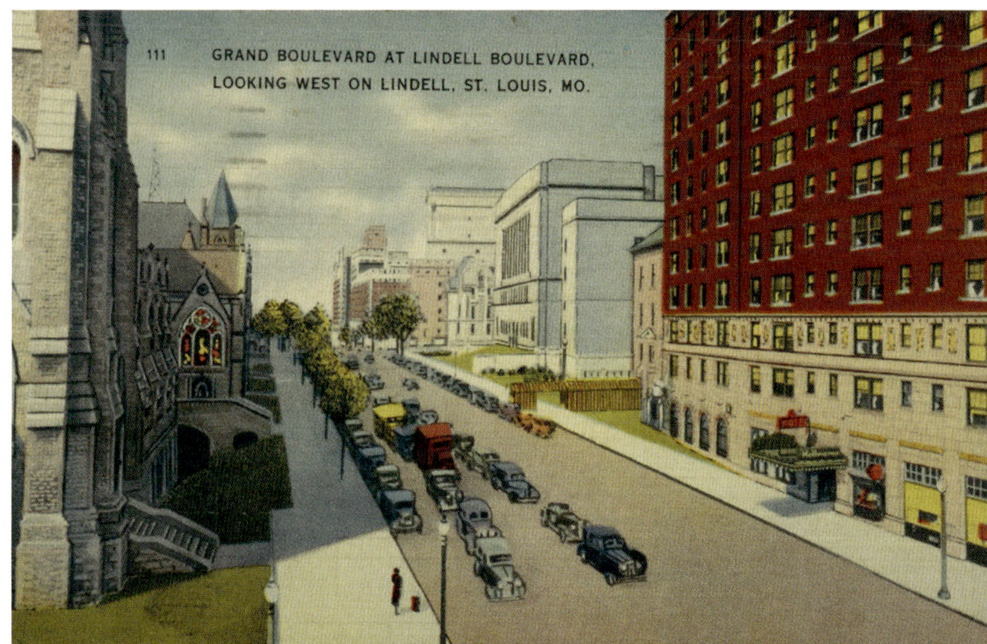

Cancelled 1940, $2-4

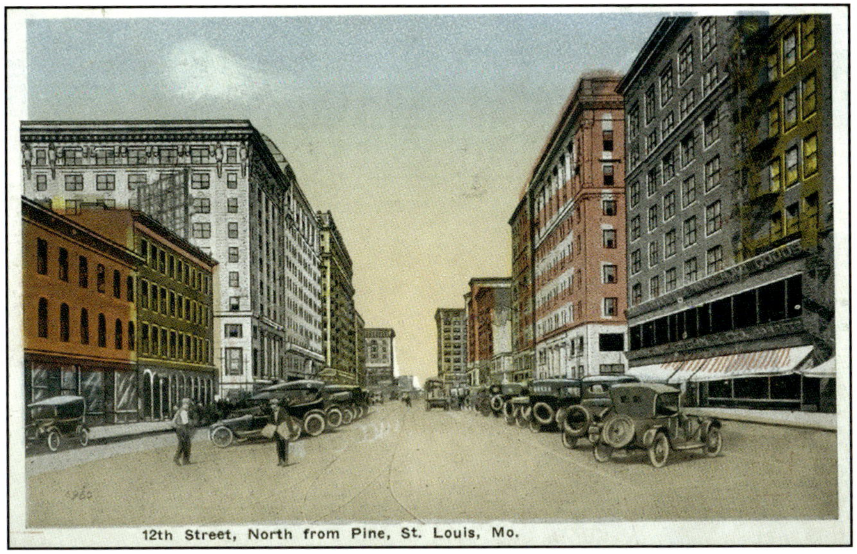

Circa 1922, $2-4

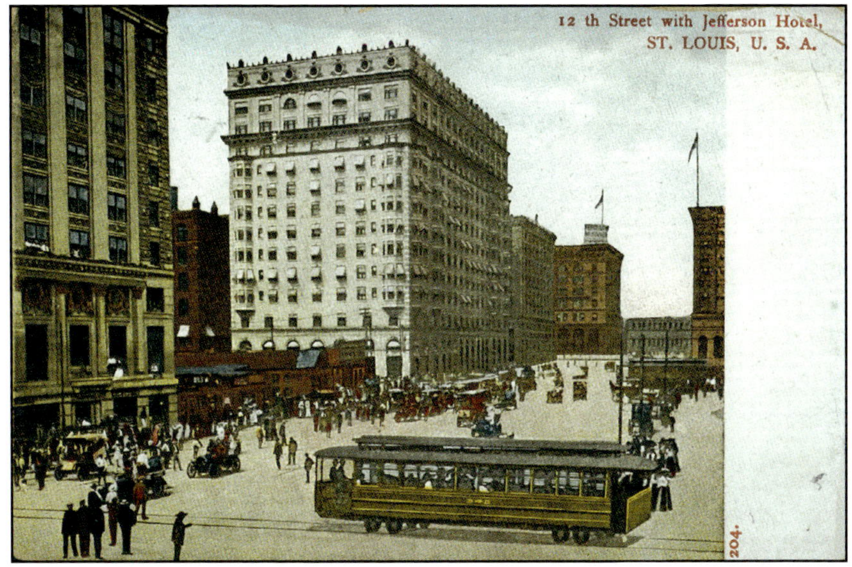

Cancelled 1905, $2-4

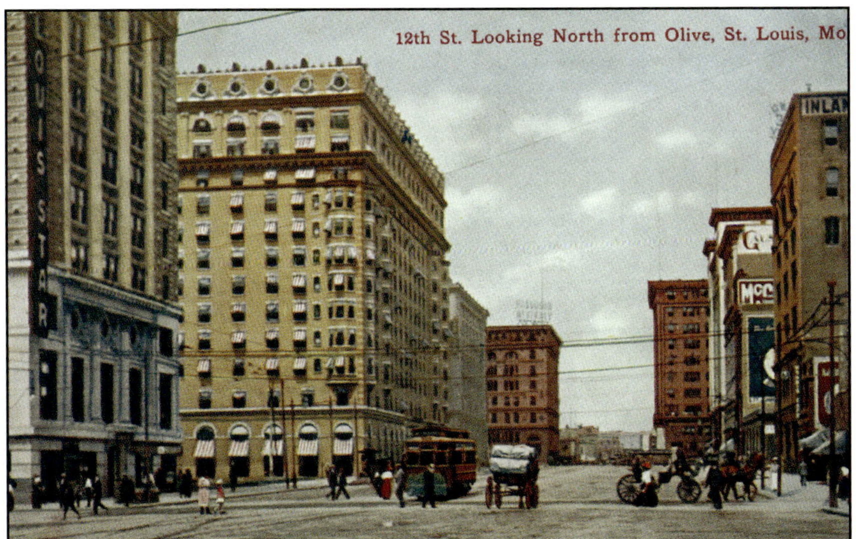

Circa 1907, $2-4

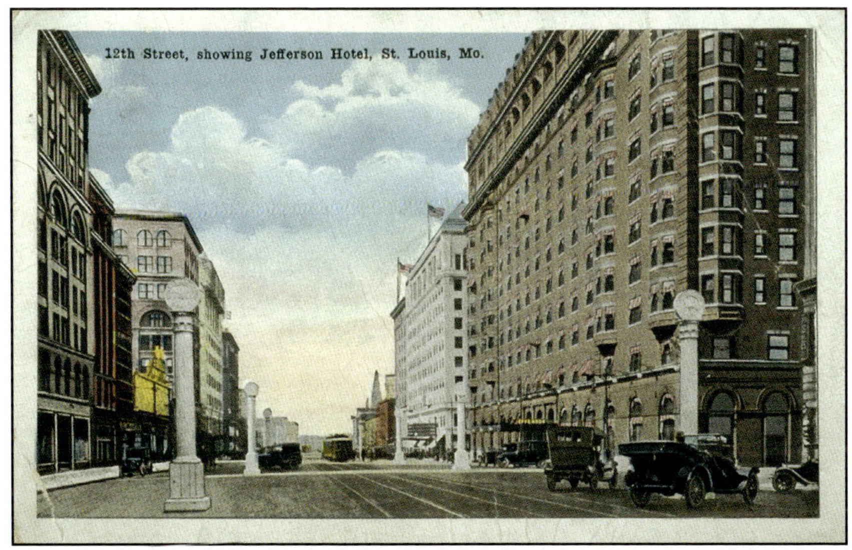

Cancelled 1918, $2-4

Four different views give us a complete picture of 12th Street. We can see such prominent buildings in St. Louis as Electric Light and Power Company and the Jefferson Hotel, which was one of the largest and most modern hotels in the city at the time.

Looking North on "Kingshighway," we see a church on our right and several other buildings lining the street.

Circa 1907, $2-4

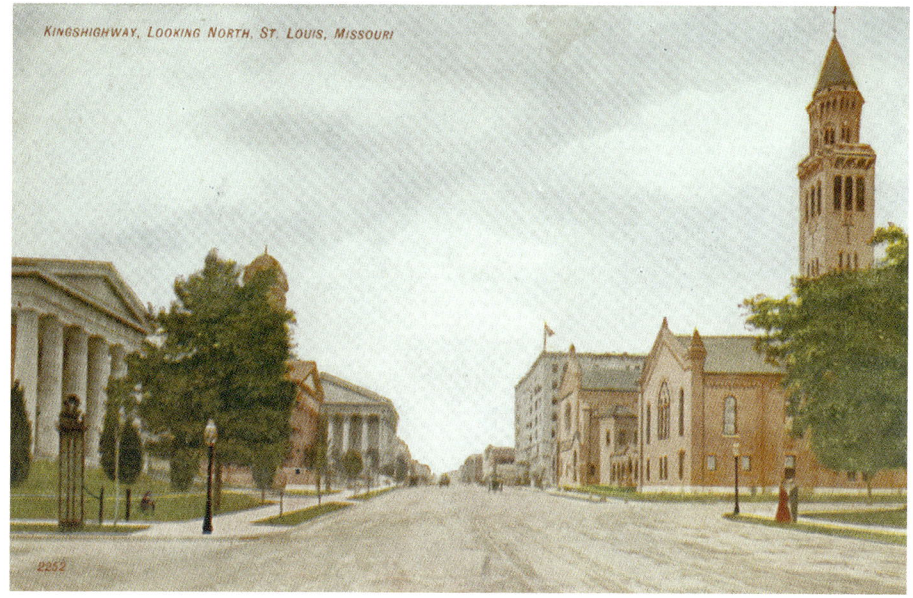

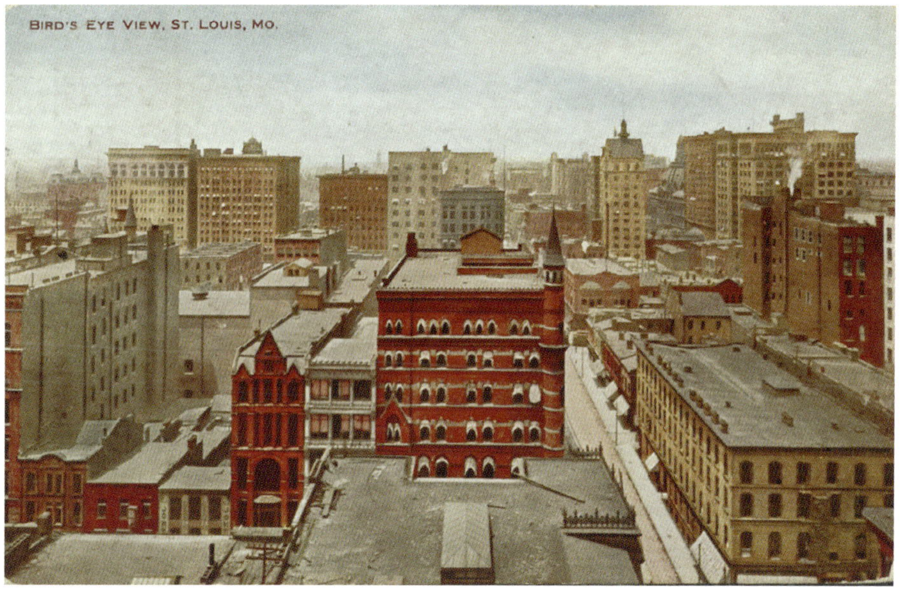

This bird's eye view of the city allows us to see the beautiful architecture and the many important buildings located in St. Louis.

Cancelled 1907, $2-4

A group of skyscrapers grazing the St. Louis city skyline.

Circa 1907, $2-4

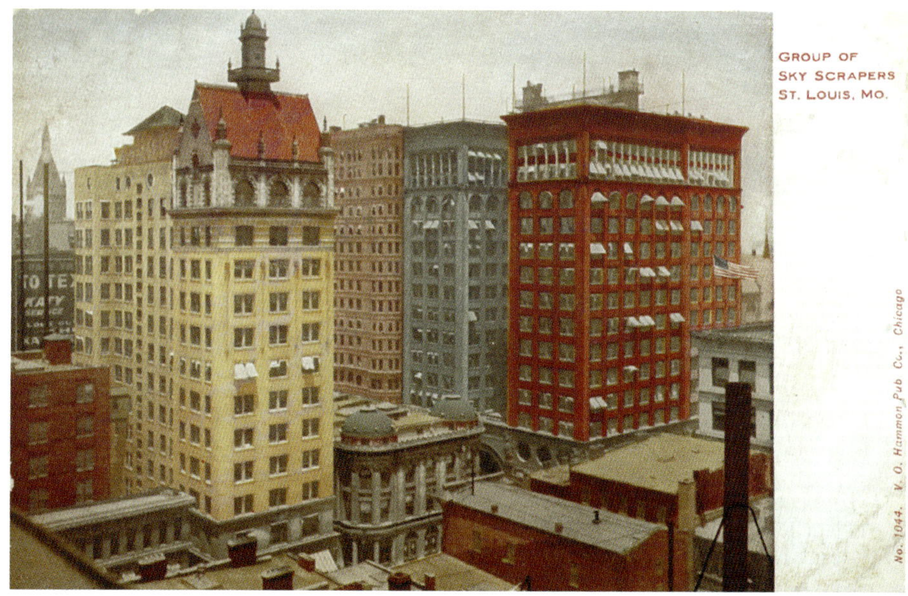

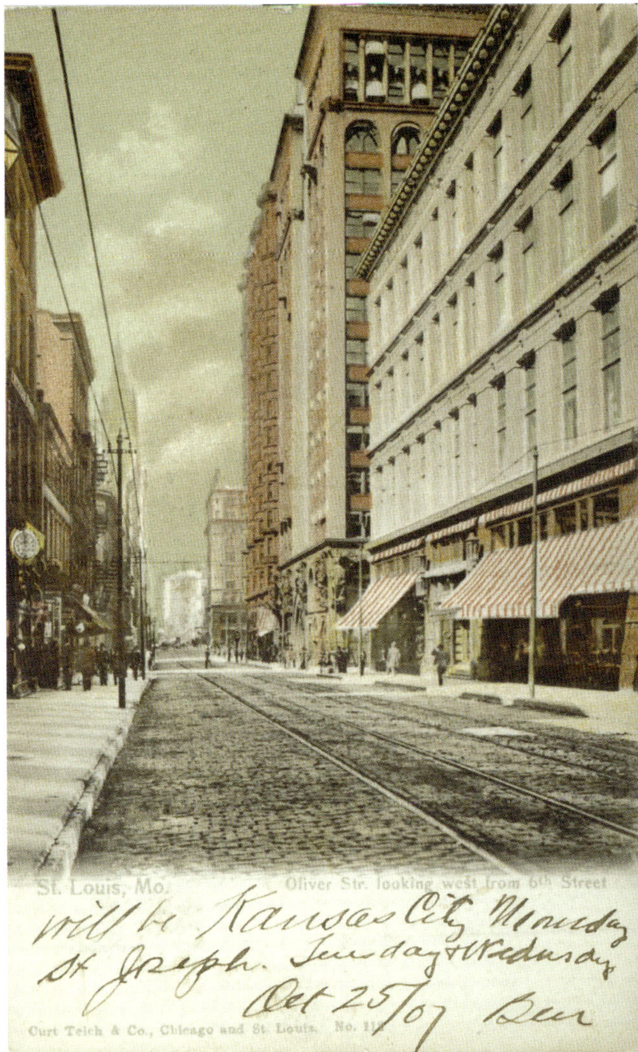

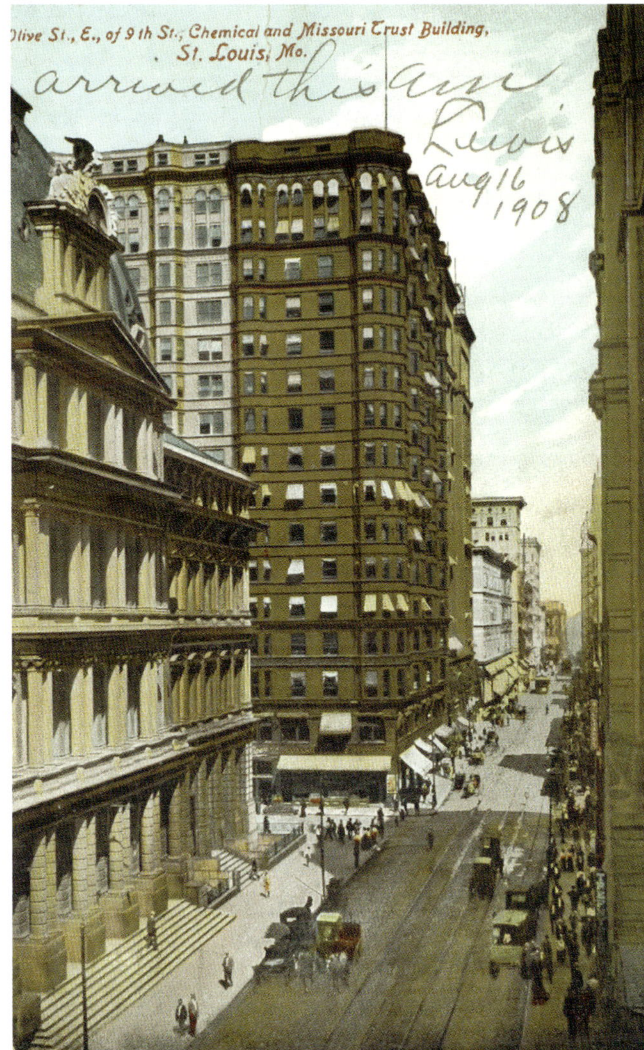

Alternate angles of Olive Street allow us to see more of the area. The Chemical and Missouri Trust Building are clearly visible.

Cancelled 1907, $2-4 (left
Cancelled 1908, $2-4 (right)

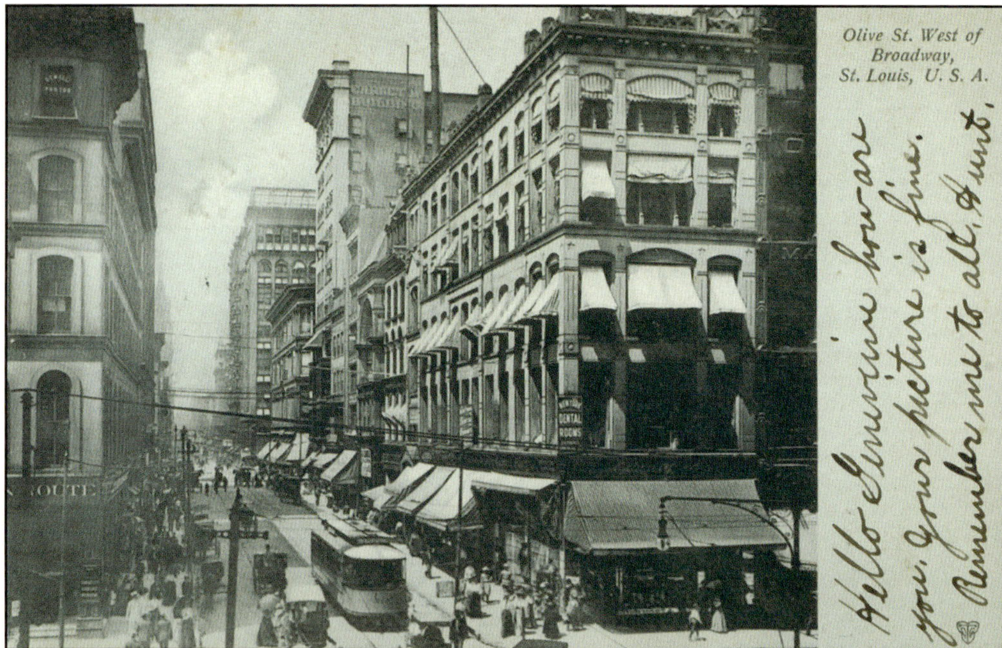

Fabulous black-and-white photo postcards show the heart of downtown St. Louis. Two separate views of Olive Street allow us to see most of the structures that attracted visitors.

Cancelled 1905, $2-4

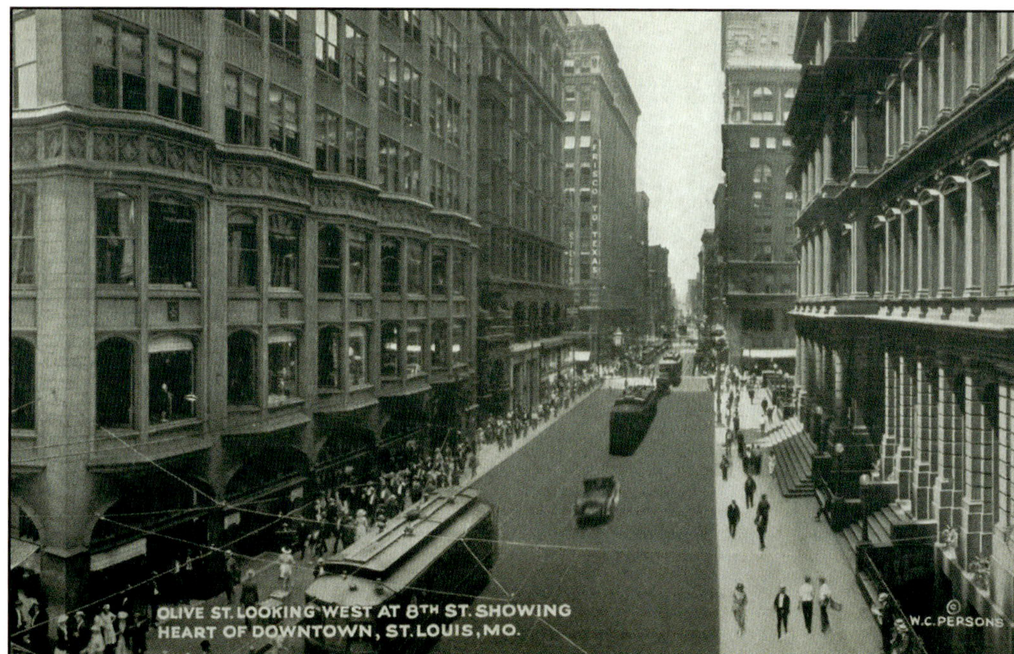

Circa 1907, $2-4

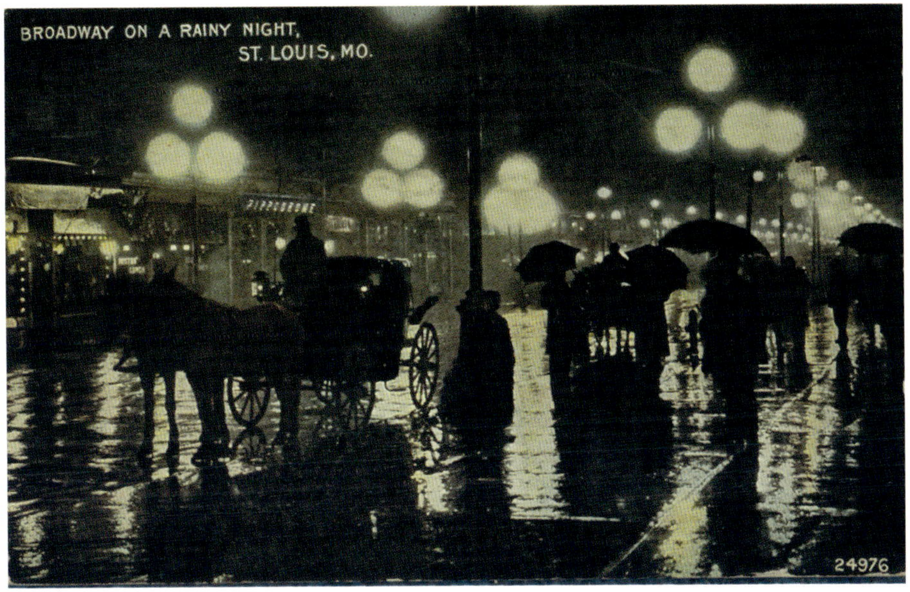

Even a rainy night on Broadway can't put a damper on these city-goers' fun.

Cancelled 1914, $2-4

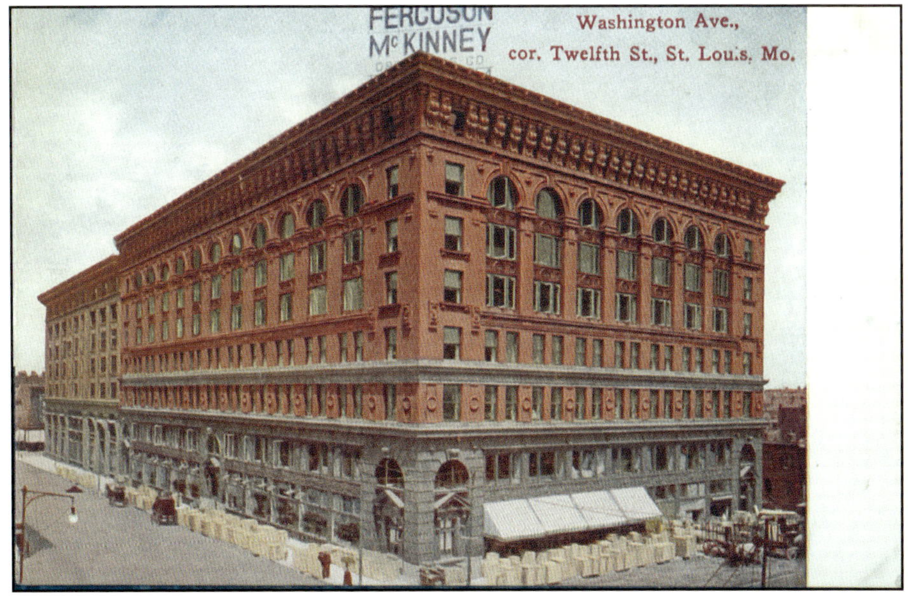

The Lesser-Goldman Building, one of the three biggest on Washington Avenue. It is located on the corner of Washington Avenue and 12th Street.

Circa 1907, $2-4

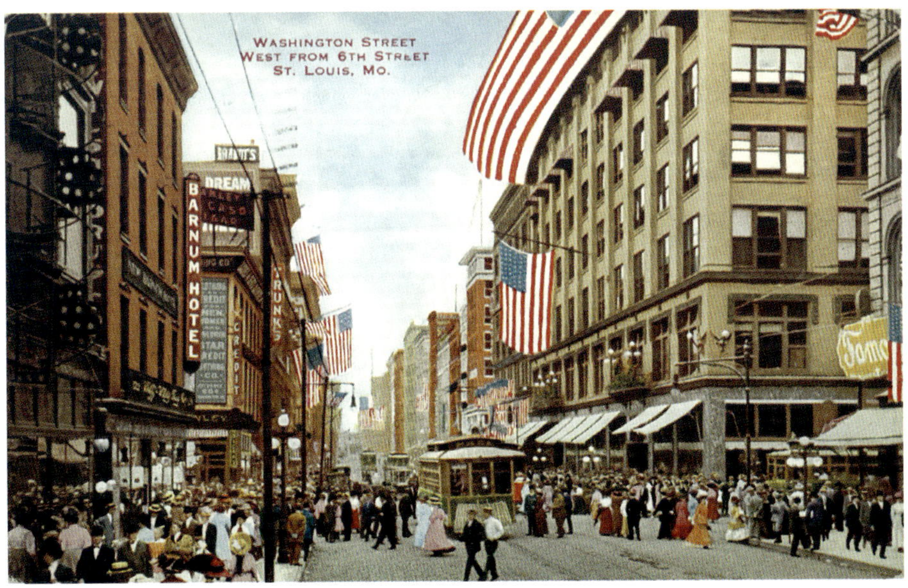

A view of Washington Avenue, looking west from 6th street. Now a vacant building, we see on the right what was once Stix Baer and then Dillard's Department Store.

Cancelled 1911, $2-4

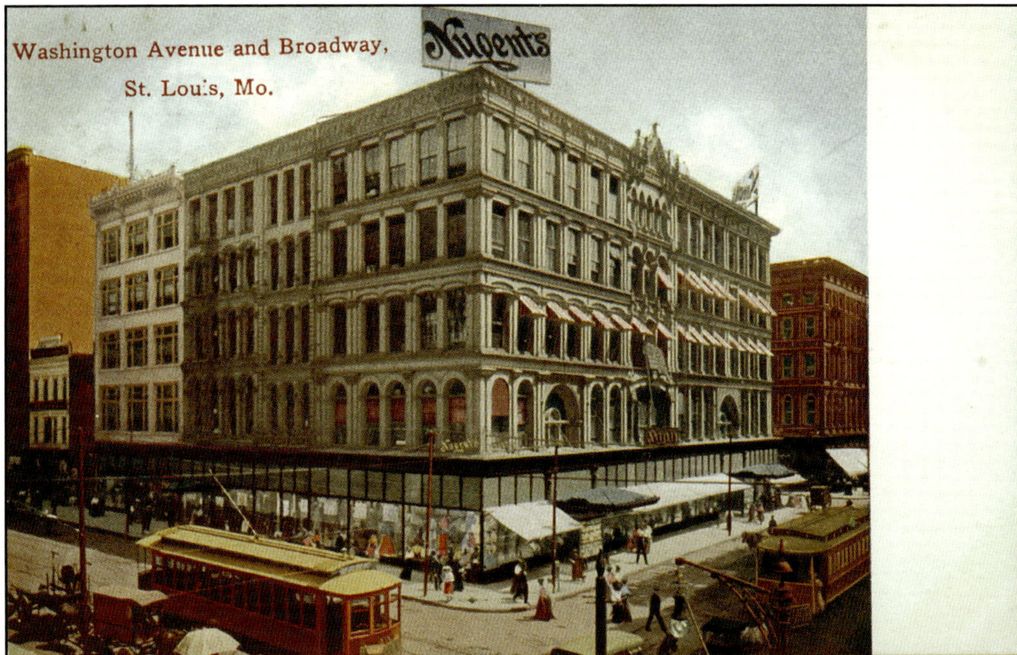

Two different views of Washington Avenue at Broadway give us a better view of the full street. You can see Nugents Department Store in each picture.

Circa 1907, $2-4

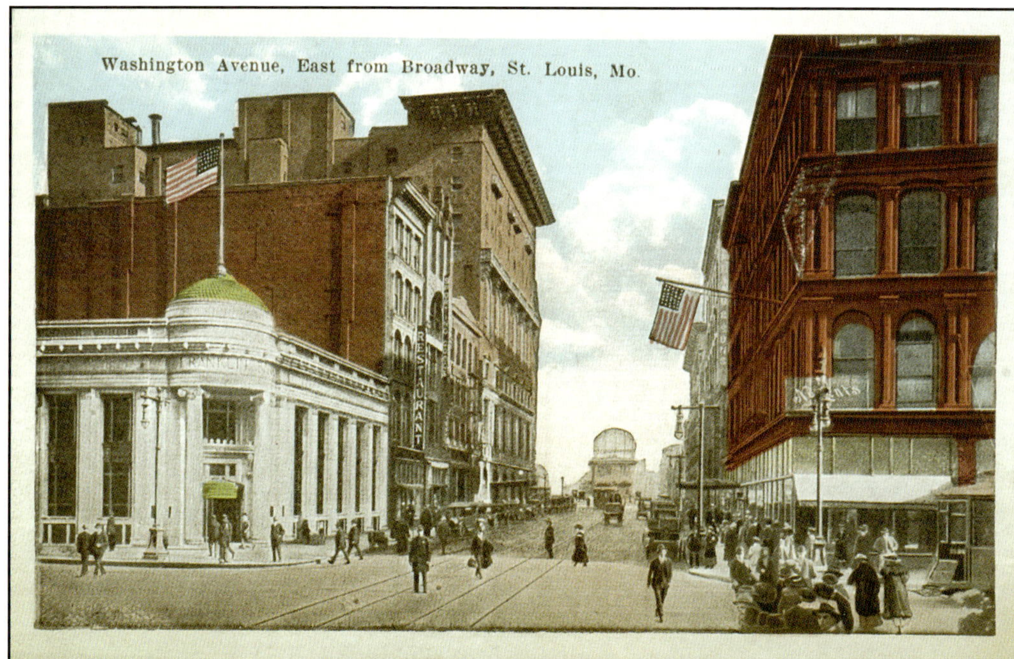

Circa 1907, $2-4

Residential Areas

St. Louis is made up of several neighborhoods that depict an era before the Depression—and unfortunately, one that showed suffering after. Displayed here are the lovely communities of Washington Terrace, Portland Place, Kingsbury Place, Fullerton's Westminster Place, Hortense Place, and others.

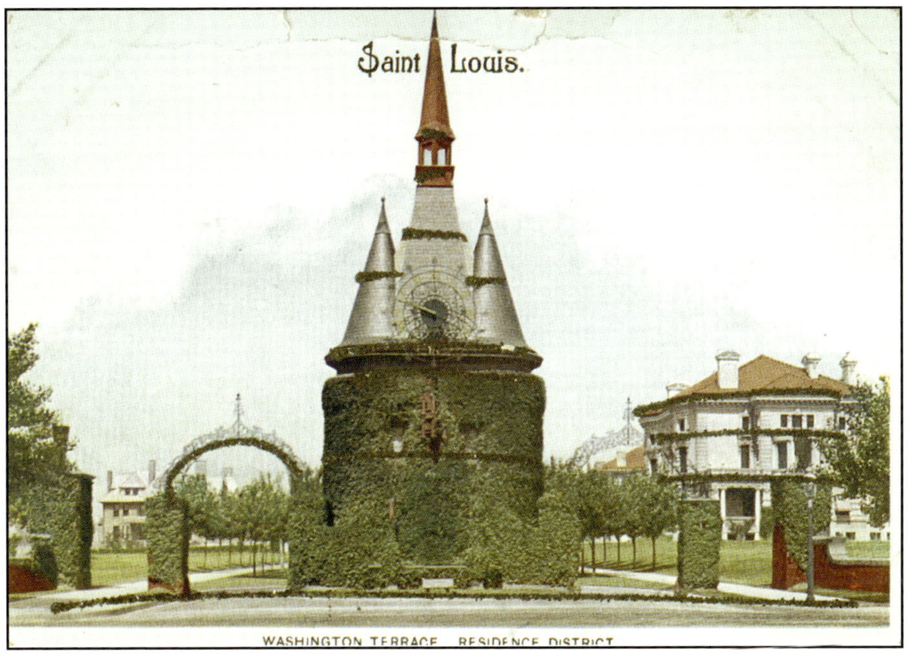

Washington Terrace was a private residential area in the central west end of St. Louis. This particular image used glitter to accent varied parts of the postcard.

Circa Early 1900s, $3-5

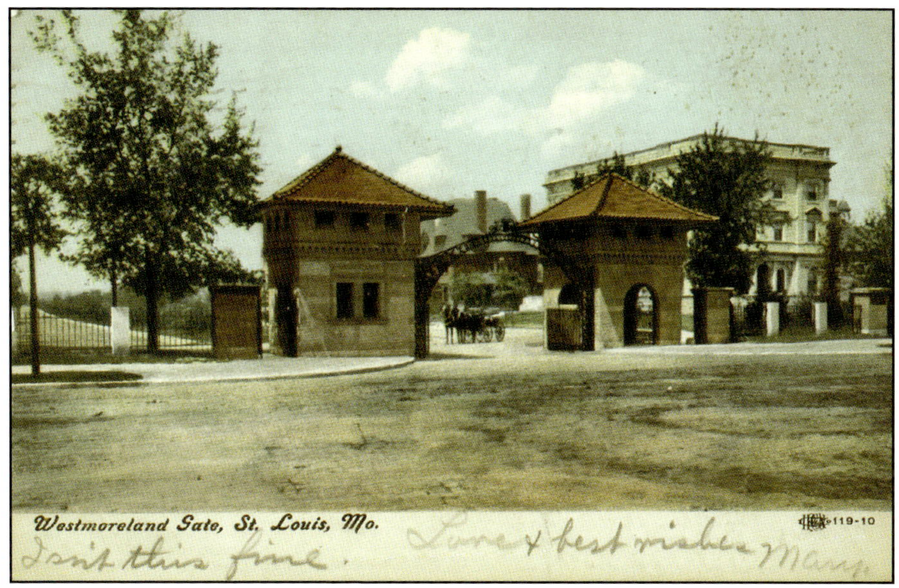

Six homes were demolished in the 1930s and 1940s in Westmoreland Place because buyers could not be found. Later in 1950, three more were taken down, and still two more by the time 1961 rolled around.

Cancelled 1907, $2-4

Lovely Portland Place still maintains most of its original homes, with the Depression only causing three to be demolished.

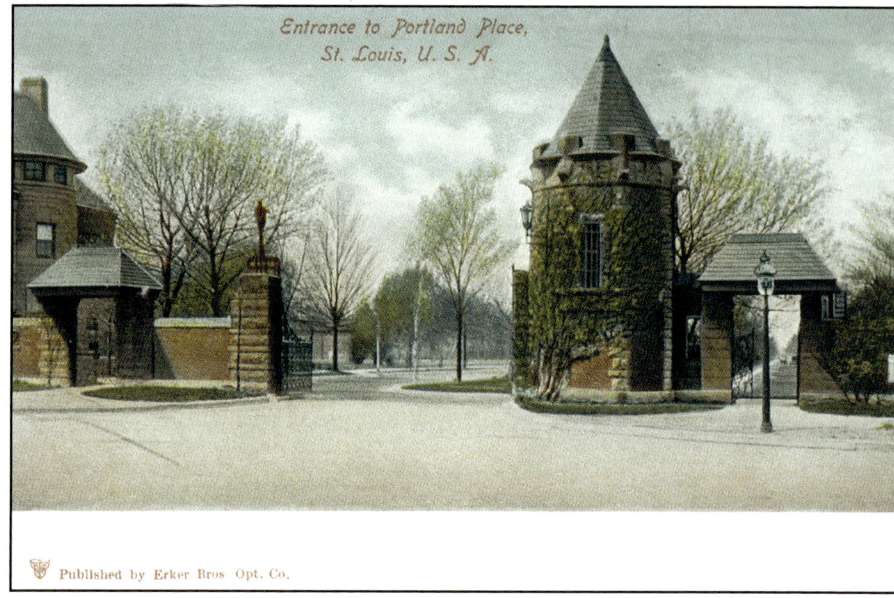

Circa 1907, $2-4

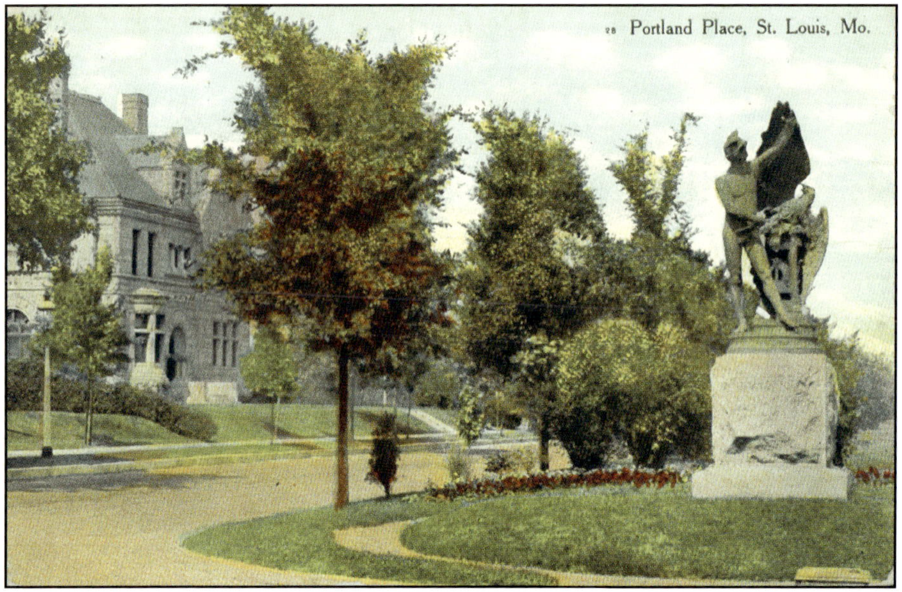

Cancelled 1912, $2-4

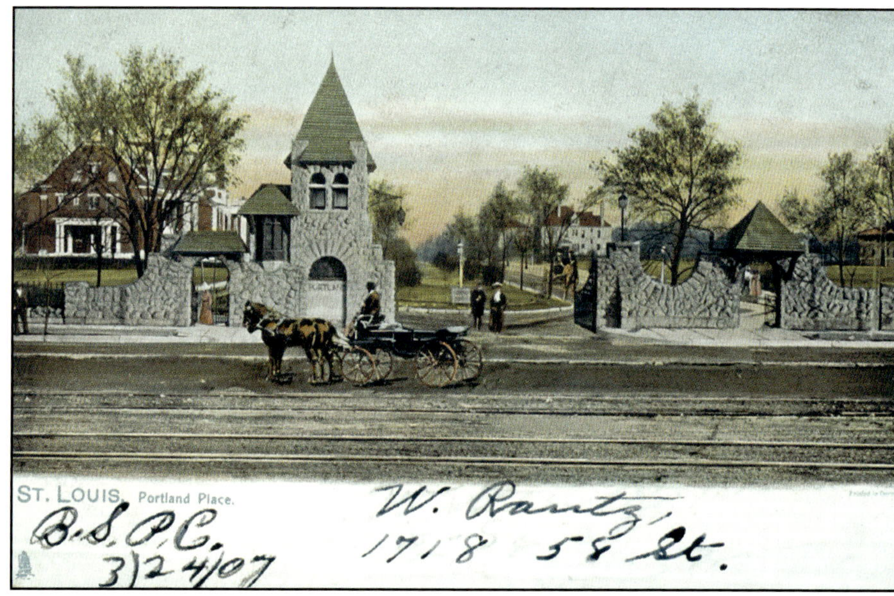

Circa Early 1900s, $3-5

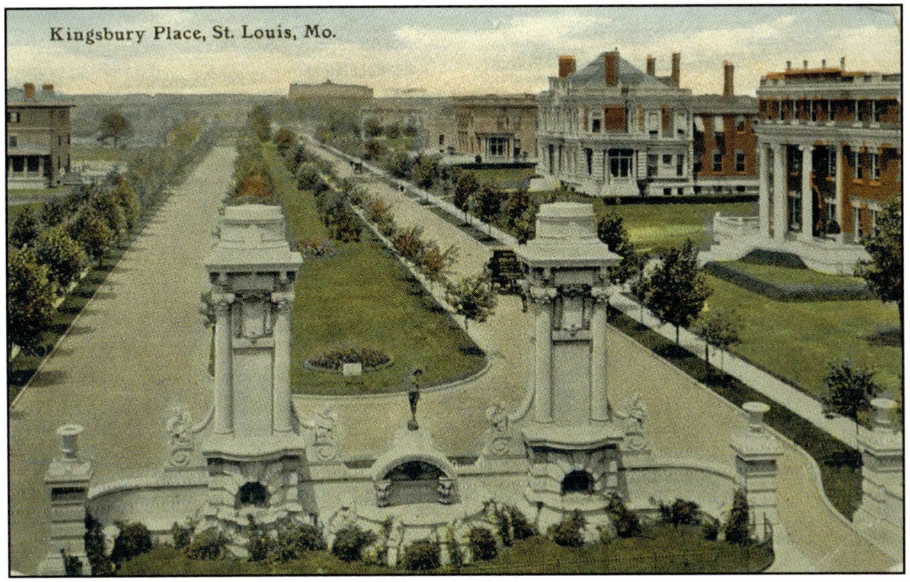

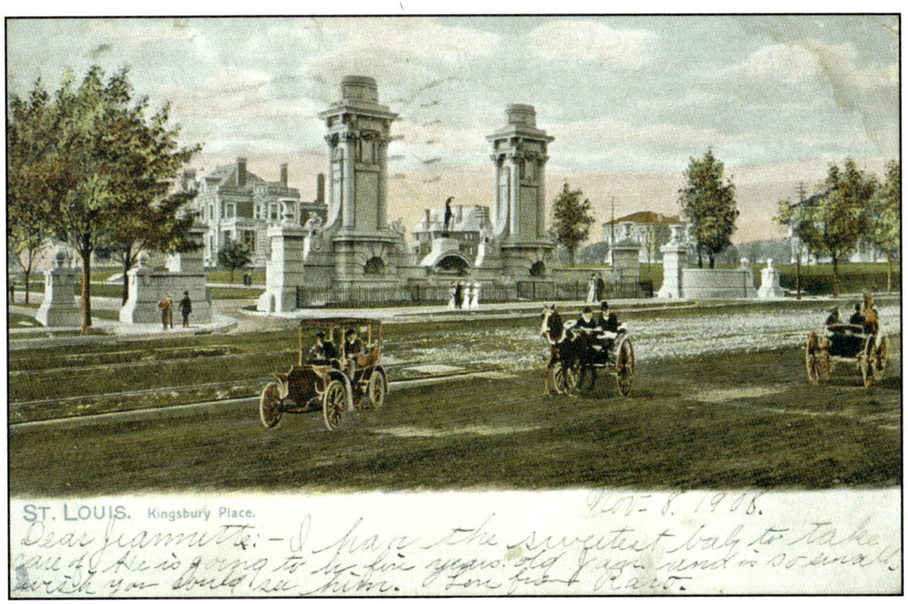

Shown here are the lovely gates of Kingsbury Place, erected in 1902 as a way to create enough interest to attract new buyers.

Cancelled 1911, $2-4 (top)
Cancelled 1908, $2-4 (bottom)

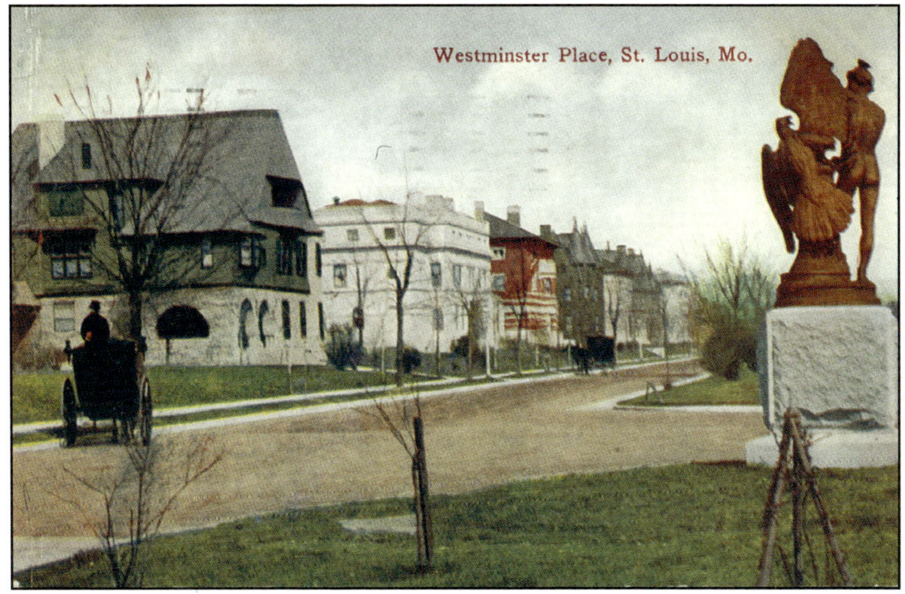

Also known as Fullerton's Westminster Place, this area was developed by Joseph Scott Fullerton, a real estate developer also responsible for other projects in St. Louis.

Cancelled 1911, $2-4

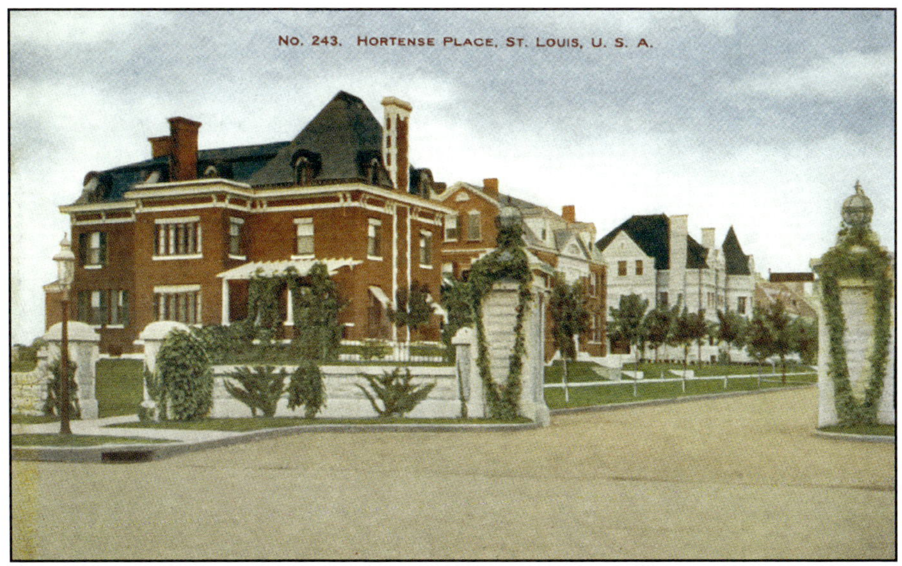

Hortense Place was developed by Jacob Goldman in 1900, and included seventeen lots—the best reserved for his own mansion home. The street is named after his daughter, Hortense.

Circa Early 1900s, $2-4

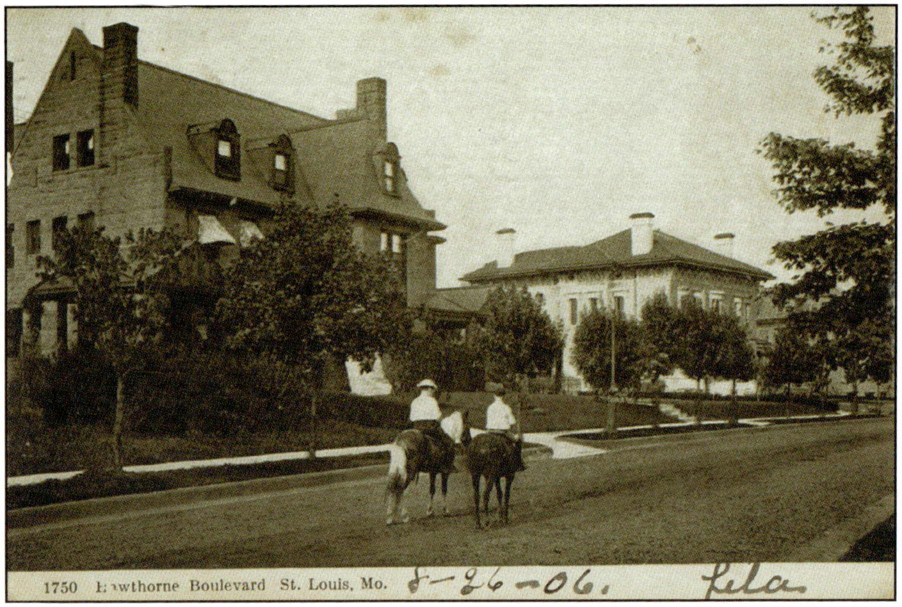

Cancelled 1906 (twice), $8-10

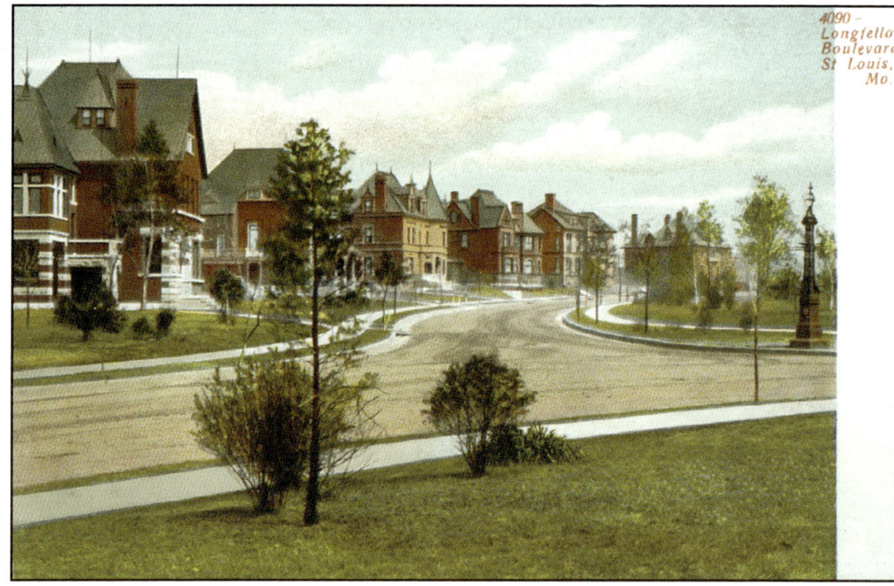

Circa Early 1900s, $2-4

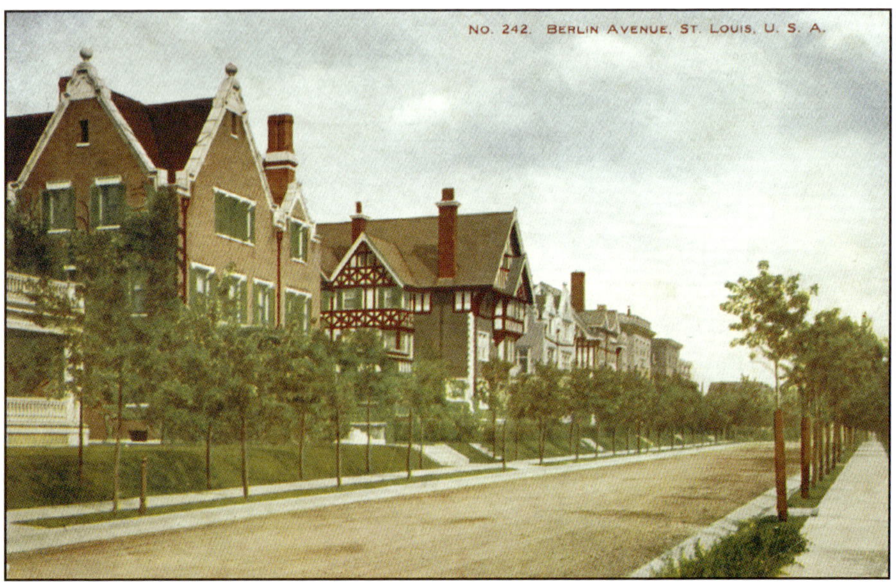

Circa Early 1900s, $2-4

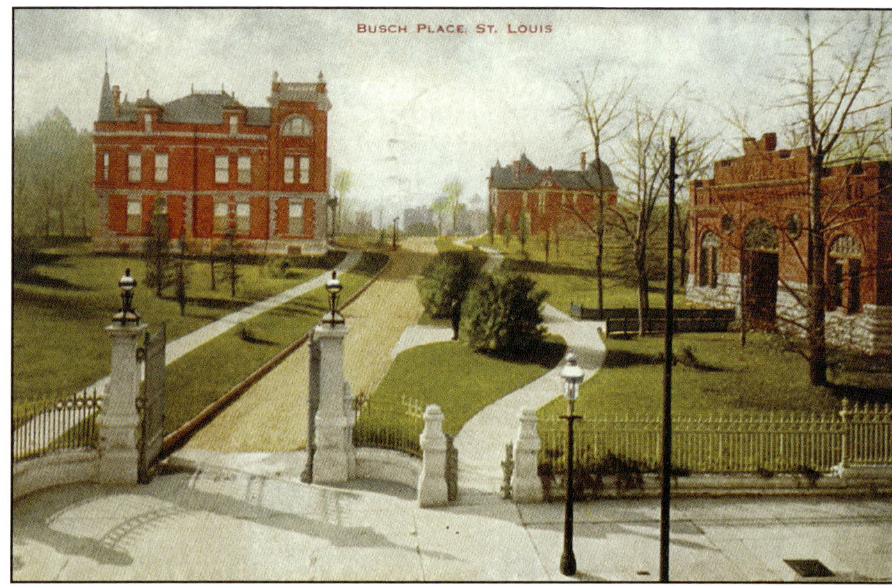

Cancelled 1911, $3-5

Hawthorne Boulevard, Berlin Avenue, Longfellow Boulevard, and Busch Place all had lovely residential homes along tree-lined streets.

More Faces of St. Louis!

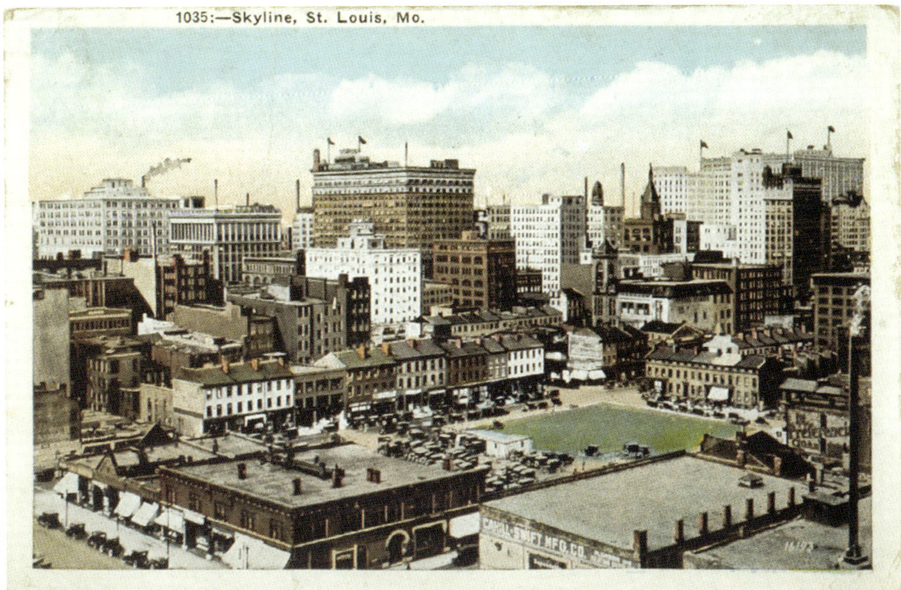

Cancelled 1924, $2-4

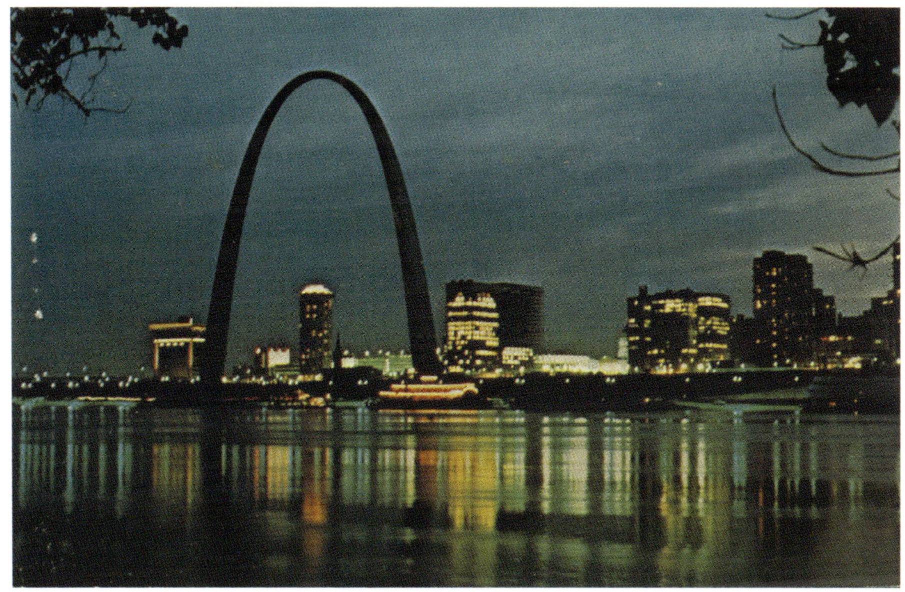

Circa 1960s, $2-4

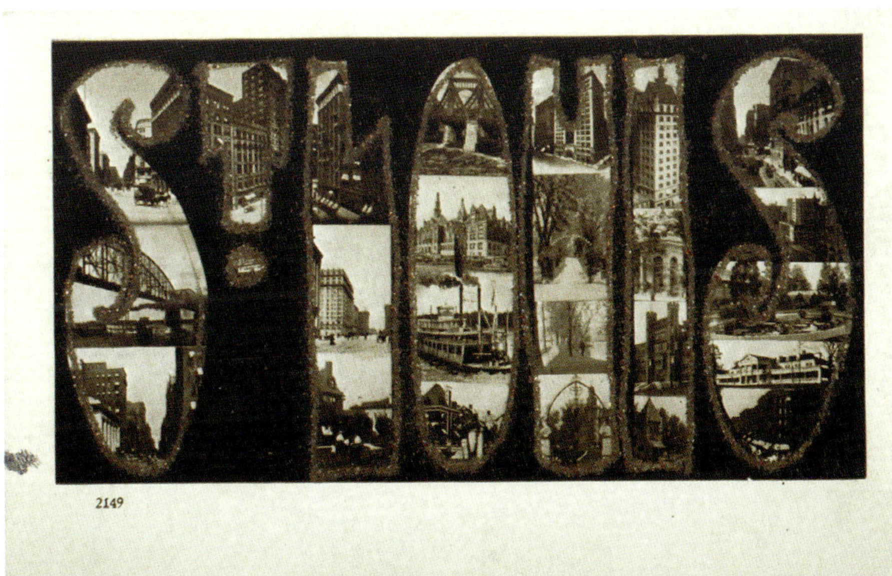

Circa Early 1900s, $3-5

Bibliography and Resources

Barnes Jewish Hospital. www.barnesjewish.org
Britannica Encyclopedia. www.britannica.com
Built St. Louis. Builtstlouis.net
Catholic Cemeteries of St. Louis Diocese. www.stlcathcem.com
City of St. Louis Development Authority. Stlcin.Missouri.org
Civil War St. Louis. www.civilwarstlouis.com
Concordia Theological Seminary. www.csl.edu
Concordia Publishing Company. www.cph.org
East St. Louis Action Research Project. www.eslarp.uiuc.edu
Evangelical Lutheran Church. www.elca.org
Explore St. Louis. www.explorestlouis.com
First Presbyterian. www.fpcstl.org
Historic Federal Buildings. W3.gsa.gov
Historic Hotels. www.historichotels.org
Jefferson Barracks. www.co.st-louis.mo.us
MICDS. About.micds.org
Missouri Folklore Society. Missourifolkloresociety.Truman.edu
Missouri History Museum. www.mohistory.org
Moolah Shriners. www.moolah.org
National Park Service. www.nps.gov
Peterson's College Planner. www.petersons.com
Real Lawyer Newsl. www.reallawyernews.com
St, Anthony's Medical Center. Stanthonysmedcenter.com
St. Louis Front Page. www.slfp.com
St. Louis Genealogical Society. www.stlgs.org
St. Louis Lofts. www.stlouislofts.com
St. Louis, Missouri. www.stlouis.missouri.org
St. Louis Public Library. www.slpl.lib.mo.us
St. Louis Time Portal. www.stlouistimeportal.com
St. Louis Union Station. www.stlouisunionstation.com
St. Louis University. www.slu.edu
St. Peter's Episcopal Church. www.stpetersepiscopal.org
Scottish Rite Freemasons. www.scottishrite-st.org
Starved Rock. www.starvedrockstatepark.org
U. S. Department of Veteran's Affairs. www.cem.va.gov
Union Avenue Church. www.union-avenue.org
Washington University. medschool.wustl.edu
World Book Encyclopedia. "Missouri." Field Enterprises, Inc. Chicago, IL, 1949.
World Book Encyclopedia. "St. Louis." Field Enterprises, Inc. Chicago, IL, 1949.

Index